Industry and Politics
United States
in
Comparative Perspective

D1622254

Industry and Politics
United States
in
Comparative Perspective

RICHARD LEHNE

Rutgers University

PRENTICE HALL, Englewood Cliffs, New Jersey 07632

Library of Congress Cataloging-in-Publication Data

Lehne, Richard.
    Industry and politics : United States in comparative perspective /
Richard Lehne.
        p.   cm.
    Includes bibliographical reference and index.
    ISBN 0-13-359118-2
    1. Business and politics--United States.   2. Industry and state-
    -United States.   I. Title.
    JK467.L45   1993
    322' .3'0973--dc20   91-44498
                                                                        CIP

Editor-in-Chief: Charlyce Jones Owen
Editorial/production supervision,
   interior design, and pagemakeup: Elizabeth Best
Copy Editor: Kathryn M. Beck
Cover Designer: Bruce Kenselaar
Interior Art: Peter J. Ticola Jr.
Prepress Buyer: Kelly Behr
Manufacturing Buyer: Mary Ann Gloriande
Editorial Assistant: Delores Mars

 © 1993 by Prentice-Hall, Inc.
A Simon & Schuster Company
Englewood Cliffs, New Jersey 07632

Printed in the United States of America

10-9-8-7-6-5-4-3-2-1

0-13-359118-2

Prentice-Hall International (UK) Limited, *London*
Prentice-Hall of Australia Pty. Limited, *Sydney*
Prentice-Hall Canada, Inc., *Toronto*
Prentice-Hall Hispanoamericana, S.A., *Mexico*
Prentice-Hall of India Private Limited, *New Delhi*
Prentice-Hall of Japan, Inc., *Tokyo*
Simon & Schuster Asia Pte. Ltd., *Singapore*
Editora Prentice-Hall do Brasil, Ltda., *Rio de Janeiro*

to
Raymond H. Bateman and John R. Mullen,
with great appreciation for their efforts
to promote understanding of relations
between government and business

Contents

List of Boxes, Illustrations, and Tables

BOXES

ILLUSTRATIONS

TABLES

Preface

Instructors responsible for courses that explore the political and social aspects of business face an unusual dilemma. Recent developments in relations between government and the marketplace have been politically stunning and economically momentous. They have altered the destiny of millions of people and captured the imagination of citizens everywhere. These developments, however, have also made obsolete many of the intellectual tools long used by instructors to make sense out of governmental and economic practices.

Students now enrolling in courses about industry and politics are challenging instructors to explain the new relationships between government and business. Internationally, the changes in these relationships are dramatic, but the relationships themselves are still in turmoil. Inside the United States, the doctrines that guided the actions of the government toward business since the 1930s are undergoing a thorough reexamination. Conceptual formulations that once seemed to convey the essence of the American experience suddenly appear terribly inadequate. Instructors must develop effective ways of analyzing and communicating the new domestic and international relationships at the time when these relationships are still being transformed.

This book is based on my answers to students wanting to know how to understand the roles of government and business in today's world and in the future. Students sense, I think accurately, that political-economic relationships remain in flux, and they are seeking guidance about how to prepare for the future.

My answers to their questions stress that both government and business are imperfect ways of solving social problems. I emphasize the value of the historic conflicts between advocates of public and private techniques for addressing the country's problems. These conflicts, I argue, have contributed a dynamism, creativity, and responsiveness to the conduct of public affairs that has been a crucial element of the American experience. Rather than seeking permanent solutions to societal problems, students should recognize that they are part of an ongoing exercise in social problem solving. The purpose of this enterprise is to create governing arrangements, corporate practices, and public policies that will safeguard the country's political decisions, enhance its material well-being, and preserve its cultural values. However successful, the solutions to today's problems will inevitably give way to newer approaches that are better suited to tomorrow's realities.

This book owes much to the students who have enrolled in the Rutgers Government and Business course in the last six years. They have forced me to reexamine questions and reconsider answers more often than I sometimes appreciated, but the result has been constructive.

Numerous distinguished guests from business and government visited class over the years and shared their insights and experiences with the students. I appreciated their generosity and benefited greatly from their contributions to the course; Albert Angel, Victor Bauer, Donald Burr, Robert J. Callander, Anton J. Campanella, Michael F. Catania, Bruce E. Coe, Aldrage B. Cooper, Jr., Christopher J. Daggett, Peter M. Dawkins, John Degnan, Richard T. Dewling, Al Fasola, Governor James Florio, Malcom S. Forbes, Jr., Hazel Gluck, Joseph E. Gonzalez, Gustav Heningburg, Michael Horn, Governor Thomas Kean, Bert Levine, Robert H. Marik, Marilu Marshall, Feather O'Connor, R. Teel Oliver, Jeffrey Owen, Richard F. Schaub, Louis P. Scibetta, Chip Stapleton, Gary S. Stein, Joseph A. Sullivan, Robert G. Torricelli, and William H. Tremayne. The course received financial support from the Eagleton Institute of Politics and personal encouragement from Alan Rosenthal, the Institute director, and both were very much appreciated.

This book would not have been possible without the earlier efforts of the scholars whose work is cited on the following pages. I am in their debt. I drew particular inspiration from a few scholars who deserve a more formal acknowledgment than academic citations alone convey: Edwin M. Epstein, Wyn Grant, and David Vogel. I also welcomed the initial encouragement to undertake this project offered by Dean David Blake. In various ways, Kent Calder, John H. Dunning, and Wolfgang Fach have introduced me to the politics of Japan, the United Kingdom, and Germany, and I am grateful.

Further thanks are due to Linda A. Pacotti for providing information on the Schering-Plough Grassroots Network, Richard F. Trabert for assistance in understanding the organization of the Merck Public Affairs Department, Christine F. Russell for information on the National Association of Manufacturers Survey of Trade Association Activities, and Floyd Stoner for discussing the staff structure of the American Bankers Association. Linda Langschied of the Alexander Library at Rutgers assembled the public opinion data used in Chapter 3 with diligence and creativity. Five students played particularly helpful roles in this project, and their assistance was much appreciated: Luis Amaro, Brian Beck, Raymond Bonwell, Joachim Fischer, and Kevin Raviol.

While working on this project, I welcomed the friendship and encouragement of Dean Mary S. Hartman of Douglass College and Dean James W. Reed of Rutgers College, and I was grateful for the financial assistance provided by the Douglass College Fellows Fund and the Rutgers College Discretionary Fund. No author could have benefited more from and appreciated more deeply the wisdom, imagination, and support offered by Henry Lehne, Susan Lewis, and Barry Qualls during the course of this project.

This book is dedicated to Raymond H. Bateman and John R. Mullen. Both have played an indispensable role in the development of this book, and both have contributed to the instruction of countless students. They have demonstrated that relations between government and business is a compelling topic that warrants the serious attention of public officials, business leaders, and scholars alike. As the domestic society becomes more complex and the international environment more challenging, their efforts to promote a fuller understanding of the interrelations of politics and industry will become even more crucial.

Industry and Politics
United States
in
Comparative Perspective

New Spotlight

on

an Enduring Topic

Dramatic changes are taking place in the relationship between government and industry in the United States and around the world. Political developments, economic trends, and emerging values are challenging the governmental arrangements that have shaped the world's economies since the end of World War II. While the institutions that have guided the American economy have achieved extraordinary success in the past, how or even whether these institutions can be reformed to face the new realities of a global economy are questions that are still unanswered.

Debates about the role government should play in the economy are both passionate and enduring. They are conducted in academic lecture halls as well as in the daily lives of citizens, companies, and government agencies. The enterprise implicit in these debates is actually *an exercise in social problem solving*. The goal is to design a governmental regime that will respect the country's political choices, promote its economic well-being, and enrich its cultural life.

Evidence of new thinking about the relationship between government and industry appears at every turn. Doctrines that have been the mainstay of government action toward business since the 1930s are being subjected to new scrutiny: trade policies are being reviewed; antitrust issues reexamined; government regulation reformed; and industrial policies reconsidered.

Policy analysts argue that existing relationships between government and industry are not suited to the competitive requirements of the global economy. The United States, they maintain, must rethink its assumptions about the responsibilities of government and business if it is to defend its political values and economic well-being in the years ahead.

Students of business administration contend that a fundamentally new "social compact" between business and society has been forged in recent decades. Business organizations can no longer be evaluated simply in economic terms; they are now responsible for helping society achieve a broad range of social objectives.

Economists have concluded that modern multinational, multiproduct enterprises are more self-sufficient than firms of past eras. Organizational developments have made it more difficult for public agencies to control these corporations and, thus, invalidated traditional assumptions about the ties between business and government.

Finally, students of politics have been impressed by the ability of Japan and the European Community to make political choices that have enhanced their economic well-being and political stature. Inside the United States, the expanding role of government has made public policy an ever more important determinant of corporate behavior. The desire to understand these developments has led political scientists to reexamine public policies toward business and to reconsider the broad nexus between the state and the economy.

It is now time to take stock of the contemporary relationship between government and business. Government is viewed in this book not as an impediment to a nation's goals but as a tool for accomplishing those goals. It is also recognized, however, that tools can be used more effectively in some circumstances than others. Governmental arrangements and corporate structures have a variety of consequences. Some are positive, and others negative. There are no perfect techniques for solving social problems. There are simply sets of practices whose results will be appraised differently as technical, social, and economic circumstances change. There can be no permanent solutions and no final victories.

Bonds between government and industry have grown up in response to discrete problems. This book focuses on government-business relationships in the United States. Other countries have responded to their problems and designed their relations between government and business in different ways. This book draws on experiences in Germany, Japan, and the United Kingdom to illustrate alternative arrangements for structuring relationships between politics and economics. These comparisons highlight the significance of the choices that have been made in the United States and suggest ways in which American practices might be improved for the future.

This book examines the relationship between government and business today and considers how this association might develop in the years ahead. It explores the setting for relations between government and industry, the institutions and policy tools affecting the government-business relationship, the strategies adopted by business to influence governmental actions, and public policies that bind industry with politics.

Part One of this book examines the features of the policy environment that shape relations between government and business. The history of government and business provides the foundation for the practices we see today. What role did government play in promoting economic development in the early years of the nation's history? How has the nature of government and industry changed over the decades, and what are the implications of these changes? What distinctive features of the country's political heritage result from its formative period, and what lessons do these events offer to those seeking to design a constructive relationship between government and business for the future? Chapter 1 addresses these questions.

The relationship between industry and government in a democracy is an uneasy one. The position of business rests upon values that contradict the dominant ethos of popular rule. Chapter 2 examines the political and economic judgments that have led to the relatively autonomous position for business in the United States, and it explores the roles of government in the economies of Japan, Germany, and the United Kingdom. From the perspective of these countries, how accurate is the judgment that an unregulated economy provides greater benefits to a society than a more directed economy?

Government-business relations are conducted within a specific system of public opinion and interest representation. Chapter 3 focuses on this advocacy environment. How trusting or how skeptical of business are Americans in the 1990s? What are the bases of their judgments? What changes have occurred in the advocacy environment in the last decades, and how do these changes affect the activities of labor unions and citizen groups? How have the media affected government and business?

Perhaps the most far-reaching change in the environment for conducting relations between government and industry in recent decades is the internationalization of the American economy. Today, essentially all major American firms are active in foreign markets, and most must defend their domestic market shares against international competitors. The growth in international economic activity has reduced the ability of the American government to fashion its own programs and pursue autonomous policy goals. Chapter 4 examines the various ways in which the American economy has become "international" and reviews the policy approaches that are available to respond to these new circumstances.

Part Two of this book analyzes the institutional features of the relationship between government and business. The American national government is composed of a series of large institutions that each have their own incentives and dynamics. Chapter 5 scrutinizes the major institutions and operations of government and compares them to the features of government in Germany, Japan, and the United Kingdom. It assesses the validity of the assertion that governments in other countries are better able to manage government-industry relations than government in the United States.

American corporations have distinct practices that craft their relations with government, and these are examined in Chapter 6. What roles are played by owners, managers, and new institutional investors in guiding corporations? What is the basis of the argument that the failures of American managers are responsible for the declining competitiveness of the United States in the international marketplace? How do the characteristics of American corporations compare with those from other countries? What practices have American firms devised for managing relations with government in the United States and in other countries?

Public policies toward business rest on common approaches for achieving public objectives. Chapters 7 and 8 review two of the most influential policy tools: antitrust laws and government regulation. How did these policy tools develop? What are their principal features? What are the strengths and the limitations of each? Under what circumstances are specific approaches more or less likely to be successful, and when are they likely to be counterproductive? What current developments are likely to affect their use in the future?

Part Three of this book examines the strategies businesses use to affect public policies. It is based on a model of the policy process that examines the role of business at specific stages in the conduct of public policy: shaping public attitudes and policy options, making governmental decisions, and implementing programs.

Business political activism has increased since the 1960s, and this activism has appeared at all stages of the policy process. Chapter 9 focuses on corporate efforts to shape public opinion and define policy options. What techniques influence most effectively the policy environment for conducting relations between government and industry? How significant are public service activities, charitable contributions, or advocacy advertising in shaping public opinion? What is the impact of corporate support for academic institutions and corporate sponsorship of research? What role do political parties play in various countries?

When pursuing their policy objectives, industry approaches government directly or through business groups. Chapter 10 examines the structure and activities of business associations. It analyzes the features of American business associations and compares them with the features of business associations in Germany, Japan, and the United Kingdom. What different roles do industry groups in these countries play? Why do some analysts argue that business associations in other countries are more successful than American associations?

As government influence over industry operations has become more pervasive in recent decades, business efforts to influence governmental decisions have multiplied. Influencing governmental decisions has become a growth industry in its own right that focuses on officeholders, election campaigns, and party affairs. Chapter 11 analyzes corporate and association programs to lobby public officials and participate in election contests. It assesses the circumstances in which businesses are active, the tactics and strategies that are used by business interests, and the advantages and handicaps of defending industry positions. The chapter concludes by appraising the impact of business lobbying on governmental decisions and on the political process.

Industry also seeks to shape the implementation of public policy by administrative agencies and the adjudication of policy issues through the courts. Activities directed toward these institutions are probably more numerous and may be more significant than business relations with either legislatures or chief executives.

Chapter 12 examines government's administrative and legal relationships with industry in the United States and compares them to relations between business and administrative and legal agencies in other countries.

Part Four examines policy areas that illustrate the importance of the relationship between government and business. Policies involving trade, industrial development, business operations, and social programs are the stakes in the competition among groups to influence government decision making.

Chapter 13 reviews the emergence of U.S. trade policies and examines the crisis those policies now face. Chapter 14 considers whether the United States should adopt industrial policies to assist individual industries patterned after those in Germany, Japan, or even the United Kingdom. What are the prospects in the 1990s for the formulation and implementation of successful American industrial policies?

Businesses do not exist in a social vacuum. They are part of the broader society, and they are affected by the country's general policies. Chapter 15 examines the relationship between business and social policy. What are the consequences for business of social policies? How does the country decide whether business or government is responsible for certain social policies? How is the relationship between industry and social policy likely to develop in the 1990s?

The relationship between business and government in the United States inspires more heated rhetoric than in any other major country. The stature afforded business in the United States reflects the overall judgment that the relative independence of industry permits society greater benefits than would be achieved through tighter governmental controls. This policy judgment, however, is a complex one that reflects the heritage of past events as well as the impact of current institutional developments, global trends, and societal expectations. Today's judgments about the balance between industry and government are not shared by everyone in the society, and they are certainly not permanent.

Judgments about government-industry relations are continually reappraised as values change and events transpire. The goal of this book is to help the reader think more clearly about the nexus between politics and the economy. It seeks less to promote doctrines than to identify issues and present analyses. The exercise in social problem solving goes on. This book's objectives will be realized when individual readers begin to make their own contribution to this decade's judgments about the most constructive relationship between government and business.

Chapter 1

Historical Perspectives on Government and Business

Government has played an influential role in shaping the American economy in every period of the nation's history. The United States had natural resources that other major nations lacked and a large domestic market that gave it an advantage over other industrializing countries. What distinguished the United States from other nations, however, was the ability of the American government at an early stage to enact policies that assisted economic growth and promoted industrial development.

Some describe the history of public policy in the United States as a chronicle of governmental responses to economic change.[1] Advocates of new manufacturing techniques, improvements in transportation, or innovations in finance all struggled against established interests defending the status quo. The results of these contests between the old and the new not only altered the nation's economic practices, they also transformed the country's social and political life.

A review of the nation's economic history sheds important light on the relationship between government and business today. An assessment of the activities of government in past eras helps us judge contemporary proposals for governmental action. An awareness of the changes that have occurred in business organization helps us appraise the corporate innovations taking place around the world today. An understanding of the evolution of American legal doctrine highlights the legal choices now being made in the United States and other countries.

While an examination of historical events is helpful, past controversies must be scrutinized carefully. Many of the words now used to discuss economic and political life have been used for centuries, but the content of these terms has changed substantially. Institutions that are as central to an understanding of economic development as *government, business,* and *law* have been recast from generation to generation. An analysis of the changes in these institutions is necessary to gauge the significance of events occurring today.

This chapter examines developments in government, business, and law in three historical periods: Colonial times to the Civil War; the Civil War to the Great Depression of the 1930s; and the Great Depression to the start of the 1990s.[2] This perspective highlights the critical features of each era. It also allows us to draw from the richness of past events to help fashion a constructive relationship between government and business for the years ahead.

COLONIAL TIMES TO 1860: LEGAL FOUNDATIONS OF ENTERPRISE

One of history's great coincidences is that both the Declaration of Independence and Adam Smith's *Wealth of Nations* appeared in the same year. Unfortunately, this coincidence is a source of confusion about the role of government in the early years of the republic. Since Smith's treatise was published in 1776, many wrongly conclude that it was used as a manual for the founding of the new nation. Smith believed that a government could never be knowledgeable enough or impartial enough to manage a country's economy successfully. Because the state lacked these qualities, Smith argued that nonintervention by the state in economic matters was the wisest policy. Smith's viewpoint, however, was not the dominant opinion of his age. He opposed the prevailing sentiment that government should direct a nation's economic life.

Role of Government

Mercantilism was the economic theory that guided British policy toward colonial America. According to mercantilism, wealth was conceived as a stockpile of treasure gathered from neighbors or colonies. Government, under this policy, should control all aspects of economic activity in order to increase the wealth, unity, and power of the state.

British trade regulations during the colonial era were designed to benefit the mother country. Manufacturing was limited in the colonies, colonies were restricted to the role of producers of raw materials, and trade was confined to the vessels and ports of the British empire. Until the 1750s, the colonies derived more benefits than burdens from the British mercantile system. They found British markets for their goods, received protection from the British navy for their shipping, and obtained British capital to help develop their economies. The growth of the colonial economies and the increased rigor with which Britain enforced trade restrictions in the 1760s were factors that contributed to the outbreak of the American Revolution.

After the American Revolution, the former colonies were faced with the task of creating an economy that could survive outside the British mercantile system. American leaders acknowledged the advice of *Wealth of Nations* but drew guidance from the activist tradition of government associated with mercantilism.[3]

Two plans from this era confirmed the influence of mercantilist assumptions by proposing an expansive role for government in economic development. Alexander Hamilton's *Report on the Encouragement and Protection of Manufactures* in 1791 urged the national government to aid fledgling industries by providing economic assistance and tariff protection. A quarter-century later, Henry Clay and John Calhoun devised a strategy, christened the "American System," that would boost economic development through a combination of tariff protection and federally funded public works projects. While neither plan was adopted by the national government, most of the activities were soon launched under the auspices of state governments.[4]

It was common in these years for states and municipalities to own stock in private companies that operated turnpikes, bridges, and canals.[5] The city of Baltimore supplied the money to found the B & O Railroad, and it then retained stock in the company. The state of Pennsylvania owned one-third of the capital of the Bank of Pennsylvania, and the Pennsylvania Railroad was literally the state's railroad. Governmental ownership of private companies aroused opposition when firms lost money, and the practice was curtailed after the Panic of 1837 when states had to appropriate funds to pay off company debts.

States and localities in these years also regulated commercial activity by controlling exports, product quality, weights and measures, and agricultural harvests.[6] Subsidies and tariffs were frequently enacted to aid specific industries.[7]

Nature of Business

Most Americans in these years were in business for themselves. They were entrepreneurs rather than employees. The United States was an overwhelmingly rural society, and, as late as 1850, twenty million of the twenty-three million Americans lived in rural areas. The great majority of Americans were farmers, and most owned the farms they worked. Those who manufactured goods did so by hand at home or in small shops.[8]

There was much economic growth in preindustrial America but little change in the nature of the firm. Most enterprises were single-unit businesses managed by their owners and employing less than fifty people.[9] Before 1840, much of the stimulus for development came from Atlantic trade and favored East Coast cities. After 1840, the growth of the American market and potential economies of scale encouraged capitalists to turn from international trade to internal investments. The American West benefited from this trend, and population in the new states soared.[10]

Law

Legal developments in this era probably had a more lasting impact on relations between government and industry than either political or economic events. American law emphasized individual liberties, limited governmental action, and favored business expansion. Befitting a new nation, the American legal system possessed an innovativeness and a vitality that was unmatched in other lands.[11]

Three features of the legal system made essential contributions to economic development: the definition of property rights, the emergence of corporations as business entities, and governmental enforcement of the terms of contracts.

Economic growth requires stable commercial relationships, but the American Revolution, like most wars, had loosened the bonds of society. During the 1780s, political disorder, fears of social disintegration, and growing concern over the security of property were common in American states.[12]

Such concerns led states to adopt new constitutions that safeguarded the value of the currency, guaranteed payment of the public debt, and protected private property. These actions advanced the movement that led to the drafting of the U.S. Constitution and the Bill of Rights. The Fifth Amendment to the Constitution stated, "No person shall be...deprived of life, liberty, or property, without due process of law; nor shall private property be taken for public use without just compensation." These guarantees reduced the risks of enterprise and encouraged entrepreneurs to undertake projects that furthered economic development.

Today, discussions of property rights sound elitist and undemocratic. In the eighteenth century, property was viewed differently. While property rights today are often thought to limit political and social rights, in the eighteenth century property rights were seen as the foundation of political rights. For people in that era, the concept of property was associated with the workplace. Property provided sustenance, and government would threaten people's livelihood by seizing their property. When the possession of property became a right that government could not revoke, people were able to enjoy political freedom and promote the country's development.[13]

The second legal innovation in this era was the emergence of the corporation as a business entity. A corporation is an artificial person that can own property, transact business, sue others, and be sued itself. During the colonial and early national periods, corporations operated under special charters granted by state legislatures. Charters were granted to organizations providing public benefits in such areas as charity, religion, or education.[14]

As the economy evolved, private groups began to offer goods and services that improved people's living conditions. Even though these groups were profit-seeking entities, they received corporate charters because their products offered "public benefits." Corporate charters were issued to banks and firms that produced such staples as textiles and glass. Until the Civil War, charters granted to profit-seeking groups identified a firm's activities and listed the public benefits it was supposed to provide.[15]

The corporation was a more popular form of economic organization in the United States in this period than in other major countries.[16] Some historians argue that the popularity of the corporate form resulted from its "democratic" rather than its economic character. Corporate organization permitted a broad range of citizenry to participate in economic development. It extended the benefits of economic stability and legal protection for investment to all citizens instead of limiting these advantages to the few who received special favors from government. The democratic nature of the corporate form was confirmed by the enactment of general incorporation laws in the middle of the nineteenth century.[17]

The third major legal innovation was government backing of contractual obligations. Stability in economic relationships was the goal of a number of clauses in the U.S. Constitution. Article I, Section 10 stipulated, "No state shall...pass any...law impairing the obligation of contracts."

Chief Justice John Marshall became a vigorous champion of the obligations of contract.[18] He insisted that state governments as well as private individuals must comply with contractual provisions. *Dartmouth College* v. *Woodward* nominally involved control of the records and seal of the college.[19] Dartmouth was founded under a colonial charter from King George III in 1769. In 1816, a dissident group sought to take over the assets of the college, and it persuaded the New Hampshire legislature to enlarge the board of trustees and give it control. The New Hampshire Supreme Court approved the acts of the legislature, but John Marshall wrote for the U.S. Supreme Court that a charter was a contract, and the provisions of a contract could not be altered by the action of a state legislature. This decision reinforced the sanctity of contract and protected corporations from legislative interference.

While this decision stressed contractual obligations, the decision in *Charles River Bridge* v. *Warren Bridge* in 1837 held that standards of community welfare could not be ignored in determining the meaning of a contract.[20] A corporation chartered to build and operate a toll bridge sought to invalidate a subsequent Massachusetts law that authorized the construction of a rival bridge. Even though the new legislation was said to violate the older contract, the U.S. Supreme Court upheld the law and ruled that no legislative charter could confer benefits that harmed the public welfare. In this decision, the Supreme Court insisted that the original contract be interpreted within the standards of community interest.

Legal doctrines from this era provided the foundation for the country's economic development. Some commentators emphasize the political objectives these actions were intended to achieve, while others stress the economic motivations. In fact, such sharp distinctions were less visible in the eighteenth century than they are today. Property rights found special favor in the Constitution, but the nature of property in the eighteenth century made this almost a populist position. Corporations became significant business entities, but corporations originally had public service orientations. Courts defended the integrity of contractual restrictions, but such decisions also compelled government to abide by the terms of its own agreements. In each of these instances, democratic values and considerations of community welfare shaped the legal doctrines that became the foundations of enterprise.

The early decades of the American republic did not leave all economic judgments to the marketplace. Opinion leaders looked to government for help in unleashing the economic potential of the new nation. While it did not impose the comprehensive restrictions that characterized European countries, government acted repeatedly to promote and sustain economic development.[21]

1860 TO 1929: THE RISE OF MODERN INDUSTRY

Between the Civil War and the stock market crash of 1929, the United States experienced an industrial revolution. The country was transformed from a sparsely populated agricultural society into the leading industrial and manufacturing power in the world. The Jeffersonian image of an agrarian, individualistic America receded, and the view of an America characterized by the factory system, the closing of the frontier, robber barons, big cities, and labor conflict emerged to take its place. The changes in the nature of economic activity upset traditional cultural and political relationships, reshaped people's lives, and tested the ability of the country's institutions to manage drastically changed social conditions.

Nature of Business

Industrialization occurred in the United States fifty years later than in Great Britain but about fifty years before it took place in Japan.[22] The pace of economic growth had accelerated in the Civil War years due to improvements in transportation, increased availability of energy supplies, and innovations in agriculture. More important than growth, however, were the changes that appeared in the structure of the economy.

These decades witnessed the revolution in production techniques associated with the factory system.[23] Power-driven machinery, continuous processing, and the interchangeability of parts became the order of the day. The American economy became noted for its standardization of goods and its high-volume, low-cost production.[24] The new techniques of mass production reduced demand for the solitary craftsman. By 1900, 60 percent of the country's workers were employed in industry, and the typical worker now faced the dependency and regimentation characteristic of a "labor force."[25]

The scale of individual businesses also increased dramatically during this era. The United States was the first nation to have its economy dominated by large firms. The Civil War had given the country a model of large-scale national organization, and the country's economic institutions soon adopted comparable organizational forms.[26] Instead of a few dozen employees, companies would employ first hundreds, then thousands, and then tens of thousands of workers.

American railroads became the nation's first big businesses.[27] They were, for a time, the largest economic organizations in the world. In the late 1880s, when no manufacturer had more than two thousand employees, the Pennsylvania Railroad employed fifty thousand workers. By the time the federal government came to employ fifty thousand civilian workers, some individual railroad companies already had more than one hundred thousand employees. Railroads also faced the era's most demanding management problems: unprecedented size, peculiar difficulties of finance, and the technical and political problems of route planning and land acquisition.[28]

The factory system and the industrial revolution made possible sharp increases in productivity and extraordinary declines in wholesale prices. Between the end of the Civil War and 1890, one index of wholesale prices declined by more than 50 percent.[29] To reduce operating costs, many American firms became involved in each stage of production, from gathering and transporting raw materials, through mass production, to mass marketing.

This pattern of vertical integration, increased efficiency achieved through economies of scale, and technological innovations resulted in more production capacity than was needed. Producers began intense efforts to limit the flow of goods by controlling competition and restricting access to the marketplace. Pooling agreements to maintain prices and divide business appeared in the decade after the Civil War, but these agreements were difficult to enforce and were finally outlawed by Congress. About 1880, pooling arrangements were replaced by trusts, in which affiliated companies surrendered their stock to trustees who operated a holding company made up of the consolidated firms. The Standard Oil Company was the nation's first important trust. It was dissolved by an Ohio court in 1892 but then reorganized under New Jersey's merger laws. A wave of mergers followed in such industries as steel, copper, rubber, and tobacco, when merged companies were found to be more profitable than trusts. As a result of mergers, individual firms controlled a larger share of the market in more industries than has occurred at any other time in the nation's history.[30]

The enormous growth in the size of American companies led to the emergence of professional management structures to replace the individualized leadership of the "captains of industry" who had founded major firms.[31] Corporations developed central management offices with specific bureaus for finance, transportation, marketing, personnel, research and development, accounting, planning, and, later, advertising. The United States pioneered in university-based management education; the first program was endowed in 1883.[32]

In this period, fundamental changes occurred in the nature of the American economy. The turbulence of the era also challenged the limited role that government had played in the society.

Role of Government

Government in this era continued to play an important but more focused version of the promotional role it had adopted in the earlier decades. Congress encouraged the development of railroads by providing massive land grants for the construction of the Union Pacific and Northern Pacific railroads. By the end of the century, it had given 131 million acres of land to assist private rail promoters, and the state governments had granted an additional 49 million acres.[33] The national government also appropriated public lands to promote scientific agriculture by supporting the establishment of land grant colleges and agricultural experiment stations in each state.

An additional role for government was also forged during this era. The creation of a national economy was achieved at the price of fierce resentment against big companies. The transformation of workers from independent entrepreneurs into salaried employees led to rancorous and sometimes violent disputes over wages, working conditions, and job security. Building a national market also resulted in the destruction of local markets and the collapse of countless small businesses that had served these markets. The bitterness of the owners and employees of these businesses combined with the hostility of farmers to ignite a prairie revolt against corporations. The growth of national companies also alienated local elites whose role in the community was challenged by big business and who later provided leadership for campaigns against business.

Opinion leaders came to fear not only governmental power but also the economic power wielded by private corporations. An extraordinary range of groups turned to government for protection. Examples arose in virtually every sector of the economy.

Meat packaging, in the years before the Civil War, had been a regional industry, with local producers and local butchers serving local markets.[34] After the Civil War, Swift, Armour, and other firms established national distribution and marketing systems that threatened the position of local meat producers. The National Butchers' Protective Association, dominated by local producers, promoted regional boycotts to keep national meat out of local markets. The association persuaded states such as Minnesota and Colorado to enact laws prohibiting the sale of meat unless the animals had been inspected by the state's officials twenty-four hours before they were slaughtered. This requirement effectively prevented national firms from selling products across state boundaries.

Legislatures also enacted specific laws regulating other practices of meat packers, railroads, and other unpopular industries. Antitrust laws and statutes prohibiting price fixing and restraints of trade were passed to address the general threat posed by giant corporations. Later, both state and national governments adopted public standards for economic activities in sensitive areas such as working conditions and banking transactions.

Most national efforts to respond to the industrial revolution in this era were more significant as symbols than as accomplishments. Despite the easy rhetoric, it was often difficult to know where the public interest in specific situations stopped and where efforts by private groups to secure commercial advantage began.[35]

As a result of the lack of consensus, landmark pieces of legislation from this period, such as the Interstate Commerce Act of 1887 and the Sherman Antitrust Act of 1890, resembled declarations of traditional values rather than clear statements of legislative purpose. The full significance of the legislative initiatives in the era would not be realized until the nation addressed the challenges of the New Deal.

Law

The economic transformation of the United States in this era prompted recourse to litigation.[36] Legal doctrines developed for an agrarian society were not suited to the problems caused by the huge concentration of industrial wealth. Two issues that generated the most controversy were the *role* of government in regulating economic activity and the *level* of government responsible for regulation.

Until the end of the nineteenth century, state governments were the centers of regulatory activity. As one source notes, "Quite literally, state legislation was the only regulatory game in town."[37] State authority to regulate economic activity was usually derived from the general powers states possessed to provide for the morals, health, safety, and welfare of their citizens—their "police powers."

The emergence of a national economy undermined state regulation. When the Fourteenth Amendment to the Constitution was adopted in 1868, its clauses prohibiting states from limiting the "privileges or immunities" of United States citizens or denying them due process of law also seemed to reduce state authority to regulate economic activity. As courts ruled on the meaning of the Fourteenth Amendment, however, judges first upheld state regulation and only later sustained national action.

The first major test of the Fourteenth Amendment came in the *Slaughterhouse Cases* in 1873.[38] The Republican-controlled legislature of Louisiana required as a health measure that all meat be slaughtered on the premises of a firm operated by its political friends. Other butchers sued, arguing that the legislature had abridged their "privileges and immunities" and taken the value of their property without due process of law. The U.S. Supreme Court upheld the Louisiana law and ruled that the Fourteenth Amendment left state authority to regulate economic activity intact.

By the end of the century, the federal judiciary began to acknowledge the dynamics of a national economy and accept the significance of national rights. In 1886, the justices struck down an Illinois law that regulated railroads within the state's borders on the grounds that intrastate regulation could affect interstate commerce, and interstate commerce could be regulated only by Congress.[39] In 1890, the U.S. Supreme Court overturned a Minnesota law and ruled that a federal court rather than a state commission should be the final arbiter of the reasonableness of railroad rates.[40]

Basic changes in the structure of commerce and industry had diminished the ability of state governments to regulate the country's economy, but the popularity of the laissez-faire philosophy among judges slowed the emergence of a national alternative to state regulation. Eventually, the federal and state judiciaries bowed to popular preferences and simply accepted the social legislation designed to square legal precedent with the new economic conditions. During the period between the Civil War and 1929, the legal foundations were laid for the expansive role that the national government would assume during the New Deal.

1929–1991: THE GROWTH OF POSITIVE GOVERNMENT

The stock market crash of 1929 symbolized the beginning of the Great Depression of the 1930s. Once under way, the decline rippled out into the economy in ever-widening circles until the country's market system had collapsed and national income had fallen by almost 60 percent.

Economic historians do not agree on the reasons for the depression. They mention excessive borrowing and speculation, the decline of international trade, a drop in the profitability of agriculture, inadequate investment, and damaging public policies. Regardless of the origins, however, the economic crisis deepened, and its scope became nationwide. Care of the hungry and the unemployed exhausted the resources of states and localities and forced them to turn to Washington for assistance. By the time the depression abated, the federal government had assumed broad new responsibilities, and the political system had been permanently altered. Before the emergence of positive government was possible, however, the changes in legal doctrine begun in previous decades had to be completed.

Law

The economic emergency brought into stark focus the historic issue of the role of government in regulating the economy. Old legal doctrines had been giving way to new realities, but the magnitude of economic deprivation tested the country's patience with the slow pace of constitutional change. New Deal legislation provoked legal confrontation.

The National Industrial Recovery Act of 1933 was the centerpiece of the New Deal.[41] It authorized the drafting of "codes" for each industry that would control supply, fix prices and wages, and regulate working conditions. The Agricultural Adjustment Act of the same year was even bolder. It sought to establish parity between industry and agriculture by raising prices for farm goods and reducing the financial burden of agricultural mortgages and debt. It also gave government power to restrict production by limiting the acreage available for cultivation. The slashing of wages and the growth in joblessness during the 1930s aroused labor militancy. The National Labor Relations Act of 1935 threw the weight of the federal government behind union organizing battles and outlawed antiunion practices.

The New Deal initiatives came under surprisingly bitter attack. The constitutionality of the National Industrial Recovery Act was challenged in *Schechter Poultry Corp.* v. *United States*.[42] The Schechter brothers were poultry wholesalers who openly violated the NIRA's Live Poultry Code to boost their profits. When prosecuted for selling "unfit" chickens at cut-rate profits, they argued that the NIRA statute was itself defective. The Supreme Court agreed. The justices ruled that Congress had exceeded its powers by regulating matters that were the responsibility of the states. The next year, the Supreme Court invalidated the Agricultural

Adjustment Act as well. In *United States* v. *Butler*, the justices wrote that the Act constituted "a statutory plan to regulate and control agricultural production" and held that such efforts were beyond the scope of federal authority.[43]

In other cases, state and federal judges provided more mixed reactions to New Deal initiatives.[44] Some measures were sustained, while others were found wanting. Conservative judges objected to New Deal restrictions and sometimes convinced moderate colleagues that the new statutes were vague and without proper constitutional foundation. The conservatives failed, however, to identify legal principles that would permit government to alleviate the economic crisis.

The election landslide of 1936 confirmed the popularity of the New Deal and placed traditional judges in conflict with both Congress and the executive branch. Threatened with plans to alter the composition and jurisdiction of the Supreme Court, conservative justices retreated from their earlier opposition to New Deal measures and accepted the new initiatives. A 1937 decision illustrates the shift.

In *National Labor Relations Board* v. *Jones and Laughlin Steel Corporation*, business groups had argued that the federal government had no power to regulate factory working conditions.[45] The Supreme Court majority, however, abandoned its earlier view and ruled that the commerce clause did grant Congress the authority to regulate industrial relations. "When industries organize themselves on a national scale," the court wrote, "...how can it be maintained that their industrial relations constitute a forbidden field into which Congress may not enter...?[46] "By the time prosperity returned, essentially all constitutional restraints on the power of federal government to regulate the nation's economy had been discarded.

Role of Government

Big government in the United States is mostly a product of the twentieth century.[47] At the start of the century, citizens could go about their lives unaware of national government decisions. Today, almost every problem is a reason for government action. The ideal of limited government has been set aside, and the ideology of positive government engulfs us.

The federal government now affects every aspect of corporate operations. The means by which firms assemble capital are defined by federal statute, and production decisions must be made with regard to public environmental and energy policies. Marketing practices, employee relations policies, equal opportunity procedures, and occupational health and safety standards are all the realm of government.

The emergence of positive government in the twentieth century is a widely appreciated development, but the reasons for the growth of government remain controversial. An examination of federal employment and revenues since 1929 reveals some reasons for that growth.

In 1929, the total civilian workforce of the federal government was 580,000.[48] More than half of that number, over 300,000 people, worked for the Post Office, and another 100,000 were employees of the Defense Department. This means that in 1929, only 180,000 workers provided all the other national services a country of 120 million people required.

The great growth in federal employment took place in the 1930s and 1940s. During the 1930s, the count of federal civilian workers grew from 580,000 to over 950,000. By the end of the 1940s, it had reached 2,100,000. In the next two decades, the pace of growth slowed, but by 1970, the number of employees had climbed to 3,000,000. In subsequent years, federal employment has remained at this level.

The growth in federal employment coincided with the two great governmental crises of the twentieth century, the depression of the 1930s and World War II. The concentration of employment growth in these periods indicates that national emergencies can lead to a permanent expansion of governmental activity. This view is confirmed by a review of the expenditure data presented in Table 1–1.

TABLE 1–1   Government Expenditures from Own Sources, 1929–1989

CALENDAR YEAR	AS A PERCENTAGE OF GROSS NATIONAL PRODUCT			
	Total (%)	*Federal (%)*	*State (%)*	*Local (%)*
1929	10	3	2	5
1939	19	10	4	5
1949	23	16	3	4
1959	27	19	4	4
1969	30	20	5	5
1979	31	21	6	4
1989 (est.)	36	23	8	5

Source: U.S. Advisory Commission on Intergovernmental Relations, *Significant Features of Fiscal Federalism*, 1987 and 1990.

In 1929, total government spending equaled $10 billion or 10 percent of gross national product. During the next decade, the years of the Great Depression, government spending as a share of gross national product almost doubled, reaching 19 percent in 1939. Government spending has continued to grow at a moderate rate in the decades since 1939, and it reached 36 percent of GNP in 1989.

The general pattern of growth in spending hides notable variations by level of government. In the years from 1929 to 1989, almost all the growth resulted from increases in federal spending. Federal spending rose from 3 percent of GNP in 1929 to 23 percent of GNP in 1989. During these same years, there was an important, but limited increase in spending by state governments and a small decline in local government spending as a share of GNP. These figures confirm the importance of national crises in expanding government, but they indicate that other factors are important as well.

The emergence of an urban-industrial economy generates problems that only positive government can address. The growth of private firms has led government to play a more active role in supervising competition and protecting society from corporate action. The importance of this role is seen in the founding *even before the New Deal* of the Interstate Commerce Commission, the Federal Trade Commission, the Federal Reserve System, and the Justice Department's Antitrust Division. An urban, industrial society also implies pollution and congestion. The Environmental Protection Agency, natural resource programs, and public transportation agencies are bureaucratic responses to these factors.

Government has also grown in the twentieth century because it provides citizens an array of social services. Education, health care, social security, housing, and the prevention of alcohol and drug abuse have all become major public responsibilities. Some programs distribute social benefits to all citizens, while others redistribute income and benefits from one group to another.

Finally, the growth of government has been stimulated by pressures from politicians and bureaucrats. Government is composed of officials and institutions that have their own interests. Governmental responses to national crises, to modernization, or to social service demands are usually bureaucratic responses. The programs enacted to address such needs sometimes take on lives of their own. They may survive because they serve the interests of officeholders rather than the goals of the broader society.

The national government has grown dramatically in the twentieth century, but its authority over private activities and institutions may have grown more rapidly than either its payrolls or expenditures. As government has responded to events, it has shaped a new public philosophy that is supportive of positive government. Whether government undertakes new initiatives in the future or cuts back specific programs, it is no longer conceivable that government could return to its pre–New Deal or even its pre–World War II scale. Positive government embodies the values and aspirations of a large majority of the American people. It is the distinctive accomplishment of the postdepression years, and it will continue to be a critical factor in relations between government and business in the future.

Nature of Business

What are the principal characteristics of American business in the twentieth century? In the post–New Deal era, industry demonstrated again that it could adapt to changing social and economic conditions. At the end of the nineteenth century, large firms expanded to reduce costs and obtain a larger market for their products. In the twentieth century, the diseconomies of huge corporations became more apparent. To protect companies from excessive bureaucracy, centrally managed firms decentralized authority over production, marketing, and personnel to division managers. To defend firms against changes in the fortunes of a single industry, single-product companies diversified into multiple product lines.

Technological innovation accelerated in these years and yielded new industries in such areas as electronics, biotechnology, telecommunications, synthetic materials, and computers. New products were developed, and the service sector of the nation's economy increased in significance. Production techniques were changed, research and development practices were reformed, and new skills were demanded from managers and other employees.

During these years, American firms also explored the advantages of overseas operations. Different firms, of course, had different goals. Some sought to guarantee control of raw materials needed for operations, others wanted low-cost foreign production, and still others tried to gain a foothold in lucrative foreign markets. Regardless of the motives, international operations changed the character of firms and added new dimensions to their relationships with government.

Small Business

Multinational operations, technological innovation, product diversification, and professionalized management characterize large American companies at the end of the twentieth century, but these firms are only part of the economy. About 95 percent of all businesses have fewer than twenty employees. Small businesses make economic and political contributions that should not be overlooked.

In 1986, American businesses employed 91 million workers. Of this number, 31 million individuals, or 35 percent, were employed by firms with less than 100 employees. Companies with fewer than 500 employees provided jobs for half of all workers, and companies with more than 500 workers provided jobs for the other half. At the far end of the spectrum, 25 million employees, or 27 percent, worked for companies that have more than 10,000 employees. Small business employment was greatest in the retail sector, and big firms employed the largest share of workers in manufacturing.

Small firms have done much to create new industries and stimulate economic growth. While they are less profitable than larger firms, small businesses provide the lion's share of new jobs and about half of all industrial innovations. Small business advocates contend that smaller firms are more dynamic and entrepreneurial than larger companies, more responsive to customers and markets, and better able to organize the skills and talents of their employees. The small entrepreneur is also seen to embody the individualism and initiative that is stressed in American tradition, and small enterprises are said to help maintain a fluid social structure, provide opportunity to new groups in the society, and restrain the excesses of big business and big government.

Source: U.S. Small Business Administration, *The State of Small Business: A Report of the President Transmitted to Congress*, (1988) pp. 62–63; Roy Rothwell and Walter Zegweld, *Innovation and the Small and Medium Sized Firm* (Boston: Klurer, Nighoff, 1981).

SUMMARY

The features of government, business, and law have changed dramatically during the different eras of American history. Table 1–2 presents an overview of these changes. Legal standards adopted in the country's first decades provided the essential foundation for enterprise. The period from the Civil War to the New Deal witnessed the development of a modern, industrial economy and the disruption of established institutions and markets. In the years since the stock market crash of 1929, the national government has grown from a minimal institution into a major force affecting all facets of American life.

TABLE 1–2 Overview of Developments in Law, Business, and Government

LAW	BUSINESS	GOVERNMENT
Colonial Times to Civil War		
Doctrines of property rights, contracts, and corporations	Agrarian society; small firms	Created societal framework; promoted economy
Civil War to Great Depression		
Reflected transition from rural to industrial society	Built industrial economy with large corporations	Selective economic promotion; expanded regulation
Great Depression to 1990s		
Legal acceptance of active role for government	Multinational operations; technology; diversification	Growth of positive government; distribution programs

Throughout American history, the central tendency of government has been to involve itself in private economic decision making.[49] The founders created a political and economic framework that fostered political stability and economic development. Since the first decades of the republic, government has also promoted the welfare of the general economy and critical industries. Government has been ready to regulate market operations when they yielded socially undesirable consequences and to impose community standards on private enterprise. Finally, government has been aware of the equity implications of enterprise and has undertaken social programs when it was deemed necessary.

The place of business in a system of popular government and the role of government in the management of a successful economy are difficult topics. The changes that have occurred in law, business, and government in recent decades are so fundamental that historic perspectives are only a limited guide to future action. The challenge of designing a constructive relationship between government and business for the future requires us to assess contemporary relationships between democracy and markets.

SELECTED READINGS

MANSEL G. BLACKFORD, *The Rise of Modern Business in Great Britain, the United States, and Japan* (Chapel Hill: University of North Carolina Press, 1988).

ALFRED D. CHANDLER, JR., *Scale and Scope: The Dynamics of Industrial Capitalism* (Cambridge, Mass.: Belknap Press, 1990).

THOMAS C. COCHRAN, *200 Years of American Business* (New York: Basic Books, 1977).

LOUIS GALAMBOS and JOSEPH PRATT, *The Rise of the Corporate Commonwealth: United States Business and Public Policy in the 20th Century* (New York: Basic Books, 1988).

KERMIT L. HALL, *The Magic Mirror: Law in American History* (New York: Oxford University Press, 1989).

END NOTES

[1]See Edward S. Greenberg, *Capitalism and the American Political Ideal* (Armonk, N.Y.: M.E. Sharpe, 1985), p. 53.

[2] For other definitions of historic eras, see Robert B. Carson, *Business Issues Today: Alternative Perspectives* (New York: St. Martin's Press, 1984); Edwin M. Epstein, *The Corporation in American Politics* (Englewood Cliffs, N.J.: Prentice Hall, 1969); and Greenberg, *Capitalism and the American Political Ideal.*

[3]Thomas C. Cochran, *200 Years of American Business* (New York: Basic Books, 1977), p. 173; and Frank Bourgin, *The Great Challenge: The Myth of Laissez-Faire in the Early Republic* (New York: Harper & Row, 1989), Chapter 4.

[4]Lawrence M. Friedman, *A History of American Law* (New York: Touchstone Books, 1973), pp. 157*ff*; and James Oliver Robertson, *America's Business* (New York: Hill and Wang, 1985), pp. 56–57, 97.

[5]Friedman, *A History of American Law*, p. 150; and Stuart Bruchey, *The Wealth of the Nation: An Economic History of the United States* (New York: Harper & Row, 1988), pp. 36–40.

[6]Friedman, *A History of American Law*, pp. 158–69, 447.

[7]Robertson, *America's Business*, p. 125.

[8]Ibid., pp. 12–13, 58, 103.

[9]Alfred D. Chandler, Jr., *The Visible Hand: The Managerial Revolution in American Business* (Cambridge, Mass.: Belknap Press of Harvard University Press, 1977), p. 14.

[10]Cochran, *200 Years of American Business*, pp. 20–25; Robertson, *America's Business*, pp. 67–68.

[11]Cochran, *200 Years of American Business*, pp. 30–32.

[12]Bruchey, *The Wealth of the Nation*, p. 16.

[13]Robertson, *America's Business*, p. 57 and 198.

[14]Ibid., p. 72; and Ronald E. Seavoy, "The Public Service Origins of the American Business Corporation," *Business History Review*, Spring 1978, pp. 30–60.

[15]Ibid.; Friedman, *A History of American Law*, pp. 167–68; Robertson, *America's Business*, p. 71.

[16]Ibid., p. 70.

[17]Oscar Handlin and Mary F. Handlin, "Origins of the American Business Corporation," *The Journal of Economic History*, May 1945, pp. 1–23; Cochran, *200 Years of American Business*, p. 76.

[18]This section relies on ibid., p. 63.

[19]4 Wheat. 518; 4 L. Ed. 629, 1819.

[20]11 Pet. 420.

[21]Sidney Pollard, *Peaceful Conquest: The Industrialization of Europe 1760–1970* (New York: Oxford University Press, 1981); and Alfred D. Chandler, *Scale and Scope: The Dynamics of Industrial Capitalism* (Cambridge, Mass.: Belknap Press, 1990).

[22]Mansel B. Blackford, *The Rise of Modern Business in Great Britain, the United States, and Japan* (Chapel Hill: University of North Carolina Press, 1988); Cochran, *200 Years of American Business*; and Louis Galambos and Joseph Pratt, *The Rise of the Corporate Commonwealth: United States Business and Public Policy in the 20th Century* (New York: Basic Books, 1988).

[23]Chandler, *The Visible Hand*, Chapter 8.

[24]Bruchey, *The Wealth of the Nation*, p. 117.

[25]Robertson, *America's Business*, p. 175.

[26]Ibid., p. 135.

[27]Chandler, *The Visible Hand*, Chapters 3–5.

[28]Ibid., pp. 3–10, 56; Robertson, *America's Business*, pp. 125–26; Thomas K. McCraw, *Prophets of Regulation* (Cambridge, Mass.: Harvard University Press, 1984), pp. 64–67.

[29]The Warren and Person index fell from 193 to 82 between 1864 and 1890. Cochran, *200 Years of American Business*, p. 72.

[30]Ibid., pp. 127–57; Blackford, *The Rise of Modern Business*, p. 55; Bruchey, *The Wealth of the Nation*, pp. 120–33.

[31]Chandler, *The Visible Hand*, Chapter 12.

[32]Blackford, *The Rise of Modern Business*, p. 57; Cochran, *200 Years of American Business*, pp. 56, 158; Galambos and Pratt, *The Rise of the Corporate Commonwealth*, pp. 80–91; and Robertson, *America's Business*, p. 126.

[33]Blackford, *The Rise of Modern Business*, p. 191.

[34]Bruchey, *The Wealth of the Nation*, pp. 122–23.

[35]Galambos and Pratt, *The Rise of the Corporate Commonwealth*, pp. 56–57.

[36]Kermit L. Hall, *The Magic Mirror: Law in American History* (New York: Oxford University Press, 1989), p. 227.

[37]Advisory Commission on Intergovernmental Relations (ACIR), *The Condition of Contemporary Federalism: Conflicting Theories and Collapsing Constraints* (Washington, D.C.: Commission, 1981), pp. 57–58; and Hall, *The Magic Mirror*, p. 234.

[38]Ibid., pp. 233–34; ACIR, *The Condition of Contemporary Federalism*, pp. 45–55.

[39]*Wabash, St. Louis, and Pacific Railway Co.* v. *Illinois*, 188 U.S. 557.

[40]134 U.S. 458, 1890; see also *Smyth* v. *Ames*, 169 U.S. 466, 1898.

[41]ACIR, *The Condition of Contemporary Federalism*, p. 79.

[42]295 U.S. 495, 1935; Hall, *The Magic Mirror*, p. 280.

[43]297 U.S. 1, 1936.

[44]Hall, *The Magic Mirror*, 279–81.

[45]301 U.S. 58, 1937.

[46]As quoted in Hall, *The Magic Mirror*, p. 282.

[47]This section relies on Robert Higgs, *Crisis and Leviathan: Critical Episodes in the Growth of American Government* (New York: Oxford University Press, 1987); Stephen Skowronek, *Building a New American State: The Expansion of National Administrative Capacities, 1877–1920* (New York: Cambridge University Press, 1982); David Lowery and William D. Berry, "The Growth of Government in the United States: An Empirical Assessment of Competing Explanations," *American Journal of Political Science*, November 1983, pp. 665–94; Greenberg,

Capitalism and the American Political Ideal; and Richard Rose, *Understanding Big Government: The Programme Approach* (London: Sage Publications, 1984).

[48]Bureau of the Census, *Historical Statistics of the United States, 1789–1945* (1945); *Historical Statistics of the United States: Colonial Times to 1970* (1975); and *Statistical Abstract* (varied years).

[49]Hall, *The Magic Mirror*, pp. 334–35.

Chapter 2

Governments and Markets

Countries create their own political and economic systems.[1] Their political-economic arrangements are not the product of irresistible forces but of a myriad of societal decisions. Some of these decisions are made at specific times, and others emerge from cultural traditions whose origins are too remote to discover.

There are as many ways of designing a country's political and economic system as there are countries. Each nation seeks arrangements that will help it achieve both material well-being and other political and social goals. The ways countries choose to structure the relationships between politics and economics are so fundamental that they often become the basis for classifying total societies.

Socialists believe that a country's economic and social needs are best served when government owns key industries and provides a comprehensive array of social services. Communist governments restrict private ownership of property and authorize public agencies to allocate the country's goods and resources to meet the nation's needs.

In the United States, Japan, and the major nations of Western Europe, privately owned firms are responsible for most employment and production decisions, and markets play a major role in allocating resources. These countries have accepted the presence of large corporations in their economies because of the contributions such firms can make to national development. The issue for these countries is to design governing arrangements that will enable them to gain the greatest benefits from economic entities at the lowest cost.

This book focuses on the political and economic arrangements in the United States and makes occasional comparisons between the U.S. and the Federal Republic of Germany, Japan, and the United Kingdom. This chapter analyzes the functions governments perform in economic affairs by drawing on the historical account of the previous chapter. It then examines the role of business in the American political process and assesses opposing views of that role. The chapter concludes by presenting capsule views of the political-economic systems of Germany, Japan, and the United Kingdom.

ROLE OF GOVERNMENT: A FUNCTIONAL PERSPECTIVE

For government to play no hand in economic decision making is not possible. Chapter 1 reported numerous examples of governmental action in the economy in all historical eras. A review of these examples reveals four types of governmental action. Table 2–1 lists these four governmental tasks and associates them with political-economic models of the role of government in the economy. The analytic models illustrate and elucidate the various governmental functions, but they are not equivalent to them.

TABLE 2–1 Functions of Government

FUNCTION	POLITICAL-ECONOMIC MODEL	OBJECTIVE OF MODEL
Framework state	Liberalism	Boost economy by reliance on market
Promotional state	Mercantilism	Boost economy by government action
Regulatory state	Market intervention	Correct operations of market
Distributional state	Marxism	Achieve economic-political equity

Framework State

Politics and markets are frequently viewed as alternative mechanisms for guiding societies. In fact, they are interrelated.[2] Societies establish a set of governing institutions that embody certain values. These institutions, in turn, construct the legal framework in which the country's economy operates and its markets function, and this framework, too, reflects important political judgments. The fact that values are inevitably embedded in the structure of markets means that there can be no markets apart from politics.

The founders of the American republic established a set of institutional rules that limited the capacity of the national government. State governments were the most influential political entities in the new system, and national authority was distributed among institutions whose agreement was required before action could be taken. This system was intended to allow a broad measure of individual liberty and inhibit the national government from abusing citizen rights, and it did. The structure also made it difficult for the national government to manage the nation's economy.

As noted in Chapter 1, the country's new political institutions did make a series of legal decisions that affected how markets would function. Private ownership of property was guaranteed, government authority was available to enforce contractual agreements, and corporations were allowed to become major vehicles of economic activity. These decisions stabilized marketplace activity and embodied values that shaped both politics and society.

The government of the framework state limits its role to creating the structure for political and economic activity. Political and economic structures are certainly not value-free, but the government in the framework state assumes that the society's interests are best served by supporting the values included in the country's basic political-economic arrangements.

The founders expected the same benefits from their reliance on markets that contemporary, market-oriented economists anticipate.[3] Perfectly competitive markets are markets in which no single producer or consumer is powerful enough to affect prices or other marketplace conditions. As producers sell their goods in competitive markets, they have an incentive to respond to consumer preferences by producing the best possible product at the lowest possible price. To do this, producers seek out new technologies and more efficient production techniques. In theory, reliance on markets should produce an efficiently functioning economy that allocates resources among competing purposes in optimal ways.

Contrary to familiar American usage, liberalism, in this context, is the belief that unregulated markets will provide a country its greatest economic benefits.

Promotional State

Early American political leaders believed that markets alone would not be adequate to promote the economic well-being of the new republic. The mercantilism of British trade policy had been part of their societal experience, and they viewed government as a positive instrument of economic policy.[4]

Seventeenth- and eighteenth-century mercantilism sought to integrate all economic enterprises into a coherent program to enhance the wealth and power of the state. American leaders regarded the state as an arsenal of practices and policies that could be used *selectively* to aid the new republic's economy. While government did not control all areas of economic activity, state and local governments frequently used their resources in the early decades to promote business, aid specific sectors of the economy, and purchase stock in private enterprises. In the middle of the nineteenth century, the national government sought to enhance the economy by providing massive subsidies for railroads, agriculture, and community development.

Contemporary governments on every front are now seeking to use their resources to promote the economic well-being of their regions. In the 1980s, state governments fashioned an active economic role for themselves by sustaining mature industries, assisting high-technology initiatives, and encouraging international enterprise.[5] The national government was also pressed to protect traditional sectors such as automobiles and steel, subsidize new projects and industries such as high-definition television and semiconductors, and develop comprehensive national economic strategies. These actions were prompted by the apparent success of foreign governments in promoting their nations' economies.

Government sponsorship of commercial affairs has become so pervasive that the present era is sometimes described as a neomercantilist age.

Regulatory State

The industrial revolution in the United States upset the nation's established social and economic patterns. Numerous groups concluded that the new industrial giants had altered the conventional terms of marketplace competition, and they sought governmental help in safeguarding their position.

Government responded with a series of creative statutes that regulated the most objectionable features of the new competition without halting its development. The national government outlawed unfair market practices and regulated the operations of controversial industries. Antitrust laws prohibited monopolies, and regulations imposed governmental standards in sensitive areas where markets were thought to function poorly, such as workplace safety and the employment of children. The regulatory state seeks to alter some consequences of market activity without losing the benefits of a competitive economy.

Market failure was the most common rationale for government regulation of marketplace activity in the nineteenth century, and it is today as well.[6] The benefits that economic theorists expect from market activity assume that markets are perfectly competitive institutions, but perfect competition in the marketplace is virtually nonexistent.[7]

Many industries are dominated by a few large firms whose market power violates the assumptions of perfect competition, and other industries, such as utilities, have structural features that make the assumptions of perfect competition unrealistic. Some economic activities affect people who are not involved in specific transactions, but markets fail to acknowledge these external effects, even though their magnitude can be enormous. Market theorists also assume that parties to a transaction have complete information about the price and quality of goods and about alternative goods that are available in the marketplace or might become available in the future. Such assumptions are, of course, false, as is the theoretical assumption that the transaction costs of marketplace activity are nil.

Market failure is the rationale for most activities of the regulatory state, but much regulation cannot be justified so politely. Many instances of government intervention are prompted by groups favoring outcomes that properly functioning markets would not provide. Such groups may believe, for example, that society would be better off with more symphony orchestras and fewer professional football teams and advocate government regulation to achieve this objective. The local butchers mentioned in Chapter 1 wanted to exclude their national competitors from local markets to help them maintain their commercial position, and they succeeded for a time in obtaining government regulations to do this.

The regulatory state is intended to provide a country the benefits of marketplace competition when markets are not fully competitive. Sometimes, however, the regulatory state can be used by groups to change the rules of well-functioning markets to produce the policy results they favor.

Distributional State

The distributional state focuses on the apportionment of material benefits among people in a society. It is particularly concerned about the impact of private economic activity and public policy on the income and wealth of the rich and poor.[8]

For Marx, property arrangements and, specifically, ownership of the means of production were the most important feature of a society. Every society could be divided into a small capitalist class that owned the means of production and a larger subject class that worked for the capitalists. Workers created value through their labor, and capitalists enlarged their fortunes by seizing the surplus produced by workers.

From a Marxist perspective, the political and legal structures of a society served the interests of the ruling class by maintaining capitalist domination. Capitalism would finally end, Marx believed, when the extremes between wealth and poverty grew so large that workers became conscious of their subjugation and recognized their common interest in overthrowing the capitalist system. The revolutionary victory of the workers would lead to a classless society in which the fruits of production would be distributed to citizens according to need. Under Marxism, the means of production would be collectively owned, and government would make economic decisions in the name of the workers.

While distributional questions are central to Marxist analysis, Marxists possess no monopoly of concern about the distribution of wealth and income. Socialists, social democrats, social reformers, and conservatives all attach special importance to distributional issues, even though their notions of equity range from egalitarian to merit-based. As a rule, the distributional state rejects the distributional patterns produced by marketplace activity and uses governmental authority to achieve a different standard of equity.

It would be a mistake to associate pure forms of the distributional state, the regulatory state, the promotional state, or the framework state with a single era or a specific government. Governments pick and choose among these functions and fashion a mixture of activities that corresponds to their distinct needs and traditions.

American government in the early national period was both liberal and mercantilist, and it regulated certain market activities to achieve the results it favored. The regulatory function of government expanded in the period between the Civil War and the New Deal, while the promotional role of government was circumscribed. Since the New Deal era, government regulations have multiplied, and increasing government attention has been paid to distributional issues. Despite this, the country still stresses market decision making and uses governmental authority to promote certain sectors of the economy.

Governments devise one set of political-economic practices to meet the problems of one era and then strike a new policy balance to fit the altered circumstances of the next era. These changes in policy are the result of the struggles that take place within a country's political system. Business influence in determining the mixture of governmental functions rises and falls in each era. A review of the ebb and flow of politics in recent decades outlines the process of change.

GOVERNMENT AND MARKETS: A POLITICAL PERSPECTIVE

The selection between government and markets as the primary domain for economic decision making is said to be a country's cardinal political-economic choice.[9] Most Americans, however, consider political issues on a concrete rather than a theoretical level. They are more concerned about immediate problems than the ideological implications of alternative solutions. Questions of governments and markets are fought out in contemporary politics, not frontally, but on the margins of such issues as employment conditions, corporate operating costs, and rates of capital investment. A survey of recent events involving the status of business in politics illustrates the conflicts that occur.

Contemporary History

In the tumultuous 1960s, the political influence of business declined when the politics of negotiation gave way to the politics of confrontation.[10] Business representatives had been comfortable with the processes of insider negotiations, and they had been able to convince the Kennedy administration to withhold legislative initiatives they opposed. Business lost its influence over the national legislative agenda when President Johnson was in office, and a flood of proposals to expand government control of business operations surfaced in departments and agencies and won consideration in Congress. During these years, business still retained enough influence to block legislative provisions it found particularly obnoxious, but its political position continued to deteriorate.

"From 1969 through 1972," one noted scholar writes, "virtually the entire American business community experienced a series of political setbacks without parallel in the postwar period."[11] Campus and public attitudes turned strongly against business, and business's ability to shape regulatory policy declined sharply. President Nixon did little to restrain an activist Congress from enacting antibusiness legislation, and his administration then used the new statutory provisions to pressure business politically. The pace of business defeats in Congress slowed during the Ford years as the economy deteriorated, but the prospects of a recovery of business influence remained dim.

In response to a string of political defeats, business began to mobilize its political resources in the mid-1970s and encourage support for its policy positions among small business, nonbusiness and grassroots groups. The tide turned in 1978 when business groups defeated a measure that would have increased the ability of unions to picket construction sites. Despite this success, business failed in these years to build significant support for its policy goals among the general public.

Business representatives began the Reagan administration in a resurgent mood, but "within a year," one commentator notes, "the honeymoon between business and the Reagan administration had ended."[12] The growth in government regulation slowed under Reagan and the cultural animosity toward business subsided, but the Reagan government did not dismantle the regulatory structures that had been created in the previous fifteen years, and it did not provide the protection business sought from domestic takeovers and foreign competition. The number of business groups increased during the Reagan years, but they expressed conflicting opinions and commanded less lobbying influence.

Public Debate

Business representatives and opponents carry on a public debate about the relative importance of government and markets when they contest specific policy issues. Beneath the surface of the disputes is an intense rivalry over the relative influence of business and nonbusiness groups in society. The rhetoric of these debates pits the image of perfectly competitive markets against the ideal of a perfectly functioning government.

Opponents of business[13] maintain that the society can be made more equitable, the performance of the economy can be enhanced, corporate decisions can be made more socially responsible, and the country's noneconomic goals can be better realized by expanding the scope of government regulation.[14] These groups are usually more concerned about the distribution of goods in the country than about the total supply of goods. They seek to enlarge the role of the public sector where they have substantial influence and diminish the societal significance of business institutions over which they have little direct control.

Business representatives respond that limitations on the autonomy of business organizations reduce their ability to provide the products and employment opportunities that society expects. They insist on the need to maintain a vibrant and autonomous private sector by which they believe the society is effectively served and in which they have substantial influence. The political agenda of the business community includes preserving the values implicit in the country's political and economic framework and undertaking policies to promote economic growth.

While the rhetoric of public debate contrasts the imagery of perfectly competitive markets with the symbolism of perfectly functioning government, reality presents the alternatives of imperfect markets and imperfect government.[15] In fact, markets frequently yield results that are suboptimal for a society and inconsistent with expected standards of conduct; and government action is often arbitrary, inequitable, and intolerant of diversity.

When presented the choice between imperfect markets and imperfect government, the United States compromised. It instructed government to expand its role in economic decision making and, at the same time, permitted the business community to use political resources to influence the course of governmental policy.

As a consequence, corporate political action has become a customary feature of the American political scene. It has also become a perennially troubling phenomenon. The juncture of economic and political power is disturbing because it threatens to overwhelm alternative political views and distort the country's policy judgments. Business involvement in politics is regarded by some as a sinister activity that advances private interests at the society's expense, but it is seen by others as a salutary factor that safeguards critical aspects of democracy. Both viewpoints should be considered.

Business Political Involvement As Desirable

Political actors participate in politics for their own purposes, but their actions can also be appraised from the perspective of the society. Those who believe that industry involvement in politics is both legitimate and desirable identify three advantages business activity provides the political system.

Defenders of business participation stress that business has provided a standard of living most people admire.[16] The country expects corporations at least to sustain the current level of material well-being in the years ahead.

A successfully functioning economy and an effectively operating business sector require a supportive policy environment. Inappropriate policies can damage the country's economy and hinder industry efforts to provide the goods and services, employment opportunities, and returns on investment the public expects.

Industry representatives understand the policy prerequisites for successful business operations. Only if business participation in politics is permitted will the policy requirements for an effective economy be expressed in the political arena. Since other interests will be present in the political arena to champion their causes, a prohibition of business involvement would exclude the group that could argue most effectively for the policies needed to support a successful economy.

Defenders of corporate political activity also argue that business participation in politics is necessary to maintain the pluralism of American democracy.[17] American democracy is based on the existence of a multiplicity of power centers within a diverse society. The expanding influence of government in American life has jeopardized the autonomy of other social institutions and reduced the capacity of those institutions to resist governmental action. Economic institutions are among the most powerful nongovernmental institutions in the society, if not the most powerful. Private business organizations are potential allies for other nongovernmental groups in their struggles against government domination. If business institutions were prevented from participating in politics, the ability of any group to stand against a domineering government would be diminished.

Finally, those who see industry involvement as legitimate contend that business organizations help safeguard individual liberties. Legally, corporations are artificial persons that have many of the same constitutional rights as regular citizens. When corporations defend their rights to freedom of speech, freedom of association, or due process, they are also strengthening the claims that individual citizens can make to these same rights. If business were excluded from political involvement, there would be one less group struggling against governmental efforts to limit constitutional rights.

Business Political Involvement As Undemocratic

From the other perspective, private corporations are not instruments of democracy but barriers to democracy. "The large private corporation fits oddly into democratic theory and vision," one distinguished author has observed. "Indeed, it does not fit."[18]

According to this view, there is no justification for business entities to participate in politics. Corporate political resources can be used to overpower other groups and subvert the country's policy process. The objective of corporations in politics is to enhance their economic position and that of their owners. Their political gains come at the expense of the general society and especially the less well-to-do. The fundamental impact of corporate involvement in politics is to accentuate existing inequities. Any benefits to society that result from corporate activities in the political arena are incidental and insignificant.

Furthermore, the political activities of modern corporations are not directed by their owners but by hired managers. In a democracy, individuals rather than concentrations of wealth are supposed to exercise political influence. Corporate managers, however, have acquired the ability to exert political influence without any legitimate basis whatsoever for having such influence. To the extent that firms are vehicles for pursuing the political goals of individuals, the country would be better served if those individuals participated in politics directly.

Finally, business involvement in politics no longer safeguards societal diversity or checks possible abuse of governmental power by officeholders. Incumbent officeholders have learned to exploit for their own purposes the resources businesses devote to political action. Incumbents in the House of Representatives, for example, capture the vast majority of campaign contributions that flow from business sources, and they use these resources to prevent the emergence of any meaningful challenge to their electoral position. Corporate involvement in politics suppresses rather than promotes social diversity.

Compromise

The political arena has responded to the issue of the legitimacy of business in politics by accepting the premises of both sides. Corporations are seen both as making essential contributions to sustaining the nation's quality of life and as exacerbating the nation's social inequalities. (See Chapter 3).

American political-economic arrangements constitute a system of *imperfect alternatives*. Instead of choosing either government or markets to make economic decisions, the country created a private economy which is both fostered and superseded by government. Government has been permitted to combine the diverse and sometimes contradictory functions of the framework, promotional, regulatory, and distributional states. Aware of the strengths and defects of both government and business, the nation shaped a political process in which both forces struggle continuously to win approval for their positions.

The choice between governments and markets as the primary vehicle for economic decision making is more complicated in the political arena than in political-economic theory. The alternatives are not a simple dichotomy between governments and markets, but a complex array of options that combine governmental and market-oriented arrangements in an infinite variety of ways. The actual functions of government and activities of industry possess a political subtlety that can only be realized by examining concrete situations. An examination of the principal characteristics of the political-economic arrangements in three other countries illustrates this complexity.

GOVERNMENT AND INDUSTRY: AN INTERNATIONAL PERSPECTIVE

Germany, Japan, the United Kingdom, and the United States are all influential nations with market-oriented economies in which private firms play a major but not unlimited role. Germany and Japan were selected for attention because they have been the world's chief examples of thriving economies for two decades. The United Kingdom, on the other hand, is a country whose time at the center of the world economic stage has passed. The UK has been regarded as a smaller, older, and sicker version of the United States, and the image of what the United States could become if it does not get its economic house in order. The United States has lost its controlling position in the global economic system, but it still possesses the world's largest national economy and numerous assets and advantages. Table 2–2 presents detailed information about other features of the four countries.

TABLE 2–2   Selected Date on Major Industrial Countries

	GERMANY	JAPAN	UNITED KINGDOM	UNITED STATES
Population (millions) 1990 (est.)	79	124	57	251
Gross National Product:				
1988 U.S. $ billions	$1,218	$2,851	$808	$4,881
1988 per capita	$19,907	$23,255	$14,152	$19,813
Annual Growth–1990	4.5%	5.6%	0.6%	0.9%
Unemployment–1990	5.1%	2.1%	5.5%	5.5%
Net National Savings As Percent of GNP–1990	26%	34%	16%	15%
Government Spending As Percent of GNP–1990	45%	33%	41%	36%

Source: *OECD Economic Outlook* (July 1991); and *Statistical Abstract of the United States 1990*, Table 1447.

Despite broad similarities, the four countries organize relationships between government and business in strikingly different ways. John Zysman has investigated the economic processes of various countries and identified the institutions that provide economic leadership in each.[19] For Zysman, the United States is a country with a *company-led* economy in which private corporations organize the economy and government intervention is limited. Japan has a *state-led* economy in which the structure of the financial system itself is an instrument of government intervention in the marketplace. Economic leadership in Germany is *negotiated*, with major decisions resulting from specific deals between finance, labor, government, and industry. Zysman describes the United Kingdom as lacking a coherent approach to managing its economy. Government occasionally seeks to take the economic initiative, but companies retain their autonomy, and powerful unions are not organized to participate in national negotiations. Closer examinations of Germany, Japan, and the United Kingdom explain Zysman's characterizations more fully.

Germany

The recovery of the German economy after World War II is often described as an "economic miracle."[20] German economic policies in the 1950s and 1960s were market-oriented, and the country profited from the expansion then occurring in the international economy. With the oil price hikes, inflationary pressures, and rising unemployment of the 1970s and 1980s, the country's economic policies became more interventionist.[21] Despite this, the postwar record of the German "social market" economy remains impressive, and, in the early 1990s, Germany was one of the world's leading trading nations.

The country's economic success is usually attributed to four factors. First, the German government is based on a series of institutional relationships that emphasize consensus and political stability. The country's parliamentary system, the influence of the bureaucracy, and the pattern of coalition governments have yielded a predictable policy environment that stresses rational decision making and encourages economic growth.

Another factor that has contributed to economic success is a harmonious system of labor-management relations. Postwar German unions have focused on worker participation in corporate governance and have accepted the importance of economic productivity. Employee representation on corporate boards of directors and the presence of workers' councils in factories have reduced tensions during periods of decline.

Banking institutions also play a stronger hand in Germany than in other major countries.[22] Banks own stock in major corporations and are also permitted to vote the stock they hold for their customers. As a consequence, banks are directly represented on corporate boards of directors, and representatives of the three largest banks chair the boards of fifteen of the country's largest companies.[23] For this reason, banks are able to provide an informed, yet somewhat detached, view of the long-term interests of companies and industries.

Finally, the success of the German economy has depended on a vigorous export program. Exports not only deliver a healthy trade surplus to the nation's economy, but they also provide marketplace discipline for German companies.[24]

Japan

In the past twenty-five years, no major economy in the world has outperformed Japan's, but Japanese economic achievement is not just a recent phenomenon. In the decades before World War II, Japan already had a large, efficient industrial sector that was supported by an active government and an influential bureaucracy.[25] Postwar reconstruction was guided by a similar coalition of industrial leaders, bureaucratic elites, and political figures who constructed a public consensus based on the primacy of economic growth.

In the 1950s and 1960s, the Ministry of Finance (MOF) and the Ministry of International Trade and Industry (MITI) worked with business panels to draft elaborate plans for economic development.[26] Through a process of "administrative guidance," the agencies gave firms and industries specific economic direction.[27] The Japanese economy was mostly closed to foreign competition in these years, and the ministries used their role in international trade to provide product protection to cooperative industries. The ministries' professional stature and their control of scarce capital, foreign exchange, and technology ensured business support for their program.

Two characteristics of this administrative system were the insulation enjoyed by the MOF and MITI from daily political pressures and their resulting ability to base decisions on substantive considerations. The two ministries probably constituted the capitalist world's most powerful economic bureaucracy, and the nation's parliament was the weakest in major industrial democracies.

Japanese economic planning was more important as a mechanism of coordination between government and industry than as a compendium of specific decisions. Collaboration and negotiation were so intense that some argued it was an error to regard government and industry as distinct institutions. Businesspeople and bureaucrats had joint jurisdiction over markets and productive resources, and both the state and private groups often worked to enhance the authority of the other.[28] As a result, public policy and private economic activity achieved a level of coordination unmatched in other industrial economies.[29]

In the 1970s and 1980s, the Japanese economy emerged to play a prominent international role. Policy attention shifted from macroeconomic policies to mercantilist efforts to foster the welfare of specific commercial sectors. In industry after industry, Japan won from the United States first place in the global marketplace, and the country's promotional policies contributed to this achievement.[30]

United Kingdom

The United Kingdom was not only the world's first industrial nation, it was also the first nation to experience widespread industrial decline. The UK's economic status has been deteriorating for more than a century as the institutions responsible for the industrial and imperial successes in the eighteenth and nineteenth centuries failed to adapt to evolving conditions.[31] Modern corporations were slow to emerge in the UK, government remained distant from industrial developments, and labor unions emphasized distributional conflicts without concern for the common stake in economic achievement. Through the 1950s, government lacked both the eyes to follow events in industry and the hands to intervene in specific situations.

In subsequent years, the United Kingdom has built the institutional capacity to sustain economic policies, but the government still failed to cure the continuing stagnation.[32] The Treasury was responsible for taxation, public expenditures, and exchange-rate policy, and individual agencies championed the interests of specific industries, but the government lacked a coherent strategy to support its policy initiatives. The government frequently intervened in the marketplace to assist specific industries, but its aid programs responded more fully to the claims of politically influential groups than to the substantive requirements of economic growth.

After 1983, the Thatcher government guided the UK away from widespread intervention in specific industries and sought instead to build an "enterprise" culture.[33] Macroeconomic policy shifted from stimulating employment to stabilizing the money supply and fighting inflation. Many nationalized industries were sold, and other areas of industrial activity were deregulated to promote competition. The final assessment of the Thatcher policies cannot yet be made, but the Thatcher era increased short-term unemployment and aggravated social tensions while at the same time improving productivity, reviving investment, increasing profits, and giving new life to persistently weak industries.

SUMMARY

American political-economic arrangements are based on a series of choices among imperfect alternatives. Privately owned firms have been allowed to play a prominent role in the economy because such firms are seen to provide the society more benefits than costs.[34] Government has been instructed to enhance the success of economic activity and to exercise the right of popular majorities to override marketplace decisions when those decisions produce social or economic distress.

The structure of the political-economic system means that conflicts between market and nonmarket groups are a recurrent feature of political life. Groups assess differently the priority to be given to maintaining an efficiently functioning economy and to moving toward a more equal distribution of opportunities and rewards in the society. They also differ in their degree of approval of the existing patterns of influence in the society and of the appropriateness of their own place in the political process.

As the role of government expands in the economy, business groups become more active in the political arena. Market-oriented and non-market-oriented groups struggle with increasing frequency to win public support for their viewpoints. These struggles occur in a specific context of public trust and criticism of both government and business. An analysis of public attitudes toward business and of the broader advocacy environment sheds additional light on the dynamics of the political process.

SELECTED READINGS

KENT CALDER, *Crisis and Compensation: Public Policy and Political Stability in Japan, 1949–1986* (Princeton: Princeton University Press, 1988).

WYN GRANT, *Business and Politics in Britain* (London: Macmillan Education, 1987).

PETER J. KATZENSTEIN (ed.), *Industry and Politics in West Germany: Toward the Third Republic* (Ithaca: Cornell University Press, 1989).

CHARLES E. LINDBLOM, *Politics and Markets: The World's Political-Economic Systems* (New York: Basic Books, 1977).

CHARLES WOLF, *Markets or Governments: Choosing between Imperfect Alternatives* (Cambridge, Mass.: MIT Press, 1988).

END NOTES

[1]This discussion draws from Marshall B. Clinard, *Corporate Corruption: The Abuse of Power* (New York: Praeger, 1990), pp. 1–3; Stephen L. Elkin, *City and Regime in the American Republic* (Chicago: University of Chicago Press, 1987), p. 11; and Wyn Grant, *Business and Politics in Britain* (London: Macmillan Education, 1987), pp. 1–2.

[2]John Zysman, *Governments, Markets, and Growth: Financial Systems and the Politics of Industrial Change* (Ithaca: Cornell University Press, 1983), pp. 17–18.

[3]See, for example, Milton Friedman and Rose Friedman, *Free to Choose: A Personal Statement* (New York: Harcourt Brace Jovanovich, 1980).

[4]Frank Bourgin, *The Great Challenge: The Myth of Laissez-Faire in the Early Republic* (New York: Harper & Row, 1989), Chapter 4.

[5]Peter Eisinger, *The Rise of the Entrepreneurial State* (Madison: University of Wisconsin Press, 1988); R. Scott Fosler (ed.), *The New Economic Role of American States* (New York: Oxford University Press, 1988); and David Osborne, *Laboratories of Democracy* (Cambridge, Mass.: Harvard Business School Press, 1988).

[6]Tyler Cowen (ed.), *The Theory of Market Failure: A Critical Examination* (Fairfax, VA: George Mason University Press, 1988).

[7]See, for example, Peter Asch and Rosalind S. Seneca, *Government and the Marketplace* (Chicago: Dryden Press, 1989), Chapters 3–5.

[8]For example, John Kenneth Galbraith, *Age of Uncertainty* (Boston: Houghton Mifflin, 1977).

[9]Charles Wolf, *Markets or Governments: Choosing between Imperfect Alternatives* (Cambridge, Mass.: MIT Press, 1988), Chapter 1.

[10]This section follows David Vogel, *Fluctuating Fortunes: Political Power of Business in America* (New York: Basic Books, 1989), Chapter 1, and pp. 11, 43, 252, and 288–89.

[11]Ibid., p. 59.

[12]Ibid., p. 252.

[13]See Seymour Martin Lipset and William Schneider, *The Confidence Gap: Business, Labor, and Government in the Public Mind* (New York: Free Press, 1983), pp. 372–73.

[14]David Vogel, "The Inadequacy of Contemporary Opposition to Business," *Daedalus: Journal of the American Academy of Arts and Sciences* (Summer 1980), pp. 47–58, especially p. 48.

[15]Wolf, *Markets or Governments*, pp. 6–7.

[16]See Michael Novak, *Spirit of Democratic Capitalism* (New York: Simon and Schuster, 1982); and Albert T. Sommers (ed.), *The Free Society and Planning* (New York: The Conference Board, 1975).

[17]See Edwin M. Epstein, *The Corporation in American Politics* (Englewood Cliffs, N.J.: Prentice Hall, 1969), p. 324.

[18]Charles E. Lindblom, *Politics and Markets: The World's Political-Economic Systems* (New York: Basic Books, 1977), p. 356; see also Chapters 13–14.

[19]Zysman, *Governments, Markets, and Growth*, pp. 92–94.

[20]This section is drawn from Ernst-Juergen Horn, "Germany: A Market-led Process," pp. 41–75, in Francois Duchene and Geoffrey Shepherd (eds.), *Managing Industrial Change in Western Europe* (London: Frances Printer, 1987); Jeffrey A. Hart, "West German Industrial Policy," pp. 161–86, in Claude E. Barfield and William A. Schambra (eds.), *The Politics of Industrial Policy* (Washington: American Enterprise Institute, 1986); and Andrew P. Black, "Industrial Policy in W. Germany: Policy in Search of a Goal?", pp. 84–127, in Graham Hall, (ed.), *European Industrial Policy* (London: Croom Helm, 1986).

[21]Juergen B. Donges, "Industrial Policies in West Germany's Not So Market-oriented Economy," *The World Economy*, vol. 3, no. 2, 1980, pp. 185–204.

[22]Andrew Shonfield, *Modern Capitalism* (New York: Oxford University Press, 1965). For an alternative view, see Wyn Grant, William Paterson, and Colin Whitson, *Government and the Chemical Industry: A Comparative Study of Britain and West Germany* (Oxford: Clarendon Press, 1988), pp. 84–97.

[23]Zysman, *Governments, Markets, and Growth*, p. 264.

[24]See the discussion of "fulcrum" industries in Christopher S. Allen and Jeremiah M. Riemer, "The Industrial Policy Controversy in West Germany: Organized Adjustment and the Emergence of Meso-Corporatism," pp. 45–64, in Richard E. Foglesong and Joel D. Wolfe (eds.), *The Politics of Economic Adjustment: Pluralism, Corporatism, and Privatization* (New York: Greenwood Press, 1989).

[25]Charles J. McMillan, *The Japanese Industrial System*, 2nd ed. (Berlin: Walter de Gruyter, 1989).

[26]Chalmers Johnson, *MITI and the Japanese Miracle* (Stanford: Stanford University Press, 1982); and Chalmers Johnson, "The Institutional Foundation of Japanese Industrial Policy," pp. 187–205 in Barfield and Schambra (eds.), *The Politics of Industrial Policy*.

[27]James Horne, "The Economy and the Political System," pp. 141–70, in J.A.A. Stockwin, et al., *Dynamic and Immobilist Politics in Japan* (Honolulu: University of Hawaii Press, 1988).

[28]See Richard J. Samuels, *The Business of the Japanese State: Energy Markets in Comparative and Historical Perspective* (Ithaca: Cornell University Press, 1987), especially pp. 8–9, 260, and 286.

[29]George C. Eads and Kozo Yamamura, "The Future of Industrial Policy," pp. 423–68, in Kozo Yamamura and Yasukichi Yasuba, *The Domestic Transformation* (Stanford: Stanford University Press, 1987).

[30]Clyde V. Prestowitz, *Trading Places: How We Are Giving Our Future to Japan and How to Reclaim It* (New York: Basic Books, 1988).

[31]John Zysman, *Governments, Markets, and Growth*, pp. 175–206; and Geoffrey Shepherd, "United Kingdom: A Resistance to Change," pp. 145–77, in Francois Duchene and Geoffrey Shepherd (eds.), *Managing Industrial Change in Western Europe*.

[32]Wyn Grant, *The Political Economy of Industrial Policy* (London: Butterworths, 1982), especially pp. 125, 146–47; and Scott Newton and Dilwyn Porter, *Modernization Frustrated: The Politics of Industrial Decline in Britain since 1900* (London: Unwin Hyman, 1988), especially pp. x and 185.

[33]See ibid., pp. 84–112; and Jeffrey B. Freyman, "Industrial Policy: Patterns of Convergence and Divergence," in Jerold L. Waltman and Donley T. Studlar (eds.), *Political Economy: Public Policies in the United States and Britain* (Jackson, Miss.: University of Mississippi, 1987), pp. 44–68.

[34]Herbert McClosky and John Zaller, *The American Ethos: Public Attitudes toward Capitalism and Democracy* (Cambridge, Mass.: Harvard University Press, 1984), Chapters 1 and 9, especially p. 7.

Chapter 3

Advocacy Process: Public Opinion, Groups, and the Media

James Fenimore Cooper, the nineteenth-century novelist and essayist, compared shaping public opinion in a democracy to staging a military coup.[1] Both, he thought, were effective means of seizing governmental power.

Public opinion today can focus governmental attention on issues and influence policy. It can determine who wins political battles and who loses.

Public impressions of government and business form the context in which political disputes between supporters and opponents of business take place. Public officials do not want to be associated with unpopular causes when elections loom. If insurance companies are thought to charge exorbitant rates, few elected officials want to be seen opposing insurance regulation. If labor union leaders are perceived as selfish and self-serving, most elected officials will keep their distance from union-endorsed political causes.

Public sentiments toward business are less friendly today than they were in the early 1960s, but less hostile than in the 1930s or the mid-1970s. Opinions change as citizens monitor corporate performance and interpret political-economic events.

This chapter examines public attitudes toward business, reviews the changes that have occurred in those attitudes in recent decades, and investigates the factors that led to the changes. A puzzling development in attitudes toward business took place in the 1980s. It appears that traditional patterns of opinion may be fading and a new opinion environment taking shape. After reviewing opinions toward business, the chapter draws back from the narrow focus on attitudes and explores the broader interest group and media context in which opinions toward business are formed.

PUBLIC ATTITUDES TOWARD BUSINESS

The public image of business leaders today is a sorry spectacle. Tune in any television drama or detective show or watch any movie, and the chances are that a businessperson is the culprit.[2] In most shows, the businessperson's selfish pursuit of profits spreads destruction and despair throughout the society.

The 1989 film *Roger and Me* humorously but effectively captured contemporary attitudes toward corporate leaders.[3] It follows the adventures of a young reporter who is seeking to interview the head of General Motors to learn why the company is closing factories and laying off workers in Flint, Michigan. The film interposes scenes of the poor being evicted from their homes with pictures of affluent neighborhoods, exclusive clubs, and posh social gatherings. It argues that corporate leaders are unconcerned about the devastation their decisions cause for communities like Flint.

Public Confidence in Business Leaders

In the 1950s and early 1960s, public opinion surveys routinely reported that citizens had substantial confidence in the leaders of the country's institutions.[4] More than 60 percent of citizens told interviewers they had great confidence in the people running colleges and universities, medical institutions, and the military. Almost half usually said that they had a great deal of confidence in people running ten different social institutions including religious organizations, the press, the Supreme Court, labor unions, Congress, and the executive branch. As late as 1966, 55 percent of those interviewed responded that they had a great deal of confidence in the leaders of major companies. (See Table 3–1.)

TABLE 3–1 Public Confidence in the Leaders of Major Institutions, 1966–1990

Question: As far as people in charge of running _____ are concerned, would you say you have a great deal of confidence, only some confidence, or hardly any confidence at all in them?

	PERCENT RESPONDING, "A GREAT DEAL OF CONFIDENCE"					
	1966	*1971*	*1976*	*1981*	*1986*	*1990*
Major Companies	55%	39%	16%	21%	16%	14%
Congress	42	24	9	15	21	12
Labor Unions	22	16	10	11	11	14
Average of Ten Institutions	48	33	20	23	24	24

Source: Louis Harris and Associates, November 1990.

Public confidence in the nation's leaders plummeted between 1966 and 1974. The collapse included leaders of both private and governmental institutions. By 1976, only 9 percent of respondents reported great confidence in the leaders of Congress, down from 42 percent ten years earlier. Only 16 percent of the sample indicated great confidence in the leaders of major companies, down from 55 percent in a decade. The drop in confidence in business leaders involved business in general and every segment of the business community.[5] The proportion of people reporting great confidence in the leaders of ten institutions fell from 48 percent in 1966 to 20 percent in 1976.

Public confidence in the nation's leaders was destroyed by two events: the Vietnam War and the Watergate scandal. Both events were profound national traumas, and they undermined public confidence in the leaders of all institutions, regardless of whether those institutions were involved in Vietnam and Watergate. The public lost faith in the leaders of religious, educational, press, labor, and business institutions as profoundly as in the leaders of the executive, legislative, and judicial branches of the national government. In the years since 1976, there has been little recovery of public confidence in the leaders of the nation's institutions.

Attitudes toward Business

Judgments about the leaders of institutions must be distinguished both from opinions about the institutions themselves and from attitudes toward the broader political and economic systems. While the public believes that the individuals running institutions are untrustworthy, they retain deep confidence in the nation's political system and its entrepreneurial economy. In contrast to uniformly negative assessments of leaders and conspicuously positive views of the political and economic systems, citizens make surprisingly complex judgments about business itself.

By a large margin, citizens believe that their personal interests coincide with the interests of business. As reported in Table 3–2, when asked if they believe that what is good for business is bad or good for the average person, 61 percent reply that what is good for business is good for the average person. Only 17 percent respond that what is good for business is bad for the average person.

Citizens also believe that large companies make a vital contribution to the nation's well-being. As reported in Table 3–3, 83 percent of respondents in 1961 agreed with the statement, "Large companies are essential for the nation's growth and expansion." In the decades since 1961, public attitudes on this item have remained remarkably stable. Agreement increased a few points in some years and declined a few points in others, but in 1989, 84 percent of those interviewed still concurred with the view that large companies are necessary for nation's economic future.

TABLE 3–2   Citizen and Business Interests, 1987

Question: Some people think what's good for business is bad for the average person.... Others think what's good for business is also good for the average person.... What do you think—what's good for business is bad for the average person, or what's good for business is also good for the average person?

	PERCENT AGREEING
What's good for business is bad for the average person	17%
What's good for business is good for the average person	61
Mixed feelings (volunteered)	19
Don't know	5

Source: Roper Organization, August 1987.

TABLE 3–3   General Assessments of Large Companies, 1961–1989

	PERCENT AGREEING							
	1961	*1965*	*1969*	*1973*	*1977*	*1981*	*1985*	*1989*
Large companies are essential for the nation's growth and expansion.	83%	88%	85%	82%	79%	83%	83%	84%
The profits of large companies help make things better for everyone.	59	67	55	46	43	39	40	39
There's too much power concentrated in the hands of a few large companies for the good of the nation.	57	52	61	74	72	76	73	73
For the good of the country, many of our largest companies ought to be broken up into smaller companies.	41	37	45	53	55	53	45	50

Source: Opinion Research Corporation, "Corporate Reputations—1989: Summary of Selected Findings...", Study No. 22121, 1990.

Not all attitudes toward large companies have been so positive or so stable. In 1961, 59 percent of the sample agreed with the view that "The profits of large companies help make things better for everyone." (See Table 3–3). Support for this positive assessment of corporate profits increased in 1965 and then fell sharply through the 1970s. In 1989, 39 percent of those interviewed concurred with the statement that corporate profits benefited everyone.

The two other questions reported in Table 3–3 address the issue of corporate power. According to another statement, "There's too much power concentrated in the hands of a few large companies for the good of the nation." In 1961, 57 percent of those interviewed shared the anxiety about concentrations of power. Fears of corporate power declined slightly in 1965 and then surged in the Vietnam and Watergate years of the late 1960s and the early 1970s. Since 1973, concerns about corporate power have been moderately high and stable.

The final statement in Table 3–3 proposes a solution to worries about the role of corporations in society: "For the good of the country, many of our largest companies ought to be broken up into smaller companies." The pattern of agreement with this statement resembles that of the previous item. In 1961, 41 percent agreed that the largest companies should be broken up. The portion sharing this view fell slightly in 1965, increased strongly during the Vietnam and Watergate years, and has remained at the 50 percent level.

The public has a more positive view of "business" and "large companies" than of the people running the firms. By better than a three-to-one margin, citizens believe that what is good for business is good rather than bad for the average person. More than eight of ten respondents agree that large companies make a vital contribution to the country's growth and expansion, and the portion of the population holding this view has been stable for three decades. At the end of the 1980s, the public was notably more critical of corporate power and less supportive of corporate profits than it had been at the beginning of the 1960s, but significant proportions of the public still express explicitly pro-corporate views on these issues.

Basis for Attitudes toward Business

While the level of support and criticism of business is important, it is even more meaningful to understand the bases of those judgments.

Historically, public attitudes toward business have been related to the state of the economy.[6] The 1880s were a period of prosperity and positive attitudes toward business. The social, political, and economic disruption caused by industrialization became acute in the 1890s, and corporations were blamed for the society's ills and the economy's depressions. Middle class antagonism toward business surfaced during the Progressive era, but this was also an era of economic growth and a rising standard of living. Probusiness attitudes were eventually ascendant as Americans concluded that the best way to achieve material progress was through private rather than governmental action.

As would be expected, confidence in business fell precipitously in the 1930s with the collapse of the nation's economy. Public confidence in business was reestablished during World War II, expanded in the 1950s, and probably reached its height in the early 1960s.

A statistical analysis of the influence of the state of the economy on confidence in business confirms the impression of the historical record. A comparison of survey data on public confidence in the leaders of major companies with measures of unemployment and inflation for the period from 1966 to 1980 finds a strong negative correlation. The statistical results demonstrate that low levels of unemployment and, to a lesser extent, low rates of inflation were associated with high confidence in the people running major companies.[7]

Public attitudes toward business are also a product of citizen judgments about the performance of companies in specific areas. Table 3–4 lists ten societal tasks which many believe are responsibilities of business and reports citizen views of how well businesses fulfilled these responsibilities.

TABLE 3–4 Responsibilities of Business, 1978 and 1988

Question: Now here's a list of things people have said are or should be responsibilities of business in this country.... For each one tell me whether you think business fulfills its responsibilities fully, fairly well, not too well, or not at all?

RESPONSIBILITY	PERCENT RESPONDING FULLY/FAIRLY WELL	
	1978	*1988*
Developing new products and services	88%	88%
Producing good quality products and services	66	77
Making products that are safe to use	65	76
Hiring minorities	74	73
Providing jobs for people	71	72
Charging reasonable prices for goods and services	33	54
Keeping profits at reasonable levels	36	51
Paying their fair share of taxes	40	45
Advertising honestly	33	42
Cleaning up their own air and water pollution	40	36
Mean of Ten Scores	54.6%	61.4%

Source: Roper Organization, *Roper Reports 89–1*, pp. 112–15.

Business gets rather high marks from citizens on items involving products and jobs.[8] Almost nine of ten respondents believed in 1988 that business fulfilled its responsibilities fully or fairly well in developing new products and services.

Producing good quality products and making products that are safe to use are the business responsibilities citizens think are most important. Three of four people interviewed in 1988 answered that business did a good job meeting these responsibilities. The proportion of people assessing business performance positively in these areas had increased by more than 10 percent in the previous decade. More than 70 percent of the sample also concluded that business discharged its responsibilities fully or fairly well in hiring minorities and providing jobs.

According to the survey, business does notably less well fulfilling its responsibilities in social areas. About half the respondents believed that business held prices and profits to reasonable levels, and less than half replied that business paid their fair share of taxes. Somewhat more than 40 percent of those interviewed concluded that business acted responsibly in advertising honestly, and only 36 percent found that business did a responsible or fairly responsible job clearing up their own air and water pollution. Despite the low ratings, public assessments of business performance in meeting social responsibilities improved in the last decade on four of the five items examined.

SUMMARY

Survey data indicate that citizens make complex judgments about corporations. The primary factor supporting the social and political role of corporations is that citizens regard corporations as the mainstay of the nation's consumer society.[9] By a large margin, they perceive their interests to be compatible with the interests of business rather than in conflict with them. Large companies are seen to make essential contributions to the growth and expansion of the economy and to do a responsible job providing products and employment.

The public appreciates the benefits of the consumer society, but it also harbors deep reservations about large companies. Business, especially big business, is distrusted because it is seen to be powerful. Americans distrust power. The unrestrained power of corporations, labor unions, or government could be used arbitrarily and could lead to the abuse of citizen rights. Remoteness appears to accentuate the distrust of power because big business is viewed far more negatively than "the businesses around you."

Businesses are also assessed negatively because they are seen as selfish and self-centered. Many citizens believe that companies place profits before the public interest. The prices businesses charge are too high, and the taxes they pay are too low. Businesses too frequently pollute the environment in pursuit of profits and act without adequate regard for the impact of their actions on the community.

Citizen assessments of business are part of the political context in which controversies about government and industry occur. Changes in the dynamics of citizen opinion may now be occurring that could affect the outcome of political controversies in the years ahead.

THE PUZZLE OF RECENT ATTITUDES TOWARD BUSINESS

Public attitudes toward business in the last decade present an intriguing puzzle. As noted, opinions toward business in the past were related to the state of the economy and citizen ratings of business performance in specific areas. In the 1980s, this relationship broke apart.

By 1990, unemployment and inflation rates had fallen sharply from the early 1980s. Citizens were twice as likely to tell interviewers that they were better off financially as they were a decade before.[10] And, public appraisals of how well business fulfilled its societal responsibilities averaged 7 percent higher in 1988 than when measured a decade earlier. (See Table 3–4.)

Despite these improvements in the economy and citizen views of how well business discharged specific tasks, business leaders remained the society's villains of choice in the 1980s. The decade witnessed no increase in confidence in the people running large companies and no evidence that general opinions of business had become more favorable. (See Table 3–3).

How come? Why did the dog not bark? Why did general attitudes toward large companies and their leaders not become more positive? What changes in the formation of opinions toward business ended the traditional relationship between improvements in employment and inflation and more positive attitudes toward business? Do the changes mean that general attitudes toward business will remain fixed at the negative levels of the mid-1970s? Answers to these questions lead to four factors that shape attitudes toward business: media treatment of business; the interest-group environment; the role of labor unions; and changes in the structure of economic policy.

Media Image of Business

Business people believe that they are routinely portrayed by the media, and especially by television, as crooks and swindlers who ravage communities and exploit workers.[11] They complain that the media emphasize the faults of American industry without acknowledging its achievements. The media indicate that success in business has nothing to do with competence or creativity and deny that individualism, fulfillment, or social concern are possible in a business environment. Business commentators believe the unsavory media image explains why the economic improvements of the 1980s were not translated into greater confidence in business leaders and more positive attitudes toward business in general.

It is an error to believe that critical portraits of business people are an invention of television or the television age. One study finds that negative images of businesspeople have characterized American life from the start.[12] This analysis reports that the "American writer mounted direct attacks on capitalism as an economic system during and shortly after the War of Independence" and continued those attacks in subsequent generations.

Literary criticisms of business originally stressed moral and cultural themes. William Dean Howell's *The Rise of Silas Lapham* (1885) is usually regarded as the first American business novel.[13] It is an account of Silas Lapham, a young Vermont man who recognized the commercial value of materials discovered on the family farm and began to manufacture paint. Needing additional capital, Lapham took on a partner, but he then forced the partner out of the business and became wealthy by seizing his partner's share of the profits. In an effort to make amends, Lapham lent money to the former partner, but Lapham's company encountered financial setbacks, his new home was destroyed in a fire, and he fell into bankruptcy. The novel concludes by suggesting that bankruptcy was a cleansing experience that redeemed Lapham from his earlier sins.

The theme that business success rested on tainted money was soon joined by the literary image of businesspeople as shallow and uncultured. In *Winesburg, Ohio* (1919), Sherwood Anderson's businesspeople were narrow and insensitive residents of a small town who denied cultural freedom to artists. Sinclair Lewis's *Babbitt* (1923) was a businessman in a middle-sized town who contributed nothing of value to the community, was attracted to products simply because they were nationally advertised, and used commercial standards to evaluate social institutions.

Explicitly political criticisms of business first appeared in novels about the ruthless tactics of the new corporations at the beginning of the twentieth century. Frank Norris's chronicle of railroad development in California, *The Octopus* (1901), focused on struggles between farmers and railroad companies, but the charges his characters made against the railroads could have been leveled against large corporations in general:[14]

> They own us, these task-masters of ours; they own our homes, they own our legislatures. We cannot escape from them. There is no redress. We are told we can defeat them by the ballot-box. They own the ballot-box. We are told that we must look to the courts for redress; they own the courts. We know them for what they are—ruffians in politics, ruffians in finance, ruffians in law, ruffians in trade, bribers, swindlers, and tricksters....
>
> They swindle a nation of a hundred million and call it Financiering; they levy a blackmail and call it Commerce; they corrupt a legislature and call it Politics; they bribe a judge and call it Law; they hire blacklegs to carry out their plans and call it Organization; they prostitute the honour of a State and call it Competition.

While Norris's embattled characters were wealthy farmers and community leaders, the country's first major proletarian novel was Upton Sinclair's *The Jungle* (1906). A Lithuanian immigrant family settled in Chicago and found work in the brutal stockyards area. The immigrants soon recognized that the workers were slaves to the machines in the factories and were no better than the animals they slaughtered. The personal jealousies inherent in capitalism destroyed the humanity of all who worked in the system, and salvation, according to the novel, could only be found through some form of socialism.

Negative portrayals of businesspeople pervade American culture, but they are not universal. The popular Horatio Alger novels of the nineteenth century taught that business virtues provided handsome rewards, and individual business figures were often associated in short stories and essays with attractive personal qualities such as inventiveness and hard work.[15] Occasionally business figures have even been cast as cultural heroes. Recall that James Stewart's hero in the classic movie *It's a Wonderful Life* (1946) was a savings and loan company executive.

Media criticisms of business have long been a prominent feature of American culture. They were not an invention of television or the 1980s, and they can not explain why attitudes toward business did not improve with the economy. Since criticisms of business are perennial cultural themes, why have the media been attacked by contemporary business commentators?

One reason is that the media are more influential than they once were.[16] While the critical themes are not new, the power of mass media to express these themes far exceeds anything James Fenimore Cooper could have imagined. In the 1960s, television emerged as a major force in the nation's politics, and a national press came together made up of *The New York Times* and *The Washington Post* and newsmagazines such as *Time* and *Newsweek*.

When the nightly network news programs expanded from fifteen to thirty minutes in the early 1960s, they were able to devote time to defining the meaning of stories for their audience. Reform movements in the United States have usually been driven by the perception that the country was not living up to its ideals. As "objective" reporting styles gave way to "advocacy" journalism, the media brought the gap between ideals and performance to a wider audience in a more vivid way. One scholar writes, "The media are, in effect, the clergy of the...society: they act as custodians of its ultimate values; they expose and denounce deviations from those values; they...have no recourse but to challenge and expose the inequities of power."[17] As powerful but imperfect institutions, business organizations are perpetual targets of journalists who demonstrate that companies fail to live up to the society's ideals. The criticisms of business are traditional, but the effectiveness with which they are broadcast is new.

Interest-Group Environment

Negative attitudes toward companies and their leaders may have persisted in the 1980s because the interest-group environment had changed. According to this position, the interest-group environment is no longer driven by grassroots opinions of citizens but by the strategies of issue entrepreneurs. To understand this view, it is helpful to recall the role of interest groups in American political theory.

Interest-group activity once constituted a vision of how democracy was supposed to work. Groups emerged from the wants, needs, and ambitions of citizens. When an important opinion arose among the people, a group was organized to promote that sentiment. Group activity represented citizen opinions to government and served as an early warning signal of public discontent. Groups detected popular unrest at an early stage and alerted public officials to the need for policy reforms before a crisis occurred.

In recent decades, the interest-group environment has changed. Groups today are more likely to be staff-dominated institutions than organizations responding to grassroots concerns.[18] New communications technologies make it possible for a few activists to create an organization to advance a policy goal and then recruit the members on whose behalf the organization supposedly speaks. Often the new groups have no citizen members and have little foundation in society.

In recent decades, there has been an enormous increase in the number of groups promoting their specialized goals.[19] Journalists report that the halls of Congress are so jammed with lobbyists that legislators have trouble moving from room to room.[20] Scholars argue that the proliferation of groups constitutes an "excess of democracy."[21] So many demands are placed on government that the system is overwhelmed. Elected officials are reluctant to adopt policies that offend any group, and, thus, government decision making is paralyzed.[22]

The new interest-group environment has additional features as well.[23] Groups and causes in society are now represented in the policy process that were previously underrepresented, such as women, consumers, environmentalists, senior citizens, and peace groups.[24] The new groups usually seek collective benefits for segments of the society rather than individual benefits, and their goals are as much ideological as material. The new movements draw support from many parts of the society rather than a single social group, and their organizational structures are less developed than those of conventional groups. Finally, the political style of the new groups is more likely to be confrontational than the style of established groups and is likely to be outside the norms of traditional politics.

Many presume that the new staff-led organizations, with ideas, copy machines, and a sense of media relations, have enriched democracy. A voice has been won by the voiceless, and issues brought to the public agenda that previously had been ignored.[25]

Other commentators stress that the new groups focus on social aspirations rather than objective conditions.[26] Issue activists seek to raise social expectations and promote dissatisfaction in order to build support for their policy objectives. Their normal tactics are to portray corporations as the cause of social problems and to discredit nongovernmental steps to deal with the issues.[27] Group entrepreneurs are most successful in building support for their positions when the economy is thriving, aspirations are rising, and the public takes prosperity for granted. The new group activists have more difficulty attracting backers for their positions when the economy is sluggish and citizens are more concerned about jobs and living standards.

This interpretation turns the traditional relationship between good economic times and support for business on its head. In the new, postmaterialistic interest-group environment, according to this view, criticisms of business multiply when unemployment and inflation rates are low, as in the 1980s, and dwindle when the economy is in recession, as in the early 1990s.

Labor Unions

A third development in the opinion environment that could affect public perceptions of business is the changing status of labor unions. Labor unions were one of "the great innovations of modern times."[28] They were a response to the emergence of the factory system and the shift in the position of workers from independent craftsmen to employees. Workers combined their individual efforts to influence decisions involving wages and hours and gain a measure of control over their working lives.

Early union efforts encountered legal barriers that resulted from English common law principles. Common law precedents prohibited commercial conspiracies in "restraint of trade" and "to injure others."[29] The earliest legal judgment in the United States involving unions occurred in 1806 and found a Philadelphia group to be an illegal conspiracy and its actions "coercive and arbitrary." The constant threat of prosecution hampered union efforts and sometimes provoked violent reactions from workers.

An 1842 decision reinterpreted common law precedents and ruled that unions were presumed to be legal unless they were outlawed by statute or actually acted to harm others. This decision gave American unions a legal status their counterparts in Britain did not achieve until 1875 and German unions did not enjoy until World War I. It also led American unions to become politically active.

Unions were originally drawn to the political arena by the need to define their legal rights and, specifically, by the need to defend themselves against the use of judicial injunctions in the 1870s and 1880s. Once in the political arena, some unions sought to persuade government to improve employment conditions for their members by mandating minimum standards in such work-related areas as wages, retirement benefits, and health care. Occasionally unions also sought to express the political views of workers on nonworkplace issues.

Individual unions such as the United Auto Workers, the Teamsters, and the International Association of Machinists are the locus of union political activity. The AFL-CIO is a federation of unions rather than a union itself.[30] It provides services to individual unions and represents common union interests, but it has little control over the activities of the member organizations. The AFL-CIO encourages local political involvement and supports policy positions and candidates when its members are in overwhelming agreement, but the federation's role is limited by the diverse interests of the member unions. Historically, the AFL-CIO has concentrated its political activity on issues concerning the legal rights of unions.

Individual unions are often more politically engaged than the federation. Some unions seek to use government to improve working conditions and to champion political causes, but union circumstances vary considerably. Unions respond to the characteristics and workplace situations of their members. Auto workers who have generations of employment with the same manufacturer, restaurant employees who work for a season, and state and local governments employees all have different political interests. Some union members make their living through defense expenditures while other unions fight to reduce defense appropriations. Some unions want more highway construction projects while others campaign for increases in social service expenditures. In the best of times, the influence of labor in politics is limited by the diversity of union interests.

In recent decades, labor's political influence has suffered further erosion because of the decline in union membership.[31] Union membership is strongest in manufacturing areas, but since the 1950s, overall employment in manufacturing has fallen. Furthermore, unions have failed to organize well the new industrial sectors, where employment has been expanding, or the new regions, such as the South, where manufacturing has been growing. Spurred by the example of the Reagan administration in the aircraft controllers strike of 1981, employers have also resisted union-organizing campaigns more diligently than in decades when the national political leadership was vigorously prounion. As a result of these trends, the proportion of nonagricultural workers represented by unions had fallen from 34 percent in 1955 to about 17 percent by 1990.

The decline in the political strength of unions has been a mixed blessing for corporations and trade associations. Even though unions are the traditional opponents of business in the workplace and the political arena, they also have much in common with business. Both labor and management are social partners who share in the benefits of a successful economy. Both managers and employees have a stake in a company's prosperity, and both suffer when the firm faces hard times.

Supporters of the newer interest groups of the 1970s and 1980s often disdain the economic concerns of labor and management and champion non-material values.[32] Labor unions and business groups sometimes join together to back job-oriented measures, such as the efforts in the 1980s to bail out the Chrysler Corporation.[33] The newer movements typically provide such efforts little support. A survey of Washington lobbyists finds that corporate representatives believe that labor unions are less antagonistic to business than citizen groups. Labor lobbyists were also found to be less critical of business than are officials of citizen groups.[34]

Companies and unions are sometimes allied on legislative matters that create jobs and boost the economy. The decline in the political strength of unions has weakened organizations that are important business allies on some economic and regulatory issues. The decline of unions makes it appear that business stands alone on economic issues and reinforces the public image of large companies as powerful and selfish.

Structure of Economic Policy

The fourth factor that could affect the formation of public attitudes toward business emphasizes substance rather than image. The Reagan era was one of the most controversial periods in American history. It was characterized by the longest peacetime economic expansion in the twentieth century, improved relations with the Soviet Union, and sharp declines in both unemployment and inflation. The

Reagan government must also be remembered as the administration that presided over the doubling of the national debt and the transformation of the United States from the world's leading creditor nation to the world's biggest debtor.

Analysts maintain that the Reagan era's radical policies were the source of fundamental problems for the U.S. economy.[35] From this perspective, the apparent prosperity of the era was false, and the economic growth was illusionary. The commonly used measures of economic well-being—levels of unemployment and inflation—were simply not adequate to gauge the state of an economy under the policies of the Reagan years. An accurate assessment of the nation's economy must recognize the enormous dangers posed by the budget and trade deficits.

Research on the relationship between the state of the economy and public opinion toward business has relied on unemployment and inflation rates as indicators of economic well-being. Confidence in business leaders and general attitudes toward business may not have improved during the 1980s because the public sensed that the economy was weaker than the unemployment and inflation rates made it appear. Even though citizens told opinion researchers that they were better off financially and that they approved the way the country was going, they may still have been troubled by news accounts of the twin deficits and corporate misconduct. From this perspective, the public's doubts about the actual health of the nation's economy prevented the development of more positive attitudes toward business leaders or business in general.

SUMMARY

Four factors that could affect the formation of public attitudes toward business have been examined: media images of business; the interest-group environment; labor unions; and the structure of economic policy. None of these factors presents a completely satisfactory answer to the puzzle of why general attitudes toward business remained critical throughout the 1980s. Each probably contains an element of truth, and each highlights a significant feature of the opinion environment in which attitudes toward business are now being formed. The media do present negative images of businesspeople, the interest-group environment has become more critical, labor unions are less influential than in the past, and traditional indicators of the well-being of the economy are not adequate to capture the complexities of the emerging international system.

Regardless of the specific reasons, large companies and their leaders will continue to be objects of criticism and distrust in the 1990s, as they were in the 1980s. Business institutions will continue to be seen as powerful and greedy, and business figures will remain convenient villains in politics and the media. Changes in the opinion environment will make it more difficult for business accomplishments to be translated into positive attitudes toward business and more likely that business failures will be fully broadcast.

The American system of imperfect political-economic alternatives yields a political process in which criticisms of business are a recurrent feature of public discourse. Business will be able to maintain an influential position in the country's political-economic system only so long as the general public believes that companies make an essential contribution to their own well-being and to the country's economic future. If these opinions fade, restrictions on business autonomy will multiply.

As will be discussed in the next chapter, the internationalization of the nation's economy poses the strongest challenge to industry's ability to satisfy public expectations since the New Deal. Whether business practices and governmental policies are adequate to meet this challenge remains to be seen.

SELECTED READINGS

MICHAEL GOLDFIELD, *The Decline of Organized Labor in the United States* (Chicago: Chicago University Press, 1987).

RONALD INGLEHART, *Culture Shift in Advanced Industrial Society* (Princeton: Princeton University Press, 1990).

SEYMOUR MARTIN LIPSET and WILLIAM SCHNEIDER, *The Confidence Gap: Business Gap: Business, Labor, and Government in the Public Mind* (New York: Free Press, 1983).

GARY MARKS, *Unions in Politics: Britain, Germany, and the United States in the Nineteenth and Early Twentieth Centuries* (Princeton: Princeton University Press, 1989).

DAVID VOGEL, *Fluctuating Fortunes: Political Power of Business in America* (New York: Basic Books, 1989).

END NOTES

[1]Cooper described public opinion in a democracy as "the lever by which all things are moved." See James Fenimore Cooper, *The American Democrat*, Liberty Classics Reprint, (New York: Knopf, 1931), p. 197.

[2]S. Robert Lichter, et al., *Watching America* (Englewood Cliffs, N.J.: Prentice Hall, 1991); and L.J. Theberge (ed.), *Crooks, Conmen, and Clowns: Businessmen in TV Entertainment* (Washington, D.C.: Media Institute, 1981).

[3]Michael Moore, *Roger and Me* (Warner Brothers, 1989).

[4]This discussion draws from the principal work on this topic, Seymour Martin Lipset and William Schneider, *The Confidence Gap: Business, Labor, and Government in the Public Mind* (New York: Free Press, 1983).

[5]Lipset and Schneider, *The Confidence Gap*, p. 37.

[6]Lipset and Schneider, *The Confidence Gap*, pp. 369–71; and Louis Galambos and Joseph Pratt, *The Rise of the Corporate Commonwealth: United States Business and Public Policy in the 20th Century* (New York: Basic Books, 1988), p. 70.

[7]Lipset and Schneider, *The Confidence Gap*, pp. 62–63. The correlation between confidence in people running major companies and the percentage of civilian unemployment was -.72, and the correlation between confidence and the increase in the consumer price index was -.38.

[8]This discussion is based on data contained in Roper Organization, *Roper Reports 89–1*, pp. 112–15.

[9]James Oliver Robertson, *America's Business* (New York: Hill and Wang, 1985), p. 193.

[10]When samples were asked in 1975, 1977, and 1979, "Would you say you are better off or worse off financially than you were a year ago?", responses were evenly divided between better and worse off. When the same question was posed in 1985, 1987, and 1989, respondents indicated by a two-to-one margin that they were better off. Opinion Research Corporation, "Corporate Reputations—1989," pp. 1–11.

[11]Martha Bayles, "Tycoons on the Tube," *Wall Street Journal*, November 18, 1985, p. 28; and "Business Thinks TV Distorts Its Image," *Business Week*, October 18, 1982, p. 26.

[12]Emily Stipes Watts, *The Businessman in American Literature* (Athens: University of Georgia Press, 1982), pp. 2–6.

[13]Ibid., pp. 55–59.

[14]Frank Norris, *The Octopus: A Story of California* (New York: Bantam Books, © 1901, pub. 1958), p. 369.

[15]Watts, *The Businessman in American Literature*, Chapter 13; and Wilson C. McWilliams and Henry A. Plotkin, "The Historic Reputation of American Business," *Journal of Contemporary Business 5* (Autumn 1976), pp. 3–18. Note other articles in the same issue.

[16]This section follows Samuel P. Huntington, *American Politics: The Promise of Disharmony* (Cambridge, Mass.: Harvard University Press, 1981), pp. 101–106.

[17]Ibid., pp. 1–2.

[18]Robert H. Salisbury, "Interest Representation: The Dominance of Institutions," *American Political Science Review* 78 (March 1984), 64–76.

[19]Jeffrey M. Berry, *The Interest Group Society*, 2nd ed. (Glenview, Ill.: Scott, Foresman, 1989), Chapter 2.

[20]Jeffrey H. Birnbaum and Alan S. Murray, *Showdown at Gucci Gulch: Lawmakers, Lobbyists, and the Unlikely Triumph of Tax Reform* (New York: Random House, 1987).

[21]Huntington, *American Politics*, pp. 105–106 and Chapters 3 and 5.

[22]For example, Mancur Olsen, *The Rise and Fall of Nations* (New Haven: Yale University Press, 1983); Lester C. Thurow, *The Zero-Sum Society* (New York: Penguin Books, 1981), pp. 10–15; and "Prepared Text of Carter's Farewell Address on Major Issues Facing the Nation," *The New York Times*, January 15, 1981.

[23]Russell J. Dalton, Manfred Kuechler, and Wilhelm Buerklin, "The Challenge of New Movements," in Dalton and Kuechler (eds.), *Challenging the Political Order: New Social and Political Movements in Western Democracies* (New York: Oxford University Press, 1990), pp. 3–20.

[24]See, for example, Jo Freeman, *The Politics of Women's Liberation* (New York: David McKay 1975); Henry J. Pratt, *The Gray Lobby* (Chicago: University of Chicago Press, 1976); Jeffrey M. Berry, *Lobbying for the People* (Princeton: Princeton University Press, 1977; and Thomas R. Rochon, *Mobilizing for Peace: The Antinuclear Movements in Western Europe* (Princeton: Princeton University Press, 1988).

[25]Michael Pertschuk, *Revolt Against Regulation: The Rise and Pause of the Consumer Movement* (Berkeley: University of California Press, 1982).

[26]David Vogel, *Fluctuating Fortunes: Political Power of Business in America* (New York: Basic Books, 1989), pp. 40–42 and 97.

[27]Pertschuk, *Revolt Against Regulation*, p. 40.

[28]These paragraphs are drawn from Gary Marks, *Unions in Politics: Britain, Germany, and the United States in the Nineteenth and Early Twentieth Centuries* (Princeton: Princeton University Press, 1989), pp. 9–10.

[29]Ibid. pp. 68–69.

[30]Harry Holloway, "Interest Groups in the Postpartisan Era: The Political Machine of the AFL-CIO," *Political Science Quarterly* (Spring 1979), pp. 117–33.

[31]Michael Goldfield, *The Decline of Organized Labor in the United States* (Chicago: University of Chicago Press, 1987); Kim Moody, *An Injury to All: The Decline of American Unionism* (New York: Verso, 1988); and Seymour Martin Lipset, "Unions in Decline," *Public Opinion*, (September/October 1986), 52–54.

[32]Ronald Inglehart, *Culture Shift in Advanced Industrial Society* (Princeton: Princeton University Press, 1990).

[33]Robert B. Reich and John D. Donahue, *New Deals: The Chrysler Revival and the American System* (New York: Penguin Books, 1985).

[34]Kay Lehman Schlozman and John T. Tierney, *Organized Interests and American Democracy* (New York: Harper & Row, 1986), p. 284.

[35]Benjamin Friedman, *Day of Reckoning: The Consequences of American Economic Policy* (New York: Random House, 1988); and Bennett Harrison and Barry Bluestone, *The Great U-Turn: Corporate Restructuring and the Polarizing of America* (New York: Basic Books, 1988).

Chapter 4

Internationalization
of
Business Activity

International corporations like Siemens, BP, and Matsushita more than tripled their ownership of American industry in the 1980s.[1] During these years the influx of capital from abroad grew eightfold, from $50 billion to almost $400 billion. A British company bought Holiday Inns, Japanese firms acquired Firestone and CBS Records, and German corporations took over A&P and Doubleday Books. By 1991, the Pillsbury doughboy, the Jolly Green Giant, E.T., and Brooks Brothers were all held by foreign investors.

The explosive growth in the international ownership of American assets underlines the fact that economic activity today occurs in a dual environment. It takes place both in a national setting and an international context. American producers are active in global markets, and international firms offer goods and services to American consumers. The international ownership of assets and the growing volume of cross-border transactions document the advent of a global economic system.

The emerging global economy results from both international agreements and technical advances. The postwar economic system was framed in a series of treaties negotiated in Bretton Woods, New Hampshire, in July 1944.[2] The Bretton Woods treaties created the International Monetary Fund to supervise exchange rates among currencies and the World Bank to provide long-term loans for postwar reconstruction and development. The Bretton Woods negotiations also led to an executive agreement establishing GATT, the General Agreement on Tariffs and Trade, whose signatories pledged to reduce international tariffs and comply with a code of fair-trade practices.

In addition, technical factors have also expanded the volume of transnational economic activity.[3] Improved technology has increased the mobility of people, goods, and capital and has made possible instantaneous, world-wide communications. Competitive pressures have prompted international corporations to cross national boundaries to realize the economies of expanded production, capitalize on specialized skills, and spread the risks of industrial activity. As a consequence, production, marketing, finance, and product development are now global activities.

The United States has been a significant player in the world economy throughout the twentieth century. In the last two decades, however, international factors have begun to have a more noticeable impact on economic conditions within the United States. No topic is discussed today with greater urgency than the international competitiveness of the American economy. This chapter begins with an examination of that issue.

Today's emerging global economy is increasingly shaped by the actions of multinational enterprises.[4] They are the most dynamic actors on the world stage and principal factors in a country's economic competitiveness. This chapter explores the development of multinational enterprises, their strategies in the industrialized world, and the impact of their operations on the countries where they are headquartered and where they are active. It focuses especially on the effects of direct foreign investment in the United States.

The internationalization of business activity has challenged established policies of the United States and the world community. Traditional practices do not fit the reality of a new economic order. The global economy poses genuine problems for the United States, but no nation has more resources available to address these new circumstances than the United States. This chapter concludes by analyzing policy issues raised by the increasing globalism of the world economy.

CARVING UP THE GLOBAL PIE

The historian Paul Kennedy, author of the best seller *The Rise and Fall of Great Powers*, appraises the geopolitical position of the United States in the years ahead in these terms: "...the only answer to the question increasingly debated by the public of whether the United States can preserve its existing (international) position is 'no'."[5]

Kennedy believes that the United States has fallen victim to a disease that has strickened great powers through the centuries, "imperial overstretch." The symptoms appear in the tendency of great powers to allow their global obligations to exceed their defense abilities. Small nations typically rise up militarily to challenge the great power at precisely the time the power's resources are most needed in its domestic economy. The decline of great powers, Kennedy believes, is inevitable because it "simply has not been given to any one society to remain permanently ahead of all the others."[6]

Kennedy's historical analysis coincided with the emergence of the popular view that there was something critically wrong with the American economy. The perception that the glory days of the U.S. economy were over was fueled by the increased prominence of other nations in the global marketplace. While the achievements of other nations have certainly gained attention, the evidence of the decline of the U.S. economy is more mixed.[7]

Position of the United States

The theme of U.S. decline has been painted too boldly. Most discussions of decline compare the economic position of the United States today with its position in the late 1940s or the early 1950s.[8] These comparisons ignore the fact that the devastation of the world's other economies in World War II made the United States appear more dominant than it actually was.

Discussions of decline note that the U.S. share of world production fell from about 42 percent in the late 1940s to 22 percent in the late 1980s.[9] The U.S. share of world production in the late 1930s, however, had been a more moderate 28 percent. A decline in the U.S. share of world product did occur between the late 1930s and the late 1980s, from about 28 percent to 22 percent, but the largest part of the dramatic drop in the years since the late 1940s simply reflected the ebbing away of temporary postwar conditions.

After World War II, living standards and per capita income in the United States were substantially higher than in every other major country. Today, living standards and per capita income in Japan and the western parts of Germany are essentially equal to those in the United States. (See Table 2–2.) The United States has not become poorer. It has experienced a decline relative to the position of other nations because the economies of other countries have grown more rapidly.

The best indicator of the health of a nation's economy is productivity. Nothing matters more to a country in the long term than productivity.[10] Labor productivity, output per unit of labor, determines in large part a country's standard of living and the real wages of its workers.

Despite journalistic accounts, the United States still leads the world in economic productivity.[11] Table 4–1 compares the *growth* in manufacturing productivity in Germany, Japan, the United Kingdom, and the United States from 1960 to 1986.

TABLE 4–1   Annual Growth in Manufacturing Productivity, 1960–1986

PERIOD	GERMANY	JAPAN	UNITED KINGDOM	UNITED STATES
1960–1986	*4.6%*	*7.9%*	*3.6%*	*2.8%*
1960–1973	5.8	10.3	4.2	3.2
1973–1979	4.3	5.5	1.2	1.4
1979–1986	2.7	5.6	4.5	3.5

Source: Office of Technology Assessment, Congress of the United States, *Paying the Bill: Manufacturing & America's Trade Deficit* (Washington, D.C.: Government Printing Office, 1988), p.45.

In the years from 1960 to 1986, productivity in American manufacturing grew by an average 2.8 percent per year. Productivity in Germany, Japan, and the United Kingdom during these years grew at a faster clip.

The post–World War II years were a period of unusual growth for many countries. Much of this growth, however, reflected a catching up for the opportunities lost during wartime. All nations then experienced a sharp decline in the growth in productivity during the 1970s. In the 1980s, productivity growth improved in the United Kingdom and the United States, was stable in Japan, and slumped in Germany.

In absolute terms, the growth in U.S. productivity presents no cause for alarm. The annual rate for the past century has been approximately 2 percent.[12] Growth in productivity in the 1980s exceeded the historic rate that had brought the country phenomenal improvements in living standards.

U.S. productivity, however, has not been growing as rapidly as productivity in some other nations. In fact, productivity has been growing at a faster rate in Japan than in the United States for four decades. Regardless of whether the Japanese growth rate is the result of higher capital investment, better management techniques, or a better trained and disciplined work force, it has been taking its toll.

Furthermore, a cross-national examination of eight key manufacturing industries finds that the United States no longer has a monopoly of the world's leading industrial practices.[13] The researchers reported that the best industry practices are increasingly found not in the United States but in other countries, and this forecasts slower productivity growth in the United States in the future.

There are also some areas in which the decline of the American economy has been absolute rather than relative. American firms dominated the U.S. market for products involving the commercial applications of technology in the 1950s and 1960s. In the last two decades, international firms have absorbed and improved American technologies and taken over U.S. markets for such characteristically American products as televisions, telephones, and tape recorders. This trend appears to be continuing in newer areas such as VCRs, 8mm video cameras, and high-definition television. American firms have lost control of the pace of technological development in many consumer markets.

More alarming than the industrial data is the evidence of deterioration in political and social areas that surround the American economy. The United States has unsound macroeconomic policies, low savings and investment rates, a severe trade deficit, and increasing infrastructure needs. Substance abuse, violent crime, and functional illiteracy are all costly problems that place substantial burdens on a competitive society. In international comparison, American high school drop-out rates are high, and levels of student achievement are low. The T-shirt slogan "Underachiever—and Proud of It" is curiously emblematic of the social problems the United States is inflicting on itself in meeting international competition.

The United States faces serious problems, but it is not without resources in dealing with them. The United States has the largest consumer market and manufacturing plant in the world. While other nations are demonstrating the ability to excel in specific technologies, there is, according to one authority, "no evidence that whole nations are beginning to overtake the United States in generating technological change."[14] The nation's work force remains the most productive in the world, and its universities and service industries are the world's best. The U.S. economy is an enormously flexible instrument whose fundamental strengths have not suddenly vanished. Furthermore, many of the country's problems were caused by U.S. policy, not by international competition. These problems can also be addressed through American policies. [15]

Position of Other Countries

Attention to the competitive challenges of the United States should not imply that other countries have no difficulties. Germany faces large public sector deficits to finance unification at a time when the country's extraordinarily high wage rates have already cut its international trade surplus.[16] Its economy has significant weakness outside its core industries and unusual rigidity. The growing turmoil in Eastern Europe and the former Soviet Union threatens to increase the burdensome immigration the country has experienced since 1988 and add to already high unemployment levels.

Japan's spectacular economic success has been driven by exports and capital investment.[17] The country faces low-cost competition from newly industrialized countries and closing markets in established countries. The nation's population is aging, labor is in short supply, and inflation is growing. While still at high levels, Japan's growth and savings rates have declined, and the country is being pressed to assume more costs of international leadership.

The United Kingdom presents the century-old tale of declines in manufacturing masked by the discovery of North Sea oil. Its research expenditures are low, its work force poorly trained, its companies and its domestic market are small, and unit production costs are high. Furthermore, the UK has a military force its limited resources can not easily support. Some rejuvenation of the economy occurred during the Thatcher years, but this was accompanied by growing social tensions.

The competitiveness of these countries' economies and others' is affected by the activities of multinational enterprises. Is national competitiveness helped by the activities of multinational firms, or is it harmed?

MULTINATIONAL ENTERPRISES IN A GLOBAL ECONOMY

Of the one hundred largest economic entities in the world, half are national governments and half are multinational enterprises (MNEs). For decades MNEs have been entering new markets through mergers, takeovers, partnerships, joint ventures, and direct investments, and they are now the world's dominant vehicle for transacting business. The new global economy has come to resemble an international industrial park. For some, MNEs are symbols of colonialism and capitalist exploitation, while for others they represent national efforts to achieve economic and social goals.

Literally, a multinational enterprise is simply a firm that has operations in more than one nation.[18] By some definitions, a firm must have *manufacturing* facilities in more than one country to qualify as an MNE or conduct a specific proportion of its business outside the country in which it is based.

In fact, being a multinational enterprise is as much an evolutionary process as a definitive condition. Typically, corporations begin to export products and then create overseas marketing organizations to boost sales. Later, the firms license foreign companies to make certain products and eventually build their own manufacturing plants in other countries. Gradually, companies internationalize their work force, management structure, and ownership; and, eventually, they organize their total operations on an international basis. Even though major companies now stand at different points in this evolution, most are becoming increasingly internationalized.

When MNEs became prominent in the 1950s and 1960s, they were perceived as a new form of colonialism.[19] MNEs typically came from the United States and focused their operations in so-called third-world nations. MNEs were regarded as instruments—or, at least as symbols—of Western domination, and the United Nations established an agency to monitor their operations. While multinationals provided nonindustrialized nations access to capital, technology, management skills, and exports markets, they were criticized for deepening the economic dependency of these countries, importing inappropriate technologies, interfering with local politics, and destroying traditional cultures.[20]

Whatever the validity of these views in the past, the world of multinational operations has changed. The image of MNEs based on experiences in the third world is of limited utility in understanding the significance of MNEs in industrialized nations with sophisticated governments. The lion's share of MNE activity today occurs in industrialized rather than nonindustrialized countries. Industrialized nations, and especially the United States, are the targets of MNEs as well as their homes. Today, third-world nations protest that they are being ignored by MNEs as frequently as they complain that they are being exploited by them.[21] Other changes in the features of MNEs are evident in Table 4–2, "The World's Largest Industrial Corporations, 1990."

Multinational firms are no longer a predominantly American phenomenon. Of the 500 largest industrial firms, only 164, or 33 percent, are based in the United States. Japan is the home of 111 (22 percent) of these firms, 43 (9 percent) come from the United Kingdom, and 30 (6 percent) are German.[22] Eleven of the 500 largest firms and two of the largest 50 (Samsung and Daewoo) are South Korean. In the last decade the service sector of MNE activity has grown at the expense of the manufacturing and extraction sectors, and nonequity forms of MNE activity such as licensing, leasing, and joint ventures, have increased more rapidly than direct investment.

TABLE 4–2 The World's Largest Industrial Corporations, 1990

CORPORATION	HOME COUNTRY	SALES ($ MILLIONS)	PROFIT/(LOSS) ($ MILLIONS)	EMPLOYEES
General Motors	U.S.	$126,126	$(1,986)	761,400
Royal Dutch Shell	UK/Neth.	107,204	6,442	137,000
Exxon	U.S.	105,885	5,010	104,000
Ford Motor	U.S.	98,275	860	370,400
IBM	U.S.	69,018	6,020	373,816
Toyota Motor	Japan	64,516	2,993	96,849
IRI	Italy	61,433	927	419,500
British Petroleum	UK	59,541	3,013	116,750
Mobil	U.S.	58,770	1,929	67,300
General Electric	U.S.	58,414	4,303	298,000
Daimler-Benz	Germany	54,259	1,042	376,785
Hitachi	Japan	50,686	1,477	290,811
Fiat	Italy	47,752	1,346	303,238
Samsung	S.Korea	45,042	N/A	N/A
Philip Morris	U.S.	44,323	3,540	168,000
Volkswagen	Germany	43,710	652	268,744
Matsushita Electric	Japan	43,516	1,649	198,299
ENI	Italy	41,762	1,697	130,745
Texaco	U.S.	41,235	1,450	39,199
Nissan Motor	Japan	40,217	808	129,546

Source: "The Global 500: The World's Biggest Industrial Corporations," *Fortune*, ©July 29, 1991, p. 245. *The Time Inc. Magazine Company.* All rights reserved.

Multinational Strategies and Tactics

General Electric recently reaffirmed its determination to become a global company by appointing the head of its London-based international operations, an Italian lawyer, to its board of directors.[23] The long-time GE executive had overseen the purchase of the controlling interest in Tungsram, the Hungarian light-bulb firm, managed joint ventures with the UK's General Electric Company, and engineered the swap of several businesses with a French corporation. Between 1985 and 1989, GE's European sales rose from $2 billion to $6 billion, and its European employment grew from 7,000 to 45,000. GE supplies half of its European sales from European production sites.

MNEs differ. They launch international operations as elements of either global, domestic market, or national markets strategies.[24] First, some firms, like General Electric, use their existing competitive advantages to build long-term global brand dominance. They invest in new capacity, cross-subsidize different geographic markets, expand across product lines, enlarge markets through product innovation, and develop global distribution channels.

Second are companies whose strategy is to defend their domestic market against foreign competition. These enterprises seek to reduce their manufacturing costs and match their competitors' investments in new plant and equipment, and they often request governmental assistance in solving their problems.

Third, some MNEs operate through largely autonomous national subsidiaries. The subsidiaries pride themselves on their responsiveness to various national markets, but the firm itself must discover ways to overcome its fragmented structure and the limitations of national markets if it is to meet the challenge of global competitors.

MNEs pursue their global, domestic market, or national markets strategies through international activities intended to gain various types of competitive advantages:[25]

1. Location-specific production advantages based on differences in factor costs;
2. Extranational production efficiencies based on large volume;
3. Access to important national markets; and
4. Global distribution policies that leverage cost and cross-product advantages.

Firms trying to defend a domestic market typically turn to the international arena to find lower-cost production facilities. They then plan to serve the domestic market from these "export platforms." Companies also move beyond national borders to create production networks that will help them realize the advantages of great volume or to gain access to important national markets that might otherwise be closed to them. Finally, international activities can be part of a plan to create a global distribution system that will allow a firm to build multiproduct identity and cross-subsidize various geographic markets.

Government Relations

The distinctive feature of MNEs is that they are active in multiple countries and thus must maintain relations with numerous governments. As they pursue their different strategies and tactics, MNEs must comply with the laws of the home country in which they are headquartered as well as the legal requirements of the host countries in which they are active. The dual identity of MNEs makes conflict inevitable.

Most home-country governments regard MNEs as vehicles to promote their political and economic interests. Firms are their modern-day gladiators. Home governments seek to expand the international role of firms headquartered in their countries and defend them against hostile action by other governments.

The U.S. government is less diligent in promoting the interests of its MNEs than are most other governments. For the United States, like most countries, foreign and international economic policies are intertwined. Although U.S. foreign policy occasionally operates on behalf of American business interests,[26] since World War II, U.S. economic concerns have normally been subordinated to foreign policy objectives. For decades, for example, the pattern of U.S. policy toward Germany and Japan has been to secure political objectives by giving up economic advantages.[27]

In addition, U.S. administrations often seek to achieve their political objectives by restricting the actions of the foreign subsidiaries of American MNEs. Under the Export Administration Act of 1979, the United States embargoed sales by European subsidiaries of American MNEs of products that could help the Soviet Union develop its oil and gas resources. The U.S. government seeks to change other countries' human rights and emigration policies by penalizing American companies whose foreign subsidiaries are active in those countries.[28] The Foreign Corrupt Practices Act (1977) makes it a crime for an American company to bribe a foreign official to obtain business, regardless of normal practices in the host country.[29]

Host-country governments, the countries where MNEs are active, welcome MNEs because of their potential to enhance the nation's economy. Host governments resent MNEs, however, because of the subordination of their countries' welfare to the policies of home-country governments and the organizational interests of the MNE. They fear MNEs because of their ability to shift factories, products, and employment from country to country, and they worry that the MNE will gather economic rewards in their country and leave them with the social and political problems.[30]

Conflicts between MNEs and host-country governments were once conducted under the threat of the nationalization of MNE assets by the host country. In recent decades, major industrial nations have avoided extreme actions and conducted relations with MNEs within a framework of bargaining and negotiation.[31]

Most major countries walk a fine line between welcoming MNEs and insisting that their national interests will not be jeopardized.[32] Foreign multinationals often find that certain sectors of the host-nation economy, such as the defense and broadcasting industries, are closed to them.[33] Host-nation governments often review the plans of MNEs when they are entering the country and establish performance requirements for firms in such areas as investment, product development, employment, and ownership by host-country nationals. The subsidiaries of MNEs must also comply with the host country's laws involving labor relations, capital flows, environmental quality, and corporate decision making regardless of the practices in their home country.

MNEs, in turn, are not defenseless in their negotiations with host governments. They control the capital, technology, and access to export markets that host governments want. MNEs can also play one country against the others while seeking investment subsidies, favorable pricing rules for their products, and special treatment under national programs for public procurement, R&D funding, job training, and infrastructure projects.

Impact of Outward MNE Investment

MNEs are accused both of damaging their home country's economy by exporting factories and jobs and hurting the host country by exploiting its markets for the benefit of the home country. Any assessment of the impact of MNEs on a country should be conducted cautiously because multinational strategies differ dramatically and negotiations between MNEs and host governments vary from case to case. Despite these problems, the importance of multinational activity demands that existing viewpoints be examined. This section considers the impact of outward investment on the MNE's home country, and the next section examines the consequences of MNEs' inward investment on a specific host country, the United States.

The argument in favor of MNE activity is a restatement of the view that competitive markets promote economic efficiency and provide goods and services to consumers at a lower price. From this perspective, outward investment by MNEs earns profits and stimulates the home country's economy. The failure of MNEs to invest outside their home country would close off profitable investment options, raise overall production costs, increase prices to consumers, lower sales, and reduce the number of jobs for home-country workers.[34]

While outward investment has a net positive affect on the home-country economy, there is no doubt that certain workers and communities are harmed by outward investment. Plants are closed, workers are fired, and communities are devastated as MNEs move investments from the home country into the global economy.

Organized labor is widely perceived to be the group most harmed by MNEs' outward investment practices.[35] Outward investment occurs in manufacturing industries in which unions are strongest. It places national labor groups in competition with each other and makes workers fearful of losing their jobs. The ability of an MNE to move capital, employment, and production enhances its bargaining power against unions and allows it to escape a country's labor-relations policies. While multinational union bargaining is an obvious response to this situation, it has been slow to emerge because of the structure of the international labor movement, the diversity of national laws, and ideological divisions among unions.

Foreign Investment in the United States

The American government "encourages" foreign investment in the United States.[36] An interagency Committee on Foreign Investment in the United States can screen foreign investments that threaten the nation's security, but the committee rarely meets. Japan, in comparison, requires every foreign investor to submit a detailed investment proposal and wait before proceeding. Investments can be prohibited on national security grounds or because they might have adverse affects on Japanese companies.

In all, foreign investment in the United States totals $2 trillion. More than 80 percent of these investments are *portfolio* investments in government securities, corporate stocks and bonds, and bank deposits. The portfolio investor is a passive investor who plays no role in managing assets. The balance of the investments are *direct* investments in U.S. companies, banks, and real estate where the investor does make decisions about how those assets will be used. Total foreign investments comprise about 6 percent of total U.S. assets.

The United States became the world's largest recipient of foreign direct investment in 1978.[37] The volume of such investment has continued to climb, and the cumulative value of foreign direct investment in the United States (FDIUS) in 1990 was estimated to be $400 billion. In a recent year, the United Kingdom was clearly the largest holder of FDIUS, followed by the Netherlands and Japan. (See Table 4–3.)

TABLE 4–3 Sources of Foreign Direct Investment in United States, 1987

COUNTRY	DOLLAR VALUE ($ BILLIONS)	PERCENT GROWTH SINCE 1980	SHARE OF TOTAL
United Kingdom	$ 74.9	431%	29%
Netherlands	47.0	146	18
Japan	33.4	611	13
Canada	21.7	78	8
Germany	19.6	158	8
Total All Countries	$261.9	216%	100%

Source: Linda M. Spencer, *American Assets: An Examination of Foreign Investment in the United States* (Arlington, VA.: Congressional Economic Leadership Institute, 1988), p.49.

Between 1980 and 1987, the total value of FDIUS grew by 216 percent. Japan recorded the largest percent increases during this period because of the small size of its investment prior to 1980. The value of Japanese investments in a single year first surpassed the value of UK transactions in 1988.[38]

Recent increases in FDIUS have been large, but the total value of direct foreign holdings in the United States remains at a modest level by international standards.[39] Total foreign holdings in most other countries are a larger share of gross domestic product than in the United States. The value of UK holdings in the United States equals 2.1 percent of U.S. gross domestic product (GDP), but the value of U.S. holdings in the UK is 5.7 percent of UK GDP. U.S. investments in the Netherlands, Canada, and Germany constitute a far larger share of their economies than the value of their investments in the United States. Japan, which has permitted little foreign direct investment, presents an exception. (See Table 4–4.)

TABLE 4–4   Magnitude of Foreign Direct Investment, 1988
                (FDI as Share of Host-Country GDP)

COUNTRY	COUNTRY'S HOLDINGS IN U.S.	U.S. HOLDINGS IN HOST COUNTRY
United Kingdom	2.1 %	5.7 %
Netherlands	1.0	6.8
Japan	.8	.5
Canada	.6	12.2
Germany	.5	1.8

Source: Economic Report of the President 1990 (Washington, D.C.: Government Printing Office, 1990), p. 125.

Direct comparisons of FDIUS with United States Direct Investment Abroad (USDIA) understate U.S. investments. Accepting this caveat, the ratio of USDIA to FDIUS has fallen from 4.6 to 1 in 1960 to .9 to 1 in 1987.[40] A different view of the magnitude of USDIA and FDIUS is gained from the fact that six million foreigners work for U.S. firms abroad while three million Americans work for international firms in the United States.[41]

MNE investment activity can affect host-country economies in either of two ways.[42] First, MNE investors can enter a region and *stimulate* the local economy. The MNE can generate new employment, introduce new techniques, create demand for local goods and services, interact with domestic firms, and be a tough competitor that prods indigenous companies to improve their operations.

Alternatively, MNE investors can come into a region and *displace* local economy activity. They can aggravate the weaknesses of the region by reducing skilled employment and shifting high-value-added functions abroad. They can steer business away from innovative local firms in favor of suppliers with whom they have an established relationship.

Among the most ardent defenders of FDIUS are state and local governments.[43] Forty states have established offices abroad to woo investors to their areas. Governors and mayors travel widely and look to foreign investment as a means of stimulating employment, increasing tax revenues, gaining new technology, improving management skills, and obtaining development capital.

The critics of foreign direct investment in the United States argue that MNEs are more likely to displace local economic activity than to stimulate it.[44] They point out that most foreign outlays are for the acquisition of existing businesses rather than the establishment of new ones.[45] In 1987, foreign investors spent $26 billion, or 84 percent of their funds, to acquire 306 existing companies and only $5 billion to establish new businesses. While three million Americans work for foreign firms, these enterprises created by one estimate only 90,000 new jobs in the years from 1980 to 1987.[46] The critics maintain that MNEs have reduced the skill level of American jobs and transformed successful firms into hollow shells for assembling products that were conceived and designed elsewhere.[47]

The issue of FDIUS will grow in the years ahead as the nation's trade deficit gives international firms more resources to take over American companies. A century ago, the United States relied on foreign, especially British, capital to develop the West.[48] A campaign against foreign ownership swept the Western states, and laws restricting British ownership were common. The best policy response to foreign investment today is to make the U.S. economy as competitive as possible. MNEs generally direct sophisticated work to countries with highly trained workers, superior educational systems, and a well-developed infrastructure.[49] Critics go further and insist that the United States must restrict those multinational investors whose actions displace U.S. economic activity, destroy local firms, and diminish American jobs.

RESPONSES TO GLOBALISM

The world is now experiencing a lag in institutional development.[50] The internationalization of business has outpaced the development of the political institutions needed to regulate the new global economy. Similar to the domestic American experience at the end of the nineteenth century, economic events at the end of the twentieth century are undermining the capacity of one set of political institutions to regulate economic activity, but the emergence of a new set of institutions to take their place has not yet occurred. In this transition era, a number of efforts are being made to adjust to the new realities, but each initiative possesses its own limitations.

Among the responses to the new globalism is a closer alignment between national governments and their multinational enterprises. As countries have recognized the importance of the international competitiveness of their economies, governments have devised programs to give home-based MNEs advantages in their competition with firms from other nations.

The difficulty in harnessing MNEs by strengthening the link between firms and governments is that the national identity of MNEs is eroding. It is increasingly difficult to determine what it means to say that a firm is an American or a British multinational.[51] While the actions of MNEs from some countries are more tempered by perceptions of national interest than others, the author of a recent article on MNEs posed the question, "Who Is Us?"[52] All of a company's directors and most of its owners and managers may be American citizens, and yet the company may still place most of its facilities, employ most of its workers, and conduct most of its research outside U.S. borders. It may be no more meaningful in the future to say a firm is an American company than it is today to view an enterprise as a Delaware or a New Jersey corporation.

A logical response to the internationalization of business is to create an international regime to regulate MNEs on a global basis.[53] There have been numerous efforts to do this, but the economic and political situations in countries are diverse. An international regime could harm MNEs from particular countries, and most governments have not yet reached the point where they are prepared to cede sovereignty over important national assets. The successes that have appeared in international regulation occur in functional areas where all parties gain from collective actions, such as in the international regulation of telecommunications and air transport.[54] A comprehensive structure for the international regulation of MNEs will probably emerge in the future, but it will be preceeded by a long period of experimentation and failure.

An alternative to global regulation is a sort of self-regulation in which small groups of like-minded nations come together to deal with a range of common issues.[55] Sometimes such groups are defined on a geographic basis, as has occurred with the European Community. Membership in the Community has grown from six to twelve nations, and it has focused its efforts on creating a single market for the Community's economy. An analogous group defined on a functional basis is composed of seven major industrial countries—the United States, Germany, Japan, Britain, France, Italy, and Canada—whose leaders meet annually to discuss international economic and political issues and coordinate their responses.[56] Specialized groups with limited memberships are able to act in contentious areas, but they can be divisive and weaken efforts to respond to international problems on a comprehensive basis.

SUMMARY

The internationalization of business activity has challenged government policies and corporate strategies. It has led to closer relationships between governments and MNEs, and it has focused public attention on international competitiveness and economic efficiency and away from equity concerns.

Integration in the world economy is both a condition and a policy option. Public policies governing the conduct of multinational firms at home and abroad affect the impact of international business activity on U.S. citizens and the U.S. economy. Existing policies are not immutable. They can encourage constructive multinational activities and restrain deleterious practices. In the years ahead, policies will regulate the conduct of MNEs with increasing precision, but the nature of those policies remains very much in doubt.

The competitiveness of a country's economy is affected by the effectiveness of its government, the competence of its corporate sector, and the choices the country makes in key policy areas. Part Two explores these issues through an examination of the structures of government, corporations, and the marketplace.

SELECTED READINGS

NORMAN J. GLICKMAN and DOUGLAS P. WOODWARD, *The New Competitors: How Foreign Investors Are Changing the U.S. Economy* (New York: Basic Books, 1989).

NEIL HOOD and JAN-ERIK VAHLNE (eds.), *Strategies in Global Competition* (London: Croom Helm, 1988).

ROBERT D. PUTNAM and NICHOLAS BAYNE, *Hanging Together: Cooperation and Conflict in the Seven-Power Summits* (Cambridge, Mass.: Harvard University Press, 1987).

JOHN M. STOPFORD and LOUIS TURNER, *Britain and the Multinationals* (New York: Wiley, 1985).

RAYMOND VERNON and DEBORA SPAR, *Beyond Globalism: American Foreign Economic Policy* (New York: Free Press, 1989).

END NOTES

[1]Norman J. Glickman and Douglas P. Woodward, *The New Competitors: How Foreign Investors Are Changing the U.S. Economy* (New York: Basic Books, 1989), pp. x–xii and 4.

[2]Theodore Geiger, *The Future of the International System: The United States and the World Political Economy* (Boston: Unwin Hyman, 1988), Chapter 2.

[3]John M. Stopford and Louis Turner, *Britain and the Multinationals* (New York: Wiley, 1985), pp. 25–39; and Raymond Vernon and Debora L. Spar, *Beyond Globalism: Remaking American Foreign Economic Policy* (New York: Free Press, 1989), p. 111.

[4]John H. Dunning, "The Organisation of International Economic Interdependence: An Historical Excursion," in John H. Dunning and Mikoto Usui (eds.), *Structural Change, Economic Interdependence and World Development*, vol. 4: "Economic Interdependence" (New York: St. Martin's Press, 1987), pp. 15–16.

[5]Paul Kennedy, *The Rise and Fall of Great Powers: Economic Change and Military Conflict from 1500 to 2000* (New York: Random House, 1987), pp. 533 and 515.

[6]Ibid., p. 533.

[7]Michael L. Dertouzos et al., *Made In America: Regaining the Productive Edge* (Cambridge, Mass.: MIT Press, 1989), pp. 23–24.

[8]See for example, Geiger, *The Future of the International System*, pp. 19–30.

[9]Joseph Nye, "Understating U.S. Strength," *Foreign Policy* (Fall 1988), p.107; and Walt Rostow, "Beware of Historians Bearing False Analogies," *Foreign Affairs* 66, no. 4 (Spring 1988). There is great variation in the data on these issues. Raymond Vernon reports that the United States had 38 percent of world output in 1950 and 27 percent in 1990, "Same Planet, Different Worlds," in William W. Brock and Robert D. Hormats (eds.), *The Global Economy: America's Role in the Decade Ahead* (New York: W.W. Norton, 1990), p. 19.

[10]William J. Baumol, Sue Anne Batey Blackman, and Edward N. Wolff, *Productivity and American Leadership: The Long View* (Cambridge, Mass.: The MIT Press, 1989). This discussion is based on Chapters 2–5.

[11]Dertouzos et al., *Made in America*, pp. 26–27.

[12]Baumol, Blackman, and Wolff, *Productivity and American Leadership*, Chapter 4.

[13]Dertouzos et al., *Made in America*, p. 26.

[14]Harald B. Malmgren, "Technology and the Economy," in Brock and Hormats (eds.), *The Global Economy*; and Rosecrance, *America's Economic Resurgence: A Bold New Strategy* (Grand Rapids, Mich.: Harper & Row, 1990).

[15]Samuel Huntington, "The U.S.—Decline or Renewal?", *Foreign Affairs* (Winter 1988–89), p. 79.

[16]Kenneth Dyson, "Economic Policy," in Gordon Smith, William E. Paterson, and Peter H. Merkl (eds.), *Developments in West German Politics* (Durham, N.C.: Duke University Press, 1989), pp. 148–67.

[17]Bill Emmott, *The Sun Also Sets: The Limits to Japan's Economic Power* (New York: Times Books, 1989).

[18]For a discussion of definitions of multinational enterprises see Alan M. Rugman, Donald J. Lecraw, and Laurence D. Booth, *International Business: Firm and Environment* (New York: McGraw–Hill, 1985).

[19]Raymond Vernon, *Sovereignty at Bay* (New York: Basic Books, 1971), and *Storm over the Multinationals* (Cambridge, Mass.: Harvard University Press, 1977). See also Rhys Jenkins, *Transnational Corporations and Uneven Development* (New York: Methuen, 1988).

[20]For an accessible discussion of these points, see Graham K. Wilson, *Business and Politics: A Comparative Introduction* (Chatham, N.J.: Chatham House, 1990), 2nd ed., Chapter 9.

[21]United Nations Centre on Transnational Corporations, *Transnational Corporations in World Development: Trends and Prospects* (New York: United Nations, 1988), Executive Summary.

[22]"The Global 500: The World's Biggest Industrial Corporations," *Fortune*, July 29, 1991, p. 239.

[23]*Financial Times* (London), December 20, 1990, p. 20.

[24]G. Hamel and C.K. Prahalad, "Creating Global Strategic Capability," in Neil Hood and Jan-Erik Vahlne (eds.), *Strategies in Global Competition* (London: Croom Helm, 1988), pp. 12–18.

[25]Ibid., p. 12; and Jack N. Behrman, "International Industrial Integration Through Multinational Enterprises," in Dunning and Usui (eds.), *Structural Change, Economic Interdependence and World Development*, p. 65.

[26]William Appleman Williams, *The Rise of the Modern American Empire: A Study of the Growth and Shaping of Social Consciousness in a Marketplace Society* (New York: Random House, 1969).

[27]See, for example, Clyde V. Prestowitz, *Trading Places: How We Are Giving Our Future to Japan and How to Reclaim It* (New York: Basic Books, 1988), Chapter 8.

[28]Vic Razis, *The American Connection: The Influence of United States Business on South Africa* (London: Frances Pinter, 1986).

[29]Sandra L. Caron, "Politics and International Business: the Impact of the Foreign Corrupt Practices Act," *Journal of Contemporary Business*, 10, no. 3 (1981), 17–28.

[30]Fernando Henrique Cardoso and Enzo Faletto, *Dependency and Development in Latin America* (Berkeley: University of California Press, 1979); and Douglas C. Bennett and Kenneth E. Sharpe, *Transnational Corporations versus the State: The Political Economy of the Mexican Automobile Industry* (Princeton: Princeton University Press, 1985).

[31]Raymond Vernon, *Sovereignty at Bay: The Multinational Spread of U.S. Enterprises* (New York: Basic Books, 1971); and Thomas A. Poynter, *Multinational Enterprises and Government Intervention* (London: Croom Helm, 1985).

[32]Stopford and Turner, *Britain and the Multinationals*, pp. 229–31. Some nations narrowly restrict the activities of MNEs. See for example, Dennis J. Encarnation, *Dislodging Multinationals: India's Strategy in Comparative Perspective* (Ithaca: Cornell University Press, 1989).

[33]A.E. Safarian, "Introductory Comments and Summary Report on Part III," in Dunning and Usui (eds.), *Structural Change, Economic Interdependence and World Development*, pp. 177–92.

[34]Peter Enderwick, *Multinational Business & Labour* (New York: St. Martin's Press, 1985), pp. 158–59; and Stopford and Turner, *Britain and the Multinationals*, pp. 186–88.

[35]Enderwick, *Multinational Business & Labour*, especially Chapter 6.

[36]This paragraph is drawn from Linda M. Spencer, *American Assets: An Examination of Foreign Investment in the United States* (Arlington, VA.: Congressional Economic Leadership Institute, 1988), pp. 19–23, 29, and 35.

[37]U.S. Department of Commerce, International Trade Administration, *International Direct Investment: Global Trends and the U.S. Role 1988 Edition* (Washington, D.C.: Government Printing Office, 1988), p. 37.

[38]U.S. Department of Commerce, International Trade Administration, *Foreign Direct Investment in the United States 1988 Transactions* (Washington, D.C.: Government Printing Office, 1989), p. 5.

[39]This paragraph follows *Economic Report of the President 1990* (Washington, D.C.: Government Printing Office, 1990), pp. 124–25.

[40]U.S. Department of Commerce, Bureau of Economic Analysis, *Survey of Current Business*, (June 1988), p. 1.

[41]Glickman and Woodward, *The New Competitors*, p. 32.

[42]John Cantwell, "The Reorganization of European Industries After Integration: Selected Evidence on the Role of Multinational Enterprise Activities," in John Dunning and Peter Robson (eds.), *Multinationals and the European Community* (Oxford: Basil Blackwell, 1988), pp. 25–49.

[43]This paragraph is based on Spencer, *American Assets*, p. 35.

[44]Glickman and Woodward, *The New Competitors*; and Martin and Susan Tolchin, *Buying Into America: How Foreign Investment Is Changing the Face of The Nation* (New York: Random House, 1988).

[45]Spencer, *American Assets*, pp. 10–11.

[46]Glickman and Woodward, *The New Competitors*, pp. 149–52.

[47]See "EC Tightens Up on Screwdriver Plants," *Japan Economic Institute Report*, March 18, 1988, p. 5.

[48]Glickman and Woodward, *The New Competitors*, pp. xxvii and 27.

[49]"Benefits from foreign flows," *Financial Times* (London), December 28, 1990, p. 8.

[50]Paul Streeten, "Interdependence: A North-South Perspective," in Dunning and Usui (eds.), *Structural Change, Economic Interdependence and World Development* pp. 19–29.

[51]See, for example, Wyn Grant, William Paterson, and Colin Whitson, *Government and the Chemical Industry: A Comparative Study of Britain and West Germany* (Oxford: Clarendon Press, 1988), p. 317.

[52]Robert B. Reich, "Who Is Us?", *Harvard Business Review*, January–February 1990, pp. 53–65.

[53]Raymond Vernon, "Codes on Transnationals: Ingredients for an Effective International Regime," in Dunning and Usui (eds.), *Structural Change, Economic Interdependence and World Development*, pp. 227–40, especially p. 238.

[54]James G. Savage, *The Politics of International Telecommunications Regulation* (Boulder, Colo.: Westview Press, 1989); and Ramon de Murias, *The Economic Regulation of International Air Transport* (Jefferson, N.C.: McFarland, 1989).

[55]Vernon and Spar, *Beyond Globalism*.

[56]Robert D. Putnam and Nicholas Bayne, *Hanging Together: Cooperation and Conflict in the Seven-Power Summits* (Cambridge, Mass.: Harvard University Press, 1987).

Chapter 5

The Dynamics of Governmental Systems

Government and business institutions were designed to deal with specific problems in their environment. As years and decades passed, those problems changed. Some institutions adapted more effectively to changes in their environment than others.

Part Two of this book examines the institutions that structure relations between government and business. Each chapter considers how some aspect of the structure of government-business relations has responded to changing political and economic conditions.

Chapter 5 focuses on the dynamics of the American governmental system. It asks whether a set of governing arrangements designed in the eighteenth century can make the political decisions needed to sustain an economy that will be competing in the global marketplace in the twenty-first century. Chapter 6 explores how corporations have adapted to two trends that have important political implications: the emergence of government as a major factor in corporate decision making and changes in the ownership patterns of corporations. Chapters 7 and 8 examine developments in the antitrust and regulatory fields in light of the changing circumstances that have appeared in both policy areas.

The success of a country's economy depends on how well it makes political decisions. Imagine a country whose public policies had these consequences: its criminal justice system imprisons more people than any comparable country without reducing crime; its elementary and secondary schools spend more per student than any major educational system with only mediocre results; its defense department expends billions of dollars per year on weapons systems and military bases its leaders don't want; and its bridges are collapsing because the country won't make the necessary maintenance expenditures.

What would you think of such a country? You would wonder whether a country whose policies imposed such costs on its economy could long survive the competition of the global marketplace.

It often appears that the United States government has lost the capacity to manage the country's policy process. American policies provide a pattern of error and misdirection that raises the question of governmental competence.

Americans normally attribute governmental error to the personal failings of officeholders. If the savings and loan system flounders or environmental initiatives languish, Americans characteristically want to "throw the bums out" or, better yet, put them in jail.

More recently, there is another answer. Policy breakdowns may result from the failure of political institutions. The structure of government itself may have become a barrier to the decisions the country needs to make to solve its policy problems.

Government decisions are important to business. This chapter begins by reviewing some types of decisions that have particular significance. How well these decisions are made is meaningful not only for business but for other groups in society as well. The chapter identifies basic features of the American political system and asks whether these features encourage or inhibit effective policy making. Finally, the chapter compares governmental arrangements in the United States with practices in Germany, Japan, and the United Kingdom to consider whether governmental systems in other countries have features that could enhance the effectiveness of government in the United States. A successful economy requires effective political decisions.

GOVERNMENT ACTIVITIES

U.S. business, in principle, holds government at arm's length. It fears that government involvement will lead to government domination. In fact, relations between government and industry are less adversarial than rhetoric suggests. The actions of government and business are more often cooperative than combative. Government performs numerous tasks that are not only valuable to business but essential.

No single agency is the focal point of contacts between government and business. A myriad of departments and agencies are important to business for diverse reasons. Table 5–1 lists some of these organizations and the programs that concern business most. Numerous other commissions and bureaus also hold life-and-death control over specific industries.

TABLE 5–1 Business-Related Activities of Departments and Agencies

DEPARTMENT OR AGENCY	ACTIVITIES
Agriculture	Price supports; the forest service; food inspection programs
Commerce	Trade programs; tourism; technical and statistic services
Defense	Massive procurement expenditures; research projects
Energy	Energy saies; energy technology; nuclear energy
Environmental Protection Agency	Numerous air, water, solid waste, toxic substance regulations
Export-Import Bank	Financing and insurance for exports
Federal Trade Commission	Regulation of commercial practices
General Services Administration	Procurement and construction
Health and Human Services	Health care financing; Food and Drug Administration; health research
Housing and Urban Development	Housing finance and construction
Interior	Public lands; minerals; mining
Justice	Antitrust; commercial litigation
Labor	Occupational safety; pension supervision; employment programs
National Labor Relations Board	Administration of labor laws
State	International commercial affairs
Transportation	Construction; auto safety; rail, air, maritime responsibilities
Treasury	Tax policy; regulates financial institutions; public debt

Government provides companies and industries numerous types of assistance. The most important forms of assistance involve the infrastructure, financial aid, research and development, government purchases, regulation, stable markets, and economic and foreign policy.

Infrastructure

Firms operate in a specific social setting, and government must maintain the necessary social systems. Discussions of infrastructure normally emphasize transportation and utilities. Companies need to transport raw materials, move goods to market, and speed employee travel, and they want energy, water, and communications systems that are reliable and moderately priced.

Recently discussions of infrastructure have begun to encompass human resources as well as the physical infrastructure. Companies benefit from high-quality educational systems, effective medical institutions, and supportive child-care facilities, and governmental actions in these areas aid business.

Financial Assistance

Government promotes economic development and other goals by giving financial assistance to individuals and institutions. This assistance takes many forms, but the most common are direct subsidies, loans and loan guarantees, and tax preferences.

Direct subsidies go to farmers for irrigation projects and market information, to Amtrak for railroad travel, and to the maritime industry for operations. Loans are provided by the Small Business Administration to expand small businesses, by the Economic Development Administration to aid firms in distressed areas, and by the Export-Import Bank to assist export sales; and loan guarantees have been used to benefit the housing industry, the Chrysler Corporation, and college students. Tax breaks promote job training, the life-insurance industry, the construction of sport stadiums, and the sale of gasohol. Some industries would not exist in their present form if public financial assistance were withheld.

Research and Development

In addition to financial assistance, government also promotes economic development by supporting research and development activities. The federal government maintains scores of laboratories to conduct research in technical areas, and it grants funds to universities, medical institutes, and corporations to help them carry on their own research. While the federal government provides tax breaks for research activities, state governments also support research through university appropriations. In addition, government stimulates technical progress through the patent system that guarantees inventors will receive the rewards of their innovations.

Government Purchases

Approximately 25 percent of the national budget is used to purchase goods and services from private companies. When government procurement is mentioned, we think first of the defense budget and expenditures for space exploration. Most of these expenditures go to purchase exotic products, but large portions of these budgets also go to buy such ordinary products as motor vehicles, clothing, medical supplies, building materials, gasoline, and communications equipment. Other government agencies are important purchasers of food, health care, office supplies, consultant services, and all the other products of a complex economy. Many companies were created to do business with government and could not survive the curtailment of government expenditures.

Government Regulation

Government regulation is a pervasive fact of corporate life. A seemingly endless list of national agencies restricts what companies can do: the Federal Trade Commission, the Food and Drug Administration, the Consumer Product Safety

Commission, the Occupational Safety and Health Administration, the Equal Employment Opportunity Commission, the Federal Communications Commission, the Environmental Protection Agency, and on and on. There is an even longer list of state agencies whose job it is to spell out the rules that businesses must follow in the various states.

While government regulation is used by politicians and academics to symbolize conflict between government and industry, companies often advocate regulation and exploit the commercial advantages regulation offers. Government regulations require drivers to purchase automobile insurance, demand the installation of pollution-control devices manufactured by a few firms, award broadcasting licenses to some companies rather than others, and establish product standards that only some corporations can meet. Regulation restricts business operations, but it also creates commercial opportunities.

Stable Markets

Economic theory and business operations traditionally focus on transactions that take place in the marketplace.[1] Markets, however, are social and political creations. They are not all alike. Markets differ from era to era, country to country, and even industry to industry. Government codifies the rules of marketplace activity, and it can change those rules.

Few business enterprises want unbridled competition. Corporations are established organizations that seek to limit the riskiness of their investments. They prefer stable markets with predictable commercial practices. They favor a live-and-let-live style of competition that offers rewards for successful operations rather than no-holds-barred competition.[2] Government policies help structure marketplace competition.

Government defines the nation's antitrust policy and determines which competitive practices are legal. It decides which corporate takeover tactics are acceptable and which violate the country's standards. Government determines whether television stations may own newspapers, whether GM may undertake joint ventures with Toyota, and whether United Airlines may buy the assets of Pan Am. Government rules can close the marketplace to some companies and grant other firms a quasi-monopoly status. Businesses compete in the marketplace, but they depend on government to defend the stability and predictability of that competition.

Economic and Foreign Policy

Economic and foreign policies affect many businesses even though they are not normally regarded as part of the relationship between government and business. Government actions influence inflation rates, the cost and availability of credit, and the general level of business activity. Foreign policy decisions can open foreign markets to a company and create commercial opportunities or poison relations with nations or regions and jeopardize a firm's very existence.

Decisions governments make in each of these areas have a critical impact on firms and industries. If well conceived, government actions can help create a flourishing economy; but, if poorly conducted, a country's policies can derail a nation's economic progress. Why are many people critical of government decision making in the United States?

PATTERNS OF AMERICAN GOVERNMENT

The U.S. government is composed of a set of institutions that were created two centuries ago to guide the affairs of three million people living in simple conditions along the Atlantic Coast. The founders of the new government sought to prevent the emergence of domestic tyrants who might act as despotically as the British monarchs. To do this, they limited the direct role of the national government in society and diffused the powers granted the Washington government among loosely linked institutions. These original decisions have served the country remarkably well, but whether these historic arrangements can yield the decisions needed to govern a complex society in an increasingly interdependent world is a fundamental question. Those who question the capacity of the United States government to make the difficult decisions needed for the future focus on three issues.

Separation of Powers

John Maynard Keynes believed that the constitutional separation of powers had been so successful in restricting governmental action that he once said to an American friend, "…you don't have a government in the ordinary sense of the word."[3] The separation of governmental powers among institutions may be so complex that it effectively denies the government the power to act in contentious circumstances.

Governmental systems can be assessed in terms of the power of government in relation to the power of the other social institutions.[4] A government is said to be *strong* when it has the political and administrative authority to make and carry out policies to deal with the country's problems. It is described as *weak* when it lacks that power.

In these terms, it is often said that the United States has created a weak governmental system. In this system, all national government institutions participate in the decision making process in most major policy areas. This was a reasonable process in the eighteenth century when few issues required national action. A weak governmental system, however, is an increasing handicap for a country facing the problems of a complex international environment.

The process of building agreement among governmental institutions can be so arduous that policy problems are left unaddressed. The inability of Congress and the president to agree on solutions to the country's budget and energy problems, for example, allowed both situations to worsen.

The complexities of reaching agreement on policy issues becomes apparent in examining the structure of Congress, the executive branch, and the presidency. Journalists and academics have likened Congress to an obstacle course.[5] Sponsors of legislative measures must avoid the obstructions presented by the substantive, appropriations, and rules committees in both chambers before their proposals even have a chance of being defeated on the floor or in a conference committee.

The process of reaching agreement was complicated in the 1970s by reforms that weakened leaders and accentuated the individuality of members. The number of select committees and party groups was increased in the House of Representatives, and the use of subcommittees was expanded. The decision process was further fragmented by the decline in the importance of seniority and the proliferation of individual and committee staff. With larger constituencies, longer terms, and a smaller size than the House, the Senate allows individual members even more latitude to pursue their personal policy interests.

Executive departments and agencies have grown in influence with the emergence of positive government. Theoretically, cabinet departments carry out congressional decisions, but, in fact, it is not possible for Congress to specify what agencies should do in every circumstance. Agencies must and do exercise discretion in determining how to interpret statutory provisions and what to do when statutes are silent on an issue. While such discretion is nominally exercised on the basis of professional objectivity, departments and agencies inevitably develop their own viewpoints and interests.

As a consequence, the executive branch is specialized and fragmented, not monolithic. When policy issues arise, the executive branch is likely to have two or three positions rather than one. Trade with Japan, for example, is perceived by the State Department as a foreign policy topic.[6] It is regarded by the Treasury as a matter of international economic policy and seen by the Defense Department as a national security issue. Agriculture, Commerce, and the U.S. Trade Representative all view trade with Japan as a commercial issue; but, even here, the U.S. Trade Representative's role in developing policy separates it from the Commerce Department, whose assignment is to administer policy. Different bureaucratic perspectives have limited the U.S. ability to develop a coherent strategy to deal with the critical issues of trade with Japan.

The president symbolizes American government and is expected to coordinate its far-flung activities. He stands atop two large bureaucracies. The White House Office employs the president's immediate staff that is organized to focus on domestic, economic, and national security policy areas, and to handle relations with Congress, the media, interest groups, and the president's personal activities. The Executive Office of the President encompasses the White House Office as well as the Office of the Vice President, the Office of Management and Budget, the Office of Policy Development, the National Security Council, the Council of Economic Advisers, the Office of Science and Technology, the Council on Environmental Quality, and the U.S. Trade Representative.

Despite the organizational apparatus, the American president grapples with leadership problems no other government head must address.[7] The president faces an independently elected Congress that is often controlled by the opposition party. The U.S. judiciary is more deeply involved in policy issues than is the judicial system in any other country and is independent of presidential control. The president cannot depend on the support of party colleagues, interest-group leaders, or the Federal Reserve System. The president is only one player in a complex system.

The complications caused by the separation of powers at the national level are compounded by the role of state governments. Dismissed not long ago as constitutional anachronisms, state governments have grown in importance in recent decades. In the 1970s, they increased their administrative attention to environmental issues and their commitment to financing public services. In the 1980s, states launched programs to promote economic development and enhance competitiveness.[8]

Ironically, the growing activism of state governments, together with the increased capacity of Congress, the bureaucracy, and the presidency, have complicated the problems of building agreement on pressing policy issues and accentuated the tendency of the American government toward stalemate.

Subgovernments

The separation of powers leads organizations with specific policy concerns to establish links with each other to get things done. The linkages among these institutions are said to constitute "subgovernments."[9] (The terms "iron triangles" and "issue networks" are also used to identify links among institutions in a policy area.) Subgovernments focus on specific policy areas such as broadcast regulation, weapons procurement, or housing construction. They are composed of legislators on subcommittees responsible for the issue area, bureau chiefs who administer the programs, representatives of interest groups affected by the policy, and semiautonomous policy analysts with specialized expertise in the area.

Subgovernments are inspired by enduring interests in policy areas rather than by sudden events. Individuals come and go, but policy forces are stable. Subgovernments have little influence on the headline issues that attract media attention, but they dominate the less dramatic topics that define most of what government does.

Business writers urge companies to emphasize communications with permanent subgovernment "insiders" when trying to influence government decisions.[10] Success depends on building relationships with congressional staff people rather than members, permanent civil servants in the departments and agencies rather than political executives, and long-time professionals in interest groups rather than outsiders who are assigned to manage an organization on a short-term basis.

Subgovernment decision making is characterized by substantial policy expertise and little political accountability. When a policy conflict arises, members of the subgovernment seek to resolve it among themselves. They resist the participation of officials who do not share their interests and perspectives.

Subgovernment decisions typically yield policies that focus on narrow concerns and disregard comprehensive issues. Airline deregulation, for example, proceeded without regard for overall transportation policy, and housing finance policies neglect urban development questions. Subgovernment decisions are also incremental and reflect limited departures from established policy. They normally escape the notice of elected officials and remain the province of policy specialists. Thus, it is not surprising that subgovernment bargains reflect the special interests of sector participants rather than the broader interests of the general public.

Instability

A description of U.S. government that emphasizes sluggishness from the separation of powers and a lack of accountability from subgovernments presents only part of the truth.[11] There are occasions when political leaders stampede into action and tolerate no delays in putting their position on the record.

This schizophrenia in the policy process is the result of a growing rootlessness and atomization in the broader political system. Television has become the primary medium of political communication in the United States. Opinions generated by the mass media, however, are less informed and less intensely felt than opinions that result from people's direct experiences.[12] It is not unusual for a topic to dominate the media for a few weeks, rise high in the surveys of public concern, and then fade quickly from people's minds.

With the media leading the public from crisis to crisis, the governing institutions are no longer able to preserve political continuity. Political parties are less meaningful to citizens than in past decades, and autonomous campaign organizations are playing a growing role in electoral politics. Open meetings and public records have made elected officials more subject to interest-group pressures and less able to resist momentarily popular but ill-conceived policies.

Governmental instability is accentuated by the rapid turnover among top officials in departments and agencies. Secretaries and assistant secretaries typically come to Washington, serve for two or three years, and then return to other careers. Changes in the leadership of the executive branch are so frequent that it has been said that the United States has a government led by "strangers" and "talented amateurs."[13]

The influence of the media and the limited institutional capacity to maintain stability have reduced the willingness of elected officials to face contentious problems. Officials can never be certain which side of an issue will be popular during the next election or how a vote on a controversial issue might be represented.

Political instability leads to policy instability. A multibillion dollar program can be launched with great fanfare and then discarded when the issue is no longer fashionable. In the late 1970s, Congress created an ambitious program to manufacture synthetic fuels to replace imported oil. President Carter said the project was comparable in scope to the NASA space program. A few billion dollars later, interest flagged, and Congress cut off funding before the program had time to achieve its legislative goals. In other areas as well, U.S. policy is said to display a "pattern of repeated initiatives and wobbly follow-up."[14]

Government in the United States is characterized by problems of inaction that result from the separation of powers, piecemeal approaches to problems associated with subgovernments, and policy instability that reflects unstable public attitudes. These problems limit the government's ability to carry out the long-term policies needed to maintain a sound economy in such areas as budgeting, energy, and trade. An examination of decision-making arrangements in other countries identifies significant contrasts with the patterns of government in the United States. Do these contrasts highlight potential areas of reform?

GOVERNMENTAL PATTERNS IN COMPARATIVE PERSPECTIVE

Governmental arrangements matter because they affect how a country understands events at home and abroad and how the country responds to those events.[15] Governing arrangements probably matter most during times of rapid political, economic, and technological change, such as we are experiencing at present.

A country's ability to manage a competitive economy is determined by three factors: its opinion environment; the capacity of its government; and its policy style. A country's opinion environment is composed of the values and attitudes of its citizens. The opinion environment can be characterized by substantial agreement on major social and economic goals, or by the lack of such agreement. A government may have the capacity to make and carry out the decisions needed to fulfill its role in the society, or it may lack that capacity. A country's policy style may bring together the various groups in the society on important issues, or it may still leave the groups at odds with each other after a policy has been chosen.[16] Our hypothesis is that a country will be able to manage its economy more effectively if its opinion environment is unified, the capacity of its government is high, and its policy style stresses agreement and accommodation.

Germany, Japan, and the United Kingdom are all parliamentary democracies where political parties guide the choice of prime minister. Despite these similarities, each country has a distinct opinion environment, level of governmental capacity, and policy style.

Germany

Since 1949, Germany has adjusted to substantial domestic and international developments without fundamental changes in its political institutions.[17] The foundation of this political stability was the impressive German economic recovery in the decades after World War II. Since economic deprivation had contributed to the collapse of the Weimar Republic and the emergence of the National Socialist regime in the 1930s, economic stability and growth have remained priorities in the country's opinion environment.

The preferred strategy for economic growth has been a vigorous export program. This strategy has been supported by a so-called "productivity coalition" composed of business, unions, and semipublic institutions.[18] The country's major institutions appreciate the rewards of a successful economy and restrain their individual actions so as to maintain the pursuit of collective benefits.

Germany has a parliamentary system in which political parties select the chancellor and dominate the policy process. The chancellor is elected for a four-year term and has the right to appoint and dismiss cabinet ministers. The effective power of the chancellor is limited, however, by the influence of party organizations, the decisions of the Federal Constitutional Court, and the latitude given individual ministers in running their own departments. Furthermore, state governments are also influential players in national politics because of their direct representation in one house of the national parliament, their role in implementing national policies, and the importance of state party organizations on the national scene. While the administrative apparatus plays a stabilizing role in German politics, the autonomy of various institutions limits the capacity of government to respond quickly to policy problems.[19]

The German policy process is a form of partnership between the government and organized groups. The policy style stresses devising consensual solutions to policy problems rather than allowing a majority to impose its own solution. While controversies do arise from sharp disagreements over important issues, a socially integrative solution is usually devised during the lengthy process of negotiation.

Opposition to the "productivity coalition" and the emphasis on economic values appeared in Germany in the 1970s.[20] A variety of popular movements articulated social concerns and sought to transform the country's political and economic system. While these movements had a visible impact on certain values and policy areas, the traditional governing institutions remained securely in place. In 1990, the political and economic structure also accommodated the integration of the eastern states without major departures from traditional practices. Table 5–2 characterizes the opinion environment, governmental capacity, and policy style of Germany and the other countries.

TABLE 5–2   Patterns of Government

	GERMANY	JAPAN	UNITED KINGDOM	UNITED STATES
Opinion environment	Stability/ Growth	Consensus on Growth	Divisive	Varied themes
Government capacity	Medium	High	Medium	Low
Policy style	Negotiation	Accommodation	Consultation	Group conflict

Japan

The stable outline of Japanese politics conceals significant changes that have occurred in recent decades.[21] In the 1950s, political leaders fused a market ideology with traditional values to overcome the political instability then gripping the country.[22] As a consequence of these efforts, a consensus on economic growth and competitiveness assumed a central role in the country's opinion environment.

Government and society in Japan are seen to "form mutually reinforcing parts of a whole."[23] The boundary between the public and private realms in Japan is not as distinct or as meaningful as in the United States. Government plays a highly interventionist role in the economy, and its key task is to integrate competing private interests through the development of a consensus on critical issues. The government is usually thought to be capable of organizing solutions to the country's problems.

The image of stability in Japanese politics emerges from three factors. First, the ruling Liberal Democratic Party (LDP) has controlled government for almost forty years, and it shows few signs of losing its grip. Second, the bureaucracy is and has been the most influential institution of government. This is especially true of the economic ministries, which were created before World War II, gained vast powers during wartime, survived the postwar years mostly intact, and have largely charted their own policy course in subsequent decades. Finally, major business interests are well organized to participate in the policy process, and they maintain close ties with important bureaucrats and political leaders. The image of government dominated by a coalition of the LDP, bureaucratic elites, and industry figures is sometimes caricatured as the "1955 System" or "Japan, Inc."

The structures of the LDP, the bureaucracy, and organized business are still prominent features of the political landscape, but the cohesiveness of the postwar system has declined. The LDP has been forced to transform its electoral base by reducing reliance on agricultural regions and expanding support in urban districts. While the parliament and the prime minister remain far weaker than comparable institutions in Western nations, Japanese bureaucracies are now increasingly attentive to the views of elected officials. The LDP's Policy Affairs Research Council and the mass media have begun to emerge as sources of alternative policies, and there are frequent conflicts between the electoral orientation of politicians and the technical concerns of bureaucrats. Major business enterprises have established themselves around the world, and they are, therefore, less dependent on domestic bureaucratic support than they once were. Regional businesses have also arisen that are not fully integrated in the country's traditional business organizations.

Bureaucratic agencies retain the strategic initiative in policy questions, but the country's policy style compels them to work toward consensus. A strong distributive orientation in Japanese politics directs compensation to disgruntled groups in policy disputes, but there are few other mechanisms for resolving policy controversies. The primacy of economic growth has traditionally been adequate to reach agreement on policy matters, but the pace of international events may prompt further changes in the Japanese policy system in the years ahead.

United Kingdom

The pattern of government in the UK is a heritage from pre-modern times. As the world's first industrial nation, Britain experienced especially intense conflicts between capitalist groups and organized labor. There is still no agreement on the appropriate role for government in the economy, and the opinion environment reflects this critical division.

Industrial enterprises were founded and became successful before government was a prominent factor in the country's economic life. Firms originally operated on a small scale without the benefits of a large domestic market, interfirm coordination, or governmental assistance. The twentieth century has witnessed frequent rounds of government activism in the economy, but these actions have been prompted by the collapse of prominent industries or surges of nationalism rather than by a coherent strategy of public action.[24]

The Thatcher era repoliticized tensions between labor and management, preached the benefits of competition, and emphasized the responsibility of firms for their own survival. Critics argue that Thatcherism was a flawed approach to the country's problems and stress the bitterness of the social divisions that appeared during the Thatcher era.[25]

The British pattern of government is sometimes described as the Westminister model of democracy: a strong cabinet; a nonpartisan civil service; programmatic, disciplined political parties; and no elected chief executive.[26] The cabinet in this system is the center of government. Ministers are individually responsible for the affairs of their departments and collectively responsible for the important decisions of the government. The prime minister plays a key role in the government but does not automatically dominate collegial decisions. The prime minister is selected from among the members of Parliament and normally has credentials as party leader. Parliament legitimizes the policies fashioned by the bureaucracy and proposed by the cabinet, but it has little law-making influence. In the British system, the cabinet has the capacity to undertake important governmental initiatives in the face of substantial political opposition.

The senior civil servants are often regarded as the strength of the British system. They are depicted as talented, bloodless, cautious careerists who sustain the government from prime minister to prime minister. They promote a policy style that emphasizes consultation and avoids challenging well-entrenched interests.[27] Civil servants routinely maintain contacts with interest-group leaders and business figures. They avoid public conflicts and involvement in electoral politics and stress informality, confidentiality, and voluntary action in the implementation of programs.

Should Europe Elect a President?

The European Community (EC) is a confederation of twelve countries. Its members have pooled their sovereignty for joint actions, such as the creation of a single European market by the end of 1992. Confederations historically have problems making decisions. The EC's difficulty defining its position in the General Agreement on Tariffs and Trade negotiations in 1991 and its poor record administering its agriculural policy demonstrate that the Community sometimes cannot "get its own act together."

The EC has three major governing institutions. Each is based on a different political principle. The Council of Ministers is composed of the representatives of the twelve member governments, and it represents the interests of the governments. The Commission is a bureaucracy headed by seventeen full-time officials appointed by the member governments for fixed terms. The Commission initiates legislative proposals, carries out Community policies, and is the "motor of integration." The European Parliament is composed of members popularly elected in the twelve countries. It has little formal law-making authority. The use of the term "parliament" here is an aspiration or a popular symbol of peaceful unification rather than an accurate description of the institution's current role.

EC decisions emerge from a dialogue between the Council of Ministers and the Commission. The process of reaching agreement on difficult issues is so tedious that EC is unable to deal with many problems.

Some governmental arrangements work better than others. The proposal to create a popularly elected European president rests on the view that an elected chief executive could bring the EC's decision-making institutions together and help the Community respond more effectively to the policy problems the peoples of Europe now face.

Source: Samuel Brittan, "The Case for a European President," *Financial Times* (London), December 13, 1990, p. 17; Juliet Lodge, "EC Policymaking: institutional considerations," in Juliet Lodge (ed.), *The European Community and the Challenge of the Future* (New York: St. Martin's Press, 1989), 27–57.

United States

There is substantial confidence in ordinary citizens in the American opinion environment and distrust of the people running government. The focus of public attention alternates from concern about the efficient functioning of the economy to interest in achieving social ideals.

In the terms discussed above, the U.S. government is weak and characterized by the separation of powers, the sectorization of policy, and the instability of political judgments. The policy style relies on interest groups to develop policy options and represent public preferences. Government initiates new policies when it secures the support of a majority of the Congress, even though important groups remain opposed to specific policies. Opposition to policies often continues after they have been enacted and delivered to the bureaucracy for implementation.

What does the review of opinion environments, governmental capacity, and policy styles tell us about conducting successful policies? What aspects of American government stand out in international comparison? What suggestions can be gained from these comparisons concerning governmental reform?

Analysis

A supportive, consensual opinion environment appears to be a prerequisite for policy success. Widespread agreement on the importance of economic objectives appeared indispensable in Germany and Japan, and the divisiveness in the United Kingdom seemed to preclude coherent policy action. In the United States, the policy emphasis has shifted from era to era, from the equity agenda in the 1960s and 1970s to greater official concern for economic efficiency in the 1980s. The changing cultural emphasis probably yields less successful policies than the relative single-mindedness of Germany and Japan, but it appears to be a viable basis for conducting policy so long as the shifting policy themes do not deteriorate into the divisiveness that characterizes Britain.

A variety of organizational arrangements can produce sufficient governmental capacity to solve a country's problems. In the German system, power is shared by the parties, the chancellor, the ministers, and the state governments. The structure of Japanese government concentrates power in administrative agencies, although competition among agencies and the traditions of accommodation can inhibit action. National authority in the United Kingdom is centralized in the cabinet, but the ideology of limited government has constrained the capacity of government. In contrast, the structure of the U.S. government diffuses authority widely, limits accountability, and hampers policy stability.

The policy style of American government stands out from those of the other countries. In each of these other countries, policy decisions emerge from efforts to build agreement among concerned groups. Consultation and accommodation are routine features of the implementation process. The American policy style rests on interest-group conflict, the winning of majority support in Congress, and the continuation of controversy during implementation.

Our review supports the hypothesis that a country will have more successful policies if it has a unified opinion environment, a government with substantial capacity, and a policy style based on accommodation rather than division. American governmental arrangements have certainly contributed to the policy successes of past generations. Despite the normal tendency to be sanguine about the effectiveness of governmental institutions, the record of recent years, provides ample grounds to be apprehensive about the ability of an eighteenth-century governmental system to solve twenty-first-century problems.

This analysis suggests two basic avenues of reform: efforts to promote consensus in the country's opinion environment and policy style; and proposals to overcome the institutional fragmentation of government.

One student of international competitiveness has concluded that "Successful societies...succeed because they have found ways to match individual self-interest to the collective good."[28] Japan and Germany have used groups and organizations to link individual and societal interests. The traditional success of the United States, in contrast, has emphasized individualism and depended on the motivation that results from a sense that individual effort will be fairly rewarded. The proliferation of groups in the United States has weakened rather than strengthened a sense of common purpose. Anything that convinces Americans that they will not be treated fairly exacerbates the divisions always present in a large and disorderly country and diminishes the prospects for successful policies.

The growing interdependence and internationalization of the U.S. economy have increased the costs that must be paid for the broad diffusion of governmental authority. The goal is not to devise reforms that would allow governmental institutions to make more policies more quickly. The goals are to advance reforms that will allow the public to be better informed about the overall consequences of governmental action and to create mechanisms to hold public officials accountable when their individual choices do not contribute to the proper functioning of government. Whether the damage now being done by poorly functioning governmental arrangements is great enough to promote institutional change is not yet clear.

SUMMARY

Relations between government and industry are more supportive and less adversarial than popular rhetoric suggests. Government provides a broad array of services that are crucial to the successful functioning of key sectors of the economy. If these services are not provided or are provided poorly, business and society suffer.

Unfortunately, the United States government is plagued by features that limit its ability to carry out long-term policies in critical areas. The separation of powers creates inertia in decision making. Subgovernments or iron triangles produce piecemeal approaches to social problems, and the country's increasingly unstable political patterns yield equally unstable policies.

The ability of countries to carry out successful policies is enhanced if public opinion on basic issues is unified, the capacity of government to make and carry out decisions is high, and the style for carrying out public policies is based on agreement and accommodation. Germany and Japan rate more highly in each of these areas than does the United States. The image of the United Kingdom is more mixed.

Efforts to improve the U.S. policy process will need to address the fragmentation of governmental authority and the persistent patterns of conflict within the country's opinion environment.

SELECTED READINGS

Bob Jessop et al., *Thatcherism: A Tale of Two Nations* (Cambridge: Policy Press, 1988).

R. Scott Fosler (ed.), *The New Economic Role of American States: Strategies in a Competitive World Economy* (New York: Oxford University Press, 1988).

Richard J. Samuels, *The Business of the Japanese State: Energy Markets in Comparative and Historical Perspective* (Ithaca: Cornell University Press, 1987).

Karel van Wolferen, *The Enigma of Japanese Power: People and Politics in a Stateless Nation* (New York: Vintage Books, 1989).

John Zysman, *Governments, Markets, and Growth: Financial Systems and the Politics of Industrial Change* (Ithaca: Cornell University Press, 1983).

END NOTES

[1]John R. Bowman, *Capitalist Collective Action: Competition, Cooperation, and Conflict in the Coal Industry* (Cambridge, England: Cambridge University Press, 1989), pp. 30 and 221–22.

[2]Ibid., p. 30.

[3]Quoted in Raymond Vernon and Debora L. Spar, *Beyond Globalism: Remaking American Foreign Economic Policy* (New York: Free Press, 1989), p. 21.

[4]Stephen Krasner, "The United States Commercial and Monetary Policy," in Peter J. Katzenstein (ed.), *Between Power and Plenty: Foreign Economic Policies of Advanced Industrial States* (Madison, Wis.: University of Wisconsin Press, 1978), p. 57.

[5]See sources cited in Steven S. Smith, "New Patterns of Decisionmaking in Congress," in John E. Chubb and Paul E. Peterson (eds.), *The New Direction in American Politics* (Washington, D.C.: Brookings Institution, 1985), pp. 203–33.

[6]Clyde V. Prestowitz, *Trading Places: How We Are Giving Our Future to Japan and How to Reclaim It* (New York: Basic Books, 1988), pp. 423–26.

[7]Fred Greenstein (ed.), *Leadership in the Modern Presidency* (Cambridge, Mass.: Harvard University Press, 1988).

[8]R. Scott Fosler (ed.), *The New Economic Role of American States: Strategies in a Competitive World Economy* (New York: Oxford University Press, 1988), especially pp. 14–18; Peter K. Eisinger, *The Rise of the Entrepreneurial State: State and Local Economic Development Policy in the United States* (Madison, Wis.: University of Wisconsin Press, 1988); and David Osborne, *Laboratories of Democracy* (Boston: Harvard Business School Press, 1988).

[9]J. Leiper Freeman and Judith Parris Stevens, "A Theoretical and Conceptual Re-examination of Subsystem Politics," *Public Policy and Administration*, 2, no.1 (1987), 9–24.

[10]Frank Shipper and Marianne M. Jennings, *Business Strategy for the Political Arena* (Westport, Conn.: Quorum Books, 1984), Chapter 1.

[11]This argument is prompted by James Q. Wilson, "American Politics, Then & Now," *Commentary*, 67, no. 2 (February 1979), 39–46.

[12]Benjamin Ginsberg, *The Captive Public: How Mass Opinion Promotes State Power* (New York: Basic Books, 1986), Chapter 3.

[13]Hugh Heclo, *A Government of Strangers: Executive Politics in Washington* (Washington, D.C.: Brookings Institution, 1977); and Vernon and Spar, *Beyond Globalism*.

[14]Vernon and Spar, *Beyond Globalism*, p. 7.

[15]This analysis was prompted by John Zysman, *Governments, Markets, and Growth: Financial Systems and the Politics of Industrial Change* (Ithaca: Cornell University Press, 1983);

and Jeffrey A. Hart, "The Effects of State-Social Arrangements on International Competitiveness: Steel, Autos, and Semiconductors in the U.S., Japan, and Western Europe" (unpublished paper prepared for delivery at 1990 Annual Meeting of the American Political Science Association, August 30 through September 2, 1990); see also Hart, *Rival Capitalists: International Competitiveness in the United States, Japan, and Western Europe* (forthcoming).

[16]Jeremy Richardson (ed.), *Policy Styles in Western Europe* (London: George Allen & Unwin, 1982).

[17]This section draws from Peter J. Katzenstein, "Stability and Change in the Emerging Third Republic," in Katzenstein (ed.), *Industry and Politics in West Germany: Toward the Third Republic* (Ithaca: Cornell University Press, 1989), pp. 307–53; Gordon Smith, "Structures of Government" and "Political Leadership," in Gordon Smith, William E. Peterson, and Peter H. Merkl (eds.), *Developments in West German Politics* (Durham: Duke University Press, 1989), pp. 24–39 and 60–76; and M. Donald Hancock, *West Germany: The Politics of Democratic Corporatism* (Chatham, N.J.: Chatham House, 1989).

[18]Katzenstein, "Stability and Change," pp. 312–13. See also Kenneth Dyson, "West Germany: The Search for a Rational Consensus," in Richardson (ed.), *Policy Styles in Western Europe*, pp. 17–46.

[19]Smith, "Structures of Government."

[20]Jost Halfmann, "Social Change and Political Mobilization in West Germany," in Katzenstein (ed.), *Industry and Politics in West Germany*, pp. 51–86.

[21]Kent Calder, *Crisis and Compensation: Public Policy and Political Stability in Japan, 1949–1986* (Princeton: Princeton University Press, 1988), Chapters 4 and 11; Karel van Wolferen, *The Enigma of Japanese Power* (New York: Vintage Books, 1989); and Takeshi Ishida and Ellis S. Krauss (eds.), *Democracy in Japan* (Pittsburgh: University of Pittsburgh Press, 1989), Chapters 3, 6 and 14.

[22]Michio Muramatsu and Ellis S. Krauss, "The Conservative Policy Line and the Development of Patterned Pluralism," in Kozo Yamamura and Yasukichi Yasuba (eds.), *The Political Economoy of Japan: The Domestic Transformation* (Stanford, Calif.: Stanford University Press, 1987), pp. 516–554.

[23]Daniel I. Okimoto, "Japan, the Societal State," in Daniel I. Okimoto and Thomas P. Rohlen (eds.), *Inside the Japanese System: Readings on Contemporary Society and Political Economy* (Stanford, Calif.: Stanford University Press, 1988), pp. 211–15.

[24]Wyn Grant, *Government and Industry: A Comparative Analysis of the US, Canada and the UK* (Hants, England: Edward Elgar, 1989), pp. 86–87.

[25]Joel Krieger, "United Kingdom," in George C. Lodge and Ezra F. Vogel (eds.), *Ideology and National Competitiveness: An Analysis of Nine Countries* (Boston: Harvard Business School Press, 1987), pp. 29–53; and Bob Jessop et al., *Thatcherism: A Tale of Two Nations* (Cambridge Policy Press, 1988).

[26]A.G. Jordan and J.J. Richardson, *Government and Pressure Groups in Britain* (Oxford: Clarendon Press, 1987); Walter Williams, *Washington, Westminster and Whitehall* (Cambridge, England: Cambridge University Press, 1988); Geoffrey Marshall (ed.), *Ministerial Responsibility* (Oxford: Oxford University Press, 1989).

[27]Grant Jordan and Jeremy Richardson, "The British Policy Style or the Logic of Negotiation?" in Richardson (ed.), *Policy Styles in Western Europe* pp. 80–110.

[28]James Fallows, *More Like Us: Making America Great Again* (Boston: Houghton Mifflin, 1989), p. 14. See also pages 187 and 208.

Chapter 6

Corporations and Public Affairs

Corporations are younger than national government institutions and quicker to adapt to changes in their economic environment.[1] Firms must continually alter their products in response to competitive pressures and technological developments. Merck became the world's largest pharmaceutical company with an outpouring of new prescription drugs, and Microsoft has become the foremost publisher of PC software by creating products for IBM-compatible computers.[2]

Corporations must also adapt to the changes that occur in their political environment. Recent developments highlight two areas of change that promise to be controversial topics in the 1990s: corporate public affairs programs and corporate governance systems.

In the last two decades, government decisions have become an increasingly important factor in shaping corporate behavior.[3] All facets of corporate operations are now affected in some way by government policies. Most large companies have established organizational units to monitor government developments and express their policy views to public officials. This chapter examines the structure of corporate public affairs programs and considers the issues such programs raise.

Questions of who actually controls corporations broke into the headlines in the 1980s when outsiders sought to take over prominent companies. Various groups affected by takeovers sought to have their voices heard in the corporate decision process. They tried to find out who controls major companies in a democracy. The second part of this chapter examines the nature of corporations, investigates the patterns of ownership, and assesses the consequences of different forms of control.

CORPORATE PUBLIC AFFAIRS PROGRAMS

The growing significance of government may be the most far-reaching development in the political environment of corporations in recent decades. As the world's largest prescription drug manufacturer, New Jersey–based Merck & Company provides products for such chronic problems as arthritis and high blood pressure. The corporation's operations are impacted by government at every level.[4]

At the supranational level, the World Health Organization (WHO) is beginning to acquire quasi-regulatory powers over the approval and sale of pharmaceutical products. WHO decisions are not binding, but some countries that lack the technical capacity to make medical rulings adopt the organization's decisions. Almost all national governments outside the United States regulate drug prices and, thus, control the revenues a firm can earn. The U.S. government affects Merck most by the Food and Drug Administration's approval of new drugs and by the government's tax decisions. State governments are important to the pharmaceutical firm because of environmental policies and programs to attract new plants. Merck also needs to remember local governments whose decisions affect the sites where the firm conducts business.

How do companies respond to the impact of government on their operations? Most CEOs lament government influence but accept it as a fact of life.[5] Since everything government does affects a company's bottom line, almost all CEOs believe that they should seek to influence the policies that impact their firms' operations. Furthermore, three of every four CEOs also believe that they should speak out on issues affecting the broader public interest.

A small portion of CEOs disagrees. They maintain that their expertise is in running companies rather than debating public policies. They believe that efforts to promote policies are more likely to inspire antibusiness groups to redouble their opposition than to achieve the company's goals. These corporate leaders argue that they have no mandate to become involved in policy debates, and they fear that "politicizing" companies will have more negative than positive consequences.

Virtually all large firms have accepted the position that they must participate in the policy process.[6] The pervasive impact of government on corporate operations has led most firms to develop an organizational structure to assess pending policy proposals and express the company's views on those initiatives.

Not all companies, of course, have the same needs. Corporate public affairs programs differ by industry and company.[7] Programs are more fully developed in industries with a history of federal regulation or where government is an important purchaser of the industry's products such as utilities, transportation, petroleum, and the defense industry. Corporate public affairs departments are found least frequently in the machinery, retailing, and metals industries.

Public affairs programs experienced a subtle shift between the 1970s and the 1980s. The programs had moved into the spotlight in the early 1970s, when firms sought to defend themselves against what they regarded as hostile interest groups and an expansive government. In the early and mid-1980s, some firms cut back their public affairs efforts because they were experiencing hard economic times and expected little to fear from the Reagan administration.

Despite occasional reductions, however, the general pattern of growth in public affairs programs continued in the 1980s.[8] In one survey, 79 percent of firms reported that the number and importance of federal actions affecting their companies increased during the Reagan years.[9] One executive commented, "More negative decisions for business have been made during the Reagan years than we could have possibly anticipated." It appears that government activity has now reached a permanent level that cannot be ignored, regardless of who the incumbent president is.

Continued growth in the 1980s also indicates that public affairs programs have become an institutionalized part of corporate life. They are now regarded as profit centers like other parts of the corporation.[10] Firms have begun to look to public affairs departments not only to defend them against government initiatives but also to help them use governmental authority to improve their operations and gain advantage over their competitors. Governmental agendas in the 1980s showed increasing evidence of efforts by firms and industries to enhance their competitive positions through governmental action.

At the beginning of the 1990s, corporate public affairs programs typically had four elements:[11]

1. *Issues Management.* Issues management identifies issues, evaluates their impact, and formulates company responses.
2. *Government Relations.* Most corporations have representatives in Washington and state capitals to explain the firm's views on pending proposals.
3. *Public Communications.* Public communications provides information about the company and its views to the public and external groups.
4. *Community Affairs.* Included here are charitable support, employee involvement programs, and community activities.

Figure 6–1 places these public affairs functions in a specific corporate context by displaying an organization chart of the Merck & Company public affairs program. Issues management (sometimes called public policy management) and government relations will be discussed in this section. Communications and community affairs are politically important as devices to enhance the effectiveness of government relations efforts, and they will be discussed below in Part Three.

Issues Management

The term "issues management" is a shorthand phrase for a slightly longer idea. It does not refer to a strategy for managing issues. Issues management is, more modestly, an approach to managing a company's response to public issues. It is "the process by which the corporation can identify, evaluate and respond to those social and political issues which may impact significantly on it."[12] According to one survey, 91 percent of *Fortune* 500 firms have issues management programs, and 74 percent of the leaders of these firms regard the programs as very important or extremely important.[13]

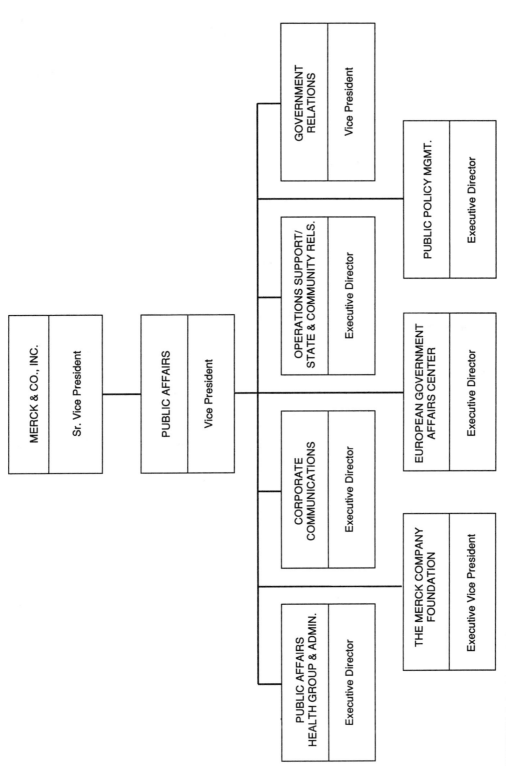

FIGURE 6–1 Merck & Company Public Affairs Department. *Source:* Adapted from material provided by Merck & Company.

An issues management system is composed of a series of steps that define a firm's response to a public issue. A typical issues management system is composed of six activities:[14]

- Monitor trends and identify issues;
- Assess the impact of issues on firm;
- Prioritize issues;
- Develop the company's position on issues;
- Design the company's strategy to achieve its goal; and
- Implement the company's strategy.

Companies seek first to identify those issues that might be of interest to the firm. They then assess the possible impact of an issue on the firm and decide which issues are most important to the firm. Companies establish their position on an issue, determine how they can best achieve their goal, and finally put their plan into action.

A corporate issues management system is based on steps that resemble the stages in the life cycle of a public issue as discussed by students of public policy.[15] Public policy analysts examine how societal problems get placed on governmental agendas, how alternative responses to the problems are formulated, how government decides among the various policy options, and how departments and agencies implement the policy option that has been selected.

Issues management systems resulted from the frustrations executives experienced when being caught by surprise by changes in governmental policy. Business commentators argued that company representatives failed to pay enough attention to issues until they broke in the media. By then, they argued, it was too late to have much impact on the course of events.[16] The earlier companies focused on an issue, it was said, the more likely they were to achieve their objectives. Issues management has an intellectual kinship to corporate strategic planning activities; but, while corporate planning concentrates on a company's products and its administrative structure, issues management emphasizes governmental policy.

Issue Identification: The first step in an issues management process is to identify emerging issues. Some analysts seek to scan the broad sociopolitical environment to detect trends that might affect their companies in the years ahead. Rising energy prices might generate citizen demands for improved public transportation systems, changes in marriage and child-raising practices could influence housing needs, and emerging standards of public accountability might lead to demands for reform of corporate governance.

Other issue analysts search out issues that are more immediate and more concrete.[17] They seek to identify issues by reading professional journals, consulting interest-group representatives, and contacting scholars with expertise about issues facing their industry. They might subscribe to the services offered by consulting firms that purport to identify upcoming issues. Corporate agents responsible for legislative affairs often visit top aides of the members of the House and Senate who sit on committees that handle issues affecting their company to learn what topics might concern the legislators in the months ahead.

Impact on Firm: Companies need to discover which issues are important to them and which are not. Issues can be classified in different ways. Among the issues identified by analysts are *operational* issues that impact directly on how the company conducts its business. Manufacturers are concerned about the regulation of chemicals used in production processes, and broadcasters worry about proposals to provide free air-time to political candidates. Issue managers also focus on *corporate* issues that affect a company's general welfare. Public utilities scrutinize proposals to reform antitrust laws, for example, and retailers are especially sensitive to matters involving personnel policies. Some companies are also concerned about broader *social* issues that affect them only indirectly, such as the budget deficit, the quality of education, or welfare reform.

Companies often rely on issue analysts to determine what consequences a proposal will have for the firm. Sometimes they assemble interdepartmental committees that draw expertise from different parts of the corporation to assess the impact of policy initiatives on the firm and its operations.

Ranking Issues: Issue analysts can easily identify scores or even hundreds of issues that could be significant to a company.[18] Since companies cannot monitor everything, issues must be prioritized.

The standards used most often to prioritize issues are the impact on the company and the probability the issue will occur. An issue that will have a greater impact on a firm is obviously important to it; but, if the chance that the issue will come to pass is extremely low, it may not warrant more than passing attention. The priority assigned issues is also affected by the ability of the company to alter the course of an issue if it did decide to act and by the relationship of an issue to the company's long-term strategic objectives.

Actual decisions on which issues should receive priority are usually made either by the company's chief executive, an executive group composed of representatives of different parts of the firm, or the public affairs group itself. The top executives at Monsanto, the chemical company, identified five issue areas on which it would concentrate as it sought to become a global company specializing in high value-added products: international trade; biotechnology regulation; intellectual property; agricultural policy; and hazardous-waste disposal.[19]

Developing Company Position: Developing a company's position on an issue is not as easy as it sounds. Most corporations today are multiproduct, multinational enterprises, and different units of firms have different positions on specific issues. In addition, companies compete with other firms, and their market position can complicate their reaction to governmental initiatives. The divisions of General Motors that sell large cars are more opposed to government regulations mandating increases in the fuel efficiency of a company's cars than are the divisions producing smaller cars. In contrast, Chrysler, which already sells a larger proportion of fuel-efficient cars, has favored governmental regulation in this area.

Given these complications, some corporate managements prefer to be *bystanders* in the policy process.[20] They may protest as they adapt their operations to satisfy new governmental standards, but they are only drawn into public disputes in extreme circumstances. Other managements recognize the continuing significance of governmental decisions and are frequent *participants* in the policy process. Still other firms are policy *activists* that seek to get a jump on their competitors by anticipating changes in the public arena and taking the initiative themselves to promote revisions in public policies.

Once issues have been identified and prioritized and the firm's position has been determined, government relations representatives develop a strategy to achieve the company's goal and implement that strategy.

Government Relations

Government relations has been described as "*the* principal new responsibility added to top corporate management's traditional functional concerns" in the last two decades.[21] The task has evolved from a matter of public relations into an analytic and technical responsibility. The enhanced attention afforded government relations is reflected in structural and behavioral aspects of corporations.

Top Management Involvement: Public policy concerns have now penetrated the ranks of top management. Concern with government appeared first in firms whose activities were particularly subject to government regulation or that sold a major share of their products to government. Most major firms have now assembled a full-time government relations staff and established a top executive committee to guide their external relations.

The chief executives of the largest corporations typically devote up to half of their time to dealing with extracorporate concerns, and government is the most important of these concerns.[22] No longer can CEOs ignore external factors and focus simply on internal operations, regardless of their individual preferences. The CEO of a major utility described the importance he attaches to government relations in these terms:[23]

> There is very little policy that I will accept that does not have some input from public affairs. I spend half my time on external affairs even though I am trying to run a business.... Government relations and issues management are probably the only way a business will survive in the future in the political arena.... If you can get legislators to stop introducing bills, I would cut down the number of resources I employ against them. As long as they keep putting in bills that impact against me, I have to be concerned.

The personal involvement of a company's chief executive in an issue is sometimes the only way to convince policy makers that the issue is important. One member of Congress from Ohio commented, "If an executive vice president wants to see me, fine if I have time. If I don't, he can see my staff. If it's really important to the company, you expect the CEO to get involved."[24] One survey of 200 CEOs reported that 56 percent spent more than ten days in Washington in the past year, and 39 percent spent more than twenty days there.[25]

Government Relations in Germany and the United Kingdom

Direct relationships between companies and the national government are less common in Germany and the United Kingdom than in the United States. In Germany, every opportunity is taken to emphasize the unity of industries, and companies rely on industry associations to conduct most relations with government. Government relations departments as found in American corporations are rare in German companies. The chancellor will meet occasionally with the heads of companies, but German firms usually seek to avoid close relations with government.

British practice combines elements of the American and German patterns. Major companies in such industries as oil, chemicals, tobacco, and electronics have government relations departments that monitor government actions and maintain direct contact with public officials. Government relations offices are rare in smaller companies and in industries such as food processing, retailing, and construction. These firms rely on business associations to maintain relations with government, or they have no relations with government at all.

Source: Wyn Grant, "Large Firms and Public Policy in Britain," *Journal of Public Policy*, Vol. 4, No. 1 (1984), pp. 1–17; and Wyn Grant, William Paterson, and Colin Whitson, *Government and the Chemical Industry: A Comparative Study of Britain and West Germany* (Oxford: Clarendon Press, 1988), pp. 103–108.

Federal Relations: Federal relations is usually the key part of a company's government relations program. These offices are responsible for monitoring the activities of legislative and executive officials and reporting to top management on existing programs and future initiatives.[26] They are expected to maintain communications with public officials who are critical to the firm's interests and provide them with information on current issues. Federal relations executives are expected to design strategies to help the firm achieve its federal policy goals and participate in implementing those strategies. In addition, federal relations offices sometimes assist other divisions of the corporation with their marketing efforts and their strategic planning.

One indication of the emergence of the federal relations function has been the frequency with which companies have decided to maintain a full-time presence in Washington. One study reports that 52 percent of manufacturing and financial companies with annual sales of $100 million have established a Washington office, and another survey indicates that 72 percent of a sample of larger firms have D.C.

offices.[27] Permanent Washington representatives help a firm maintain contacts with officials working on key issues, better understand the nuances of ongoing events, and bring cohesion to the government relations activities of different parts of the company.[28] The recession of the early 1980s and the takeovers and consolidations of the mid-1980s led to a reduction in the Washington presence of old-line manufacturers, but high-tech firms like Apple Computer, Genentech, and Intel moved in at the end of the decade to establish themselves in Washington.

State Government and International Offices: Much of the expansion in government relations programs in the last few years has occurred in the areas of state government and international affairs. The decline in policy activism in Washington in the 1980s contributed to a revitalization of state governments, and this, in turn, led to a trend toward the creation of state government relations units in major corporations.[29] Companies focus their attention on states in which they have extensive operations and on states such as California which they think provide leadership for other states in adopting new policies.

The internationalization of business has also led to the emergence of international public affairs strategies. Historically, companies wanted to assess the risk of investing in particular nonindustrialized countries.[30] The growing concentration of international business activity in major industrial countries has shifted the focus of analysis. International enterprises are now engaging in negotiations and lobbying with stable foreign countries. Companies that have relationships with governments in countries such as Germany and the United Kingdom are now utilizing there the same techniques they employ in domestic government relations programs.

Political Activities: Some firms also sponsor political activities. If a company sponsors a political action committee, it is usually administered in the government relations office and regarded as an activity that helps company representatives develop contacts with federal and state officials. Some companies organize grass-roots networks of employees, suppliers, and shareholders to communicate company positions to legislators on critical issues, and these networks are usually guided by government relations departments as well. Many firms encourage employees to vote and participate in community affairs. These policies may be administered by personnel offices or government relations departments.

SUMMARY

The emergence of public affairs as a management function reflects the increased importance of government in the political environment of corporations. Corporate public affairs offices include both an issues management capacity that identifies issues, evaluates their impact, and formulates company responses, and a government relations unit that maintains communications with elected and appointed officials. These offices were usually established in reaction to governmental initiatives. They have now become important instruments that help firms increase the effectiveness of their operations and gain competitive advantage.

WHO CONTROLS MODERN CORPORATIONS?

A less immediate but no less meaningful change occurring in the political environment of corporations is seen in the patterns of corporate ownership and control. When one asks who controls corporate America, the answer beginning to be heard with increasing frequency is Dale Hanson. Dale Hanson is a pleasant man with an easy smile and an informal manner.[31] He does not like the ways some corporations are governed. He thinks corporate chiefs are paid too much and that some defenses against corporate takeovers do more to protect the interests of managers than shareholders. Hanson's statements on such issues are studied meticulously because he may be the country's most powerful corporate owner. Hanson is executive director of the California Public Employee's Retirement System, the largest public employee pension fund in the United States, with $56 billion in assets.

In 1988, pension funds like Hanson's owned nearly 17 percent of all outstanding stock in public corporations, up from 9 percent in 1970. Investment companies, trust funds, insurance companies, savings banks, and educational endowments owned another 20 percent of corporate America. As owners of a growing share of American business, pension funds and other institutional investors are beginning to play an active role in setting policy for corporate America. They are key participants in takeover battles and frequent advocates for reform in corporate governance.[32] Before discussing their role, it is necessary to consider other groups that share control over modern corporations.

Shareholders

Shareholders are the legal owners of business corporations. They have purchased a "share" of the company's assets and profits and theoretically control its activities. Shareholders meet once a year to review the firm's performance and elect members to a board of directors. When the ownership of stock in a company is widely dispersed, the company is said to be "publicly held."[33]

Boards of directors of companies are supposed to represent the interests of the shareholders.[34] They are symbols of power, but they have been called pawns as well as potentates.[35] Boards establish general policies and select the top managers who are responsible for carrying out those policies. The typical board meets monthly or quarterly and has fourteen members. "Inside" boards are dominated by the company's high-level executives, and "outside" boards draw most of their members from external organizations such as law firms, banks, universities, foundations, or other corporations.

Outside directors sometimes exercise power during periods of crisis or management transition, but in normal times they do nothing more than ratify the decisions of the incumbent management. Since part-time board members know less about the company's operations than the full-time management and have trouble agreeing among themselves on a course of action, they usually have little impact on corporate policy. One scholar concludes: "…directors in large mainstream corporations normally tend to play a passive role, as invited guests, characteristically tied to the inside hosts by some sort of personal or business relationship."[36]

Management

The diffusion of ownership and the weakness of boards of directors has left a power gap in the control of modern corporations. A famous study by Berle and Means argues that corporate managers have filled the gap by extending their responsibility for a firm's operations into de facto control over its policies.[37] A company's management is widely seen today as the dominant force in guiding its destiny. The management recruits members for the board of directors, controls the process by which directors are elected, fixes the agenda for board meetings, and runs annual shareholder gatherings. With their knowledge of company affairs and their control of critical procedures, managers can become a self-perpetuating elite that places its personal interests above those of the shareholders or of the firm.

Managers have different interests from those of shareholders, and they may use their position to increase their own rewards at the expense of the shareholders. Shareholders may want to have a larger portion of profits distributed as dividends, while managers may want to retain profits for use in the firm's operations. Shareholders may favor investments in pioneering areas, while managers may favor investments in less-risky undertakings. Shareholders may object to high salaries, generous fringe benefits, lucrative stock deals, and "golden parachute" severance payments that protect top managers from unanticipated departures. Managers contend that these benefits are necessary to attract and retain talented executives.

Employees

A company's employees also exercise some de facto control over the company's operations. The interests of employees in the United States are legally expressed through labor unions and bargaining. The National Labor Relations Act guarantees to employees the right to join unions and bargain collectively with employers. Management and labor representatives are required by law to bargain in good faith over wages and working conditions.

The large majority of American workers, as noted in Chapter 3, are not members of unions. Most employees believe that their interests overlap, to some degree, the interests of their employers. Since they know that companies need competent workers, such employees conclude that they are better off relying on company practices and legal guarantees than in seeking the presence of labor unions.

The interests of workers are represented differently in Germany. Management teams of large German companies are chosen by supervisory boards, half of whose members are selected by company employees. German law also requires firms to have workers' councils in individual plants. The approval of these councils is needed before companies can alter their operations in ways that significantly affect workers.

In the 1980s, direct employee ownership of firms attracted attention as a means of accommodating the competing demands of shareholders and employees. Employee stock-ownership plans (ESOPs) received favorable tax treatment, and they became a popular device for saving the jobs of workers threatened with the plant closings.[38] American unions have shown little enthusiasm for alternatives to collective bargaining as means of exercising employee influence, but the 1990s may test whether forms of employee ownership can play an effective role in corporate governance.

Financial Institutions

There is no doubt that the 1990s will see growing influence of financial institutions in the governance and operations of corporations.[39] By the end of the 1990s, according to one estimate, pension funds, mutual funds, insurance companies, banks, and other financial institutions will control two-thirds of the stock of major corporations.[40] Traditionally, financial institutions have been passive investors, supporting a company's management or sitting on the sidelines. Those days are passing quickly. Financial institutions are now beginning to act like owners of companies rather than simple investors.

The amount of money invested in corporations that is controlled by pension funds, mutual funds, and insurance companies is growing so rapidly that these institutions cannot sell their stockholdings without driving down the price of the stock and taking losses. The trend toward investment fund activism has usually been prompted by the desire to improve corporate performance and increase the value of a fund's holdings, but investment funds sometimes seek to achieve social and political goals.[41]

Dale Hanson, executive director of the California Public Employee's Retirement System, and his counterparts in Wisconsin, New York, Massachusetts, and New Jersey participated in efforts in the 1980s to pressure companies to cease doing business in South Africa, and they then urged Exxon to change its environmental procedures after the disastrous Alaska oil spill in 1989. More recently, activist funds have concentrated on corporate governance issues. Several funds compelled Honeywell Corporation to alter its policies for electing directors, convinced Lockheed to change its rules to resist takeovers, and urged TRW and Occidental Petroleum to establish stockholder advisory committees.

The trend toward investment fund activism draws sharply mixed reviews. Most corporate executives are wary of investment fund managers. They resent outsiders telling them how to run companies they think the funds know little about. They charge that fund managers focus on short-term rather than long-term results and contend that the funds' willingness to sell out companies to "fast-buck" manipulators aggravated the takeover mania of the 1980s.[42] Others respond that investment funds are in a better position to serve as watchdogs defending the interests of stockholders than any other institution. In an era of dispersed stock ownership and weak boards of directors, investment funds are in the best position to identify chief executives who treat public companies as personal fiefdoms and blow the whistle on management proposals that benefit executives rather than companies.

Features of Japanese Corporations

Before World War II, many Japanese companies belonged to one of four groups of corporations, or *zaibatsu*, that together controlled 32 percent of the country's corporate investment and 50 percent of bank deposits. These groups were broken up in the postwar years but were later succeeded by similar groups called *keiretsu*. These companies own stock in other firms in the group, share project risks, and favor each other in commercial activities.

Two characteristics of Japanese firms are said to be most influential in shaping their conduct. First, stock ownership and stock market activity have less influence on a company's operations than in the United States. About 30 percent of the stock of companies in a group is owned by other firms in the group. Thus, management does not need to worry about hostile takeovers or stockholders' rights. This pattern of ownership allows firms to focus on product development and market share and downplay the importance of profits and dividends.

Second, major Japanese firms have a strong commitment to their current employees. Employees are considered to be an essential component of the firm, and the task of management is to mediate between the shareholders and employees. The commitment to employees is seen in lifetime employment practices, salary levels based on seniority, and the absence of rigid job classifications. Large Japanese firms usually have fewer employees than comparable American companies, so they can maintain a homogeneous workforce and protect their employees during periods of recession. Subcontractors absorb most of the burden of economic shocks, and employment conditions in these firms are harsh.

Sources: Merton J. Peck, "The Large Japanese Corporation," in Meyer and Gustafson (eds.), *The U.S. Business Corporation*, pp. 21–42; and Masahiko Aoki, "The Japanese Firm in Transition," in Kozo Yamamura and Yasukichi Yasuba (eds.), *The Political Economy of Japan: The Domestic Transformation* (Stanford, Calif.: Stanford University Press, 1987), pp. 263–88.

Criticisms of Corporations

Corporations have preserved much of their autonomy in the United States because of their contribution to the nation's standard of living and their record in providing citizens economic and social opportunities. Despite this, corporations remain the subject of significant criticism. These criticisms emphasize the themes of legitimacy and performance.

Corporations are said by some observers to be fundamentally undemocratic institutions in a democratic society.[43] Corporate decisions about products, employment, and investment affect the total society, but the general public has no say in selecting corporate leaders. When corporate managers misinterpret events and bungle strategies, consumers and employees suffer, but top executives are usually insulated from the worst consequences of their own errors. There is no necessary relationship, it is noted, between corporate profitability and social welfare. When corporate profits soar, the costs may fall on the general public. Commentators who question the legitimacy of corporations usually advocate increased federal regulation of corporate decision making.[44]

The second set of criticisms of corporations focuses on global competitiveness and maintains that different segments of corporations are not performing adequately. Some observers point to the failures of management.[45] American managers are said to have a short-run bias. Quarterly profits and the nightly stock market reports are more important to executives than long term investments and product developments. Business schools are also said to concentrate on financial tactics and neglect the importance of production issues. American companies are seen to have poor labor-relations policies and to have been slow to appreciate the importance of overseas markets and the internationalization of business. In what is the unkindest criticism of all, contemporary executives are said to have lost the entrepreneurial spirit that once characterized American business.

Analysts also identify failures of other elements of corporations. Boards of directors are said to tolerate subpar management practices and to allow the market value of their companies' stock to fall so low that the firms become targets for corporate takeovers.[46] American workers are blamed for demanding higher wage levels than improvements in productivity justify and for failing to develop the skills needed for an increasingly technological economy.[47] Critics of corporations maintain that the market alone does not impose sufficient sanctions for substandard performance and propose that new government standards for corporate performance be devised.

SUMMARY

Modern corporations are usually dominated by the top executives who manage the firms' activities on a daily basis. The theoretical control of shareholders is rarely exercised because ownership is broadly dispersed and boards of directors are uninvolved in a company's operations. The growing volume of stock owned by pension and investment funds has made fund managers a potential new force in controlling corporations.

The implications of this development could be a pivotal issue of the 1990s as the proportion of corporate America controlled by fund managers continues to grow. The need to respond to new patterns of stock ownership could be a challenge for corporate managers in the 1990s comparable in magnitude to the need to adjust to the increased significance of government in the 1970s and 1980s.

SELECTED READINGS

BENNETT HARRISON and BARRY BLUESTONE, *The Great U-Turn: Corporate Restructuring and the Polarizing of America* (New York: Basic Books, 1988).

JAY W. LORSCH and ELIZABETH MACIVER, *Pawns or Potentates: The Reality of America's Corporate Boards* (Boston: Harvard Business School Press, 1989).

SEYMOUR LUSTERMAN, *Managing Federal Government Relations* (New York: Conference Board, 1988).

ALFRED A. MARCUS, ALLEN M. KAUFMAN, and DAVID R. BEAN, (eds.), *Business Strategy and Public Policy: Perspective from Industry and Academia* (New York: Quorum Books, 1987).

JOHN R. MEYER and JAMES M. GUSTAFSON, (eds.), *The U.S. Business Corporation: An Institution in Transition* (Cambridge, Mass.: Ballinger, 1988).

END NOTES

[1]Thomas K. McCraw, "The Evolution of the Corporation," in John R. Meyer and James M. Gustafson (eds.), *The U.S. Business Corporation: An Institution in Transition*, (Cambridge, Mass.: Ballinger, 1988), pp. 1–20.

[2]Karen Zagor, "Resilient Merck bucks trend with 20% advance for quarter," *Financial Times* (London), January 23, 1991, p. 16; and Louise Kehoe, "Microsoft surges on sales of Windows," *FT*, January 21, 1991, p. 17.

[3]Mike H. Ryan, Carl L. Swanson, and Rogene A. Buchholz, *Corporate Strategy, Public Policy and the Fortune 500: How America's Major Corporations Influence Government* (New York: Basil Blackwell, 1987).

[4]"Corporate Structure for Public Affairs," Rutgers University presentation, February 19, 1986.

[5]David G. Moore, *Politics and the Corporate Chief Executive* (New York: Conference Board, 1980), Chapter 3.

[6]Kirk Victor, "Being Here," *National Journal*, August 6, 1988, pp. 2021–2025.

[7]Seymour Lusterman, *Managing Federal Government Relations* (New York: Conference Board, 1981).

[8]Alfred A. Marcus and Mark S. Irion, "The Continued Viability of the Corporate Public Affairs Function," in Alfred A. Marcus, Allen M. Kaufman, and David R. Beam (eds.), *Business Strategy and Public Policy: Perspectives from Industry and Academia* (New York: Quorum Books, 1987), pp. 267–81.

[9]Lusterman, *Managing Federal Government Relations*, pp. 21–22.

[10]David Vogel, *Fluctuating Fortunes: Political Power of Business in America* (New York: Basic Books, 1989), p. 287.

[11]This list draws from P.N. Andrews, "The Sticky Wicket of Evaluating Public Affairs: Thoughts about a Framework," *Public Affairs Review*, vol. 6 (1985), 94–105.

[12]Jon Johnson, "Issues Management—What are the Issues?," *Business Quarterly*, 48, no. 3 (Fall 1983), p. 22.

[13]Robert L. Heath and Richard Alan Nelson, *Issues Management: Corporate Public Policymaking in an Information Society* (Beverly Hills, Calif.: Sage Publications, 1986), p. 21.

[14]These elements are discussed differently in various works. See, for example, Johnson, "Issues Management," p. 23; and Heath and Nelson, *Issues Management*, p. 20.

[15]See the formulation presented by Charles O. Jones, *Introduction to the Study of Public Policy* (Monterey, Calif.: Brooks/Cole, 1984).

[16]Joseph T. Nolan, "Political Surfing When Issues Break," *Harvard Business Review*, (January 1985), pp. 72–81.

[17]James K. Brown, *Guidelines for Managing Corporate Issues Programs* (New York: Conference Board, 1981), Chapter 4.

[18]Brown, *Guidelines for Managing Corporate Issues*, pp. 13–16.

[19]Stephen E. Littlejohn, "Competition and Cooperation: New Trends in Issue Identification and Management at Monsanto and Gulf," in Marcus, Kaufman, and Beam (eds.), *Business Strategy and Public Policy*, p. 22.

[20]These distinctions are suggested by Ryan, Swanson, and Buchholz, *Corporate Strategy, Public Policy and the Fortune 500*, p. 95.

[21]Richard G. Darman and Lawrence E. Lynn, "The Business—Government Problem: Inherent Difficulties and Emerging Solutions," in John T. Dunlop (ed.), *Business and Public Policy* (Cambridge, Mass.: Harvard Graduate School of Business Administration, 1980), p. 49.

[22]George A. Steiner, *The New CEO* (New York: Macmillan, 1983), p. 26.

[23]"A Chief Executive's View of Public Affairs," Rutgers University presentation, February 16, 1984.

[24]Quoted in John M. Barry, "CEOs Make The Best Lobbyists," *Dun's Business Month*, February 2, 1986, p. 28.

[25]Ibid., p. 32.

[26]Lusterman, *Managing Federal Government Relations*, 1988, p. 6.

[27]Lusterman, *Managing Federal Government Relations*, p. 24; and Barry, "CEOs Make The Best Lobbyists," p. 32.

[28]Kirk Victor, "Being Here," *National Journal*, August 6, 1988, pp. 2021–2025.

[29]Seymour Lusterman, *Managing Business-State Government Relations* (New York: Conference Board, 1983).

[30]Thomas L. Brewer (ed.), *Political Risks in International Business: New Directions for Research, Management, and Public Policy* (New York: Praeger, 1985); and Stephen J. Kobrin, *Managing Political Risk Assessment* (Berkeley: University of California Press, 1982).

[31]This paragraph relies on Martin Dickson, "Investors Wake Up To Their Power," *Financial Times* (London), December 3, 1990, p. 16.

[32]See, for example, Moira Johnston, *Takeover: The New Wall Street Warriors* (New York: Penguin, 1987), pp. 188–89.

[33]Some argue that family ownership of firms remains important. See Philip H. Burch, *The Managerial Revolution Reassessed* (Lexington, Mass.: Lexington Books, 1972).

[34]Winthrop Knowlton and Ira M. Millstein, "Can the Board of Directors Help the American Corporation Earn the Immortality it Holds So Dear?," in Meyer and Gustafson

(eds.), *The U.S. Business Corporation*; The Business Roundtable, "The Role and Composition of the Board of Directors of the Large Publicly Owned Corporation: Statement of the Business Roundtable," *The Business Lawyer*, (July 1978), 2096–3012; and C. P. Alderfer, "The Invisible Director on Corporate Boards," *Harvard Business Review*, (November 1986), 38–46.

[35]Jay W. Lorsch, with Elizabeth MacIver, *Pawns or Potentates: The Reality of America's Corporate Boards* (Boston: Harvard Business School Press, 1989); and Charles A. Anderson and Robert W. Anthony, *The New Corporate Directors* (New York: Wiley, 1986).

[36]Edward S. Herman, *Corporate Control, Corporate Power* (New York: Cambridge University Press, 1981), p. 48.

[37]Adolf A. Berle and Gardiner C. Means, *The Modern Corporation and Private Property* (New York: Macmillan, 1932).

[38]Corey Rosen, Katherine Klein, and Karen M. Young (eds.), *Employee Ownership in America: The Equity Solution* (Lexington, Mass.: Lexington Books, 1986).

[39]This paragraph draws on L. Lowenstein, *What's Wrong with Wall Street: Short-term Gain and the Absentee Shareholder* (Reading, Mass.: Addison-Wesley, 1988). See, as well, David Vogel, *Lobbying the Corporation* (New York: Basic Books, 1978).

[40]Ira Millstein, reported in Sarah Bartless, "Big Funds Pressing for Voice in Management of Companies," *The New York Times*, February 23, 1990, pp. A1 and D5.

[41]Lauren Talner, *The Origins of Shareholder Activism* (Washington, D.C.: Investor Responsibility Research Center, 1983).

[42]This paragraph relies on Martin Dickson, "Investors Wake Up To Their Power," *Financial Times* (London), December 3, 1990, p. 16.

[43]Ralph Nader and Mark J. Green (eds.), *Corporate Power in America* (New York: Grossman, 1973).

[44]See, for example, Ralph Nader, Mary Green, and Joel Seligman, *Taming the Giant Corporation* (New York: W.W. Norton, 1976.)

[45]Michael L. Dertouzos et al., *Made In America: Regaining the Productive Edge* (Cambridge, Mass.: MIT Press, 1989); Bennett Harrison and Barry Bluestone, *The Great U-Turn: Corporate Restructuring and the Polarizing of America* (New York: Basic Books, 1988); Robert B. Carson, *Business Issues Today: Alternative Perspectives* (New York: St. Martin's Press, 1984), pp. 99–102; and William J. Abernathy and Robert H. Hayes, "Managing Our Way to Economic Decline," *Harvard Business Review* (July 1980), pp. 67–77.

[46]Arch Patton and John C. Baker, "Why Directors Won't Rock the Boat," *Harvard Business Review* (November 1987), pp. 10–18.

[47]Ezra J. Vogel, *Japan as Number One* (Cambridge, Mass.: Harvard University Press, 1976).

Chapter 7

Antitrust Laws
and
Competition Policy

Corporate mergers, takeovers, and restructurings made the 1980s the most turbulent decade for American business in the twentieth century. In 1989, almost five thousand merger transactions were announced with a combined value of $378 billion.[1] At the start of the 1980s, AT&T had been the world's largest corporation. The breakup of the company under a court decree revolutionized the communications industry and constituted the country's largest corporate divestiture. The buyout of RJR Nabisco by an investment firm was the largest corporate takeover in American history and inspired journalistic denunciations of greed and barbarism.[2]

These events emerged from the maelstrom of controversy that has surrounded the country's antitrust laws in the last fifteen years. Antitrust policy is intended to promote economic competition and discourage monopolies, mergers, and restraints of trade. For almost a century, it was one of the most significant features of the nation's business environment. Now antitrust has lost the unqualified allegiance of economists, has been challenged by trends in domestic and international business, and has been partially abandoned by the federal government.[3] An antitrust Rip Van Winkle who had slept from the 1970s to the early 1990s would discover that antitrust laws were no longer the looming presence in the country's boardrooms they once had been.

The purpose of this chapter is to examine the antitrust traditions from which contemporary events emerge and consider whether antitrust laws are still a suitable basis for promoting the country's economic and political objectives. This chapter explores the origins of antitrust laws and the economic assumptions associated with them; it examines the policy's evolution and the rationale for recent criticisms.

American antitrust laws are unique. No country has tried more consistently to structure economic competition and supervise marketplace behavior than the United States. The uniqueness of the American approach to antitrust is best appreciated by comparing U.S. policies to those of other countries. This chapter reviews the policies of Germany, Japan, and the United Kingdom. In its final section, the chapter assesses the recent wave of takeovers and mergers from the perspective of antitrust policy.

AMERICAN ANTITRUST POLICY

Antitrust policy was a passionate issue in the early decades of this century.[4] It stood at the center of presidential campaigns and reflected a vigorous struggle over the country's future. It is significant that Americans use the phrase "anti-trust policy" while Europeans speak more soberly of "competition policy." The difference in usage reflects the fact that American laws were inspired more by political fears than economic theories.

In the decades after the Civil War, U.S. citizens were fearful of railroads, cartels, Standard Oil, the size of eastern banks, and the plight of farmers. American industry was being reshaped during this period, and mergers took the form of *trusts* in which the ownership of companies was turned over to the board of trustees of a supercorporation in exchange for a share of the new corporation's earnings. By the end of the century, trusts controlled the production of petroleum, sugar, tobacco, beef, whiskey, harvesting machinery, and other everyday products.

Nineteenth-century legislators did not understand economic theories of competition,[5] but they did recognize that the new corporations represented concentrations of economic and political power that jeopardized their way of life. Since trusts had the power to restrict the supply of goods and increase prices, government, they concluded, should regulate the development of trusts and control their practices.

Economic Rationale for Antitrust

During the last century, economic analyses of antitrust issues have become more sophisticated. For antitrust purposes, a monopoly can be defined as a situation in which a seller or group of sellers can affect patterns of competition by changing the price at which a product is sold.[6] Trusts and other monopolistic restraints of trade are important in economic terms because they violate the assumptions of a perfectly competitive market. Perfect competition assumes that no buyer or seller has control over prices and that new firms can enter the market whenever they want.

Monopolistic restraints of trade are thought to be economically inefficient on several grounds. It is necessary first to distinguish *allocative* from *productive* efficiency. Productive efficiency occurs when a firm is manufacturing its product at the lowest possible cost. Allocative efficiency appears when a society distributes resources among economic activities in a manner that provides it the greatest possible benefit.

Monopolistic arrangements are inefficient because monopolists can impose higher prices on the society than is economically warranted. They are allocatively inefficient because the higher prices direct more resources to areas where monopolists are active than is appropriate. Monopolies are also inefficient in production because monopolists face few competitive pressures and have less incentive to cut operating costs.

The most common defense of monopolistic market structures is that monopolies can sometimes achieve lower production costs than other firms. In certain industries, the average cost of manufacturing a product declines as the number of products made increases. The more items produced, the less it costs to produce each item. Declining average costs, or *economies of scale*, usually result from the specialization of labor and the spreading of fixed costs over a higher level of production. Monopolists who control an entire industry can benefit from economies of scale and from their greater ability to mount large research and development programs.

Antitrust Statutes

Antitrust policies have evolved slowly.[7] The Sherman Act of 1890 has been the foundation of the country's antitrust policy for a century. Section 1 of the law prohibits agreements to fix prices and restrain trade, and Section 2 makes it illegal for firms to "monopolize" particular markets or industries. Table 7–1 summarizes the main provisions of the Sherman Act and subsequent antitrust laws.

TABLE 7–1 Major Provisions of Antitrust Laws

ACT	PROVISIONS
Sherman Act (1890)	Prohibits agreements to fix prices or restrain trade and bans actions that seek to monopolize a market
Clayton Act (1914)	Prohibits price discrimination, restrictions on retailers, and mergers, if they lessen competition
Federal Trade Commission Act (1914)	Creates the Federal Trade Commission and prohibits unfair methods of competition
Robinson-Patman Act (1936)	Strengthens Clayton Act rules against price discrimination
Wheeler-Lea Act (1938)	Expands authority of Federal Trade Commission to protect consumers as well as competitors
Celler-Kefauver Act (1950)	Extends Clayton Act's prohibition to encompass various types of mergers
Antitrust Improvement Act (1976)	Requires firms to notify government in advance of pending mergers

The history of the Sherman Act illustrates the problems that have plagued the enforcement of antitrust laws from the start. The prohibition of agreements between companies to fix prices had the perverse impact of prompting companies to merge with their competitors so they could escape the restrictions of the new law. In addition, the Supreme Court interpreted the ban on actions to "monopolize" a market in Section 2 to mean that only "unreasonable" or coercive attempts to monopolize were prohibited while monopolies produced by conventional commercial means were perfectly legal.[8]

Calls for stronger antitrust laws were a major issue in the 1912 presidential election. The Clayton Act and the Federal Trade Commission Act were part of President Woodrow Wilson's broad economic package that also included creation of the Federal Reserve System, reduction of tariffs, and enactment of a federal income tax. The Clayton Act prohibited specific actions that lessened competition, such as requiring retailers to purchase all their products from one supplier, and it banned corporate mergers accomplished through the acquisition of stock. The Federal Trade Commission Act created the Federal Trade Commission to enforce the Clayton Act, and it also gave the new agency the sweeping authority to prevent companies from "using unfair methods of competition."

These two statutes also had limited impact when first enacted because the Federal Trade Commission had little power to enforce its rulings and the Supreme Court interpreted the ban on mergers accomplished through the acquisition of stock to mean that mergers accomplished through the acquisition of assets were permissible. The Robinson-Patman Act of 1936 strengthened the Clayton Act's rules against price discrimination to help small retailers compete with large chain stores, and the Wheeler-Lea Act of 1938 authorized the Federal Trade Commission to protect consumers as well as companies. In 1950, the Celler-Kefauver Act extended the Clayton Act's antimerger rules to cover asset as well as stock mergers and to ban other forms of mergers. The Antitrust Improvement Act of 1976 required large corporations to notify the government of pending mergers and give the authorities time to investigate potential violations of law.

Antitrust Litigation

The Antitrust Division of the Justice Department and the Federal Trade Commission are responsible for enforcing antitrust laws. Antitrust suits can also be brought by private parties who believe that they have been harmed by a company's anticompetitive practices. Table 7–2 provides an overview of the implementation of antitrust laws in different time periods.

There was little enforcement of antitrust rules between 1890 and 1905, but Supreme Court decisions did establish precedents that helped shape antitrust policy in later periods.[9] *United States* v. *Trans-Missouri Freight Association*, the first major case involving an agreement among companies to fix prices, was decided in 1897.[10] The defendants acknowledged the existence of a rate-setting association but contended that their rates were fair. They maintained that Section 1 of the

Sherman Act only prohibited price-fixing agreements that imposed unreasonable rates. By a five-vote majority, the Supreme Court rejected the companies' position and ruled that agreements to fix prices are per se illegal, regardless of the fairness of the prices.

TABLE 7–2 Implementation of Antitrust Laws By Time Period

PERIOD	ACTIVITIES
1890–1905	Little enforcement action, but court decisions established important legal precedents
1906–1920	Spectacular corporate break-ups and the creation of the judicial Rule of Reason
1921–1938	Little enforcement action
1939–1980	Antitrust laws assume modern features and have broad relevance for corporate action
1981–1990	Enforcement concentrates on price fixing and certain types of merger activities

Source: Based on Donald Dewey, *The Antitrust Experiment* (New York: Columbia University Press, 1990), pp. 6–11.

Section 2 of the Sherman Act, banning corporate actions to monopolize a market, was tested in *United States* v. *Northern Securities Company*.[11] J.P. Morgan and James Hill used the Northern Securities Company to gain control of the only two railroads that served the northern parts of the Midwest and West. The government charged Northern Securities with monopolizing rail transportation in the region in violation of the Sherman Act, and by a five-to-four margin the Supreme Court agreed. More importantly, the justices ordered the merger between the two railroads to be dissolved even though the Sherman Act had not given the Court the authority to impose this type of remedy. The significance of the divestiture precedent became clear in the period from 1906 to 1920.

United States v. *Standard Oil Company of New Jersey* is probably the most famous antitrust case in the nation's history.[12] Standard Oil symbolized everything the public disliked about corporate trusts. The government charged that Standard Oil had employed a catalogue of illegal and improper practices to gain control of 85 percent of the market for refined oil. In 1911, a unanimous Supreme Court agreed with the government, found that Standard Oil had violated the Sherman Act, and ordered the company dissolved.

The significance of the *Standard Oil* decision was not just the spectacular dissolution of a notorious company. It was also the rationale for the Court's action. Chief Justice White defined a two-step process for deciding if a company had "monopolized" a market. According to White, a court first determines if the company had sufficient market power to be considered a monopoly. If the company had enough market power, a court then decides if the market power had been acquired properly or improperly. A Rule of Reason, the justice wrote, should help a court distinguish "normal methods of industrial development" from those that were unacceptable. Since there was abundant evidence that Standard Oil had acted illegally, the Supreme Court ruled that the company had violated the Sherman Act and should be broken up.

The implications of the Rule of Reason's distinction between normal and abusive business practices were pursued in *U.S. v. United States Steel Corporation*.[13] U.S. Steel had been formed in 1901 through the merger of twelve independent companies and was the nation's largest industrial enterprise. It controlled 60 percent of total U.S. iron and steel output when the government alleged that it had violated the Sherman Act. The Supreme Court rejected the government's charge, found that the company's position had been achieved through "normal" rather than abusive tactics, and determined that the firm had never tried to eliminate its competitors. For the court, U.S. Steel was a "good" rather than a "bad" trust, and it was acquitted.

The Rule of Reason placed an enormous burden on would-be trust-busters. They had to prove that a firm had a dominant market position, had obtained its position through predatory tactics, and had used its power to eliminate its competitors. Because of the burden of proving each of these elements, there was little antitrust enforcement activity between 1920 and 1938.

The New Deal period of the late 1930s restored considerable vitality to the antitrust field. Congress enacted the Robinson-Patman and Wheeler-Lea acts, and the Roosevelt administration stepped up enforcement actions by bringing an indictment against the Aluminum Company of America (ALCOA). The *ALCOA* case dealt a sharp blow to the Rule of Reason standard for interpreting antitrust issues and set the tone for enforcement actions in subsequent decades.[14]

In 1937, the Justice Department charged that ALCOA had monopolized the aluminum market, even though there was little evidence that ALCOA had engaged in improper activities. The government relied on the fact that ALCOA controlled the overwhelming share of the market. After lengthy litigation, the Supreme Court finally ruled that Congress had not intended to condone good trusts and condemn bad ones. Congress had, the Court insisted, forbade all monopolies. On this basis, the justices rejected the Rule of Reason, declared that market share alone was sufficient evidence of a violation of antitrust laws, and found ALCOA guilty of monopolizing the aluminum industry. The clarity of this ruling led the Justice Department to step up its enforcement activities and prompted Congress to strengthen antitrust standards.

The *ALCOA* era ended sometime in the late 1970s. By this time, the Supreme Court had begun to back away from the *ALCOA* principle that market share alone was evidence of wrongdoing. When the government charged that DuPont had monopolized the cellophane industry, the Supreme Court accepted the company's defense that cellophane was only a small part of a larger flexible-wrapping-materials industry in which DuPont played a limited role.[15] When a competitor argued that Kodak had used its market power in film to expand the sales of its cameras, the justices wrote that successful marketplace competition should not be an excuse for "legal castigation" and ruled mostly in Kodak's favor.[16]

The start of a new stage in the implementation of antitrust laws was symbolized by the dismissal in January 1982 of a suit the government had launched against IBM thirteen years earlier. The Justice Department had charged in 1969 that IBM monopolized the market for general-purpose computers by bundling its services to require customers to purchase entire computer systems, by offering reduced prices in educational markets, and by announcing new products in a manner that damaged competitors. After twelve years, 100,000 pages of trial transcripts, and tens of millions of pages of documents, the head of the Justice Department's Antitrust Division concluded in 1982 that the suit was "without merit" and ordered it dismissed. The dismissal of the IBM suit constituted another step away from the *ALCOA* ruling and back toward a Rule of Reason standard for adjudicating monopoly cases.

Enforcement Issues

Most contemporary examinations of antitrust issues devote less attention to the actions of Congress than to the efforts of administrative agencies. Key decisions about the meaning of the antitrust laws are being made today by the administrators who are responsible for enforcing the laws. The antitrust goal of maintaining free and fair competition generates debates on four topics: monopolies, mergers, price fixing, and anticompetitive practices. Each has presented distinct enforcement problems.

Monopolies: The Sherman Act outlaws efforts to monopolize an industry. This assumes, however, that the boundaries of a market can be clearly delineated. This is often not the case. In the DuPont case, are cellophane and flexible wrapping materials part of one market, or do they represent different markets? Does beer constitute its own market, or is it part of a larger beverage market? The more broadly the product market is defined, the less monopolistic any company is likely to appear.

The same issue arises in determining the relevant geographic market. The more expansive the geographic borders, the less prominent is any single producer.

Analysts also disagree about the appropriate remedy to apply when a monopoly is discovered. There is little evidence that consumers benefited from the dissolution of Standard Oil. Furthermore, companies may be monopolies because they are efficient. If the Justice Department had succeeded in breaking up IBM in 1982, the result may well have been a less effective computer industry.

Mergers: The Clayton Act as amended by the Celler-Kefauver Act prohibits mergers that lessen competition. There are three types of mergers. A *horizontal* merger is the union of two or more companies that sell the same product; for example, if Ford Motor were to join with Chrysler. A *vertical* merger occurs when companies that operate at different stages of a production-distribution process combine; for example, if Ford were to combine with U.S. Steel because steel is heavily used in manufacturing cars. *Conglomerate* mergers involve companies that sell different but related products, operate in different regions, or are active in completely unrelated product areas, for example, if Ford were to link up with a book publisher.

In 1982 and 1984, the Justice Department issued new Merger Guidelines spelling out standards for reviewing proposed mergers that were more lenient than earlier rules.[17] Horizontal mergers among companies are usually motivated by efforts to increase a firm's market share. The guidelines defined the market circumstances in which the department would accept or oppose such mergers. The Justice Department also indicated that its review of proposed mergers would consider the financial condition of the firms, the ease with which new firms could enter the industry, the pace of technological change, and the importance of international competition.

Vertical mergers have no direct effect on the concentration in particular markets, but they attract enforcement attention because they could close markets to independent suppliers and limit opportunities for new firms to enter the market. According to the guidelines, vertical mergers would be examined if there was substantial concentration in the market most affected by the merger. In fact, the Reagan administration allowed vertical mergers that would probably have been challenged in earlier periods.

The courts have approached the issue of conglomerate mergers cautiously. Both the costs and the benefits of conglomerate mergers remain unproven. They have been opposed on the economic grounds that they inhibit potential competition and the political basis that they constitute undesirable concentrations of wealth and power. Under the Justice Department guidelines, very few conglomerate mergers have been or would be challenged.

Price Fixing: Price fixing and collusion among firms to restrain trade are prohibited by Section 1 of the Sherman Act and by the Federal Trade Commission Act. Explicit price-fixing agreements among firms in the electrical equipment industry were prosecuted in the 1950s. Price fixing may also occur, although it is more difficult to prove, when firms act in ways that allow them to benefit from coordinated action even though they had no explicit agreement to fix prices.

Essentially all commentators, scholars, and practitioners oppose collusive activity to fix prices. The Reagan administration doubled the number of price-fixing cases in its early years. Active prosecution is usually regarded as an effective deterrent against further collusion.

Anticompetitive Practices: The Clayton, Robinson-Patman, and Sherman acts outlaw a variety of commercial practices that can reduce competition. Price discrimination occurs when a producer sells the same product to different retailers at different prices. Price discrimination is illegal when it is intended to harm competitors. The practice occurs when firms seek to boost their sales by favoring high volume dealers or by selling at lower prices in communities in which they face strong competition. Price discrimination prosecutions are difficult because sellers argue that price differences are justified and are not intended to harm competitors.

Contractual relationships between producers and retailers are also illegal if they have anticompetitive consequences. Among potentially illegal "vertical restrictions" are tying agreements, which occur when a producer only allows a retailer to purchase a popular product if the retailer also agrees to purchase a quantity of a less-desirable product. Exclusive dealing agreements that require a retailer to purchase all products from a single producer and resale price maintenance arrangements that allow the manufacturer to set the price of a product charged by the retailer may also be illegal. Each of these practices can be used by producers to limit competition and damage competing companies. The Reagan administration was criticized for its lack of enthusiasm in investigating and prosecuting cases involving price discrimination and vertical restrictions.

A review of the origins and evolution of U.S. antitrust policy highlights the ebb and flow of governmental action, but it understates the American commitment to the desirability of marketplace competition. A further perspective on U.S. antitrust policy is gained by comparing U.S. policy with features of competition policy in Germany, Japan, and the United Kingdom.

COMPARATIVE ANTITRUST POLICIES

U.S. antitrust policy rests on the assumption that competition is politically and economically desirable. Other countries assess competition more equivocally and more instrumentally. They are as likely to fear "excess" competition as they are to applaud full and fair competition. They often seek as well to use competition as a policy tool to accomplish other governmental objectives, but if competition interferes with achieving these other objectives, they are not reluctant to set it aside.

Countries develop their competition policies in their own sociopolitical context. U.S. policy was created to deal with domestic conditions in the late nineteenth and early twentieth centuries. The competition policies of Germany, Japan, and the United Kingdom are a heritage from the post–World War II era, when each country recognized its dependence on the international economy.

Table 7–3 outlines the major features of antitrust policies in Germany, Japan, the United Kingdom, and the United States. It notes first whether a country's approach to antitrust issues is to prohibit flatly any reduction of competition or to regulate the level of competition in the interests of achieving other goals. Table 7–3 then indicates whether the goals of a country's antitrust policies are simply to promote competition, or whether it uses these policies to manage the decline or "rationalization" of an industry or to accomplish other public purposes. The table also indicates whether the countries allow exemptions to their antitrust policies and whether the antitrust policies are systemically or only occasionally enforced.

TABLE 7–3   Comparative Antitrust Policies

	GERMANY	JAPAN	UNITED KINGDOM	UNITED STATES
Approach:				
In Theory	Regulate	Prohibit	Regulate	Prohibit
In Practice	Regulate	Regulate	Regulate	Mixed
Goals:				
Competition	Yes	Yes	Yes	Yes
Rationalization	Yes	Yes	Yes	No
Public Good	Yes	Yes	Yes	No
Exemptions:				
Economic	Yes	Yes	Yes	Rare
Technological	Yes	Yes	Yes	Limited
International	Yes	Yes	Yes	Limited
Enforcement:				
Government	Mixed	Weak	Mixed	Demanding
Private	Rare	Rare	None	Rigorous

Source: Based on Report of the President's Commission on Industrial Competitiveness, *Global Competition: The New Reality*, Vol.2 (Washington, D.C.: Government Printing Office, 1985), p. 191; supplemented by David B. Audretsch, *The Market and the State: Government Policy Towards Business in Europe, Japan and the United States* (New York: New York University Press, 1989), pp. 77–118.

Germany

Modern cartels, associations of companies that set prices and limit production, appeared first in Germany in the 1870s.[18] They were organized by industries, banks, and even the government to help companies survive recessions, reduce excess production capacity, and sustain prices. The German Law Against Restraint of Competition was enacted in 1958 and reflects the government's lukewarm commitment to promoting competition. It states that "competition is not in and of itself the goal, but rather the means for improving efficiency and technical progress."[19] Mergers among competing firms are permitted if they help an ailing industry or serve the broad public interest.

German law emphasizes corporate behavior rather than industry structure. The existence of a monopoly is not illegal in Germany. The government can only proceed against a company if the firm has abused its monopoly position by charging excessive prices, providing inferior goods, or restricting sales. German law exempts from antitrust rules corporate agreements that promote efficiency, advance technical developments, or expand foreign trade. Approximately three hundred cartels have been approved by the German government and continue to function.[20]

The Federal Cartel Office is responsible for administering antitrust laws. Details of proposed mergers must be submitted for review, but the office can only block a merger with the concurrence of other government agencies. Large German companies in core industries rarely face antitrust problems. Daimler Benz, the auto manufacturer, was recently permitted to take over the leading companies in the German defense industry.

Japan

Japan had no antitrust policies before the American occupation after World War II.[21] Zaibatsu had symbolized the development of the Japanese economy in the early decades of the twentieth century, and the Japanese government opposed allied efforts to impose antitrust laws. One scholar writes:[22]

> It will be recalled that at the time of the Occupation a wide-spread Japanese interpretation of the antitrust program for Japan was that the United States sought to weaken the Japanese economy...it is clear that many Japanese government officials think...competition is always "excess competition." Competition (i.e., excessive competition) is considered inefficient, resulting in firms too small, firms unable to cope with cyclical changes, unable to compete effectively in international trade.

Despite the resistance of Japanese officials, Occupation authorities imposed measures dissolving the zaibatsu, major corporations, and cartels in what has been described as "the greatest single use of government power in postwar Japan."[23] The Antimonopoly Law enacted in 1947 encouraged reliance on marketplace competition and opposed mergers that lessened competition, but the law was never stringent and was soon relaxed.

The objectives of Japanese competition policy since the post war era have been to increase economic efficiency, stabilize critical industries, and improve the country's position in international trade. The nation's Fair Trade Commission failed to enforce the antimonopoly statutes in the 1950s and 1960s because of pressure from business groups and other government agencies.[24] Exemptions to antitrust laws are permitted to limit competition among small companies, reduce production capacity in declining industries, and gain advantage in import-export transactions.

Some scholars conclude, "Few other developed countries have relegated competition policy to such a subservient position" as has Japan and contend that Japan's "merger policy at best resembles a sieve."[25] Others, however, insist that the market structure of the Japanese economy has become more competitive in recent years: "The most remarkable change in Japanese industrial organization (in the 1970s and 1980s) has been the decline in cartel-like practices."[26] They point out that the Antimonopoly Law was strengthened in 1977 and maintain that the Fair Trade Commission has moved effectively against price fixing and collusion by publicizing anticompetitive practices and appealing to Japan's consumer movement, even though the agency lacks statutory power to prohibit such practices.

United Kingdom

Competition policy in the United Kingdom has emerged in the post-World War II period, but it has not been a government priority.[27] It is entwined with other social and economic objectives and is continually balanced against such pressing concerns as public safety, local employment, and regional disparities.

Under UK law, there is no presumption against monopolies or mergers.[28] The policy seeks to regulate only those monopolies whose actions harm the public interest. The Thatcher government of the 1980s stressed its view that takeovers and marketplace decisions constituted a superior basis for identifying the public interest. Exemptions from British antitrust rules are permitted for economic, technological, and international purposes.

The British process for enforcing monopoly and merger policies is purely administrative.[29] It is based on civil rather than criminal law, involves few explicit sanctions, and depends on cooperation between government and industry. The Office of Fair Trading (OFT) identifies possible monopoly situations and refers them for investigation to the Monopolies and Mergers Commission (MMC). If the MMC concludes that action is warranted, the Secretary of State directs the OFT to meet with the dominant firm and seek assurances that the public interest will be protected in the future. Neither companies nor individuals who believe that they have been damaged by monopolistic actions may bring legal action to recover damages.

United States

The important features of U.S. antitrust policy are summarized in Table 7–3. In theory, U.S. policy stands totally against monopolies and restraints on competition; but, in practice, the policy has reflected a mixture of standards. The goal of U.S. policy has been to promote competition. Labor unions, public utilities, agricultural cooperatives, export associations, and joint research projects have been exempted from U.S. antitrust laws, but the significance of these exemptions is limited. Antitrust laws have been enforced more diligently in the United States than in the other countries. While the Reagan administration emphasized the prosecution of price fixing and anticompetitive practices, the Bush administration has promised closer scrutiny of mergers and anticompetitive practices.[30] Litigation brought by private companies is a major technique for enforcing U.S. antitrust laws.

U.S. antitrust policies have been fiercely debated in the last fifteen years. Scholars associated with the University of Chicago have argued that antitrust policies should have no other purpose than to maximize consumer welfare by promoting economic efficiency and minimizing prices.[31] They argue that antitrust policies have been stretched beyond their original purpose. In general, proponents of the Chicago school believe that corporate mergers and takeovers increase efficiency and seldom reduce competition. According to the Chicago school, antitrust reforms are needed if U.S. corporations are to meet the challenge of international competition.

The Structuralist opponents of the Chicago ideology maintain that existing laws have balanced the competing objectives of U.S. antitrust policy quite effectively. They criticize the efficiency orientation of the Chicago school as "minimalist" and regard its marketplace assumptions as "simplistic."[32] They argue that there is no systematic evidence that large corporations enhance long-term economic efficiency, and they point out that the United States has opposed concentrations of power for political as well as economic reasons. The debate between the Structuralists and the supporters of the Chicago school had governmental significance in the 1980s in the area of public policy toward corporate takeovers.

PUBLIC POLICY TOWARD CORPORATE TAKEOVERS

Corporate takeovers were a headline issue of the 1980s that has persisted into the 1990s. They involved RJR-Nabisco, AT&T,[33] Philip Morris, and Federated Department Stores, and captured the attention of newspapers, magazines, and the broadcast media. Takeovers are denounced by some as the semilegal plundering of innocent companies and lauded by others as an essential free-market technique for promoting efficiency and growth.

Corporate Takeover Glossary

Merger: Situation in which two companies agree to combine to form one company.

Acquisition: One company buys some or all of the assets of another company.

Takeover: An outside force buys a controlling amount of stock in a company.

Target Company: A company that is being taken over.

Hostile takeover: A takeover that is opposed by the target company's management.

Buyout: A group of investors buys the stock of a publicly-traded company and takes the company private, meaning that its stock is no longer publicly traded.

Leveraged Buyout: A buyout funded by loans in which the company's assets are pledged as collateral for the loans.

Junk Bonds: High-risk bonds that pay a higher-than-average return to investors and are often used to raise funds for buyouts, takeovers, or acquisitions.

Raider: A person who seeks to take over companies through hostile takeovers to realize short-term financial gains.

Greenmail: A defensive tactic in which the target company buys a block of its stock from a potential raider at a price in excess of the market price to prevent the takeover.

Poison Pill: A defensive tactic against hostile takeovers in which a target company is authorized to issue new securities to increase the cost of the takeover to a raider.

Hostile takeovers begin when an investor or raider concludes that the assets of a company are worth more than the company's stock. Raiders believe that they can make a profit by borrowing money, buying all of the firm's stock, selling off assets to reduce the loans used to buy the stock, and then retaining the remaining assets as profit. After a takeover has occurred, companies are often compelled to close factories, lay off employees, and cut capital and R&D expenditures to pay off their debts. Critics believe that hostile takeovers distract managers from important operating tasks and force them to concentrate on immediate controversies.

The economics literature takes a more positive view of hostile takeovers.[34] The overwhelming proportion of takeovers, it is noted, are not the sensational coups that grab headlines but ordinary corporate decisions initiated by managers seeking to improve their firm's long-term position. According to most economists, takeovers prod managers to use the company's assets more productively, increase operating efficiency, and realize the value of the shareholders' investment. The fact that the price of a company's stock normally rises 20 to 30 percent when it is being taken over is seen as evidence that takeovers are beneficial.

Unfortunately, there is no clear evidence that takeovers do more harm or good.[35] Opponents of takeovers point to instances in which companies, communities, and workers have been devastated by takeovers, and proponents rely on neoclassical economics to insist that market competition leads to an efficient use of resources that eventually benefits everyone.

Corporate takeovers are affected by three bodies of public policy.[36] First, the Williams Act of 1968 requires investors seeking to take over a company to disclose stock purchases and sources of funds. Second, they must also satisfy federal procedural requirements in making the takeover offers, as overseen by the Securities and Exchange Commission (SEC). Third, takeovers are affected by the federal tax code, which allows companies to deduct interest expenses for loans used to finance takeovers and to increase depreciation deductions when takeovers lead to increased asset values. And, of course, takeovers must also comply with the prevalent interpretation of the antitrust statutes.

There is a broad range of possible policy responses to takeovers.[37]

- There is no problem and no policy response is needed. The dominant academic view is that the market system is working reasonably well. Hostile takeovers help overcome the inertia of entrenched managements and promote corporate accountability.
- There is a problem, but it will cure itself. Increases in corporate debt, disruptions of established operations, and the short-term focus of managers are damaging American companies. The negative consequences of takeovers will be apparent in the next recession when firms go bankrupt because they cannot make their debt payments. Investors in takeovers and junk bonds will lose money, and interest in new takeovers will quickly subside. Reliance on the self-correcting features of the market will be less damaging to the economy than a new round of government regulations.
- There is a problem that should be addressed through changes in tax and antitrust policies. Takeovers and mergers are detrimental to the economy, but the speculative fever can be cured by the vigorous enforcement of antitrust laws and amendments to the tax code.

- There is a problem that should be addressed through strengthening federal take-over procedures. The Williams Act should be amended to require sounder financing for takeovers, longer time periods for shareholders to evaluate proposals, and tighter controls on stock manipulation and insider trading.
- Takeovers are a serious problem that require tough new laws. Many bills have been introduced in Congress that allow a company's outside directors to veto a takeover proposal, prohibit companies from buying stock in other firms, and require bidders to provide community-impact statements explaining how they plan to protect workers and communities from harm.

New corporate takeovers or the collapse of firms under the burden of debt from old takeovers will probably attract media attention to the takeover issue in the future. Elected officials will then feel pressure to reconsider public policies governing takeovers. The policymakers' task will be to strike a balance that protects the vitality of established companies and the interests of workers and communities without entrenching mediocre managers who have little concern about the future of their companies, the people who depend on those companies, and the general welfare of the nation's economy.

SUMMARY

Antitrust policy is intended to promote economic competition and secure the consumer benefits that competition is assumed to produce. Antitrust policies have evolved slowly and now focus on restricting monopolies, anticompetitive mergers, price fixing, and sales practices that have anticompetitive consequences. Theorists of the Chicago school argue that antitrust policies should maximize consumer welfare by promoting efficiency and minimizing prices, even if this means relaxing traditional antitrust standards. Structuralists maintain that the domination of markets by monopolists should be prohibited on economic and political grounds, even if minor benefits are lost in the process. Germany, Japan, and the United Kingdom see less harm in allowing individual firms to dominate important sectors of their economies than does the United States.

Antitrust policies seek to structure the marketplace so competition may flourish. In some circumstances, however, competition is not possible. In these situations, governments may try to restore the benefits of lost competition through regulation. Government regulation is examined in the next chapter.

SELECTED READINGS

DAVID B. AUDRETSCH, *The Market and the State: Government Policy Towards Business in Europe, Japan and the United States* (New York: New York University Press, 1989).

BRYAN BURROUGH and JOHN HELYAR, *Barbarians at the Gate: The Fall of RJR Nabisco* (New York: Harper & Row, 1990).

Tim Frazer, *Monopoly, Competition and the Law: The Regulation of Business Activity in Britain, Europe and America* (New York: St.Martin's Press, 1988).

William F. Shughart, *Antitrust Policy and Interest Group Politics* (New York: Quorum Books, 1990).

Murray L. Weidenbaum and Kenneth W. Chilton(eds.), *Public Policy Toward Corporate Takeovers* (New Brunswick, N.J.: Transaction Books, 1988).

END NOTES

[1]Nikki Tait, "Values of mergers declines by a third," *Financial Times* (London), December 27, 1990, p. 3. Article relies on data calculated by Securities Data.

[2]Bryan Burrough and John Helyar, *Barbarians at the Gate: The Fall of RJR Nabisco* (New York: Harper & Row, 1990).

[3]John E. Kwoka and Lawrence J. White (eds.), *The Antitrust Revolution* (Glenview, Ill.: Scott, Foresman, 1989).

[4]Robert A. Katzmann, "The Attenuation of Antitrust," *The Brookings Review*, vol. 2, no. 4 (Summer 1984), 23–27.

[5]These paragraphs are based on Don E. Waldman, *The Economics of Antitrust: Cases and Analysis* (Boston: Little, Brown, 1986), pp. 2–17.

[6]The definition is based on Richard A. Posner, *Antitrust Law: An Economic Perspective* (Chicago: University of Chicago Press, 1976), p. 8.

[7]The account of events in these sections is based on A.D. Neale and D.G. Goyder, *The Antitrust Laws of the United States of America: A Study of Competition Enforced by Law*, 3rd ed. (Cambridge, England: Cambridge University Press, 1980); Dominick T. Armentano, *Antitrust and Monopoly: Anatomy of a Policy Failure*, 2nd ed. (New York: Holmes & Meier, 1990); Martin J. Sklar, *The Corporate Reconstruction of American Capitalism, 1890–1916: The Market, the Law, and Politics* (New York: Cambridge University Press, 1988); and Timothy J. Waters, "Antitrust Law and Policy: Rule of Law or Economic Assumptions," in Robert J. Larner and James W. Meehan (eds.), *Economics and Antitrust Policy* (New York: Quorum Books, 1989), pp. 151–77.

[8]*Standard Oil of N.J.* v. *United States*, 221 U.S. 1 (1911).

[9]Unusually helpful reviews of antitrust issues are found in Douglas F. Greer, *Business, Government, and Society* (New York: Macmillan, 1987), Chapters 5–10; Damodar Gujarati, *Government and Business* (New York: McGraw-Hill, 1984), Chapters 6–10; and Martin C. Schnitzer, *Contemporary Government and Business Relations* (Boston: Houghton Mifflin, 1990), Chapters 4–9.

[10]166 U.S. 290, 1897.

[11]192 U.S. 197, 1904.

[12]221 U.S. 1, 1911.

[13]251 U.S. 417, 1920.

[14]148 F.2d 416, 1945.

[15]*United States* v. *E.I. duPont de Nemours* 351 U.S. 377, 1956.

[16]*Berkey Photo* v. *Eastman Kodak Co.* 603 F.2d 263, 1979.

[17]E. Thomas Sullivan, "The Antitrust Division as a Regulatory Agency: An Enforcement Policy in Transition," in Murray L. Weidenbaum and Kenneth W. Chilton (eds.), *Public Policy Toward Corporate Takeovers*, (New Brunswick, N.J.: Transaction Books, 1988), pp. 106–40.

[18]Thomas K. McCraw, "Mercantilism," in Claude E. Barfield and William A. Schambra (eds.), *The Politics of Industrial Policy* (Washington, D.C.: American Enterprise Institute, 1986), pp. 33–62.

[19]Quoted in David B. Audretsch, *The Market and the State: Government Policy Towards Business in Europe, Japan and the United States* (New York: New York University Press, 1989), pp. 66–76.

[20]Ibid. p. 69.

[21]Audretsch, *The Market and the State*, pp. 87–118.

[22]Eleanor M. Hadley, *Antitrust In Japan* (Princeton: Princeton University Press, 1970), pp.447–48.

[23]Masu Uekusa, "Industrial Organization: The 1970s to the Present," in Kozo Yamamura and Yasuichi Yasuba (eds.), *The Political Economy of Japan: The Domestic Transformation* (Stanford, Calif.: Stanford University Press, 1987), pp. 469–515; here, p. 477.

[24]Ibid., p. 477.

[25]Audretsch, *The Market and the State*, pp. 94 and 115.

[26]Masu Uekusa, "Industrial Organization," p. 481.

[27]Wyn Grant, *Government and Industry: A Comparative Analysis of the US, Canada and the UK* (Hants, England: Edward Elgar, 1989), pp. 96–101.

[28]See Tim Frazer, *Monopoly, Competition and the Law: The Regulation of Business Activity in Britain, Europe and America* (New York: St. Martin's Press, 1988), pp. 24–30.

[29]Ibid., pp. 35–38.

[30]Peter Riddell, "US to step up anti-trust policy," *Financial Times* (London), November 6, 1989, p. 20.

[31]Robert H. Bork, *The Antitrust Paradox: A Policy at War with Itself* (New York: Basic Books, 1978); and William F. Shughart II, *Antitrust Policy and Interest Group Politics* (New York: Quorum Books, 1990).

[32]Rowe, "Antitrust in Transition: A Policy in Search of Itself," *Antitrust Law Journal* 54 (1985), p. 5.

[33]See AT&T's $5 billion proposal to take over NCR, the computer and office machine corporation. See also Milton L. Rock (ed.), *The Mergers and Acquisition Handbook* (New York: McGraw-Hill, 1987).

[34]Richard E. Cook, "What the Economics Literature Has to Say about Takeovers," in Weidenbaum and Chilton (eds.), *Public Policy Toward Corporate Takeovers*, pp. 1–23.

[35]John C. Coffee, Louis Lowenstein, and Susan Rose-Ackerman, *Knights, Raiders, and Targets: The Impact of the Hostile Takeover* (New York: Oxford University Press, 1988), Chapters 11–14.

[36]Murray L. Weidenbaum, "Strategies for Responding to Corporate Takeovers," in Weidenbaum and Chilton (eds.), *Public Policy Toward Corporate Takeovers*, pp. 141–67.

[37]This section relies directly on Murray L. Weidenbaum, "Strategies for Responding to Corporate Takeovers," in Weidenbaum and Chilton (eds.), *Public Policy Toward Corporate Takeovers*, pp. 146–48.

Chapter 8

Understanding Government Regulation

The meltdown of the savings and loan industry has been described as the "greatest regulatory fiasco in American history."[1] Ed Gray, chairman of the Federal Home Loan Bank Board and chief regulator of the industry, remembers being called to a private meeting at a lavishly marbled Senate office building.[2] It was April 1987, and Senator Dennis DeConcini of Arizona took the lead at the meeting. He was joined by senators Alan Cranston of California, John Glenn of Ohio, and John McCain, also of Arizona.

The Senators, DeConcini said, were concerned about Lincoln Savings and Loan, a California S&L, or "thrift" institution, that had been bought by Charles H. Keating. They wanted to know why Gray's examiners were being harsh and unfair in their examination of Lincoln's records. A few weeks earlier the Bank Board had imposed a new regulation limiting investments in speculative ventures by thrifts such as Lincoln. DeConcini asked Gray to withdraw the regulation.[3] The meeting continued for an hour with Gray defending the need for the new rule.

The Senators called a second meeting a week later with the Bank Board officials from San Francisco who were directly responsible for regulating Lincoln. This time, they were also joined by Senator Riegle of Michigan. As the Senators continued to defend Lincoln, the San Francisco officials stressed that procedures at Keating's S&L violated common sense, the Bank Board's regulations, and the law. They compared Lincoln to a ticking time bomb, said it was the worst situation they had ever seen, and promised that a criminal complaint would soon be filed. Shortly after this meeting, the San Francisco regulators recommended to Washington that Lincoln be taken out of Keating's control because it was squandering federally insured funds and violating legal requirements.

Ed Gray soon completed his term at the Bank Board and was succeeded as chair by a former Senate aide. The Lincoln case was then transferred from the San Francisco office to Washington, nothing more was heard about the criminal referral mentioned by the San Francisco regulators, and Lincoln negotiated a favorable new agreement with the Bank Board that allowed Keating to remain in business. Less than a year later, however, in April 1989, Lincoln was finally taken over by the Bank Board, the cost to taxpayers was then estimated to be $2.5 billion, and Charles Keating was subsequently arrested, indicted for fraud, and convicted.

During this period newspapers carried accounts of Charles Keating's extensive political contributions and donations. At a news conference held after Lincoln Savings and Loan was seized by federal regulators, Keating said: "One question, among the many raised in recent weeks, had to do with whether my financial support in any way influenced several political figures to take up my cause. I want to say in the most forceful way I can: I certainly hope so."[4]

One way to interpret the savings and loan industry collapse is to see it as an instance of criminals buying political protection to cover up misconduct and eventually getting caught. Some observers argue, however, that the S&L debacle involved more than crooks and payoffs. They note that financial losses at Lincoln and similar S&Ls "did not account for a significant share of [S&L] association losses."[5] They maintain that the dynamics of the S&L industry need to be understood to explain why the regulatory mess actually occurred.

To open a saving and loan association or a bank, potential owners invest a specific amount of their own funds to serve as the institution's capital and assure it a margin of safety. S&Ls and similar financial institutions then have two operating tasks: first they collect savings, and then they use the savings to earn income.[6] Historically, saving and loan associations undertook these tasks in distinct ways. Originally, deposits made in S&Ls could only be withdrawn after six months, one year, or some specific period of time. In contrast to these "time deposits," accounts in commercial banks were available whenever the depositor wanted funds. These were called "demand deposits." S&Ls originally used the time deposits only to make twenty- or thirty-year mortgage loans to help people purchase homes. Commercial banks earned income by offering a greater variety of loans and services. S&Ls and commercial banks made a profit by earning more from their loans than they had to pay in interest to depositors. To maintain confidence in the banking system, the federal government guaranteed that depositors would not lose their money if individual banks went bankrupt.

During the 1970s, the saving and loan industry faced two major problems. First, interest rates soared. By the end of the 1970s, rates reached 20 percent. Second, advances in communications and data processing made money market funds, a new form of savings account offered by other financial service companies, available throughout the country. Money market funds gathered people's savings and lent those savings to government agencies willing to pay 13 or 14 percent interest. S&Ls were limited by law to paying about 5 percent interest on savings accounts.

As a result of these two developments, S&Ls lost deposits as people shifted their savings from thrifts into money market funds that paid higher interest. Yet the S&Ls were still committed to long-term mortgage loans that yielded only 7 or 8 percent interest per year. As the level of deposits fell, S&Ls lost most of their capital. They turned to Washington for help.

First, Congress ended the rule limiting the rate S&Ls could pay in interest so that they would stop losing deposits to the money market funds. Regulators then reduced the minimum amount of capital required of S&L institutions so that hundreds of S&Ls would not be forced out of business. Third, Congress and the regulators together allowed S&Ls to invest in activities other than home mortgages so they could earn higher returns on their investments. Finally, Congress increased savings insurance to $100,000 per account to make S&Ls more attractive to depositors.

By 1983, Congress and the regulators had responded to four specific S&L problems, but together the four piecemeal changes produced a dangerous regulatory situation. Normally, the managers of banks and S&Ls act responsibly so as not to jeopardize the capital invested by the people who own the bank. By 1983, however, hundreds of S&Ls had lost all their capital. These decapitalized institutions remained in business only because the federal government guaranteed depositors that it would refund their money if the S&L went bankrupt.

The managers of these decapitalized S&Ls had no reason to act prudently. They had nothing to lose. They made risky loans on speculative ventures, often to friends and associates. They recognized that they would reap substantial rewards if the gambles paid off and knew that the federal government would be required to pay off the depositors if the loans went into default.

Furthermore, S&Ls earn immediate profits by processing loans, and they can increase profits by increasing their volume of loans. Decapitalized S&Ls paid abnormally high interest rates to attract deposits from throughout the country so they could sustain a surging tide of loans. During this period the most reckless S&Ls grew to mammoth size. Depositors were unconcerned about the reckless nature of the loans being made by the S&Ls because the federal government had guaranteed them that their deposits would be protected.

In 1985, federal regulators began to recognize the consequences of the regulatory changes that had been made a few years earlier. They asked Congress to grant them authority to halt the developing trends, but they were opposed by S&L managers like Keating and the United States League of Savings Associations, which did not want regulators to take any action against its members. By 1986, regulators could no longer close the worst S&Ls because they lacked funds to pay off the depositors.[7] The issue that brought Ed Gray to the meeting with Senator DeConcini was a Bank Board regulation to limit the riskiest ventures of the decapitalized S&Ls.

While delaying definitive action and hoping the problem would cure itself, legislators like the so-called "Keating Five" Senators diligently solicited political contributions from the S&L industry. Neither the Republican nor the Democratic party wanted to address the S&L fiasco until after the 1988 presidential election season because neither candidate wanted to debate who was most responsible. Regrettably, each day the decapitalized S&Ls remained in operation, the volume of reckless loans increased. Because many of those loans would never be repaid and the federal government had guaranteed the funds of depositors, each day of operations ran up an estimated $30 million in losses that federal taxpayers would eventually be required to pay. This refusal to deal with the regulatory problems of the savings and loan industry in a timely manner turned a $20 billion or $30 billion debacle into a $300 billion disaster. When, in 1990, the federal government faced up to its responsibility to pay off the depositors whose funds it had guaranteed, some observers estimated the total cost to taxpayers would reach $500 billion.

Even the sorriest spectacle can be instructive. This chapter uses the example of the savings and loan industry to consider how best to understand government regulation. The chapter first outlines different perspectives on regulation that emerge from the analyses of scholars and the activities of businesspeople. It then reviews the history of regulation and identifies the features of new and old patterns of regulation. In the last section, the chapter focuses on deregulation and regulatory reform and reviews the stakes that were involved in these movements. The savings and loan saga is certainly not a typical regulatory event, but it can help us decide how to understand best the dynamics of government regulation.

PERSPECTIVES ON REGULATION

Government regulation is "a distinctively American approach to balancing public and private interests."[8] Regulations insist that public purposes must be respected in business operations. While antitrust policies control the competition-related activities of business, regulation restricts business actions involving specific products. (Sometimes the distinctions between antitrust and regulatory policies are blurred.)

Two analytic perspectives have dominated our understanding of the place of regulation in the relationship between government and business: the public interest perspective and the private interest perspective.[9]

Public Interest Perspective

Most analyses present regulation as a response to market failure.[10] Regulation seeks to protect consumers and achieve the benefits of marketplace competition in situations in which competition does not occur.[11] Sometimes the technical factors of an industry's operations prevent competition. Such industries are often called *natural monopolies*. They include local telephone, electric, or water utilities, in which high capital investment makes competing utility systems too costly; and radio and television broadcasting, in which operating rules are needed to prevent broadcasters from disrupting each other's signals.

Regulation may also appear because of a different form of market failure: the failure of the price mechanism. In some industries, prices are not an accurate measure of the true social costs of business activity. Some businesses are regulated because their operations pollute the environment, yet the marketplace prices of the business's product do not include the full social costs of pollution. In other instances, a product is more valuable to the society than to the individual consumer, and it is regulated to assure that enough of that product is provided to meet the society's needs.

Finally, market failure may occur because consumers lack the information needed to make proper judgments about products and producers. S&Ls and other financial institutions are regulated because individual consumers cannot know enough to determine if a firm's lending practices are sound and if the institution itself is safe. Medical products and medical practitioners are required to meet government standards because individual consumers have no basis on which to make medical judgments.

In each of these instances, regulation emerges as a cure for the failures of the marketplace. If regulation fails to achieve its objectives, it is assumed that the regulatory process had been poorly designed or subverted. According to the public interest perspective, the regulation of the saving and loan industry was intended to provide a safe and secure place for citizens to save money, and the collapse of the industry occurred because regulators lacked the intelligence and resources to supervise the industry properly and because unscrupulous managers and politicians exploited the regulatory process for their own selfish goals.

Private Interest Perspective

According to the private interest perspective,[12] it is a pretense to maintain that regulation is a public interest activity.[13] According to this view, people pursue their private interests in the regulatory arena with the same diligence as they pursue their individual interests in the private sector. Regulation should be understood as nothing more than an effort to use governmental authority to redistribute income from one group to another. Since numerous studies show that the actual consequences of many regulatory policies are to enrich specific private groups, students of regulation should acknowledge that the actual effects of regulation are, in fact, the intended effects.

Three groups are in the best position to benefit from regulation. First is business. Business does not act as a class, but as companies or industries. When a company faces a decline in sales, it can cut the price of its product, improve quality, increase its advertising budget, or invest in a lobbying effort to secure beneficial regulatory action.[14] When the S&L industry faced problems in the late 1970s, it launched a campaign to change the governmental rules under which it operated. As a result, it was allowed to pay higher interest rates, reduce its capital, and invest federally guaranteed funds in speculative ventures. Some firms in the industry profited handsomely from these changes until the governmental costs of their actions were publicly recognized.

Members of Congress can also benefit by transforming regulation into pork-barrel politics.[15] Regulatory actions affect specific geographic areas in distinct ways, and members of Congress seek to promote the economic interests of their regions. The corporate headquarters of Charles Keating's firm was in Arizona, and Lincoln Savings and Loan was located in California. The Senators from these states were most active in promoting their cause in the Lincoln S&L case. Members of Congress have influence over regulatory agencies, and the expectation that they will exercise that influence helps legislators raise campaign funds. Keating contributed well over $1 million to the political causes of the five Senators with whom Gray met.

Regulators are in a position to benefit individually and organizationally from regulation.[16] Extensive regulatory authority can lead to bureaucratic aggrandizement with surging budgets and growing personnel rosters. Regulation also benefits individual bureaucrats by giving them an opportunity to advance their careers either by garnering professional esteem or by displaying their qualifications for private sector jobs.

From the private interest perspective, an understanding of regulation is enhanced by acknowledging that regulatory intervention in the marketplace is usually an effort by some group to increase its own wealth and income at the expense of others. Benefits to private groups are neither a subversion nor an aberration but reflect the fundamental nature of regulation.

Empirical Perspective

Regardless of whether regulation is seen as an effort to promote public or private interests, businesspeople recognize that regulations inevitably assist some groups at the expense of others.[17] The old rule that limited S&Ls to paying no more than 5 percent interest on savings accounts helped money market fund managers persuade depositors to withdraw their savings from S&Ls. The federal guarantee of S&L deposits erased for depositors the difference between a prudently managed and a recklessly managed S&L and thus benefited poorly run institutions by making them as attractive as well-managed firms.

Since each company operates in a unique way, the impact of government regulation differs by firm. Nevertheless, there is no escaping the fact that every economic enterprise in the country is affected by the costs and benefits of a myriad of government regulations.

The impact of regulation depends on the details of specific situations, but regulatory disputes follow normal patterns: consumers vs. producers; producers vs. producers; or consumers vs. consumers. Some regulatory issues are disputes between consumers and producers. When a regulated public utility wants to raise the fees it charges for its product, its opponents are those who must pay the higher costs.

Other regulatory disputes are contests between two different groups of producers. In part, the S&L controversy pitted the decapitalized S&Ls against those S&Ls that were well managed. It is common for regulatory issues to be contests between truckers and the railroads, high-cost and low-cost manufacturers, or export-oriented firms and companies serving a domestic market.

Finally, regulatory questions can place the interests of one group of consumers against the interests of others. Automobile insurance rates, for example, can be higher for the residents of crime-ridden urban areas or safer suburban districts, for careful drivers or the accident-prone, for men or women, for experienced drivers or those who have recently learned to drive. Regardless of the original motivation, every governmental regulation has impact on various segments of the economy.

DIMENSIONS OF FEDERAL REGULATION

Government regulation is not a complicated topic. Regulations are policy tools. They are rules that restrict business operations in order to accomplish governmental purposes. Regulation is made to appear more complex than it is when commentators focus on administrative arrangements rather than public purposes. Government regulation is conducted in an infinite variety of ways, but an emphasis on the purposes of regulation rather than the techniques makes regulation easier to comprehend.

There are scores of federal regulatory agencies but only two basic forms of regulation. Governments engage in *economic regulation* when they require firms in a particular industry, such as the savings and loan industry, to behave in specific ways regardless of the forces of the marketplace. Governments' *social regulations* impose rules on how all firms, regardless of industry, conduct specific functional activities, such as labor-management relations or environmental protection. Table 8–1 lists four agencies involved in the economic regulation of specific industries and four other agencies responsible for the social regulation of specific functions. The table also identifies the years in which the agencies were created and their jurisdictions.

TABLE 8–1 Selected Federal Regulatory Agencies

AGENCY	YEAR CREATED	JURISDICTION
Economic Regulation		
Interstate Commerce Commission	1887	Railroads; trucking; some water shipping
Federal Home Loan Bank Board	1932	Savings and loan industry; abolished 1990
Federal Communications Commission	1934	Interstate, foreign telephone; television and radio
Federal Energy Regulatory Commission	1977	Replaced Federal Power Commission (1920); natural gas, electricity
Social Regulation		
Equal Employment Opportunity Commission	1964	Enforces 1964 Civil Rights Act banning discrimination
Environmental Protection Agency	1970	Environmental pollution
Occupational Safety & Health Administration	1970	Health and safety standards in the workplace
Consumer Product Safety Commission	1972	Safety and labeling standards for consumer products

Economic Regulation

Federal economic regulation began with the creation of the Interstate Commerce Commission (ICC) in 1887. Article I of the U.S. Constitution gives Congress the power to regulate interstate commerce, but Congress left this authority to the states until 1887.

The emergence of an industrial economy and the growing impact of railroads on society led many states to begin to regulate commerce on their own. In 1877, the U.S. Supreme Court confirmed the authority of government to regulate economic activity in *Munn* v. *Illinois*.[18]

Munn was one of the most unscrupulous grain elevator operators in Illinois. He stored grain for shipment in interstate commerce. Munn was convicted in state court of violating an Illinois law regulating prices that could be charged for storing grain. His attorney argued that the Illinois law was unconstitutional because the state had no power to regulate items in interstate commerce and no power to reduce the value of Munn's property by limiting his prices. The U.S. Supreme Court upheld the Illinois law and defined a doctrine that has sustained government regulation in subsequent decades, "When private property is devoted to a public use, it is subject to public regulation."[19]

Within the next decade, twenty-five states began to regulate rail operations, but the growing volume of state regulation soon impeded interstate commerce. In *Wabash, St. Louis, and Pacific Railway Co.* v. *Illinois*, the Supreme Court severely restricted state regulation of rail operations by expanding congressional power under the commerce clause.[20] This decision led Congress to pass the Act to Regulate Commerce in 1887 that created the ICC and instructed the agency to promote safe, adequate, and economical surface transportation.

The ICC was the federal government's first independent regulatory commission. Independent commissions with five or seven members appointed to lengthy terms developed into a popular administrative device for regulating private economic activity. Commissions were stable agencies that would base their decisions on expert analyses rather than partisan electoral considerations. Their decisions would reflect the collective judgment of a group rather than idiosyncratic opinions of a single administrator. The popularity of the commission form for regulating economic activity reflects a distrust of government, confidence in expertise, and recognition of the need for a predictable environment in which to make investments and conduct business.

Despite widespread support for the creation of the ICC, the commission was generally ineffective in the first three decades of its history.[21] The ICC's statutory powers were unclear, and most of its actions were challenged in the courts. Congress subsequently passed a series of laws shoring up the commission's authority that culminated in the Transportation Act of 1920. This last law authorized the ICC to establish railroad rates and oversee the development of the industry, and it led to a tremendous expansion of the ICC's role.

During the Great Depression of the 1930s, competition between railroads and lower-cost trucking firms intensified. The ICC consistently took the side of the railroad industry by requiring truckers to match the higher rates charged by the railroads. In the 1960s and 1970s, the Congress and the ICC devised numerous plans to assist the financially troubled railroads, but none of their schemes was able to reverse the industry's decline. In the deregulation era of the late 1970s and early 1980s, Congress said that the industry's problems had been caused by federal regulation and granted railroads more freedom to set prices and govern their own operations.[22]

The Interstate Commerce Commission served as a prototype for other independent regulatory commissions. It focused originally on a single industry, railroads, and later assumed some responsibility for the associated industries of trucking and water shipping. It exercised its authority over the industry by making decisions in three economic areas: *entry*, or what firms are allowed to participate in the industry; the *price* firms may charge for their products; and the *conditions of service*, or the features of the product that is provided consumers. The ICC also regarded itself as the defender of the industry it was to regulate rather than as a watchdog for consumers' interests. Social regulation differs from economic regulation in that it cuts across industry boundaries and seeks to achieve policy goals that extend beyond industry operations.

Social Regulation

Federal social regulation is associated with the expansion of federal regulatory authority that occurred in the 1960s and 1970s. Most of this new regulatory authority involved the areas of equal employment opportunity, environmental protection, occupational safety and health, and consumer protection. Much social regulation, however, comes from an earlier era and concerns such business functions as labor-management relations, corporate finance, and marketing.

Part of the justification for social regulation is the view that imperfections in the market system cause the problems social regulation is intended to correct. A perfectly functioning price system, for example, would somehow account for the social costs of environmental pollution and occupational disease. More importantly, social regulation embodies society's aspirations. It indicates that the society wants to promote certain objectives, such as fair labor-management relations or clean air. Social regulation represents the governmental judgment that these objectives can be achieved by restricting the operations of business and other private institutions.

The Environmental Protection Agency (EPA) was created in December 1970 and embodies the common features of social regulatory agencies. The structure of the newer social regulatory agencies reflects disenchantment with the classic independent regulatory commissions.[23] The older commissions were usually seen to be "captured" by the businesses they were intended to regulate, unconcerned about consumers, and unable to take the actions needed to solve the industry's long-term problems.

The newer social agencies are more likely to be located in the executive branch than be independent and headed by an administrator than a commission. A single administrator is more visible than a commission and held more easily accountable for an agency's actions or inactions. An administrator is also a presidential appointee, and the president will pay the political costs for an administrator's shortcomings. The newer social regulatory agencies administer rules that cut across sectors of the economy, and, thus, these agencies are less likely to be unduly influenced by a single industry or corporation.

The EPA bears symbolic responsibility for the society's anxieties about acid rain, the greenhouse effect, holes in the ozone layer, toxic wastes, and other environmental nightmares, but its actions are based on specific statutes. The agency's authority is derived from single-purpose statutes covering clean air, clean water, solid wastes, toxic wastes, radon, noise, and other pollutants.

Within each of these areas, the EPA first establishes *broad program standards*. In air pollution, for example, the EPA has defined national air-quality standards for common pollutants, factory emission levels for specific substances, emission standards for newly constructed factories, and motor vehicle emission standards. The EPA then defines *narrow performance and design standards* that restrict how companies operate or mandate how products perform so as to achieve the broad program standards. For example, automobile emission standards specify how many grams per mile of hydrocarbons, carbon monoxide, and nitrogen oxides cars are permitted to release. Social regulatory agencies usually enforce compliance with their standards through a system of permits and certifications that firms must obtain to demonstrate that they are abiding by the agencies' rules.

Inherent in the standard-setting and enforcement process are specific problems that social regulatory agencies inevitably face. First, it is often difficult to relate narrow performance and design standards to broad policy objectives.[24] How many grams of nitrogen oxides per mile are permissible? How much health risk is allowable for workers who are employed in factories that use cancer-causing substances like benzene? Second, social regulation invariably involves compliance costs to business, and these costs generate antagonism. Theoretically, although not in every instance, the value of the benefits to the society exceed the costs, but the parts of the society that pay the costs of social regulation are often not those who receive the benefits. Finally, social regulation can be used in a strategic and political way. Eastern coal producers and labor unions, for example, combined to require new power plants to install expensive equipment to remove sulfur emissions regardless of the sulfur content of the coal being burned in the power plant. This regulation used governmental authority to end the cost advantage and reduce sales of western coal, which was naturally low in sulfur content.[25] Table 8–2 summarizes the key differences between economic and social regulation.

TABLE 8–2   Key Features of Economic and Social Regulation

REGULATION FEATURES	ECONOMIC REGULATION	SOCIAL REGULATION
Focus of agency	Single industry	Multi-industry activity
Structure	Commission	Executive agency
Focus of rules	Entry, price, service	Standards
Political context	Producers, officials	Diverse interests

Discussions of regulation sometimes emphasize peculiar historic events or administrative structures and lose sight of the general patterns of governmental action.[26] Much of government operates by imposing restrictions on business and other private institutions, even though the term regulation is only applied to specific situations. Criticisms of regulation are motivated by complaints about specific forms of economic and social regulation as well as by unhappiness with government's broader goals and activities.

CONTEST BETWEEN REFORM AND DEREGULATION

Deregulation was a worldwide trend in the 1980s. The movement away from government control of economic decisions took different forms in different countries, but it dominated domestic policy in the United States and the United Kingdom and was quite visible in Germany and Japan. Even though deregulation is associated with the Reagan era, its intellectual origins and some of the key events in the deregulation process occurred in the 1970s. A review of the various criticisms of regulation foreshadows the political conflicts that emerged in the 1980s.

Criticisms of Regulation

The Reagan era's opposition to regulation was based on academic criticisms that had widespread support in the 1970s, but these nonpartisan criticisms were turned to political purposes in the 1980s that were not fully justified.[27] The critiques of economic regulation emphasized different points than the appraisals of social regulation.

The journalistic critics of economic regulation argued that producers had too much influence in the operations of independent regulatory commissions. The Federal Home Loan Bank Board, for example, was more concerned about the problems of S&Ls as institutions than about the overall health of the country's banking system or the welfare of consumers. The ICC sought to protect railroad companies instead of concentrating on the development of a comprehensive surface transportation system.

Economic critics accepted the goals of economic regulation but maintained that the actions of regulatory commissions had blocked rather than facilitated the achievement of statutory goals. Airlines, truckers, railroads, and other regulated industries were incurring unnecessary costs, providing worse service, and sacrificing economic efficiencies because of the regulatory frameworks established by the various commissions. The statutory goals of providing safe and efficient services in these industries could be achieved more effectively if the regulatory commissions abandoned or at least changed their regulatory approach.

The criticisms of social regulation argued with both its goals and its techniques. The critics insisted that the health, safety, environmental, and equity objectives were not worth the costs the society would incur to achieve them. In one observer's words, "…the problem is mainly that there are too many instances of regulations that generate large social costs without commensurate social benefits…."[28]

Furthermore, the statutes creating social regulatory programs frequently contained rigid goals that no political system could realistically achieve.[29] Precise deadlines focused attention on short-term, quick fixes that often stood in the way of long-term solutions to basic problems. The statutes asserted the importance of one policy and were often unwilling to acknowledge alternative approaches to achieving goals in that policy area or the need to balance one social goal with a variety of competing objectives. Analysts recommended that regulatory agencies rely on market incentives rather than command-oriented regulations to achieve their goals.

In the 1970s and early 1980s, there was substantial economic evidence to support the view that some deregulation and some regulatory reform would better achieve the public goals of industry-oriented, economic regulation. There was political disagreement about the goals of social regulation, and some ambiguous evidence that the techniques of the social agencies were costly and ineffective. In the 1980s, various criticisms of economic and social regulation were combined into a general attack on regulation that ignored the merits of individual programs and was offered as evidence of the need for comprehensive deregulation.

Deregulation

Presidential interest in regulation had been infrequent until the 1970s, when Presidents Ford and Carter spotlighted the importance of regulatory issues. The period from 1978 to 1982 witnessed a flurry of legislative activity that deregulated a number of critical industries. (See Table 8–3.)

TABLE 8–3   Major Deregulation Statutes, 1978–1982

YEAR	NAME OF ACT	PURPOSE
1978	Airline Deregulation Act	Ended price, entry, route, regulation by 1985
	Natural Gas Policy Act	Eliminated intra- and interstate price controls by 1989
1980	Motor Carrier Reform Act	Allowed more flexible pricing in trucking industry
	Staggers Rail Act	Allowed railroads flexibility in pricing and in discontinuing uneconomical routes
	Depository Institutions Deregulation Act	Eliminated ceiling on S&L interest rates
1982	Bus Regulatory Reform Act	Allowed price, entry competition in bus industry
	Depository Institutions Act	Expanded range of permissible investments for S&Ls

The statutory initiatives of the years between 1978 and 1982 appeared exclusively in the areas of economic regulation and attracted bipartisan support.[30] During the later years of the Reagan administration, however, regulation became a more partisan issue. The Reagan government regarded both social and economic regulation as unnecessary burdens that had to be relieved if the country's economy was to be revitalized. The statutory framework for social and economic regulation changed little after 1982, but the administration reduced the significance of regulation by reducing the budgets of regulatory agencies and appointing officials to run the agencies who were more sympathetic to the administration's policy goals than to the agencies priorities. Throughout the Reagan years, there was a contest between those who sought to deregulate various areas of social and economic life and others who proposed to reform the regulatory process by making regulation less burdensome but more effective.

Regulation, however, remains a policy tool. The standard for evaluating regulatory initiatives is whether they have a positive or negative effect on society. The regulation of the S&L industry offers one example of the significance of regulation. Since the airline industry was the first major industry to be deregulated, it offers another basis for making judgments about deregulation.

Impact of Airline Deregulation

The Airline Deregulation Act of 1978 gave companies greater flexibility to enter the airline industry, determine prices, and decide themselves how they would service different routes.[31] The legislation did not, however, remove all controls. Carriers are still required to demonstrate that they meet financial and technical qualifications before they begin service and to satisfy safety and maintenance standards during operations.

Most analysts agree that airline deregulation has resulted in lower fares. By one study, the cost of flying fell 23 percent between 1977 and 1986; and, by another estimate, airline deregulation is saving passengers approximately $16 billion per year in comparison with preregulation prices.[32] Fare reductions, of course, have not occurred on every flight. Fares fell most sharply between major airports served by competing airlines, and fares rose between lesser airports that were only served by a single carrier. About one hundred smaller communities have lost jet service, but most are now served by commuter airlines that usually operate more frequently.

The long-term downward trend of airline accident rates continued during the deregulation period.[33] Between 1979 and 1987, accidents on large jet carriers fell 36 percent in comparison with the 1970 to 1978 years, and fatalities declined 32 percent. Concerns about airline safety are prompted by fears that airlines will cut back on maintenance expenditures as marketplace competition rises, that new airlines will be less safe than established carriers, and that the air travel infrastructure will be inadequate to meet the needs of new passengers attracted by lower fares. To date, however, there is no evidence that these fears have been justified.

Critics of airline deregulation point out that the airline industry has become more concentrated in the years since deregulation. In 1988, the top eight carriers controlled 94 percent of the domestic passenger market, and an increasing number of communities are being served by only one or two carriers.[34] Mergers and consolidations have had a devastating effect on workers who have lost their jobs and communities that have lost all service. Furthermore, fares will inevitably rise in the years ahead, the critics argue, as the anticompetitive consequences of consolidation take their toll.

SUMMARY

Government regulations are rules that restrict business operations to accomplish government purposes. Regulations constitute an elaborate network of restrictions that affect every facet of business activity.

Economic regulation was designed to provide the benefits of competition in industries where genuine competition was not possible, such as railroads and public utilities. Social regulation seeks to achieve social objectives by specifying how business operates in specific situations. Regulation is often regarded as a device to achieve public purposes, but there is increasing evidence that it is used by business and public officials to advance their private objectives.

In the 1970s, most academic commentators concluded that independent regulatory commissions were impeding rather than assisting the performance of firms in the industries they were created to oversee. Other critics argued that the goals of social regulation were too costly and that the performance of social regulatory agencies was arbitrary. These criticisms were carried into the political arena and became the basis for the decade's contest between those who sought to deregulate various areas of social and economic life and others who strived to make regulation less burdensome and more effective.

SELECTED READINGS

GEORGE C. EADS and MICHAEL FIX, *Relief or Reform? Reagan's Regulatory Dilemma* (Washington, D.C.: Urban Institute Press, 1984).

LARRY N. GERSTON, CYNTHIA FRALEIGH, and ROBERT SCHWAB, *The Deregulated Society* (Pacific Grove, Calif.: Brooks/Cole, 1988).

EDWARD J. KANE, *The S&L Insurance Mess: How Did It Happen?* (Washington, D.C.: Urban Institute Press, 1989).

ROGER E. MEINERS and BRUCE YANDLE (eds.), *Regulation and the Reagan Era: Politics, Bureaucracy and the Public Interest* (New York: Holmes & Meier, 1989).

LEON N. MOSES and IAN SAVAGE (eds.), *Transportation Safety in an Age of Deregulation* (New York: Oxford University Press, 1989).

END NOTES

[1]Ned Eichler, *The Thrift Debacle* (Berkeley: University of California Press, 1989), p. vii.

[2]This account relies on James Ring Adams, *The Big Fix: Inside the S&L Scandal: How an Unholy Alliance of Politics and Money Destroyed America's Banking System* (New York: Wiley, 1990), pp. 238–54.

[3]The Senators deny any illegality or that Gray was asked to withdraw the regulation. See James Ring Adams, *The Big Fix*, p. 245.

[4]David J. Jefferson, "Keating of American Continental Corp. Comes Out Fighting," *Wall Street Journal*, April 18, 1989, quoted in Adams, *The Big Fix*, p. 254.

[5]Eichler, *The Thrift Debacle*, p. 104.

[6]These paragraphs rest on Edward J. Kane, *The S&L Insurance Mess: How Did It Happen?* (Washington, D.C.: Urban Institute Press, 1989).

[7]Eichler, *The Thrift Debacle*, p. 101.

[8]Louis Galambos and Joseph Pratt, *The Rise of the Corporate Commonwealth: United States Business and Public Policy in the 20th Century* (New York: Basic Books, 1988), p. 56.

[9]Barry M. Mitnick, *The Political Economy of Regulation: Creating, Designing, and Removing Regulatory Forms* (New York: Columbia University Press, 1980), Chapter 3.

[10]Marver H. Bernstein, *Regulating Business by Independent Commission* (Princeton: Princeton University Press, 1955).

[11]Thomas K. McCraw, *Prophets of Regulation* (Cambridge, Mass.: Harvard University Press, 1984).

[12]The viewpoint is also called the *public choice* perspective.

[13]This discussion is based on Sam Peltzman, "Toward a More General Theory of Regulation," *Journal of Law and Economics* (August 1976); Robert E. McCormick, "A Review of the Economics of Regulation: the Political Process," in Roger E. Meiners and Bruce Yandle (eds.), *Regulation and the Reagan Era: Politics, Bureaucracy and the Public Interest* (New York: Holmes & Meier, 1989), pp. 16–37; and William F. Shughart, *Antitrust Policy and Interest Group Politics* (New York: Quorum Books, 1990), Chapters 1–2.

[14]Bruce M. Owen and Ronald Braeutigam, *The Regulation Game: Strategic Use of the Administrative Process* (Cambridge, Mass.: Ballinger, 1978).

[15]This idea is derived from the concept of the antitrust pork barrel outlined in Richard A. Posner, "The Federal Trade Commission," *University of Chicago Law Review*, 37 (1969), pp. 47–89.

[16]William A. Niskanen, *Bureaucracy and Representative Government* (Chicago: Aldine, 1971); James Q. Wilson, "The Politics of Regulation," in James W. McKie (ed.), *Social Responsibility and the Business Predicament* (Washington, D.C.: Brookings Institution, 1974), pp. 135–68.

[17]Roger C. Noll and Bruce M. Owen, *The Political Economy of Deregulation: Interest Groups in the Regulatory Process* (Washington, D.C.: American Enterprise Institute, 1983).

[18]94 U.S. 113, 1877.

[19]Kermit H. Hall, *The Magic Mirror: Law in American History* (New York: Oxford University Press, 1989), pp. 234–36.

[20]118 U.S. 557, 1886.

[21]For a well-presented review of the ICC's development, see Damodar Gujarati, *Government and Business* (New York: McGraw-Hill, 1984), pp. 251–59.

[22]This theme was expressed in the Railroad Revitalization and Regulation Act of 1976 and the Staggers Rail Act of 1980. The Motor Carrier Act of 1980 relaxed the ICC's regulation of the trucking industry.

[23]Marver Bernstein, "The Regulatory Process: A Framework for Analysis," *Law and Contemporary Problems*, 26 (Spring 1961), 329–46; and Roger C. Cramton, "Regulatory Structure and Regulatory Performance: A Critique of the Ash Council Report," *Public Administration Review*, vol. 32, no. 4 (July 1972), 284–93.

[24]Eugene Bardach, "Social Regulation as a Generic Policy Instrument," in Lester M. Salamon (ed.), *Beyond Privatization: The Tools of Government Action* (Washington, D.C.: Urban Institute Press, 1989), pp. 197–229.

[25]Bruce A. Ackerman and William T. Hassler, *Clean Coal Dirty Air* (New Haven: Yale University Press, 1981).

[26]James Q. Wilson (ed.), *The Politics of Regulation* (New York: Basic Books, 1980).

[27]American Bar Association, Commission on Law and the Economy, *Federal Regulation: Roads to Reform* (No site: American Bar Association, 1979); Michael S. Baram, *Alternatives to*

Regulation: Managing Risks to Health, Safety and the Environment (Lexington, Mass.: Lexington Books, 1982); Leonard W. Weiss and Michael W. Klass, (eds.), *Case Studies in Regulation: Revolution and Reform* (Boston: Little, Brown, 1981); and Lawrence J. White, *Reforming Regulation: Processes and Problems* (Englewood Cliffs, N.J.: Prentice Hall, 1981).

[28]White, *Reforming Regulation*, p. 225.

[29]Larry E. Ruff, "Federal Environmental Regulation," in Weiss and Klass (eds.), *Case Studies in Regulation*, pp. 235–61; and Robert E. Litan and William D. Nordhaus, *Reforming Federal Regulation* (New Haven: Yale University Press, 1983), pp. 89–99.

[30]George C. Eads and Michael Fix, *Relief or Reform? Reagan's Regulatory Dilemma* (Washington, D.C.: Urban Institute Press, 1984).

[31]This discussion is based on Jonathan D. Ogur, Curtis L. Wagner, and Michael V. Vita, *The Deregulated Airline Industry: A Review of the Evidence* (Washington, D.C.: Federal Trade Commission, 1988); Paul Stephen Dempsey, *The Social and Economic Consequences of Deregulation: the Transportation Industry in Transition* (New York: Quorum Books, 1989); and Leon N. Moses and Ian Savage (eds.), *Transportation Safety in an Age of Deregulation* (New York: Oxford University Press, 1989).

[32]Leon N. Moses and Ian Savage, "Introduction," in Leon N. Moses and Ian Savage (eds.), *Transportation Safety in an Age of Deregulation*, p. 4.

[33]Moses and Savage, "Summary and Policy Implications," in Moses and Savage (eds.), *Transportation Safety in an Age of Deregulation*, pp. 308–31; here, p. 310.

[34]Dempsey, *The Social and Economic Consequences of Deregulation*.

Chapter 9

Corporations
and
Political Action

Businesses compete every day in the marketplace to sell their products. They also compete in the political arena. Businesses employ nonmarket, political tactics to gain favorable operating rules, expand sales, reduce costs, and impede the success of competitors. Occasionally they enter the political arena to pursue ideological goals. As the role of government in society has swelled, the importance of nonmarket tactics in determining the marketplace success of firms has increased.

This chapter and the three that follow examine the tactics used by business to influence public policy. Public policies can be analyzed in terms of a series of discrete steps. First, a specific policy problem is identified. Second, the views of different groups and organizations about the issue are gathered. Third, government makes a formal decision selecting a particular policy option; and, finally, the chosen policy is implemented by administrative agencies and reviewed by the judiciary. Each step in this process provides opportunities for business and other societal groups to influence the content of the policy.

Business tactics to influence public policy can seek to affect the climate of opinion in which issues are considered or influence directly the policy decisions that governments make. This chapter examines the indirect techniques of influence that involve public opinion, the sponsorship of research, and corporate social responsibility. It also explores the relationship between business and political parties and the role of parties in influencing policy decisions. Subsequent chapters examine techniques of influence involving business associations, lobbying strategies, and activities directed toward administrative agencies and the judiciary.

MODELS OF POLITICAL ACTION

No topic provokes more sharply divergent assessments than the role of business in politics. Some commentators contend that business is an illegitimate force that distorts the political process and seeks to protect the interests of a small ruling class. Different observers see business struggling rightfully but ineffectually to maintain its dwindling position in society; these observers contend that the political actions of business result from the pressures of marketplace competition. A comparison of the market-oriented and the ruling-class interpretations of the politics of business helps clarify the disputes that recur in the analyses of the political role of business.

Market-Oriented Politics

Empirical studies of corporate involvement in politics stress the diversity of positions adopted by business. These studies attribute the differences among companies to the competitive situations of individual firms in the marketplace.[1] The principal objective of a company is to assure its survival by generating an acceptable level of sales and profits.[2] Exporters stand against importers, small companies have needs that are different from those of big corporations, and high-technology firms operate in a vastly different environment from that of heavy industry. Each firm must secure its marketplace position before any other political concern is relevant.[3]

The view that the politics of business is driven by the need to sell products extends an element of democratic legitimacy to business's political actions. The purchase of products by consumers implies the acceptance of the actions business undertook to bring the goods to market.

The political actions of business also gain legitimacy because of the role of business in sustaining a pluralistic society. A pluralistic society is composed of a variety of groups representing various economic, political, and cultural interests of citizens. Each group competes with the others to promote its own interests, but no single group is able to dictate the society's policies. Business groups help restrain government, maintain social diversity, and reduce the chance of political repression. A textbook written for students of business administration describes the role of business in politics in these terms: "In the United States, pluralism is a basic reality of the modern business culture.... (Whether businesspeople) prefer pluralism is not the issue. It, like the weather, is here."[4]

Ruling-class Politics

The alternative view is that the politics of business is guided by the interests of corporate owners and managers. Business is seen as a unified force that dominates the country's politics. As Gabriel Kolko writes, "The real questions are (1) Do a small *group* of very wealthy men have the power to guide industry and thereby much of the total economy, towards ends that they decide are compatible with their own interests? (2) Do they own and control major corporations? The answers must *inevitably* be affirmative."[5]

Proponents of the ruling-class model view business not as a collection of competing firms but as a network of essentially indistinguishable companies that have similar motivations and patterns of behavior. Sometimes business owners and managers are presented as members of a national upper class who come from advantaged backgrounds, attend preparatory schools, join exclusive clubs, and are listed in the social register.[6] Shared social backgrounds lead businesspeople to interpret political events in the same ways, and social ties help them coordinate action to serve the interests of their class.

Other studies see operating relationships among firms as mechanisms of coordination for achieving business political interests.[7] These studies investigate the business affiliations of top company managers and the members of corporate boards of directors.[8] They document patterns of corporate borrowing, joint ventures, and purchasing practices. They explore the degrees of concentration in particular industries and in the economy in general. Each of these operating relationships is regarded as evidence that companies act in concert to promote shared political objectives.

Finally, still other analyses find that an inner circle of corporate leaders guides the politics of business through participation in a series of intercorporate business associations. These elite, pan-business organizations are "the real motors of business political motion,"[9] and they represent the development of the class-consciousness that is an increasingly important determinant of corporate political behavior.

According to the ruling-class view, political authority is an extension of economic power. Corporate economic power is transformed into political power in two ways.[10] First, corporations participate in the political process through interest groups, lobbying, and other direct and indirect methods of swaying governmental decisions. They dominate the country's political ideology, dictate its governmental agenda, and determine the content of its public policies.

The second way business exercises political influence is through the economy. Firms make decisions about production, investment, and employment, and these decisions affect the living standards of the nation's citizens and the resources that are available to the public sector. If government policy damages business, corporations will retaliate by using their resources in ways that provide citizens and government fewer benefits. If this happens, levels of production, investment, and employment will fall, living standards will decline, and the resulting public wrath will endanger the electoral prospects of elected officials.

Political Mobilization of the 1970s

Supporters of both the market-oriented and ruling-class models of business politics can examine the same events and find support for their contradictory positions. An example of this is the political mobilization of business that occurred in the early 1970s, as discussed in Chapter 2.

Most observers agree that businesses increased their political activity in the early 1970s. Business groups had suffered a series of political defeats in Congress in the late 1960s and early 1970s that were without parallel in the postwar period.[11] They faced new regulatory requirements, more rigorous product standards, increased costs, and diminished operating autonomy. Businesspeople viewed the defeats as an attack on their place in society.[12] As one commentator observed, "It is not the products themselves that are under attack but the system that produces them and the character and credibility of their producers...."[13]

In addition, business also recognized in these years that American hegemony in the world was ending and they now faced international rivals who enjoyed higher growth rates, lower labor costs, greater increases in productivity, and more supportive political environments.[14] The profitability and even viability of major corporations was under assault at home and abroad.

In response to these developments, corporations upgraded their organizational capacity to deal with governmental issues, as seen in Chapter 6. Critical commentators describe these actions as an "unprecedented expansion of corporate political activities" and "one of the most remarkable campaigns in the pursuit of political power in recent history."[15] They attribute much of the conservative mood of the 1980s to the increased political activism of business.[16]

Advocates of the ruling-class model depict the events of the 1970s as a case study of the ability of economic leaders to assert political power.[17] They maintain that disputes among business interests are of secondary importance.[18] When corporate chiefs recognized a potential threat, they utilized their resources to engineer a stunning shift to the political right. Essentially without public support, business achieved virtual dominance of the legislative process. It defeated the first elected incumbent president since the 1930s, installed the most ideologically conservative president since the 1920s, and achieved changes in tax and labor relations policies that were previously unimaginable.

Proponents of the market-oriented model of business politics argue that the events of the 1960s and 1970s prove that business does not at all dominate governmental decision making. Business was on the defensive in these years and reeling from the attack. It recovered its position through a process of criticism and reform, as it had done in previous generations. The absence of a vigorous movement to abolish private enterprise is not evidence of corporate domination of political decision making but of a popular judgment that the country is better served by a system of private enterprise than by the alternatives.

How should the market-oriented and ruling-class models of business participation in politics be appraised? It is not necessary to choose between them. Both viewpoints are valuable and, to an extent, complementary. Social science models are not meant to be precise descriptions of actual events but aids in understanding basic patterns of behavior.

The market-oriented model is indispensable in assessing the political disputes that fill the daily press. It provides a framework in which conflicts over taxes, operating regulations, and production costs can be examined. The ruling-class model highlights the long-term advantages, if not the omnipotence, that economic leaders in a private enterprise system possess when they enter the political arena. It explains why politicians and others extend to them some measure of deference.

Both viewpoints identify important factors in the policy process that may otherwise be ignored. Both are helpful as we proceed to explore the direct and indirect means by which business participates in political decision making.

INDIRECT FORMS OF POLITICAL INFLUENCE

Corporations, interest groups, and individuals act more and more often to influence governmental decision making. Some of their actions focus on specific decisions, such as the enactment of a law or the adoption of an administrative regulation. Other actions seek to affect the climate of opinion in which governmental decisions occur. This section examines corporate efforts to create a supportive atmosphere for their policy objectives.

Public Opinion and Advocacy Advertising

Public issues emerge in the context of specific patterns of opinion, and these opinions, sometimes more than reality, may determine the nature of governmental action. Not every potential issue receives public attention. In the 1960s, issues of social equity were at center stage, while in the 1980s, questions of economic competitiveness attracted public concern. The political definition of an issue is also affected by public attitudes. The U.S. trade deficit may be seen as an issue that concerns the failures of corporate managers, underskilled workers, international trade barriers, or inappropriate governmental policies. The choice of issues that receive attention and the political definition given those issues go a long way toward determining the significance of a country's policies.

Business and other groups sometimes seek to shape the public attitudes that give rise to public issues. Some business groups believed that the policy process in the 1960s and 1970s proceeded without an adequate understanding of the functioning of the nation's economic system. Business lacked credibility in policy circles, they concluded, because people did not understand how a market economy operates. In response, companies and business associations developed programs to promote economic education among employees, students, and shareholders.[19] Whether the economic education movement had any impact on public attitudes is doubtful, but it does illustrate efforts to shape the context of opinion from which public issues emerge.

Legal Status of Corporate Political Activity

Corporate political activity occurs within a constitutional and statutory framework that authorizes some actions and prohibits others. In constitutional terms, corporations are "artificial" persons. They receive the same constitutional rights as "natural" persons, unless there is a compelling reason for denying them these rights.

Freedom of speech on policy issues is a constitutional right that is protected for both corporations and "natural" persons. According to the U.S. Constitution, corporations are free to use their funds to advocate positions on public issues, to influence public opinion on ballot questions, and to present corporate views to public officials. These activities are constitutionally protected forms of "speech."

Candidate elections are a different matter. Here the need to prevent the "appearance of corruption" is enough to justify government regulation. Contributions by both corporations and individuals to candidate campaigns may be restricted. The federal government regulates the contributions and expenditures of presidential and congressional candidates, and the states each regulate their candidate elections in their own way. The federal government and most state governments limit or occasionally ban corporate financial contributions to candidate campaigns. Other states do not restrict corporate donations at all.

Source: John A. Cray, "Corporate Identity and Corporate Political Activities," *American Business Law Journal*, 21 (Winter 1984), pp. 438–61. Key court decisions are *First National Bank of Boston* v. *Bellotti*, 435 U.S. 765 (1978) and *Consolidated Edison of New York* v. *Public Service Commission*, 447 U.S. 530 (1980).

Corporations, business associations, unions, and other interests also employ advertising campaigns to promote their policy views.[20] Advertising campaigns to advocate the sponsor's views on public issues are not new. In 1906, AT&T conducted a surprisingly successful print campaign to convince the public, troubled by the emergence of giant corporations, of the benefits of an integrated, monopolistic telephone system.[21]

In practice, it is difficult to distinguish issue ads from advertisements designed to sell a company's products or improve its image. An oil company's commercial assurance that it shares the public's concern about the environment may be intended to increase the sale of its products, enhance its corporate image, or deflect political efforts to impose new restrictions on its operations. Since the costs of product ads are tax-deductible expenses while the costs of advocacy advertising are not, corporate advertisers have little incentive to distinguish among types of advertising.[22]

The most famous series of advocacy advertisements is sponsored by Mobil Oil Corporation.[23] These ads present the company's viewpoints on questions affecting both the oil industry and broader public concerns. They stand out because of their aggressiveness and the persistence of the company's efforts. United Technologies' advocacy advertising has stressed ideological themes, and W.R. Grace sponsored provocative ads on the dangers of the federal budget deficit. Newspapers such as the *Washington Post* and the *New York Times* welcome advocacy advertising, but television networks shun such ads which they fear may violate their obligation to present all sides of controversial issues.[24]

The question with advocacy advertising, of course, is whether anyone pays attention.[25] There is little systematic evidence that the ads accomplish the goals of their sponsors. Institutional advertising does appear to enhance a company's image, but the general public, as a rule, pays little attention to advocacy advertising. There are no indications that advocacy advertising, for example, has reduced public distrust of corporate leaders. Officeholders and other specialized groups are more aware of issue advertising, but they are also more skeptical.

Research Institutes

A more effective corporate effort to alter the terms of policy debates has been the support of research centers that champion market-oriented solutions to public problems.[26] Through the 1970s, organizations such as the Ford Foundation, the Brookings Institution, and the Institute for Policy Studies achieved quasi-monopoly status in "think-tank" policy development. The proposals devised by such organizations usually involved an expansion of the role of government in society and a diminution of the autonomy of private organizations.

In the 1970s, private foundations and corporations directed funds to existing and emerging research organizations that did the scholarly groundwork for proposals that stressed nonbureaucratic approaches to public issues. Among the most prominent of these organizations were the American Enterprise Institute, the Heritage Foundation, the Institute for Contemporary Studies, and the Hoover Institution at Stanford University. The most prestigious center to benefit from enhanced corporate funding was the National Bureau of Economic Research in Cambridge, whose analyses were responsive to the concerns of the corporate community.

Corporations and private foundations did not buy policy conclusions from these organizations, but they did encourage the development of intellectual perspectives that were more compatible with the continued importance of nongovernmental institutions in society. Respected scholars were encouraged to elaborate views that had remained undeveloped, and funding was provided to disseminate research findings that had previously received little notice.

Social Responsibility

Some business figures argue that the most effective way for business to affect the climate of opinion is to behave as good corporate citizens.[27] Business, they submit, must be socially responsible and look beyond the immediate demands of the marketplace. As a major community institution, it has an obligation to protect and improve the welfare of the society.[28] Only by doing this will business be able to play a meaningful role in shaping the course of public events.

The phrase "social responsibility" is used to describe a broad range of business activities that are said to benefit society. Only some of these activities, however, are motivated by a desire to improve the welfare of society. The significance of corporate social responsibility can only be assessed by distinguishing among different types of corporate behavior. (See Table 9–1.)

TABLE 9–1   Perspectives on Social Responsibility

BASIS OF COMPANY ROLE	FOCUS OF MANAGEMENT CONCERN	
	Market Activities	*Nonmarket Activities*
Shareholders & employees	Enlightened self-interest	Political legitimacy
Larger society	Marketplace efficiency	Social improvement

Table 9–1 identifies different perspectives on social responsibility by examining the basis of the company's social role and the focus of management concern.[29] Few corporate activities are purely altruistic efforts to improve society. Most corporate activities presented as examples of social responsibility are forms of enlightened self-interest. They are intended to serve the interests of a company's shareholders and employees by improving the firm's sales.

Corporate philanthropy and community service are often marketing devices.[30] McDonald's regards community relations and its Ronald McDonald Houses, which provide free or low-cost accommodations to families visiting children's hospitals, as part of its marketing program. "Twenty years ago," noted its marketing chief, "we decided we wanted an image beyond food, based on strong virtues. We put up a value structure that's difficult to penetrate. It makes us dependable in a world of strange new things...."[31] The decision of Coca-Cola to sponsor Hands Across America was based on similar considerations.[32] New Jersey Bell works to improve that state's education system because many of its future employees will be graduates of state schools and because it believes that improvements in education will benefit the economy, which, in turn, will benefit New Jersey Bell.[33]

Some scholars argue that the doctrine of social responsibility has significant political implications.[34] From this perspective, actions presented as examples of social responsibility are intended to encourage public acceptance of corporate actions and increase the political legitimacy of corporate power. The doctrine of social responsibility became prominent shortly after the emergence of national corporations had disrupted traditional patterns of economic and social life.

Corporate support for popular causes at that time increased the political legitimacy of corporations and dampened enthusiasm for increased government regulation. Expenditures on behalf of social causes are still thought to boost corporate legitimacy and further the long-term interests of shareholders and employees.

Classical economic thought holds that firms best serve the interests of the larger society by ignoring social causes and concentrating on their marketplace efficiency.[35] A company's highest social responsibility, according to this view, is to offer consumers the best possible goods at the lowest price. By responding to consumer preferences, a firm provides jobs for employees, fair returns for investors, and products for the society. Companies have no right to engage in activities that are not related to their products. Such activities impose hidden costs on consumers, employees, and investors, and they give corporations influence over social institutions that should remain independent. From this perspective, a company's social responsibilities are expressed through its products, not its support of charitable causes.

Business efforts to demonstrate social responsibility have had only limited impact. The magnitude of purely altruistic corporate action is small. Corporate charitable contributions equal about 1 percent of profits, and this figure includes expenditures that are at least partially motivated by marketing concerns. Opinion surveys provide little evidence that the general public recognizes corporate support of charitable and community services. Elite groups probably appreciate corporate contributions more fully, but they also tend to be more cynical. Socially responsible conduct provides business few general rewards, but the disregard of community standards would surely generate antagonism.

Another technique corporations use to improve the climate for considering policy issues is to support political parties. In some countries, such support is the most effective tactic available to influence public decisions.

BUSINESS AND POLITICAL PARTIES: A COMPARATIVE PERSPECTIVE

Political parties represent social interests to government and influence governmental policy. Formal affiliations between business and political parties are rare.[36] Businesses typically maintain working relations with all parties that may participate in government. Despite this, it is clear that business leaders prefer some parties to others. They have an affinity for parties whose programs promote the economy and an aversion to parties that restrict private enterprise. The centrist or center-right parties favored by business advocate policies intended to spur economic growth. Left-center or leftist parties usually define themselves in terms of workers' economic and social rights.

Table 9–2 displays party divisions in Germany, Japan, the United Kingdom, and the United States by characterizing parties as oriented toward economic growth or workers' rights. Parties in all countries have broader concerns than this chart implies, and the differences among parties are more pronounced in some nations than others. Despite this, a review of the heritage and structure of party systems sheds valuable light on relationships between government and industry in each country.

TABLE 9–2 Political Party Orientations

COUNTRY	ECONOMIC GROWTH	WORKERS' RIGHTS
Germany	Christian Democratic Union/Christian Social Union Free Democratic party	German Social Democratic party
Japan	Liberal Democratic party	Japan Socialist party
United Kingdom	Conservative party	Labour party
United States	Republican party	Democratic party

Germany

German political parties dominate the policy process.[37] In large measure, the party system is a product of the post-World War II era and reflects a break from earlier antidemocratic traditions.[38] German electoral laws limit representation in the national parliament to parties that receive at least 5 percent of the vote. In recent decades, only two major parties and one smaller party have had a role in government.

German political parties are rooted in the country's social and economic divisions.[39] The German Social Democratic party (SPD) has the strongest ties with past eras and remains the favored party of industrial workers and trade union families. In recent decades, it has abandoned its earlier advocacy of the nationalization of industry, supported the existing economic system, and sought to expand worker participation in corporate decision making. The Christian Democratic Union and its Bavarian affiliate, the Christian Social Union, attract particular support from Catholics, practicing Protestants, white-collar workers, farmers, and the traditional middle class. The Christian Union parties (CDU/CSU) present a nonsectarian appeal, maintain ties to labor and social groups, and are sensitive to the interests of civil servants.

The Free Democratic party (FDP) is a small, middle-class party that has played a key role in governing coalitions with both the CDU/CSU and the SPD. The party has supported market-based economic policies, civil liberties, and governmental assistance to small business. Its centrist position has checked the more extreme tendencies of the two larger parties.

In 1983, the Green party became the first new party to be represented in the national legislature in thirty years. It gained support by emphasizing pro-environmental and antiestablishment positions, but internal divisions have limited the party's impact. In 1990, the Greens failed to attract 5 percent of the national vote and lost their national representation.

German political parties are, by international standards, "conspicuously rich" institutions that have built "huge party staffs."[40] Germany began public financing of political parties in 1959, and, in 1985, the system provided legislative parties, party organizations, and party foundations approximately $130 million, or approximately 75 percent of their income.[41] In election years, the parties receive substantially more. In addition to public funds, parties receive significant amounts from membership dues and private, usually corporate, contributions. Public financing has sustained the minor parties and reduced, although not ended, the influence of private donors.[42]

The direct participation of business leaders in German party politics today is described as "almost non-existent."[43] Another scholar concludes, "Various studies have shown that most members of the present business elite believe that they have neither the time nor the skill to devote themselves very much to party politics."[44] This, of course, does not mean that there are no ties between business and the parties. About 10 percent of the members of the national legislature are middle-level businesspeople; and the FDP, in particular, has close financial and policy bonds with business groups.[45] Business representatives participate in the meetings of the CDU/CSU and FDP that develop party policy.

Japan

Japan provides the world's foremost example of a political system with free elections dominated by a single party.[46] The Liberal Democratic party (LDP) has been Japan's governing party since 1955. The LDP overcame the country's ideological polarization in the 1950s and fashioned a political consensus based on economic growth and higher standards of living. The party's success in retaining power over the years has rested on its ability to adapt its policies to the country's social and economic changes.

Political factions are the dominant unit of party organization. The LDP today is composed of four major factions and one minor faction.[47] Factions have evolved into collegial structures that command impressive resources. They are nonideological groups that play little role in policy development but are represented in the party's governing coalitions. Japanese parties lack the mass membership base that characterizes German or Western parties and have little local party structure.

The LDP has become Japan's governing party, and the Japan Socialist Party (JSP) has become the permanent opposition. In the 1950s, the JSP won support by defending the democratic features of the country's constitution and opposing rearmament and the United States–Japan Security Treaty. As these issues receded, the party lost hope of assuming power. Although the JSP never championed an uncompromising brand of socialism, it has sometimes given more attention to safeguarding socialist thought than to winning elections.[48]

Japan has an expensive system of electoral politics. The absence of local party organization means that individual candidates must build and finance their own campaign apparatus. The amounts of money required for these efforts produce the financial scandals that recur in Japanese politics.[49]

The LDP is far better financed than its campaign opponents, and business groups provide essentially all the funds. It is a measure of the relative influence of party units that contributions received by the LDP are dwarfed in size by the money raised by the factions and even by some individual leaders. In the 1990 election, business groups were reported to have provided LDP candidates at least $200 million in donations and credits.[50]

The permanent governing role of the LDP has led Japanese business to deviate from international patterns and build close working relationships with the party. Both financial contributions and policy advice link the political and industrial worlds in Japan. Traditional businesses emphasize relationships with administrative officials, but newer businesses are in closer contact with LDP representatives in parliament.

United Kingdom

The UK has a highly organized party system that reflects the country's status as the first industrial nation.[51] Party leaders direct electoral campaigns and parliamentary life, but the traditional class-based party system shows signs of deterioration.

The British Labour party emerged from the social dislocation of industrialization and is rooted in the union movement. All major industrial unions are affiliated with the Labour party and provide most of its financial support.[52] The party has always been divided between rigid socialists who demand widespread nationalization and social democrats who seek to increase social welfare expenditures and expand the economic role of the government. The party had been held together by its commitment to the working class, but this unifying principle has been weakened as traditional industries have declined and the industrial work force has contracted. Intraparty conflicts have intensified as the historic foundation of the party has eroded.

Historically, the British Conservative party has been less ideological than the Labour party. One British scholar has noted that the defining characteristic of the Conservative party is the personal preeminence of the party leader.[53] In the decades after World War II, Labour and Conservative governments agreed on the extent of government intervention in the economy and on labor-management issues. In the 1980s, however, Prime Minister Thatcher introduced a strident ideological element into British politics by championing free-market policies to revive the nation's faltering economy.

The Conservative party benefits from the division of the anti-Conservative vote among Labour and two smaller parties. The electoral system has allowed the party to dominate the nation's politics for the last decade with only 40 percent of the popular vote. Most British voters express less support for their party than antagonism to opposing parties.

British business is overwhelmingly sympathetic to the Conservative party, and its support for Labour is "negligible."[54] Despite this, "senior business leaders do not generally seek public office or play important roles within the Conservative Party...."[55] Business played essentially no role in forming Thatcher's program for creating an "enterprise culture."

British political parties are modestly funded.[56] They receive free broadcast time during election seasons and some support for legislative staff, but there is no general public financing of parties. At the national level, the Labour and the Conservative parties receive about equal funding from unions and corporations respectively. At the local level, the Conservatives have a two-to-one financial advantage over Labour because of their active local membership and donations from regional corporations. About 15 percent of major British firms contribute to the Conservative party, but only about twenty firms donate significant amounts. The trend is that business financial support of parties is declining.[57]

United States

The United States has the only unqualified two-party system in the world.[58] Despite this, American parties have rarely been imitated in other countries.

When American parties originated, governmental authority was decentralized, and parties developed a state and local base. In recent decades, party reforms have asserted the primacy of national over state rules. Campaign technology, communications patterns, and fund-raising practices have also contributed to the nationalization of the party system, and the growth and professionalization of party staffs in Congress and at national party committees have furthered the nationalizing trend. Despite these developments, the federal system still sustains the vitality of state and local parties.

American parties are candidate-centered in comparison to the parties discussed above, and the ties between social groups and political parties are loose. The Republican party was once the party of Northeastern liberals and conservative Midwesterners, but the growth of the South and the Southeast has moved the party to a middle-class conservative base.[59] The Democratic party once functioned as the agent of disadvantaged economic groups, labor union leaders, and conservative Southerners, but it has encountered difficulty in presenting an attractive national program, as it has lost the allegiance of Southern groups, industrial union membership has contracted, and international economic concerns have become more prominent.

Election costs have increased dramatically in the United States in the last two decades. American campaign finance is usually candidate-oriented, and the largest share of funds come from citizens who support individual candidates, issues, or ideologies. The Republican party, like the British Conservatives, finds it easier to raise citizen contributions than do the Democratic or Labour parties. Government finances presidential campaigns and many state election contests, and public funding of legislative staffs constitutes, in part, public funding for legislative parties.

Businesses contribute substantial amounts to parties and campaigns in the United States, but the contribution patterns differ from those in other countries. The most prominent donors in the U.S. business community are not major corporations but associations of local businesses, such as car dealers, real estate agents, doctors, and local builders. Unlike the three countries discussed above, the use of corporate monies to finance national elections is restricted. Corporate political action committees are supported by employee rather than company funds, and most corporate PACs are modestly funded. (See Chapter 11). Corporate funds may be used to assist national conventions, subsidize some legislative and party activities, and finance campaign activities in a few states.

The pattern of business contributions in the United States is less partisan than in other countries. Corporations and business groups in Japan, the United Kingdom, and even Germany direct the overwhelming share of their donations to parties concerned about economic growth and limit contributions to parties that stress workers' rights. Partisan divisions in the United States are less clear. The Republican party receives substantial backing within the business community, but prominent business leaders endorse Democratic candidates in every election. Certain industries, such as the entertainment industry, routinely favor Democratic majorities, and business-oriented political action committees deliver almost half of their contributions to Democratic candidates. The political representatives of business in the United States are less ideological and more accommodationist than those in the other three countries.

SUMMARY

Business seeks to influence the conduct of public policy by affecting the climate of opinion through advocacy advertising, research support, and claims of corporate social responsibility. Although advocacy advertising attracts attention, there is little evidence that it has much impact. In contrast, corporate research support has expanded the range of nonbureaucratic options considered in policy debates. Corporate social responsiblity is a multifaceted concept that is often used as a component of ambitious marketing programs. While it does have marketing significance, the non-market consequences of corporate social responsibility are probably limited to forestalling political attacks rather than advancing positive objectives.

American businesses are less involved with political parties than businesses in Germany, Japan, and, perhaps, the United Kingdom, and the pattern of support shows less respect for party lines. Political actions of U.S. business are more candidate-oriented than in the other countries and more closely related to specific policy areas.

Business also seeks to affect the conduct of policy though business associations, lobbying, and contact with administrative agencies and the courts. These activities are examined in the next three chapters.

SELECTED READINGS

JOHN R. BOWMAN, *Capitalist Collective Action: Competition, Cooperation and Conflict in the Coal Industry* (Cambridge, England: Cambridge University Press, 1989).

GERALD L. CURTIS, *The Japanese Way of Politics* (New York: Columbia University Press, 1988).

JEROME L. HIMMELSTEIN, *To the Right: The Transformation of American Conservatism* (Berkeley: University of California Press, 1990).

STEPHEN PADGETT and TONY BURKETT, *Political Parties and Elections in West Germany: The Search for a New Stability* (London: C. Hurst & Company, 1986).

MICHAEL USEEM, *The Inner Circle: Large Corporations and the Rise of Business Political Activity in the U.S. and U.K.* (New York: Oxford University Press, 1984).

END NOTES

[1]E. E. Schattschneider, *Politics, Pressure and the Tariff* (New York: Prentice Hall, 1935); Raymond A. Bauer, Ithiel de Sola Pool, and Lewis Anthony Dexter, *American Business and Public Policy: The Politics of Foreign Trade* (Chicago: Aldine-Atherton, 1972); Bruce A. Ackerman and William T. Hassler, *Clean Coal and Dirty Air* (New Haven: Yale University Press, 1981); and Richard A. Harris, *Coal Firms under the New Social Regulation* (Durham, N.C.: Duke University Press, 1985).

[2]This analysis is prompted by John R. Bowman, *Capitalist Collective Action: Competition, Cooperation and Conflict in the Coal Industry* (Cambridge, England: Cambridge University Press, 1989), pp. 29–30, 221–22, and 232–34.

[3]Some believe that the political process can be understood as a reflection of differences in the competitive position of firms. See Thomas Ferguson and Joel Rogers, "The Reagan Victory: Corporate Coalitions in the 1980 Campaign," in Ferguson and Rogers (eds.), *The Hidden Election: Politics and Economics in the 1980 Presidential Election* (New York: Pantheon Books, 1981), pp. 7–8.

[4]Keith Davis and William C. Frederick, *Business and Society: Management, Public Policy, Ethics*, 5th ed. (New York: McGraw–Hill, 1984), p. 134.

[5]Gabriel Kolko, *Railroads and Regulation: 1877–1916* (New York: Norton, 1965), p. 169.

[6]Edward Digby Baltzell, *The Protestant Establishment* (New York: Random House, 1984); William G. Domhoff, *Who Rules America?* (Englewood Cliffs, N.J.: Prentice Hall, 1967).

[7]Michael Schwartz, *The Structure of Power in America: The Corporate Elite as a Ruling Class* (New York: Holmes & Meier, 1987), Part I.

[8]Donald Palmer, Roger Friedland, and Jitandra Singh, "The Ties That Find: Organizational and Class Bases of Stability in a Corporate Interlock Network," *American Sociological Review*, (December 1986), 781–96.

[9]Michael Useem, *The Inner Circle: Large Corporations and the Rise of Business Political Activity in the U.S. and U.K.* (New York: Oxford University Press, 1984), especially pp. 3, 74–75, and 148–49; and Joseph G. Peschek, *Policy-Planning Organizations: Elite Agendas and America's Rightward Turn* (Philadelphia: Temple University Press, 1987).

[10]Charles E. Lindblom, *Politics and Markets: The World's Political-Economic Systems* (New York: Basic Books, 1977); and David Marsh, "Interest Group Activity and Structural Power: Lindblom's *Politics and Markets*," and David Marsh and Gareth Locksley, "Capital in Britain: Its Structural Power and Influence over Policy," in David Marsh (ed.), *Capital and Politics in Western Europe* (London: Frank Cass, 1983), pp. 3–13 and 36–60.

[11]David Vogel, *Fluctuating Fortunes: Political Power of Business in America* (New York: Basic Books, 1989), p. 59

[12]Leonard Silk and David Vogel, *Ethics and Profits: The Crisis of Confidence in American Business* (New York: Simon and Schuster, 1976).

[13]Michael Novak, *The American Vision* (Washington, D.C.: American Enterprise Institute, 1978), p. 37.

[14]Jerome L. Himmelstein, *To the Right: The Transformation of American Conservatism* (Berkeley: University of California Press, 1990), Chapter 5. Michael Useem reports that the politicization of business in the United Kingdom also resulted from challenges to companies by labor unions; see his book, *The Inner Circle*, p. 171.

[15]Useem, *The Inner Circle*, p. 4; and Thomas Byrne Edsall, *The New Politics of Inequality* (New York: W.W. Norton, 1984), p. 107.

[16]See Thomas Ferguson and Joel Rogers, *Right Turn: The Decline of the Democrats and the Future of American Politics* (New York: Hill and Wang, 1986); and the works cited above.

[17]Dan Clawson and Mary Ann Clawson, "Reagan or Business? Foundations of the New Conservatism," in Schwartz (ed.), *The Structure of Power in America*, pp. 201–217.

[18]Lindblom, *Politics and Markets*, pp. 203–206 and 210–12.

[19]Myron Emanuel et al., *Corporate Economic Education Programs: An Evaluation and Appraisal* (New York: Financial Executives Research Foundation, 1979).

[20]Herbert Waltzer, "Advocacy Advertising and Political Influence: The Campaigns of Corporations to Cue the Public and Tether the Press," unpublished paper presented at the Annual Meeting of the American Political Science Association, August 28–31, 1986. See also S. Parkash Sethi, *Advocacy Advertising and Large Corporations: Social Conflict, Big Business Image, the News Media, and Public Policy* (Lexington, Mass.: D.C. Heath, 1977); and S. Parkash Sethi, *Handbook of Advocacy Advertising: Concepts, Strategies, and Applications* (Cambridge, Mass.: Ballinger, 1987).

[21]Richard L. Heath and Richard Alan Nelson, *Issues Management: Corporate Public Policymaking in an Information Age* (Beverly Hills: Sage Publications, 1986), p. 57.

[22]U.S. Congress, Senate, Committee on the Judiciary, Subcommittee on Administrative Practice and Procedure, *Sourcebook on Corporate Image and Corporate Advocacy Advertising*, 95th Congress 2nd, 1978.

[23]Herbert Schmertz and William Novak, *Good-bye to the Low Profile: The Art of Creative Confrontation* (Boston: Little, Brown, 1986).

[24]Ronald Alsop, "TV Networks Balk at Broadcasting Ad on Federal Deficit," *Wall Street Journal*, January 24, 1986, p. 30; and David Wessel, "Businessmen Use Ad to Urge U.S. Budget Cuts, But Fight to Keep Tax Breaks for Their Firms," *Wall Street Journal*, November 19, 1987, p. 70.

[25]Waltzer, "Advocacy Advertising and Political Influence," pp. 23–25.

[26]Sidney Blumenthal, *The Rise of the Counter-Establishment: From Conservative Ideology to Political Power* (New York: Harper & Row, 1988), pp. 51–58; John S. Saloma, *Ominous Politics: The New Conservative Labyrinth* (New York: Hill and Wang, 1984), Chapters 2–3; Edsall, *The New Politics of Inequality*, pp. 117–20; Ferguson and Rogers, *Right Turn*, pp. 103–105; and Himmelstein, *To the Right*, pp. 143–45.

[27]See, for example, Committee for Economic Development, *Social Responsibilities of Business Corporations* (New York: CED, 1971); and Robert K. Ackerman, *The Social Challenge to Business* (Cambridge, Mass.: Harvard University Press, 1975).

[28]This definition is derived from Jerry W. Anderson, *Corporate Social Responsibility: Guidelines for Top Management* (New York: Quorum Books, 1989), p. 9.

[29]This typology was suggested by Daryl G. Hatano, "Should Corporations Exercise Their Freedom of Speech Rights?," *American Business Law Journal*, 22, no. 2 (Summer 1984), 165–87.

[30]Louis W. Fry et al., "Corporate Contributions: Altruistic or For-Profit?," *Academy of Management Journal* 25, no.1 (1982), 94–106.

[31]"McDonald's Combines A Dead Man's Advice with Lively Strategy," *Wall Street Journal*, December 12, 1987, pp. 1, 12.

[32]James E. Post and Sandra A. Waddock, "Social Cause Partnerships and the 'Mega-Event': Hunger, Homelessness and Hands Across America," in James E. Post (ed.), *Research*

in *Corporate Social Performance and Policy: A Research Annual—Volume 11, 1989*, "Corporate Social Policy: 1980s to the 1990s" (Greenwich, Conn.: JAI Press, 1989), pp. 181–205.

[33]Speech at Rutgers University, February 16, 1984.

[34]Neil J. Mitchell, *The Generous Corporation: A Political Analysis of Economic Power* (New Haven: Yale University Press, 1989), especially pp. 56, 62, and 141.

[35]Theodore Levitt, "The Dangers of Social Responsibility," *Harvard Business Review*, 36, no. 5 (September 1958), 41–50; Milton Friedman, *Capitalism and Freedom* (Chicago: University of Chicago Press, 1962), pp. 132–33; and Milton Friedman, "The Social Responsibility of Business is to Increase Its Profits," *New York Times Magazine*, September 13, 1970, pp. 122–26.

[36]John P. Windmuller and Alan Gladstone (eds.), *Employers Associations and Industrial Relations: A Comparative Study* (Oxford: Clarendon Press, 1984), p. 27.

[37]Peter J. Katzenstein, *Policy and Politics in West Germany: The Growth of a Semisovereign State* (Philadelphia: Temple University Press, 1987), p. 36. See also Lewis J. Edinger, *West German Politics* (New York: Columbia University Press, 1986), p. 227.

[38]William M. Chandler, "Party Transformations in the Federal Republic of Germany," in Steven B. Wolinetz (ed.), *Parties and Party Systems in Liberal Democracies* (London: Routledge, 1988), p. 70; and Gordon Smith, "The 'Model' West German Party System," in Peter H. Merkl, (ed.), *The Federal Republic of Germany at Forty* (New York: New York University Press, 1989), pp. 249–64.

[39]See Merkl (ed.), *The Federal Republic of Germany at Forty*; H.G. Peter Wallach and George K. Romoser (eds.), *West German Politics in the Mid-Eighties: Crisis and Continuity* (New York: Praeger Special Studies, 1985); and Stephen Padgett and Tony Burkett, *Political Parties and Elections in West Germany: The Search for a New Stability* (London: C. Hurst, 1986).

[40]William E. Paterson, "West Germany: Between Party Apparatus and Basis Democracy," pp. 181, in Alan Ware (ed.), *Political Parties: Electoral Change and Structural Response* (Oxford: Basil Blackwell, 1987); see also, Arthur B. Gunlicks, "The Financing of German Political Parties," pp. 228–45, in Merkl (ed.), *The Federal Republic of Germany at Forty*.

[41]Karl-Heinz Nassmacher, "Oeffentliche Parteienfinanzierung in Westeuropa: Implementationsstrategien und Problembestand in der Bundesrepublik Deutschland, Italien, Oesterreich und Schweden," *Politische Vierteljahresschrift*, vol. 28, no. 1. (March 1987), 109.

[42]Arnold J. Heidenheimer, "Adenauer's Legacies: Party Finance and the Decline of Chancellor Democracy, " and Arthur B. Gunlicks, "The Financing of German Political Parties," pp. 213–45, in Merkl (ed.), *The Federal Republic of Germany at Forty*.

[43]B. Wessels, "Federal Republic of Germany: Business Profits from Politics," p. 148, in M.P.C.M. van Schendelen and R.J. Jackson (eds.), *The Politicisation of Business in Western Europe* (London: Croom Helm, 1987).

[44]Edinger, *West German Politics*, p. 200.

[45]Katzenstein, *Policy and Politics in West Germany*, 14.

[46]This section is based on Hans Baerwald, *Party Politics in Japan* (Boston: Allen & Unwin, 1986); Gerald L. Curtis, *The Japanese Way of Politics* (New York: Columbia University Press, 1988); Michio Muramatsu and Ellis S. Krauss, "The Conservative Policy Line and the Development of Patterned Pluralism," pp. 515–54, in Kozo Yamamura and Yasukichi Yasuba (eds.), *The Political Economy of Japan*, vol. 1 (Stanford: Stanford University Press, 1987); J.A.A. Stockwin, "Parties, Politicians and the Political System," pp. 22–53, in Stockwin et al., *Dynamic and Immobilist Politics in Japan* (Honolulu: University of Hawaii Press, 1988); and J.A.A. Stockwin, "Japan: The Leader-Follower Relationship in Parties," pp. 96–116, in Ware (ed.), *Political Parties.*

[47]Curtis, *The Japanese Way of Politics*, p. 82.

[48]Ibid., pp. 127–33.

[49]Ibid., pp. 177–82.

[50]"Long-Ruling Party Regains Control in Japanese Vote," *New York Times*, February 19, 1990, pp. A1 and A5.

[51]See Stephen Ingle, *The British Party System* (Oxford: Basil Blackwell, 1987); Peter Byrd, "Great Britain: Parties in a Changing Party System," pp. 205–24. in Ware (ed.), *Political Parties*; and George Breckenridge, "Continuity and Change in Britain," pp. 203–21, in Wolinetz (ed.), *Parties and Party Systems in Liberal Democracies*.

[52]Byrd, "Great Britain," p. 212, in Ware (ed.), *Political Parties*.

[53]Ingle, *The British Party System*, p. 67.

[54]Wyn Grant with Jane Sargent, *Business and Politics in Britain* (London: Macmillan Education, 1987), p. 172.

[55]A.G. Jordan and J.J. Richardson, *Government and Pressure Groups in Britain* (Oxford: Clarendon Press, 1987), p. 242.

[56]Vernon Bogdanor, "Financing Political Parties in Britain," in Bogdanor (ed.), *Parties and Democracy in Britain and America* (New York: Praeger, 1984); Grant, *Business and Politics in Britain*, Chapter 8; and Byrd, "Great Britain: Parties in a Changing Party System," in Ware (ed.), *Political Parties*.

[57]Grant, *Business and Politics in Britain*, p. 184; and Bogdanor, "Financing Political Parties in Britain," p. 141.

[58]See Alan Ware, "United States: Disappearing Parties?," pp. 117–36, in Ware (ed.), *Political Parties*; and Steven B. Wolinetz, "The United States: A Comparative View," pp. 269–95, in Wolinetz (ed.), *Parties and Party Systems*.

[59]For a somewhat different interpretation, see Thomas Byrne Edsall, *The New Politics of Inequality* (New York: W.W. Norton, 1984), pp. 67–68.

Chapter 10

Business Associations and Common Interests

Visitors to Washington see the headquarters building of the U.S. Chamber of Commerce across Lafayette Park from the White House. It is a weighty structure from the 1920s that sits on land that was once the site of a mansion occupied by Daniel Webster. From the front windows of the Chamber building, guests look past the statue of Andrew Jackson on horseback in Lafayette Park toward the front, pillared entrance to the White House.

A plaque in the Chamber's foyer explains that the Chamber of Commerce is dedicated to promoting the "national economic welfare". The problem, of course, is that there are different opinions about that welfare. The view of the "national economic welfare" at the Chamber building is not always shared by the leaders of other business associations. Aircraft companies in Seattle have a different perspective on economic welfare than do coal miners in West Virginia or furniture manufacturers in North Carolina.

How are the various views of business represented in the policy process? As noted in Chapter 6, large American companies have established public affairs departments to monitor governmental events and express corporate positions on policy issues. Companies have also created numerous organizations like the Chamber of Commerce to communicate the interests of firms, industries, and regions directly to government.

Systems of representing business interests in the policy process differ by country. The U.S. system of autonomous groups and corporate offices contrasts with the more orderly networks of business associations used to define and communicate business viewpoints in other countries. Some structures for expressing business purposes and perspectives serve a nation's interests more effectively than others. This chapter asks whether the U.S. system for representing business in the policy process helps the country define its common interests or whether it complicates and obscures the pursuit of those interests.

The chapter begins by examining the characteristics of the complex array of American business associations. It then compares these associations to business groups found in Germany, Japan, and the United Kingdom. It investigates the role of business groups in the different countries and assesses their impact on government policy. The chapter concludes by considering whether the practices of business associations in other countries might be used to improve policy making in the United States.

BUSINESS ASSOCIATIONS IN THE UNITED STATES

Business associations in the United States serve three purposes.[1] Some groups provide *management services* that help member firms improve their operations. Associations distribute information on product innovations, train workers, sponsor insurance programs, advise on managerial tasks such as labor relations, undertake advertising campaigns, and gather industry statistics. Most firms could not provide these services alone, or could do so only at greater cost.

Some associations establish *product standards* that assure product quality and facilitate use. In the past, business associations also organized cartels that controlled production levels, fixed prices, and allocated markets. Such anticompetitive practices are now illegal in the United States in most circumstances, but they are permitted in specialized areas such as international trade.[2]

Third, business associations conduct *government relations* activities for their members. Groups monitor events in Congress and the executive branch and disseminate information about new government programs. They also develop policy positions on issues that affect their members, represent the views of members to government officials, and encourage member firms to become politically active.

There is an abundance of business associations in the United States. They are independent of each other and, often, competitors with each other. There are leadership associations with broadly based memberships, limited business groups that have specialized functions, and trade associations that represent members in a specific industry or sector. Table 10–1 lists different associations, the year they were founded, the number of members, and the size of the group's staff and budget.

Leadership Associations

The country's most prominent general business associations are the Chamber of Commerce, the National Association of Manufacturers, and the Business Roundtable.[3]

TABLE 10–1　American Business Associations

ORGANIZATION	YEAR FOUNDED	MEMBER FIRMS	STAFF SIZE	BUDGET ($MILLIONS)
Leadership Associations				
National Association of Manufacturers	1895	13,500	180	$14
Chamber of Commerce of the U.S.	1912	180,000	1100	$65
Business Roundtable	1972	200	16	–
Specialized Business Associations				
The Business Council	1933	230†	3	*
Committee for Economic Development	1942	225†	44	$4
National Federation of Independent Business	1943	520,000	200	$44
American Business Conference	1980	100	10	$2
Selected Trade Associations				
Chemical Manufacturers Association	1872	175	200	$15
American Bankers Association	1875	11,000	400	$62
Motor Vehicle Manufacturers Association	1913	7	109	$14
National Automobile Dealers Association	1917	19,600	320	$10
National Association of Broadcasters	1922	7,500	150	$13
American Trucking Association	1933	3,594	280	$30
Air Transport Association of America	1936	29	125	$8
Pharmaceutical Manufacturers Association	1958	105	90	$10

Sources: D. Burek et al. (eds.), *Encyclopedia of Associations 1990*, Vol.I, Part 1–3 (Gale Research, 1989); and B. Bachman and A. O'Shea, (eds.), *National Trade and Professional Associations of the United States 1988* (Washington, D.C.: Columbia Books, 1988).
* Less than $500,000
† Members are individuals rather than firms.

The National Association of Manufacturers (NAM) is the country's oldest general business group. It has a membership of 13,500 manufacturing firms, an annual budget of $14 million, and a staff of 180. Even though most of its members have fewer than 500 employees, it accounts for about 75 percent of the nation's manufacturing production and employment.

The NAM originally concentrated on the labor relations matters and became a platform in the 1930s for attacks on New Deal policies. Its antiunion, anti–New Deal heritage gave the organization an obstructionist image that has been difficult to shed.

NAM membership peaked in 1957 at 22,000 companies and then began to decline.[4] To slow the membership loss and participate more effectively in national affairs, the association moved its headquarters from New York to Washington. The organization now sponsors policy groups on business subjects and represents the views of its members on national and international topics. It seeks to develop positive positions on economic and industrial issues, but the diversity of its membership has limited its ability to advance forceful positions on controversial topics.[5]

The United States Chamber of Commerce is the largest and most representative business association in the country. It was founded in 1912 at the suggestion of President Taft to provide a sounding board that could represent all segments of the economy, not just manufacturing. The Chamber now has 180,000 corporate members plus several thousand memberships from state and local chambers and trade associations. The large majority of its members are small firms with fewer than ten employees, but large firms also participate vigorously in Chamber affairs.

In the early 1960s, the Chamber stressed its opposition to communism, big government, and welfare expenditures.[6] In recent decades, its positions have become more moderate, and its claim to be the principal representative of business has been more widely accepted. The Chamber has thirty committees and councils that develop policy positions on a range of business issues. Its representatives testify before congressional committees, lobby governmental leaders, and organize litigation to support business positions.

The distinctive features of the Chamber are its elaborate communications apparatus, its extensive grassroots membership, and its influential staff. The Chamber produces a weekly television program and a daily news show, and it publishes the *Nation's Business*, its *Washington Report*, and the *Voice of Business*. The Chamber has used its computer facilities and its network of local chambers to organize district action committees whose members communicate Chamber positions to officials in Congress and the executive branch.

The Chamber's need to consult its members on policy questions restricts its ability to respond to fast-moving issues. Despite this, the Chamber's position at the center of relations among corporations and associations, the ability of its staff to promote its issue positions, and the Chamber's well-organized grassroots network have won it a conspicuous place among the country's most influential business associations.

The Business Roundtable is the newest and one of the most effective business associations. It was established in 1972 from a merger of two small groups concerned about construction costs and labor law.[7] What distinguishes the Roundtable from the NAM or the Chamber of Commerce is that it is made up of the chief executive officers of two hundred major corporations. Membership is by invitation. The chief executives agree to participate directly in Roundtable meetings, chair task forces on specific policy questions, and take part in the organization's lobbying program.

The Roundtable focuses on broad policy questions and avoids single-industry issues. Its Washington activities are guided by a Steering Committee composed of the Washington representatives of twenty-five member companies. The group has developed a pragmatic, accommodationist approach to policy issues and a preference for working behind the scenes. It rarely testifies before Congressional committees, and its nonpublic approach allows the group flexibility in the compromises that occur during the legislative process.

The Roundtable has an uneasy relationship with other business groups. It represents the views of major corporations that are often less antagonistic to labor unions and government regulation than small and medium-sized firms. The Roundtable is criticized by NAM and Chamber lobbyists for being too quick to compromise free enterprise principles in its efforts to reach short-term accommodations.[8] In a recent battle over federal spending, the Chamber of Commerce and the NAM resisted tax-hike proposals, while the Roundtable acknowledged the need for increased revenues.[9]

Specialized Business Associations

General business associations command the most media attention, but specialized groups also play a notable, albeit more limited, role in representing business to government.

The Business Council was established at the beginning of the New Deal era to provide a forum through which government officials and business leaders could exchange views on economic and industrial policy issues. As a quasi-official advisory body, the Council was originally a part of the Commerce Department, but it declared its independence in 1961 when a Commerce Secretary tried to control the group's meeting agenda.

The Business Council is composed of 230 company chairmen or presidents, many of whom are also members of the Business Roundtable. Unlike the Roundtable, however, the Council does not lobby or take formal policy positions. It convenes a few times each year to discuss issues. Administrations use the meetings to build political support for their programs or for an upcoming election, and business leaders attend to promote their firms' causes and display their credentials for future government appointments.

The Committee for Economic Development (CED) was organized in 1942 to help the country avoid economic hardship in the years after World War II. True to its origins, the CED remains a research and information organization. Since its creation, the CED has published several hundred monographs on such topics as hard-core unemployment, the social responsibility of business, the structure of government in metropolitan areas, urban education, international trade, and the like. Its publications generally represent responsible opinions on socially-relevant issues. The organization does not engage in lobbying, but its reports influence the course of policy debates.

The National Federation of Independent Business (NFIB) is the largest group in the country representing the views of small business. About half of its approximately 500,000 members are retailers, and the rest come from construction, manufacturing, wholesaling, finance, agriculture, and professional services.[10]

The organization communicates the opinions of small business to both state and national officials, and the range of its activities has expanded in the last two decades as government has become more active. The distinctive feature of the NFIB is that it regularly polls its members on business issues and then reports the results to Congress and the executive branch. It has an aggressive lobbying program with important grassroots support. The symbolic appeal of small business and its local lobbying sometimes make the NFIB an important ally of the general business associations.

A different segment of the business community is represented by the American Business Conference. Founded in 1980, this organization is an association of chief executives of 100 mid-sized, high-growth companies. Its members head companies with moderate sales and an annual growth rate of 15 percent. These companies often have interests that are different from those of the larger firms represented by the Business Roundtable, and they have been impatient with the pragmatism of the senior organization.

Trade Associations

The resources and influence of trade associations representing specific industries are, in the aggregate, many times larger than those of the more famous leadership associations. While the decade of the 1980s was a period of stability for the general business organizations, it was a time of growth for the trade groups that represent particular industries. The number of trade, business, and commercial associations in the United States grew from 2,900 in 1970 to 3,100 in 1980, an increase of 7 percent. Between 1980 and 1989 the number of associations grew from 3,100 to 3,800, an additional rise of 23 percent.[11]

Many trade associations are small operations with a narrow scope, such as the Frozen Potato Products Institute or the Fresh Garlic Association. Others, however, are prominent organizations such as the American Bankers Association or the American Petroleum Institute that have staffs and budgets that rival or exceed in size those of the broader associations. A 1988 source lists more than one hundred industry and trade groups with annual budgets in excess of more than $5 million.[12] Some associations, such as the Motor Vehicle Manufacturers Association, are composed of a handful of national or international corporations, while other groups, such as the National Automobile Dealers Association, are made up of thousands of local retailers. (See Table 10–1.)

One snapshot of the activities of trade associations is obtained by examining the organization chart of one of the country's largest trade groups, the American Bankers Association, as displayed in Figure 10–1.[13] The ABA was founded in 1875, and its major purpose is to enhance the role of banks in providing financial services. It has a staff of 400 and an annual budget of $62 million. It is directed by a large board and a five-person executive committee.

ABA member banks possess 95 percent of the banking industry's assets. Ten thousand of the ABA's 11,000 members, however, are small community banks. Only a few score are money-center institutions with familiar names.

The ABA focuses its services on smaller banks. One-third of ABA staff comprise the Membership and Administrative Services group that plans conventions, manages publications, and responds to information requests. The Banking

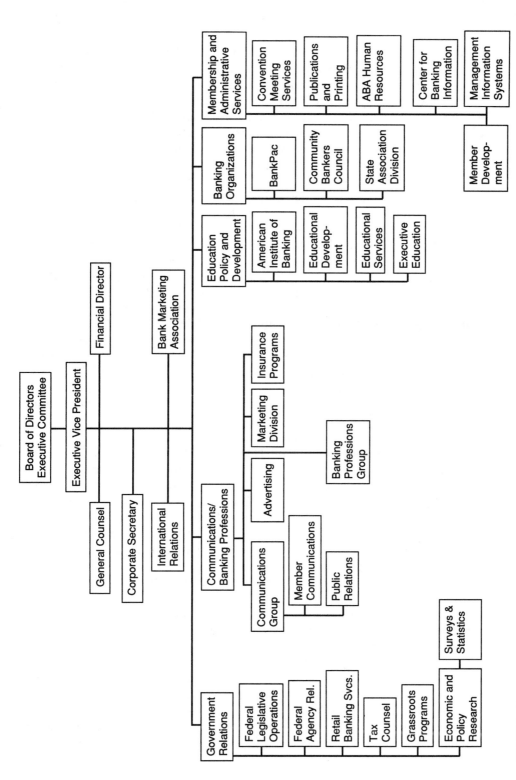

FIGURE 10-1 American Bankers Association Staff Organization Chart. *Source* Adapted from American Banjer's Association, November 1989.

Organizations section works with members to assure that the association is responsive to specialized member concerns. The ABA trains bank employees through its American Institute of Banking and promotes executive development through its educational services program. The Banking Professions group disseminates information about new products, services, and developments in banking occupations. Government relations activities are fundamental to the ABA's members, but they consume only a fraction of the organization's staff and resources.

A similar view of the activities of trade groups comes from recent surveys of associations in manufacturing industries.[14] Eighty-five percent of these trade associations assemble data on their industry's operations, three out of four support public information programs, and about half manage education and training programs for industry employees. Somewhat less than half engage in product-related tasks such as establishing technical standards, developing sales and marketing programs, and encouraging product research and safety. Importantly, the surveys also report that "...the extent to which associations have placed their emphasis on government relations has grown significantly over the last several years."[15] Associations typically create government affairs committees, lobby regulatory agencies and Congress, and hold government affairs conferences.

Despite the extensive array of leadership associations, specialized groups, and trade associations, U.S. companies often break away from established business groups and go their own way. Firms frequently conclude that their associations are not representing their particular interests. Recently, the chief executive of the John Hancock Financial Services corporation testified before a Senate committee in support of a bill that would allow nonbanking companies to operate banks.[16] The bill had been written by the Financial Services Council, a consortium of eighteen companies including John Hancock, American Express, Ford Motor Company, Citicorp, Merrill Lynch, and Sears, Roebuck. The Council had been formed because the companies' primary trade associations, the American Bankers Association, the Securities Industry Association, and the American Council of Life Insurance, opposed the bill and sought to restrict the entry of new firms into the banking industry. The associations represented the fears of their small members who were concerned about increased competition from large companies. Acknowledging the opposition of the established associations, the John Hancock representative said, "...sometimes it makes us wonder why we are paying dues to an organization that lobbies against us."

Even with the variety of business groups, firms often abandon traditional associations and form ad hoc coalitions or operate independently when important issues arise. Each major firm has its own marketplace characteristics and its own relations with suppliers, distributors, employees, and government. The country's cultural traditions emphasize the autonomy of individual firms, and the legal system stresses competition among firms rather than cooperation.[17]

As a consequence of the uncertain tie between associations and individual companies, business groups can never depend on the allegiance of their members. The need to retain the support of their members compels associations to emphasize their ongoing contribution to the specific goals of individual corporations. They also seek to demonstrate to members that they are doing more to advance their goals than other business groups. For this reason, U.S. business associations are reluctant to endorse policies that are opposed by member firms, even if the policies would benefit the national economy or specific industries. Business associations in other countries are stronger and more stable than U.S. groups and are better able to participate in complex policy debates.[18] Other dimensions of these differences become clear when American business associations are compared with groups in other countries.

BUSINESS ASSOCIATIONS: A COMPARATIVE PERSPECTIVE

Business associations can serve the interests of individual firms, promote the health of specific industries, or advance the goals and policies of the government or society. These three orientations are reflected in different models of interest representation: individualism; associationalism; and corporatism.[19]

From the perspective of business associations, individualism is a system of interest representation in which companies act alone or with other firms in a purely voluntary manner to pursue their own particular interests. Individualistic business associations are dependent on member support, independent of government, and have nonhierarchical organizational arrangements.

Associationalism is a system of interest representation in which the focus shifts from firms to entire industries.[20] Companies here assume that their success depends on the health of their industry. Under this model, industry associations acquire an independent status that allows them to champion policies that promote the long-term interests of the industry, even when these policies harm specific companies. Such associations develop financial and organizational independence from the particularistic demands of member companies. They almost become the industry's governing body. The state may help these associations develop the ability to win the endorsement of member firms for proposals that harm their immediate interests.

In a corporatist system, companies are organized into a limited number of functionally defined business associations that have the legal sponsorship of the state. Membership in such associations is often compulsory, and the groups may be authorized by the state to speak for the industry in the public arena. These organizations have a semipublic status, are related to each other hierarchically, and may perform public functions. The boundary between the public and private realm in these circumstances is sometimes blurred. While individualistic business groups express the preferences of companies to government, business organizations under a corporatist model constitute a structure through which governmental decisions are communicated to companies.

The structure of business representation in the United States is individualistic. This system of representation allows companies to pursue their own interests as they see them, and it provides no coercive mechanism to promote the broader interests of an industry or the society. Companies may act alone, as part of an association, or as members of an ad hoc coalition when they believe it is in their benefit to do so. No single business voice emerges from this system of multiple groups, and business representatives often advocate contradictory positions. Firms in Germany, Japan, and the United Kingdom have created business associations whose characteristics differ in significant ways from those of U.S. groups.

Structure of National Associations

Business groups in Germany and Japan are large, hierarchical, and inclusive organizations that have both associational and corporatist characteristics. There is one general business organization in each country for political and economic questions, a separate national group that concentrates on labor-management issues, and a third association that focuses on regional business questions. (See Table 10–2.)

TABLE 10–2   National Business Associations

ASSOCIATION	STRUCTURE
Federal Republic of Germany	
Federation of German Industry	Peak
Confederation of German Employers' Associations	Peak
Diet of German Industry and Commerce	Peak
Japan	
Japan Federation of Economic Organizations	Mixed
Japan Federation of Employers' Associations	Peak
Japan Chamber of Commerce and Industry	Peak
United Kingdom	
Confederation of British Industry	Mixed
Institute of Directors	Direct
Association of British Chambers of Commerce	Peak
United States	
National Association of Manufacturers	Direct
Chamber of Commerce of the United States	Mixed
Business Roundtable	Direct

The members of national business associations in these countries, in contrast to the American practice, are usually other business groups rather than individual companies. The Federation of German Industry is that country's principal business organization.[21] It is made up of forty associations that represent such industries as chemicals, aerospace, textiles, and machinery.[22] These industry associations are, in turn, composed of narrowly defined product associations whose members then are individual companies. A total of 550 specific associations are represented in the Federation of German Industry, which, because of its hierarchical structure, is called a "peak" association. The membership of the individual associations includes 95 percent of all industrial firms but does not include banks and insurance companies. The Federation plays the key role in developing business positions on major economic and political issues and is the principal spokesperson for business viewpoints. The component industry associations deal with issues of concern to their members, but they seek to resolve conflicts with other associations that are Federation members. In this system, business often speaks with a single voice.

The Japan Federation of Economic Organizations is that country's most influential business association.[23] It is a mixed association that may be even more prestigious than the Federation of German Industry and whose membership is more comprehensive.[24] The group is made up of 110 associations representing banks, insurance firms, and the wholesale and retail trade as well as industrial companies. One study notes, "The system approximates a hierarchy in which each level aggregates and reconciles the interests represented at that level."[25] The top executives of the country's largest private enterprises provide the leadership for the Japan Federation of Economic Organizations. It is so highly regarded that its president is often referred to as the "prime minister of business"!

The Confederation of German Employers' Associations and the Japan Federation of Employers' Associations[26] are also peak associations composed of business groups, but they concentrate on industrial relations matters.[27] Employer associations devoted to labor relations questions are common outside the United States, and they resemble the groups that appear in the United States in industries with small employers and dominant unions, such as coal, hotels, or trucking.[28]

Neither the Japanese nor the German employers' association is the actual bargaining agent for employers. Both, however, play a strong hand by devising employer strategies and establishing parameters for the bargaining that occurs between industry groups and unions. Both also seek to influence legislation that defines legal relationships between employers and employees or affects corporate personnel costs.

The Diet of German Industry and Commerce is a different type of business association.[29] The Diet is an obligatory, quasi-public organization composed of sixty-nine local chambers of industry and commerce. Businesses are required by law to be members of the local chamber and pay dues. The local chambers are legally subordinate to the ministries of various state governments, but they preserve substantial operating autonomy. They are legally responsible for representing the economic interests of a region to state and local governments, and they assist in job training programs and assembling regional financial and technical information.

The Japanese Chamber of Commerce and Industry also represents smaller businesses and is composed of regional associations.[30] As with the Diet of German Industry and Commerce, its individual associations are often more influential than the national group, and they can be major players in local government decision making.

Business associations in the United Kingdom combine a few of the associational features of German and Japanese groups with the more individualistic characteristics of American associations.

The foremost British business association is the Confederation of British Industry (CBI).[31] It was created in 1965 from a merger of three independent groups representing large firms, small businesses, and companies in their role as employers. The membership of the CBI is composed of individual firms, industry groups, employer associations, and a few nationalized companies. The CBI staff numbers more than 360, but the organization today has limited influence on its members.[32]

Even with a single, encompassing business association, British business seldom develops a unified position on national policy issues, and it often fails to develop any position at all. The CBI has traditionally represented the opinions of large firms in heavy industries, but these firms now contact government directly whenever priority issues arise. One contemporary study concludes, "the CBI has had relatively limited impact on the major issues which have dominated British politics since its formation."[33]

Recent years have witnessed the emergence of competitors to the CBI. The Institute of Directors was founded in 1903 as a social club, but it expanded its staff and transformed itself in the 1970s into a effective lobbying organization. The group represents the free-market attitudes of individual managers rather than the established, institutional positions of large corporations. The Institute of Directors broke with the CBI to support efforts of the Thatcher government to cut public subsidies to declining industries.

The Association of British Chambers of Commerce has also won an expanded national role in the last decade as a representative of small business.[34] The Association is a weak federation of local chambers, but many local chambers have vigorous and influential regional memberships.

Activities of National Business Associations

Modern business appeared in its present form in the United Kingdom and the United States before the national governments in these countries became dominant factors in economic life. The strength of free-enterprise philosophies in both nations encouraged firms to maintain their autonomy from government and other firms. Business associations in the United Kingdom and the United States remain underdeveloped in comparison to associations in Germany and Japan, and individual companies are more likely to break with business associations when actions of the groups displease them. This limits the ability of groups in the U.S.

and the UK to develop unified positions on policy issues or take stands that are opposed by individual firms.

German and Japanese business associations grew up in an environment in which government was already a principal factor in economic decision making. As a consequence, business associations in these countries are less likely to resent government. The legal systems in these countries are supportive of business associations, communications between government officials and business groups are frequent, and government often provides business groups direct financial support.

Business organizations in Germany and Japan are expected to adopt positions that promote societal and industry interests, not just the interests of individual companies. Business groups in both countries have a quasi-public status that is acknowledged in their countries' constitutions. Henry Jacek has described how business organizations achieve this role:[35]

> As the (business) organization develops from a purely member-dependent voluntary association concerned with urgent, immediate problem-solving to one with a diversified and dependable financial, personnel and status resource base...then the organization staff develops sufficient autonomy to influence both members and potential members.... Indeed, by having such resources the association staff should develop the ability to control member behaviour sufficiently, so as to act as a private interest government.... In this way the special interests of current association members are replaced by more general public interests.

German business associations are expected to help government develop policy solutions to economic problems and then build support for those initiatives. Conflicts among companies are typically resolved in negotiations among association and industry figures. In the United States, in contrast, conflicts among firms and industries are frequently carried into the governmental arena.

Japanese companies are permitted to establish product-oriented associations when their industries face a recession, have excess capacity, or face technological challenge. These associations are authorized to limit competition by setting prices or closing unneeded factories.[36] Japanese associations also receive exemptions from antitrust laws to export goods, divide international markets, monitor foreign commercial and technical developments, and undertake collaborative research. American business groups have no institutional basis for taking positions that could promote social or industry objectives at the expense of individual firms.

Should American business associations be strengthened so that they can develop unified policy positions and advocate proposals that are independent of the parochial interests of individual members? Some maintain that the current pattern of fragmented business representation in the United States leads individual firms and interests to pursue short-term goals without concern for the long-term interests of their industries or of the society.[37] Business organizations and corporations adopt so many conflicting positions that their views have little impact. Such commentators contend that American business associations must be better organized if the United States is to meet the challenges of international competition.[38] Only stronger business groups, they maintain, can play an effective role in promoting efficiency and limiting excessive competition. The individualistic traditions of American and British business mean these countries lack a potentially valuable vehicle for shaping informed, yet dispassionate public policy.

Other scholars maintain that business organizations already dominate the country's political process.[39] Corporations and business associations now constitute an omnipotent force that is able to subvert the popular will at every point in the policy process. The way to improve economic policy making would be to restrict the political activities of individualistic corporations instead of enhancing the effectiveness of business associations.

SUMMARY

The viewpoints of American business on public policy issues are communicated to government officials through corporate government relations offices and an extensive array of business associations. The individualistic pattern of interest representation coincides with the tenets of American political ideology and reflects the country's fear of economic concentration. U.S. business groups have less influence in the policy process than groups elsewhere, are less able to develop unified positions, and less frequently endorse policies that harm individual members.

The political philosophies of Germany and Japan emphasize the positive benefits of collective action. The patterns of interest representation reflect associational and corporatist principles. These countries believe that influential business groups can enhance economic efficiency and improve the conduct of public policy by guiding corporate decision making in responsible ways. Policy proposals hammered out in business associations and then presented to government are thought to be based on a fuller understanding of economic and technical issues and a greater awareness of the need to advance the nation's broad economic and social interests. A strengthening of U.S. industry associations vis-à-vis their member companies could be a constructive option for American business in the 1990s.

SELECTED READINGS

LEONARD H. LYNN and TIMOTHY J. MCKEOWN, *Organizing Business: Trade Associations in America and Japan* (Washington, D.C.: American Enterprise Institute for Public Policy Research, 1988).

GORDON SMITH, WILLIAM E. PATERSON, and PETER H. MERKL, (eds.), *Developments in West German Politics* (Durham, N.C.: Duke University Press, 1989).

WOLFGANG STREECK and PHILIPPE C. SCHMITTER (eds.), *Private Interest Government* (London: Sage Publications, 1985).

M.P.C.M. VAN SCHENDELEN and R.J. JACKSON, (eds.), *The Politicisation of Business in Western Europe* (London: Croom Helm, 1987).

STEPHEN WILKS and MAURICE WRIGHT, (eds.), *Comparative Government-Industry Relations: Western Europe, the United States and Japan* (Oxford: Clarendon Press, 1987).

END NOTES

[1]Louis Galambos, *Competition and Cooperation: The Emergence of a National Trade Association* (Baltimore: Johns Hopkins University Press, 1966), pp. 11–36; and Louis Galambos, "The American Trade Association Movement Revisited," in Hiroaki Yamazaki and Matao Miyamoto, (eds.), *Trade Associations in Business History* (No site: University of Tokyo Press, 1988), pp. 121–35.

[2]The Webb-Pomerene Act of 1918 exempts cartels engaged in foreign trade from the Sherman Antitrust Act.

[3]This section draws upon information from the individual groups and upon Sar A. Levitan and Martha R. Cooper, *Business Lobbies: The Public Good and the Bottom Line* (Baltimore: Johns Hopkins University Press, 1984), Chapters 2–3.

[4]Levitan and Cooper, *Business Lobbies*, p. 16.

[5]David Vogel, *Fluctuating Fortunes: The Political Power of Business in America* (New York: Basic Books, 1989), p. 288.

[6]Vogel, *Fluctuating Fortunes*, p. 34.

[7]Kim McQuaid, *Big Business and Presidential Power: From FDR to Reagan* (New York: William Morrow, 1982), pp. 285–308.

[8]Levitan and Cooper, *Business Lobbies*, p. 39.

[9]Curtis M. Grimm and John M. Holcomb, "Choices Among Encompassing Organizations: Business and the Budget Deficit," in Alfred A. Marcus, Allen M. Kaufman, and David Beam (eds.), *Business Strategy and Public Policy: Perspectives from Industry and Academia* (New York: Quorum Books, 1987), pp. 105–18.

[10]Levitan and Cooper, *Business Lobbies*, p. 41.

[11]*Statistical Abstract of the United States 1990* (Washington, D.C.: Government Printing Office, 1990), p. 786.

[12]B. Bachman and A. O'Shea, (eds.), *National Trade and Professional Associations of the United States 1988* (Washington, D.C.: Columbia Books, 1988), pp. 403–4.

[13]This discussion is drawn from ABA publications and the sources cited for Table 10–1.

[14]National Association of Manufacturers, *Manufacturing Trade Associations: Their Changing Focus and Management*, 1985–1989 editions (Washington, D.C.: NAM, 1985, 1987, and 1989).

[15]NAM, *Manufacturing Trade Associations, 1985*, p. 36.

[16]George Mellon, "What to Do When Your Own Lobby Is Against You," *The Wall Street Journal*, February 16, 1988, p. 37.

[17]Juergen Hartmann, *Verbaende in der westlichen Industriegesellschaft* (Frankfurt: Campus Verlag, 1985), pp. 76–77, 162–87.

[18]Leonard H. Lynn and Timothy J. McKeown, *Organizing Business: Trade Associations in America and Japan* (Washington, D.C.: American Enterprise Institute for Public Policy Research, 1988), pp. 67–68, 172–73, and 56–57.

[19]For a discussion of comparable terms, see Philippe C. Schmitter, "Still the Century of Corporatism?", pp. 7–52, in Schmitter and Gerhard Lehmbruch, (eds.), *Trends Toward Corporatist Intermediation* (Beverly Hills: Sage Publications, 1979); Peter Katzenstein, *Corporatism and Change* (Ithaca: Cornell University Press, 1984); Wolfgang Streeck and Schmitter,

"Community, Market, State—and Associations? The Prospective Contribution of Interest Governance to Social Order," pp. 1–29, in Streeck and Schmitter (eds.) *Private Interest Government: Beyond Market and State* (London: Sage Publications, 1985); Alan Cawson, "Introduction: Varieties of Corporatism: The Importance of the Meso-level of Interest Intermediation," pp. 1–21, in Cawson (ed.), *Organized Interests and the State: Studies in Meso-Corporatism* (London: Sage Publications, 1985); Franz Traxler, "Patterns of Associative Action," Chapter 2, and Henry J. Jacek, "Business Interest Associations as Private Interest Governments," Chapter 3, in Wyn Grant (ed.), *Business Interests, Organizational Development and Private Interest Government: An International Comparative Study of the Food Processing Industry* (Berlin: Walter de Gruyter, 1987); and Michael G. Huelshoff, "West German Corporatism at Forty," Chapter 7, in Peter H. Merkl (ed.), *The Federal Republic of Germany at Forty* (New York: New York University Press, 1989).

[20]Wolfgang Streeck, "Between Pluralism and Corporatism: German Business Associations and the State," *Journal of Public Policy* vol. 3, no. 3 (1983), 265–284.

[21]The name in German is the Bundesverband der Deutschen Industrie (BDI). For the history of German associations see Karl Josef Uthmann and Hermann Freiherr von Wolff-Metternich, *Der Bundesverband der Deutschen Industrie* (Dusseldorf: Droste Verlag, 1974); and Walter Simon, *Macht und Herrschaft der Unternehmerverbaende: BDI, BDA und DIHT im oekonomischen und politischen System der BRD* (Koeln: Pahl-Rugenstein Verlag, 1976).

[22]See Hartmann, *Verbaende in der westlichen Industriegesellschaft*, pp. 81–108.

[23]The name of the group is Keizai Dantai Rengokai (Keidanren). For a history of Japanese associations, see Matao Miyamoto, "The Development of Business Associations in Prewar Japan," pp. 1–45; and Takeo Kikkawa, "Functions of Japanese Trade Associations Before World War II," pp. 53–83, in Yamzaki and Miyamoto (eds.), *Trade Associations in Business History*.

[24]This discussion is drawn from Lynn and McKeown, *Organizing Business*, pp. 78–81; see also Charles J. McMillan, *The Japanese Industrial System*, 2nd ed., (Berlin: Walter de Gruyter, 1989).

[25]Lynn and McKeown, *Organizing Business*, p. 81.

[26]The names of these organizations are, respectively, Bundesvereinigung der Deutschen Arbeitgeberverbaende (BDA) and Nippon Keieisha Dantai Renmei (Nikkeiren).

[27]See Ronald F. Bunn, "Employers Associations in the Federal Republic of Germany," pp. 169–201, and Solomon B. Levine, "Employers Associations in Japan," pp. 318–56, in John P. Windmuller and Alan Gladstone (eds.), *Employers Associations and Industrial Relations: A Comparative Study* (Oxford: Clarendon Press, 1984).

[28]See Milton Derber, "Employers Associations in the United States," pp. 79–114, in Windmuller and Gladstone, *Employers Associations and Industrial Relations*.

[29]The association is called the Deutscher Industrie und Handelstag (DIHT). See Hartmann, *Verbaende in der Westlichen Industriegesellschaft*, pp. 96–98, 102.

[30]Nippon Shiko Kaigisho (Nissho).

[31]This discussion is based on Wyn Grant and David Marsh, *The Confederation of British Industry* (London: Hodder and Stoughton, 1977); Grant, *Business and Politics in Britain*, Chapter 6; Hartmann, *Verbaende in der westlichen Industriegesellschaft*, pp. 109–26; and E.G.A. Armstrong, "Employers Associations in Great Britain," in Windmuller and Gladstone (eds.), *Employers Associations and Industrial Relations*, pp. 44–78.

[32]William Coleman and Wyn Grant, "The Organizational Cohesion and Political Access of Business: A Study of Comprehensive Associations," *European Journal of Political Research* 16 (1988) 467–87.

[33]Grant and Marsh, *The Confederation of British Industry*, p. 207; and A.G. Jordan and J.J. Richardson, *Government and Pressure Groups in Britain* (Oxford: Clarendon, 1987), p. 167.

[34]Wyn, *Business and Politics in Britain*, pp. 128–29.

[35]Henry J. Jacek, "Business Interest Associations as Private Interest Governments," in Grant (ed.), *Business Interests, Organizational Development and Private Interest Government*, pp. 48 and 52.

[36]Lynn and McKeown, *Organizing Business*, pp. 18–45.

[37]Ian Maitland, "Collective Versus Individual Lobbying: How Business Ends Up the Loser," in *Business Strategy and Public Policy*, pp. 96–99.

[38]William G. Ouchi, *The M-Form Society: How American Teamwork Can Recapture the Competitive Edge* (Reading, Mass.: Addison-Wesley, 1984). For an analysis of the United Kingdom, see Wyn Grant, with Jane Sargent, *Business and Politics in Britain* (London: Macmillan Education, 1987).

[39]See, for example, Michael Useem, *The Inner Circle: Large Corporations and the Rise of Business Political Activity in the U.S. and U.K.* (New York: Oxford University Press, 1984) or Mark Green and Andrew Buchsbaum, *The Corporate Lobbies: Political Profiles of the Business Roundtable & the Chamber of Commerce* (Washington, D.C.: Public Citizen, 1980).

Chapter 11

Lobbying Government

Charls Walker is chairman of the board of Charls E. Walker Associates, chairman of the American Council for Capital Formation, and Washington's most acclaimed business lobbyist.[1] With offices down Pennsylvania Avenue from the White House, Walker heads a prestigious lobbying firm that represents fifteen major corporations on a continuing basis and three dozen more as project clients. Walker grew up in northcentral Texas, earned an MBA degree at the University of Texas, and received a doctorate in economics from the University of Pennsylvania's Wharton School. He was a college instructor and an economist for the Federal Reserve Bank in Dallas before he came to Washington as an assistant to the secretary of the Treasury. He later became an official of the American Bankers Association, helped launch the Business Roundtable, and was deputy secretary of the Treasury.

Walker is famous for his gregariousness, shrewdness, energy, and delight in exercising political influence. He specializes in taxation and trade issues, and his clients include such firms as AT&T, DuPont, Ford, and IBM. Walker offers clients his substantive insights, his understanding of Washington customs, and his contacts with top decision makers. Walker flourished during the tax-reform battles of the 1980s. He personified the slow-walking, smooth-talking advocate of tax incentives for savings and investment and promoted his ideas in Congress by framing them in terms of jobs, payrolls, and economic growth.[2]

When major businesses seek to influence congressional decisions, they can retain Charls Walker or one of Washington's 12,500 other contract lobbyists. They can also call on business associations, rely on their public affairs offices, or create an ad hoc coalition to deal with the situation. The form of lobbying usually depends on the impact of the issue and the frequency with which such issues occur. Table 11–1 relates the four patterns of lobbying to the characteristics of issues.

TABLE 11–1   Patterns of Business Lobbying

FREQUENCY OF ISSUE	IMPACT OF ISSUE	
	Specific to Firm	*Uniform among Firms*
Recurring	Public affairs office	Business association
Occasional	Contract lobbyist	Ad hoc coalition

Source: Adapted from Allen M. Kaufman, Ernest J. Englander, and Alfred A. Marcus, "Structure and Implementation in Issues Management: Transaction Costs and Agency Theory," in James E. Post (ed.), *Research in Corporate Social Performance and Policy: A Research Annual—Vol. 11* (Greenwich, Conn.: JAI Press, 1989), pp. 257–71.

When policy issues arise, businesses think first of established business associations. They pay dues to these organizations and believe they should get something in return. If an issue is a recurring one that affects all firms in an industry in a uniform way, a company will turn to a business association. These organizations are eager to defend the interests of their members and prove their worth. Since business groups want to retain the support of all their members, however, they try to avoid issues that involve internal warfare. When an issue pits one member company against another or has a unique impact on a firm, firms cannot depend on their associations for help.

A company's own public affairs department is well suited to lobby on issues that occur frequently but affect the firm in a specific way. A corporation's lobbyists are experts in their own operations, and they can speak authoritatively about how an issue affects their employees and their customers. Corporate lobbyists are loyal to the firm and can take a long-term perspective on the company's problem, but they are ill-prepared to deal with the confrontation and compromise of highly charged controversies.

When an issue affects a company in a specific way but occurs only occasionally, companies often retain contract, for-hire lobbyists, like Charls Walker. Contract lobbyists are extremely knowledgeable about the governmental process, adept at working with people from diverse institutions, and familiar with the pressures of public controversy. They also charge huge fees, but contract lobbyists can provide the specialized expertise that is needed for specific situations.

Some policy proposals affect specific business and nonbusiness interests in unique ways. In these circumstances, representatives of affected groups often create ad hoc coalitions to promote their common objectives. When legislators recently proposed rules that would endanger the future of big cars, for example, representatives of senior citizen groups whose members have trouble getting in and out of small cars, volunteer organizations that transport their members by car, and police associations who prefer powerful cruisers joined with business lobbyists to delay the measure.[3]

Major corporations have options for influencing governmental decisions that most citizens lack. Americans have long feared that the options available to business lobbyists combine to give business excessive influence in the political process. This chapter considers this issue. It begins by examining the types of activities that Charls Walker and other business lobbyists pursue and the informal rules they follow as they practice their craft. The chapter then analyzes the strategies of business lobbyists in a specific situation, the Superfund debate, and it concludes by assessing the impact of business lobbying on public policy.

WHAT DO BUSINESS LOBBYISTS DO?

Business lobbyists have both advantages and handicaps in comparison to representatives of other groups. In a world of elected officials, businesses are not membership groups and, thus, control few votes. They also embody an objective—corporate profitability—that has little popular appeal. On the other hand, business lobbyists generally have good reputations, substantial expertise, broad networks of contacts, and adequate funding.[4] Furthermore, their firms provide products that people want. Business lobbyists draft legislation, find sponsors for bills, develop arguments, shape coalitions, and steer a proposal through the pitfalls of the legislative process. Successful lobbyists follow a set of rules that reflects principles common to all lobbying activities but has particular significance for business. What are the rules for being a successful lobbyist?[5]

Cultivate Key Figures

Two decades ago, the tone of business representation in Washington was set by a small group of elite lobbyists from firms like Procter & Gamble, U.S. Steel, General Motors, and American Cyanamid, and lobbying activities were based on personal access to a few powerholders.[6] Lobbyists from this era knew where to buy good cigars, find the best restaurants, and obtain tickets to Redskins games.

Today, the nature of the lobbying process has changed. The circles of the influence in Washington in the 1990s are wider than in the past. Top legislative leaders share influence with subcommittee chairs, individual members, and even senior staff aides. Furthermore, the ability of a few corporate lobbyists to set the political strategy of business has waned. New corporations and industry groups from the South and the West have gained prominence, and they are not willing to follow the lead of a few established figures.

Private contact with a handful of top public officials is not all there is to lobbying today, but lobbyists still play golf at prestigious clubs and cultivate personal relationships. Being known by key people and maintaining communications provide the basis for cooperation when controversies arise. Business representatives usually have the stature and the resources to sustain these contacts. Corporate groups sometimes hire former legislators, ex-staff aides, and consultants who build on personal relationships with officeholders to present corporate positions.[7]

Develop a Good Argument

Lobbying has become a more analytic and substantive process in recent years. As Congress responds to a growing array of social problems, government involves itself ever more deeply in business operations. As proposals for legislative intervention in business become more sophisticated, assessments of their impact become more analytic. Lobbyists today are no longer trained as salespersons but as attorneys, MBAs, accountants, policy analysts, economists, and technical people.

Elected officials are not experts in substantive matters, but they want to have publicly defensible, analytically sound reasons for supporting a proposal. To satisfy the need for a good argument, supposedly objective studies by independent experts are often commissioned by Washington lobbyists as a part of lobbying campaigns. Outside consultants can be retained today to study almost any facet of a legislative proposal and assess its impact on specific companies and congressional districts.

Consulting firms insist that their work is unbiased, but they are not hired to contradict the positions of the groups that pay them.[8] A recent account of tax-reform legislation discovered that opponents had funded dozens of studies of the allegedly disastrous effects of proposals they opposed. According to the studies, the new tax plan would raise apartment rents by 20 percent to 40 percent, displace millions of workers in export industries, and jeopardize "the oral health of the American people." Horse breeding would fall 18 percent, canned tuna would become obsolete, and American Samoa would be devastated. Whatever their shortcomings, these studies provide a measure of the thinking of their sponsors, and they have a meaningful impact on the legislative process.

Nurture the Grassroots

The aphorism that all politics are local underlines the fact that members of Congress are elected from specific districts.[9] Electoral cycles require legislators to be attentive, at least periodically, to the sentiments of their constituents. Politicians, however, are usually less concerned about the amorphous opinions of the general public than about the more focused views of a smaller group of attentive citizens who care intensely about a issue and may base their future electoral support on that issue.

Washington lobbyists have long relied on "grassroots" techniques to remind legislators that important constituents are interested in what they do on specific issues. Lobbyists often have local citizens meet with legislators to "educate" them about the perspectives of their group and convince the lawmakers of the seriousness of their views. Organizations like the Chamber of Commerce and corporations like Schering-Plough have built impressive networks of local activists who can be relied upon to contact district legislators.[10] Ninety percent of trade association lobbyists and 80 percent of corporate representatives recruit influential constituents to carry their message to district legislators.[11]

In the 1960s, a high-tech form of grassroots lobbying was popularized by Common Cause when it sent computerized appeals to its contributors urging them to contact senators and representatives on specific issues.[12] Ideological groups later realized that they too were able to orchestrate "spontaneous" expressions of citizen concern; and, finally, corporations and business associations recognized that their networks of suppliers, dealers, employees, stockholders, and customers could be encouraged to speak out on critical proposals.[13]

The most famous instance of grassroots lobbying occurred in the 1980s when Congress decided to increase tax revenues by withholding some of the interest paid on savings accounts.[14] Bankers were angry about the new requirement because withholding would increase their paperwork costs and require them to explain to angry customers why their money had been withheld from them.

In the era of high-tech grassroots lobbying, the American Bankers Association hired a market-research firm to hold a series of small-group discussions. When the legislation was explained, citizens were irate. They were unconcerned about the administrative problems of bankers, but they were incensed that government wanted to withhold money from kids with paper routes, senior citizens, and the poor. To encourage citizens to express their views, the ABA distributed an information kit that included sample letters to be sent to local newspaper editors, brochures for customers, and special statements for senior citizens.

As a result, customers sent 22 million pieces of mail to Congress opposing the new withholding scheme, more mail than Congress had ever received on a single issue. Legislation repealing the withholding plan was passed by both houses and enacted into law over the president's objections.

The ABA succeeded in winning repeal of the withholding measure because the group's objective coincided with a widely held public sentiment and because the ABA had the ability to mobilize millions of citizens to express their views.

Build Coalitions

Contemporary lobbying conditions frequently lead business representatives to form specialized legislative coalitions. Individual legislative proposals usually affect some corporations in important ways but leave most firms apathetic and unconcerned. Established business or industry associations often find their members divided over the desirability of supporting or opposing specific measures. As a consequence, broad business groups often remain silent on critical issues and ad hoc coalitions emerge to exchange information and coordinate strategies on specific pieces of legislation.[15]

Business groups have been most successful in achieving their legislative objectives when they are able to forge coalitions with citizen, labor, and community organizations. These coalitions are an important vehicle for coordinating grassroots and other types of lobbying activities.

Understand PACs

Money has been a prominent tool of business involvement in politics for a century, but the mechanisms of participation have changed. In 1896, the head of the Republican National Committee financed the McKinley presidential campaign through systematic assessments on large corporations.[16] In response, the Tillman Act of 1907 made it illegal for businesses to contribute to federal campaigns. This law was often evaded. After the 1972 election, twenty-one companies were found guilty of having made illegal campaign contributions, mostly to the campaign of President Nixon.

Political Action Committees

PACs originated in the labor movement in 1943. When Congress extended to unions the rule that organizational funds could not be contributed to political candidates, the CIO set up a fund to receive and disperse voluntary contributions from its members.

Campaign reform laws in the 1970s popularized the use of PACs. Corporations, unions, trade or membership associations, agricultural cooperatives, and partnerships were all authorized to use their funds to establish PACs and pay their administrative costs. PACs can also be independent of outside sponsorship.

PACS can receive donations from individuals or other PACs, give funds to federal candidates, or use the funds for political purposes that are independent of specific federal campaigns. Corporations and other sponsors are still prohibited from giving organizational funds to federal candidates.

The maximum amount any individual can contribute to a PAC is $5,000 per year, and PAC contributions are limited to $5,000 per candidate per election. Individuals may contribute no more than $25,000 per year to federal candidates, directly or through PACs, and no more than $1,000 to an individual candidate's campaign committee per election. Most contributions to corporate PACs come from the company's executives.

Source: Edward Zuckerman, *Almanac of Federal PACs: 1988* (Washington, D.C.: Amward Publications, 1988).

New campaign finance laws in the 1970s redefined the rules for funding federal elections and established political action committees (PACs) as the most conspicuous vehicle for financing campaigns.[17] PACs are either sponsored by an organization or unconnected to any specific group. The PACs that contribute the largest amounts to federal candidates are sponsored by membership associations such as the realtors, doctors, or trial lawyers; or by labor unions, such as the Teamsters, auto workers, or letter carriers. In the period from 1989 to1990, seven of the ten largest PAC contributors to federal candidates were associated with unions, and three were sponsored by trade and membership associations.[18] The realtors' PAC was the largest contributor, with donations of more than $3 million, and the runner-up was the PAC sponsored by the American Medical Association, which contributed $2.4 million.

Corporate PACs are smaller than labor or association PACs, but are more numerous. (See Table 11–2.) During the years 1989 to 1990, the largest corporate PAC, sponsored by AT&T, ranked thirteenth on the overall list of PAC contributors, and only five of the fifty largest PACs were sponsored by corporations. The AT&T PAC gave federal candidates $1.5 million between 1989 and 1990, while the typical "large" corporate PAC donated between $250,000 to $400,000 to federal candidates.

TABLE 11–2 Largest Corporate PACs, 1989–1990

NAME OF PAC	CONTRIBUTIONS TO FEDERAL CANDIDATES
1. AT&T PAC	$1,457,360
2. Federal Express Corporation PAC	$756,950
3. RJR Nabisco PAC	$720,500
4. UPS PAC	$661,332
5. Philip Morris PAC	$573,410
6. Union Pacific Fund for Effective Government	$512,614
7. Barnett Banks People for Better Government	$462,050
8. American Family Corporation PAC	$430,250
9. Lockheed PAC	$425,159
10. Northrop Employees PAC	$411,775

Source: Federal Election Commission, March 31, 1991.

Despite the relatively modest size of individual corporate PACs, contributions from corporate PACs in the aggregate are still quite significant. In the period 1989 to 1990, corporate PACs contributed $58 million to federal candidates, or 36 percent of the $159 million federal candidates received from all PAC sources. Membership association PACs contributed $44 million to federal candidates in that election cycle, and labor-sponsored PACs gave $35 million.

PACs generally favored incumbents and Democrats. Four out of every five PAC dollars went to incumbents in the period 1989 to 1990, as is displayed in Table 11–3, and three of every five dollars were received by Democrats. Not all PACs act in same ways. Labor PACs directed 93 percent of their contributions to Democratic candidates and were somewhat more likely to support challengers than other PACs.

TABLE 11–3 Contributions of PACs to Federal Candidates, 1989–1990

TYPE OF PAC	NUMBER OF PACS	TOTAL CONTRIB.	PARTY OF RECIPIENT		STATUS OF RECIPIENT		
			Dem.	*Rep.*	*Incum.*	*Chall.*	*Open*
All PACs	4681	$159M	62%	38%	79%	10%	11%
Corporate	1965	$58M	47%	53%	83%	9%	8%
Membership	796	$44M	55%	45%	83%	7%	10%
Labor	372	$35M	93%	7%	71%	15%	14%
Other	1548	$22M	64%	36%	74%	12%	14%

Source: Federal Election Commission, March 31, 1991.

The behavior of corporate PACs has changed from election to election. In general, however, they are cautious. They contribute an even greater share of their funds to incumbents than the average PAC and slightly more to Republicans than to Democrats.[19] Corporate PACs give the largest share of their contributions to legislators who are members of committees that handle issues that concern them.[20] They also favor candidates who have supportive ideologies, have backed the firm on important issues, and represent districts where the corporation has facilities. In contrast, membership PACs and labor PACs place greater emphasis on how legislators have voted on a few key issues.

Use Other Political Money Carefully

PACs receive considerable media attention, but they are only one way of using money to participate in politics, and, from some perspectives, not the most important way. There are a variety of non-PAC avenues for dispensing money that are available to corporations, unions, and others seeking to influence governmental decisions.

Individuals contribute a larger share of campaign funds than do PACs. While little influence attaches to a single contribution, corporate representatives can become prominent fundraisers for a candidate and gather numerous contributions from people affiliated with a single firm. Trade associations can also support a candidate by collecting personal checks from individuals and then presenting the checks to the campaign in a bundle. These practices allow the fundraisers to gain "credit" for large contributions that would be illegal if presented in a single check.

PAC laws regulate campaign donations to federal candidates, but they leave other types of political contributions unchecked.[21] Corporations and unions are permitted to make contributions from their treasuries to support national party operations, voter registration drives, party-building activities, and even some state-level campaigns. Such donations are called "soft" money, and, according to journalistic reports, they soared from $55 million per year in the early 1980s, to more than $140 million in 1988.[22]

In recent years, some legislators have established or become affiliated with foundations that receive large tax-deductible contributions from organizations and individuals with legislative interests. Sometimes these charitable foundations contribute to the election activities of the political figure with whom they are aligned. A foundation associated with California's Senator Cranston conducted voter registration drives with funds received from financially shaky savings and loan associations, the Teamsters union, the trial lawyers, and the National Association of Letter Carriers.[23] On other occasions, members of the House or Senate solicit funds for conventional charities or even for presidential libraries, but these activities, too, provide lobbyists an opportunity to gain the thanks of officeholders.

A more direct way of focusing the attention of legislators on an organization's issues is to pay legislators appearance fees. Moneyed groups have paid Senators and House members "honoraria" to attend their functions, speak to their groups, and brief them on issues. Such organizations as the Tobacco Institute and the Outdoor Advertising Association have paid legislators more than $100,000 per year to meet with their officials and discuss their legislative problems.[24] A standard fee is $2,000 per appearance, and all expenses are covered when the meeting is held at a posh resort in a faraway setting.

Assist in Campaigns

In general, business people stay away from electoral politics in droves.[25] A few corporate leaders participate in presidential, gubernatorial, or senatorial campaigns, but they avoid less visible races and shun ongoing party activities. While 88 percent of corporate lobbyists contribute to election campaigns, only 28 percent of business organizations publish information on voting records, 14 percent donate services to campaigns, and 8 percent endorse candidates.[26] Representatives of nonbusiness interests contribute less often to campaigns but participate more frequently in other forms of campaign activity.

Despite the reluctance of business, legislators want all the campaign support they can get. Lobbyists who participate in campaigns do so for one of two reasons. They either want to enhance the election chances of officeholders who are sympathetic to their cause or to affect the conduct of officials who are going to win anyway. Campaign activities in one election indicate to politicians that an organization will probably be active in upcoming elections. Such an organization might throw its support to another candidate if the official is insensitive to its goals. The frequency with which campaign consultants become contract lobbyists is a measure of the effectiveness of assisting in campaigns as a technique for gaining access for lobbying.[27]

SUPERFUND: A CASE STUDY

The significance of various lobbying techniques and the effectiveness of business lobbying can be assessed by discussing a specific legislative issue: the response of the chemical industry to proposals to create a federal Superfund to clean up hazardous-waste dump sites.[28]

The basic issue in the Superfund debate in the 1980s was whether the clean-up of waste sites would be paid for by ordinary revenues or a special tax on the chemical industry. Representatives of the Commerce Department, the Council of Economic Advisers, and the Office of Management and Budget preferred government funding of clean-up sites, while the EPA, the Council on Environmental Quality, and the Occupational Safety and Health Administration argued for industry payments. The president originally favored an 80 percent/20 percent split between industry and government.

The chemical industry's frequent involvement with pollution issues had led to an expansion of the public affairs role of the Chemical Manufacturers Association (CMA) and the establishment of public affairs units in the industry's largest firms. The CMA's position on the Superfund was that cleaning up hazardous waste sites was a public responsibility that should be financed by the federal government. "The Administration's bill unfairly singles out the chemical and related industries," the CMA argued. "In doing so, it fails to adequately reflect the society's responsibility for resolving a problem which everyone has helped create and for whose solution everyone should help pay."[29] The CMA strategy was to have the proposal referred to numerous subcommittees, confuse the legislative issues, and hope the bill would die of complications.

Major firms in the industry approached the bill in terms of their own situations. Union Carbide had a large public affairs program with a headquarters unit, a Washington office, and several regional offices for dealing with states and localities. It was noted for assigning "issue managers" to key topics and involving operating executives in its public affairs effort. The Monsanto public affairs structure resembled that of Union Carbide and added a vigorous grassroots program. Dow Chemical had a corporate-level public affairs office but no regional offices. It was recognized as a leader in PAC spending and organization. Public affairs at DuPont devoted substantial attention to issue analysis and forecasting and left lobbying to the legal department. DuPont did not have a PAC, but it was headed by a activist CEO (Irving Shapiro) who was a crusader for corporate social responsibility.

Dow advocated a hard-line strategy of resistance to Superfund proposals. Dow insisted that it was already paying the costs of treating its own wastes in its own facilities and reasoned that it did not want to pay to clean up others' waste dumps. Dow was joined by Union Carbide and DuPont in pushing the CMA to stand against industry funding of the Superfund. Monsanto was concerned about the industry's public image and advocated a compromise to limit the companies' eventual costs, but it publicly supported the CMA position.

The opposition of hard-liners and Monsanto's grassroots program had slowed the pace of Superfund legislation, but the industry then made a critical blunder. The head of the CMA appeared on ABC's *Nightline* and said that the industry supported a bill that would apportion 75 percent of the costs of clean-ups to the industry and only 25 percent to government. The next day he announced that his statement had been misinterpreted, but the damage was done, and a bill requiring industry to pay 75 percent of the costs promptly passed the House of Representatives.

It appeared that the legislation might get caught up in an election-year rush in the Senate, but differences of opinion within the CMA began to surface. Union Carbide became convinced that the industry could not win a public debate over the Superfund issue and began to press for moderation and compromise. The CEO of DuPont then expressed his support in an interview in the *New York Times* for immediate legislation to clean up hazardous waste sites. The CMA position fragmented even further. Senate sponsors of the legislation sensed victory and pressed ahead with a bill that required the industry to contribute 87.5 percent of the costs, and this bill was soon passed by the Senate, accepted by the House, and signed by the president. The Superfund was renewed in subsequent years and increased in size, but it has been an administratively cumbersome law that has cleaned up relatively few waste sites.

What light do the events surrounding the creation of the Superfund shed on the effectiveness of business lobbying?

Foreign Lobbying in the United States

Newspaper accounts of the activities of lobbyists for foreign governments and international corporations remind Americans of George Washington's warning in his Farewell Address against the "insidious wiles of foreign influence."

Lobbyists who undertake political or public relations tasks for foreign clients are required by the Foreign Agents Registration Act to register as "foreign agents" with the Justice Department. Campaign spending by the U.S. subsidiaries of foreign firms is regulated according to the standards that are used to regulate the conduct of U.S. firms. The effectiveness of these laws is now being called into question by former officials who seek out foreign clients immediately after they leave office and by the growing involvement of international organizations in the U.S. election process.

Pat Choate in *Agents of Influence* has recently focused attention on the activities of lobbyists for Japanese organizations in the United States. Choate argues that "...the Japanese have the most extensive, sophisticated, and successful political-economic machine in the United States." He reports that

Japanese companies and government agencies employed 140 U.S. lobbying and public relations firms in 1990, at a cost of $100 million, to influence Washington decision making. According to Choate, the Japanese goal is to "co-opt politicians, shape public opinion, finance political campaigns, silence or isolate critics, and blackball appointees to high federal positions."

Source: Deborah M. Levy, "Advice for Sale," *Foreign Policy* (Summer 1987), pp. 64–86; and Pat Choate, *Agents of Influence* (New York: Knopf, 1990), pp. xiii–xvi.

BUSINESS LOBBYING: PLURALISM OR HEGEMONY?

The fear that lobbying, especially business lobbying, gives moneyed groups disproportionate influence in the political process is an abiding concern of American voters. Every year corporations and other groups spend hundreds of millions of dollars to influence congressional decisions because they think these expenditures are effective. The Washington pressure-group community overrepresents business interests and neglects those who lack the resources to make themselves heard.[30] While supporters regard business involvement in politics as a legitimate and usually defensive activity, critics see the linkage of economic with political power as a particularly ominous phenomenon.

Despite citizen concerns, political scientists are surprisingly unable to provide systematic evidence that lobbying has an independent impact on congressional decisions. To assess business lobbying and understand the inconsistency between popular and academic views, the following section explores the arguments of those who maintain that business lobbying has little impact on policy decisions.

Rationale for Limited Impact of Business Lobbying

Four explanations are offered for the view that business lobbying has limited influence on congressional decisions: poor use of resources; countervailing pressures; primacy of public opinion; and normal patterns of interest-group support.

Commentators recognize that business is a resourceful participant in the political process, but observers maintain that business lobbyists do not utilize their resources effectively. They note that business generally has poor political intelligence and is forever seeking to catch up with events after they occur.[31] Part of the reason that business suffered a series of political defeats in the 1960s and 1970s, from this perspective, was that business representatives continued to rely on a lobbying style that emphasized insider negotiations after the congressional system had opened up and power had been fragmented.[32] Business lobbyists often misread events, became inflexible when they should have compromised, and abandoned their goals when victory was at hand.

Business also fails to coordinate its efforts adequately or to develop coalitions with small business and non-business groups. A recent study of legislation that increased corporate taxes concluded that the firepower of business "was potentially fatal to any piece of legislation," but also pointed out that business groups "never managed to form an effective 'killer' coalition."[33] Business frequently fails to achieve its policy objectives, according to this view, because it manages political resources poorly. The leaders of the CMA and DuPont made public statements during the Superfund debate that significantly undermined the industry's position.

Second, analysts believe that the lobbying power of business can be formidable when the business community is mobilized and united, but they maintain that this almost never occurs. Business interests are fundamentally diverse, and nothing can offset this diversity. Few issues mobilize the business community as a whole; but even on these topics, business representatives espouse disparate viewpoints.[34] When some business advocates take a public position on an issue, they are usually met by a chorus of lobbyists from other business groups championing a contradictory policy.[35] One liberal House member assessed the lobbying of the financial community in these terms:

> Business PACs invest in incumbents. It's the banks against the thrifts, the insurance companies against the banks, the Wall Street investment banks against the money center commercial banks. There's money any way you vote.[36]

In such conditions, the efforts of business lobbyists to push public policy in one direction or another have little impact on the decisions that are eventually made. The divisions among companies on the Superfund issue illustrate this point.

Third, some studies of congressional lobbying question whether business is as influential as is usually thought under any circumstances. On the basis of their review of congressional action on regulatory issues, Derthick and Quirk write:

> We suspect that, whatever may have been true in the past, interest group regimes today derive much of their apparent power merely from the absence of challenges...and not from any reliable ability to defeat such challenges when they occur.... (B)ehind their bloodless victories...lies far more vulnerability than has generally been supposed.[37]

These authors maintain that particularistic political pressures are less important in determining the outcome of an issue than broader patterns of public sentiment. A study of environmental legislation and a cross-national review of business lobbying also conclude that business success in influencing legislative decisions depends less on lobbying tactics than on broad currents of public opinion.[38] Throughout the Superfund debate, participants based their strategies on assessments of public sentiments toward the chemical industry and the environment.

Finally, some investigations do find a modest relationship between business lobbying, particularly PAC contributions, and the actions of individual legislators, but these cases still do not demonstrate that lobbying caused the actions that followed.[39] Legislators receive lobbying attention and campaign support from a group because they are disposed to support that group. The coincidence of lobbying activities and the subsequent action of members of Congress could illustrate the normal practice of interest group support and the belief of legislators that their constituents would agree with the arguments made by the lobbyists.

Synthesis: The Context of Lobbying

The case for the limited impact of business lobbying has some appeal, but the argument fails to explain why journalists and businesses attribute such importance to lobbying activities. It fails to consider the context in which lobbying occurs.[40] Rather than reaching an overall conclusion about the impact of lobbying, it is more valuable to identify the circumstances in which business advocates have greater or lesser impact.

Consistent with the arguments presented above, business lobbyists have less impact in situations that involve well developed public attitudes, dozens of competing lobbyists, and a multitude of divergent perspectives. Proposals to abolish private enterprise and the market economy would presumably unify and mobilize business. Such viewpoints make little headway, in part, because of the anticipation of business opposition, but also because of the absence of public support. Issues that pit labor unions against management usually inspire unified business opposition, but the outcome typically depends on which side can persuade the public of the validity of its position.

Most legislative issues, however, are specialized questions that involve a single industry or firm. Such issues attract little public attention and little countervailing lobbying activity. In these circumstances, the blandishments of a few resourceful lobbyists can have a decisive effect on congressional decisions. (Recall the discussion of the savings and loan issue in Chapter 7.)

Those who describe business lobbying as either omnipotent or inconsequential paint too simple a picture. Industry advocates are sometimes powerful, sometimes self-serving, and sometimes supportive of issues that benefit consumers. Judgments about the impact of business lobbying must be made in terms of specific situations. The overall conclusions of analysts, however, frequently depend more on the ideological premises with which they began than on the evidence they encountered.

SUMMARY

Corporations communicate their views to officeholders through business associations, their public affairs offices, contract lobbyists, or ad hoc coalitions. The selection of the particular form of lobbying depends on the frequency of the issue and its impact on specific firms.

Corporate lobbyists have distinct advantages and disadvantages in the political process, but they follow a set of rules that are common to all lobbying activities: cultivate key figures; develop good arguments; nurture the grassroots; build coalitions; understand PACs; use other political money carefully; and assist in campaigns.

Suspicions that business lobbyists have excessive political influence are widely held, but academics have had little success in demonstrating the impact of lobbying on political decisions. Business lobbying tends to be most influential when an issue attracts little attention and generates little organized opposition or when business objectives coincide with public sentiments. Lobbying has less impact when issues are widely debated and when the positions of specific public officials will be widely known.

SELECTED READINGS

JEFFREY H. BIRNBAUM and ALAN S. MURRAY, *Showdown at Gucci Gulch: Lawmakers, Lobbyists, and the Unlikely Triumph of Tax Reform* (New York: Random House, 1988).

PAT CHOATE, *Agents of Influence* (New York: Knopf, 1990).

THEODORE J. EISMEIER and PHILIP H. POLLOCK, *Business, Money, and the Rise of Corporate PACs in American Elections* (New York: Quorum Books, 1988).

BROOKS JACKSON, *Honest Graft: Big Money and the American Political Process* (Washington, D.C.: Farragut, 1990).

ROBERT B. REICH and JOHN D. DONAHUE, *New Deals: The Chrysler Revival and the American System* (New York: Penguin Books, 1985).

END NOTES

[1]This section is drawn from Elizabeth Drew, "Charlie: A Portrait of a Lobbyist," in Allan J. Cigler and Burdett A. Loomis (eds.), *Interest Group Politics* (Washington, D.C.: CQ Press, 1983), pp. 217–50; and *Beacham's Guide to Key Lobbyists: An Analysis of Their Issues and Impact* (Washington, D.C.: Beacham, 1989), pp. 522–27.

[2]See Jeffrey H. Birnbaum and Alan S. Murray, *Showdown at Gucci Gulch: Lawmakers, Lobbyists, and the Unlikely Triumph of Tax Reform* (New York: Random House, 1988), pp. 16–18, 48, 50, and 200.

[3]Robert E. Norton, "Can Business Win in Washington?", *Fortune*, December 3, 1990, p. 80.

[4]Edwin M. Epstein, *The Corporation in American Politics* (Englewood Cliffs, N.J.: Prentice Hall, 1969), pp. 67–69.

[5]The following discussion is drawn from a presentation by Raymond H. Bateman, "How To Be a Successful Lobbyist," Rutgers University Political Science Department, March 26, 1988.

[6]Thomas Byrne Edsall, *The New Politics of Inequality* (New York: Norton, 1984), pp. 113–15.

[7]See, for example, Robert B. Reich and John D. Donahue, *New Deals: The Chrysler Revival and the American System* (New York: Penguin Books, 1985), p. 113.

[8]This example is drawn from Birnbaum and Murray, *Showdown at Gucci Gulch*, pp. 111–12.

[9]This section is based on Kay Lehman Schlozman and John T. Tierney, *Organized Interests and American Democracy* (New York: Harper & Row, 1986), pp. 184–98.

[10]See Schering-Plough's *Voice*, "Grassroots Network: A Program of Political Development," Fall 1989 and subsequent issues.

[11]Scholtzman and Tierney, *Organized Interests and American Democracy*, (New York: Harper & Row, 1986), p. 173.

[12]Andrew S. McFarland, *Common Cause: Lobbying in the Public Interest* (Chatham, N.J.: Chatham House, 1984).

[13]Burdett A. Loomis, "A New Era: Groups and the Grass Roots," pp. 169–90, in Cigler and Loomis (eds.), *Interest Group Politics*; and Charles S. Mack, *Lobbying and Government Relations: A Guide for Executives* (New York: Quorum Books, 1989), Chapter 8, "Grass-Roots Lobbying."

[14]Robert L. Heath and Richard Alan Nelson, *Issues Management: Corporate Public Policymaking in an Information Age* (Beverly Hills: Sage Publications, 1986), pp. 101–103.

[15]Sar A. Levitan and Martha R. Cooper, *Business Lobbies: The Public Good and the Bottom Line* (Baltimore: Johns Hopkins University Press, 1984), pp. 140–42.

[16]George Thayer, *Who Shakes the Money Tree? American Campaign Financing Practices from 1789 to the Present* (New York: Simon and Schuster, 1973), pp. 48–50; and Michael J. Malbin, "Looking Back at the Future of Campaign Finance Reform: Interest Groups and American Elections," pp. 232–76, especially 243–47, in Michael J. Malbin (ed.), *Money and Politics in the United States: Financing Elections in the 1980s* (Chatham, N.J.: Chatham House, 1984).

[17]For fuller reviews, see Robert E. Mutch, *Campaigns, Congress, and Courts: The Making of Federal Campaign Finance Law* (New York: Praeger, 1988); Larry J. Sabato, *PAC Power* (New York: W.W. Norton, 1984; and Frank J. Sorauf, *Money in American Elections* (Glenview, Ill.: Scott, Foresman, 1988).

[18]See Federal Election Commission, "PAC Activity Falls in 1990 Election," March 31, 1991.

[19]Theodore J. Eismeier and Philip H. Pollock, *Business, Money, and the Rise of Corporate PACs in American Elections* (New York: Quorum Books, 1988); and Edward Handler and John R. Mulkern, *Business in Politics: Campaign Strategies of Corporate Political Action Committees* (Lexington, Mass.: Lexington Books, 1982).

[20]See J. David Gopoian, "What Makes PACs Tick? An Analysis of the Allocation Patterns of Economic Interest Groups," *American Journal of Political Science* 28 (May 1984), 259–81; and Schlozman and Tierney, *Organized Interests and American Democracy*, p. 240.

[21]Elizabeth Drew, *Politics and Money: The New Road to Corruption* (New York: Macmillan, 1983); and Herbert E. Alexander, *"Soft Money" and Campaign Financing* (Washington, D.C.: Public Affairs Council, 1986).

[22]Brooks Jackson, *Honest Graft: Big Money and the American Political Process*, rev. ed. (Washington, D.C.: Farragut, 1990); "Bush, Dukakis Presidential Campaigns Each Spent More than $100 Million," *Wall Street Journal*, December 12, 1988, p. A14; and "Democrats Identify Sources of Unregulated Money," *New York Times*, May 26, 1990, p. A9.

[23]Richard L. Berke, "Cranston Inquiry Widens to Include Signups of Voters," *New York Times*, December 6, 1989, p. 1, B10; and Berke, "How Cash Is Given to Politicians' Interests," *New York Times*, December 10, 1989, p. E1.

[24]"Interest Groups Pay Millions in Appearance Fees to Get Legislators to Listen as Well as to Speak," *Wall Street Journal*, June 4, 1985, p. 62; "Virginian Defends Paying Congressmen Who Toured Coal Mines," *New York Times*, June 16, 1986, p. B10; and "Fees that Lobbyists Routinely Pay Lawmakers to Get Acquainted Raise Questions About Ethics," *Wall Street Journal*, December 17, 1987, p. 64.

[25]There are, of course, exceptions. See, Ronald Brownstein, "So You Want To Go Into Politics?", *Inc.*, November 1985, pp. 98–107; and Nicholas Lemann, "New Tycoons Reshape Politics," *New York Times Magazine*, June 8, 1986, pp. 51, 94, 101, and 102.

[26]Schlozman and Tierney, *Organized Interests and American Democracy*, p. 211.

[27]Monica Langley, "Black, Manafort & Stone Cuts Controversial Path Between Campaign Consulting and Lobbying," *Wall Street Journal*, December 23, 1985, p. 38; and Thomas B. Edsall, "The Power Is Inside, but the Money Is Outside," *Washington Post National Weekly Edition*, December 5, 1985, pp. 11–12.

[28]This discussion is drawn from John F. Mahon and James E. Post, "The Evolution of Political Strategies During the 1980 Superfund Debate," in Alfred A. Marcus, Allen M. Kaufman, and David R. Beam (eds.), *Business Strategy and Public Policy: Perspectives from Industry and Academia* (New York: Quorum Books, 1987), pp. 61–78.

[29]*Chemical and Engineering News*, June 25, 1979, quoted in *ibid.*, p. 67.

[30]Schlozman and Tierney, *Organized Interests and American Democracy*, pp. 66–68.

[31]Levitan and Cooper, *Business Lobbies*, pp. 68–82.

[32]Vogel, *Fluctuating Fortunes*, p. 11.

[33]Birnbaum and Murray, *Showdown at Gucci Gulch*, p. 287.

[34]For a classic statement of this position, see Raymond A. Bauer, Ithiel de Sola Pool, and Lewis Anthony Dexter, *American Business and Public Policy*, rev. ed. (Chicago: Aldine, 1972), Parts IV–VI.

[35]Dickinson, McGaw and Richard McCleary, "PAC Spending, Electioneering & Lobbying: A Vector ARIMA Time Series Analysis," *Polity*, 17 (Spring 1985), 574–85.

[36]Quoted in Robert Kuttner, "Ass Backward," *The New Republic*, April 22, 1985, p. 22.

[37]Martha Derthick and Paul J. Quick, *The Politics of Deregulation* (Washington, D.C.: Brookings Institution, 1985), p. 258.

[38]Ronald Brownstein, "Trench Warfare," *National Journal*, September 14, 1985, 2047–53; and Alan Gladstone, "Employers Associations in Comparative Perspective: Functions and Activities," in John P. Windmuller and Alan Gladstone (eds.), *Employers Associations and Industrial Relations: A Comparative Study* (Oxford: Clarendon Press, 1984), p. 27.

[39]The classic statement of this view is found in Alexander Heard, *The Costs of Democracy* (Chapel Hill: University of North Carolina Press, 1960). See also W. P. Welch, "Campaign Contributions and Congressional Voting: Milk Money and Dairy Price Supports," *Western Political Quarterly*, 35 (December 1982), 478–95; John R. Wright, "PACs, Contributions, and Roll Calls: An Organizational Perspective," *American Political Science Review*, 79 (June 1985), 400–414; and Janet M. Grenzke, "Shopping in the Congressional

Supermarket: The Currency is Complex," *American Journal of Political Science*, 33 (February 1989), pp. 1–24.

[40]Michael T. Hayes, *Lobbyists and Legislators* (New Brunswick, N.J.: Rutgers University Press, 1981).

Chapter 12

Business, Administrative Agencies, and Legal Traditions

U.S. telecommunications policy was affected more profoundly by the decision to break up AT&T in the 1980s than by any other decision in a half-century. Even though Congress is the nation's primary policy-making institution, the decision to separate local telephone service from AT&T's long-distance, manufacturing, and research operations was not made on Capitol Hill or even in the White House. This fundamental step in the nation's telecommunications policy was taken by an assistant attorney general in the Justice Department and supported by a federal district judge in Washington.

Bill Baxter was an obscure law professor at Stanford when he was selected by President Reagan to head the Justice Department's Antitrust Division.[1] He was a dark-eyed, dark-haired, severe-looking man in his early fifties who was regarded by his colleagues as brilliant as well as arrogant. He was dispassionate to the point of being cold, and he was convinced that government regulation was excessive and antitrust laws were applied too broadly for the nation's good.

Harold Greene had been a civil rights attorney in the Justice Department in the 1960s when he attracted the attention of then Attorney General Robert Kennedy. He had drafted the Civil Rights Act of 1964 and the Voting Rights Act of 1965 and later spent a decade as a municipal court judge in the District of Columbia. Greene had been a short, slightly rotund jurist with gray hair and tortoise-shell glasses when he was appointed to the federal district court by President Carter. His goal was to prove that the federal courts could handle complex litigation like the AT&T case.

In 1974, the federal government had charged AT&T with violating antitrust laws by having its operating companies favor equipment manufactured by another AT&T subsidiary, but no trial on the charge had begun when Ronald Reagan became president. Because Reagan's attorney general and deputy attorney general had legal contacts with AT&T subsidiaries in the past, they were not permitted to participate in decisions related to the case against AT&T. Thus Bill Baxter became the department's senior official in matters involving AT&T.

Many Reagan administration figures wanted Baxter to dismiss the suit against AT&T. At a meeting of the Cabinet Council on Commerce and Trade, the secretaries of Defense and Commerce argued strongly to President Reagan that the suit against AT&T should be dismissed because breaking up AT&T would destroy the unified communications system needed for national security and dismember a company that was helping to relieve the country's international balance-of-payments problems. Much to the group's surprise, Baxter delivered a stinging rebuttal of the views of the senior members of the Reagan cabinet and insisted that the case should continue.

As the vociferous debate died down, the group turned to President Reagan, but the president stood up and left to have lunch with Vice President Bush. The meeting adjourned without any decision on the AT&T case, and Baxter allowed the Justice Department's prosecution of the case to continue.

Greene inherited the AT&T case when he joined the federal bench, and he did everything he could to expedite its consideration. The case was to be decided by Greene alone since it was too lengthy and technical to be considered by a jury. Before and during the formal proceedings, Greene issued a series of rulings that made the AT&T attorneys increasingly pessimistic about their prospects.

Some months into the trial, at a time when most of the staff was attending the Justice Department's Christmas party, AT&T attorneys notified Baxter that they wanted to negotiate a settlement. Baxter's terms were intellectually simple but far more sweeping than anything that had previously been taken seriously. Baxter believed that the operating companies providing local telephone service would require regulation in the years ahead. He insisted that these local operating companies be separated from AT&T's long-distance, manufacturing, and research divisions, which he thought could be free of long-term regulation.

Seeking to put an end to the litigation and fearing Judge Greene's decision, AT&T accepted Baxter's terms with remarkable swiftness. The company surrendered two-thirds of its assets in the hope that it could move more quickly into the new, high-technology world of advanced communications on the basis of Baxter's terms than on the basis of any telecommunications policy decisions that were likely to come from Congress, the Federal Communications Commission, the Commerce Department, or the White House. Judge Greene allowed the antitrust suit to be dismissed on the basis of the agreement between the Justice Department and AT&T, and a fundamental shift occurred in the country's telecommunications policy.[2]

While Congress has the constitutional authority to make policy, decisions of administrative agencies and the courts, as in the AT&T case, also have an enormous impact on business and the economy. Business lobbyists seek to influence decisions wherever they are made. More than 90 percent of lobbyists for corporations and trade associations say that congressional decisions are "very important" for their objectives.[3] This does not mean, however, that other lobbying targets are ignored. Fully 75 percent of business representatives report that executive agencies are also very important, 63 percent regard the White House as equally critical, and 20 percent say that lobbying the courts is significant.

This chapter examines relationships between business on the one hand and administrative agencies and the judiciary on the other. The first section reviews relationships between industry and government agencies and explores the strategies businesses employ to influence administrative decisions. The second section concentrates on legal issues. It considers the role of the court system in the administrative and policy processes and the legal opportunities for groups to gain commercial advantage. The final section of the chapter explores the administrative-judicial relations of business from a cross-national perspective.[4] It investigates bureaucratic and legal practices in other countries and considers whether the international patterns of legal-administrative relationships contain lessons that could be useful for the United States.

ADMINISTRATIVE DECISIONS AND BUSINESS

Administrative agencies play three important roles in the policy process. Agencies are one of society's repositories of expertise on specific policy subjects, and they present their opinions during the development of legislative programs. Second, agencies are the institutions that translate statutes into detailed administrative rules. They fill in the gaps in legislation and reconcile conflicting statutory provisions. Finally, agencies determine how administrative rules are to be applied to specific cases and individuals.[5]

American democratic theory stresses that government derives its authority from the consent of the people. From this perspective, the actions of bureaucratic agencies should be determined by elected officials. Agencies should do what elected officials would want if the officials were adequately informed about an issue. This theory, however, is impossible to maintain in practice. Since legislators have opinions that are both diverse and changing, agencies can not know what elected officials would do in specific situations. Bureaucrats, therefore, must use their own judgment to resolve the issues they face.

The ways in which administrators exercise their discretion have enormous significance. Bill Baxter determined himself what the antitrust laws meant when applied to AT&T, and his judgment defined a fundamentally important element of the country's telecommunications policy. Under the Clean Air Act, the EPA decides what air-quality standards are needed to "protect the public health...allowing an adequate margin of safety." The more stringent the EPA's standards, the greater the compliance costs. When the Food and Drug Administration wanted to ban saccharin because it failed to satisfy the statutory standard of "safety" required of food additives, it threatened to wipe out entire industries and cause widespread health problems.

Given the stakes involved in administrative decisions, it is no surprise that business groups seek to influence administrative decisions. Since administrative judgments are more substantive and less responsive to popular opinion than legislative decisions, corporations are usually better able to gain a hearing for their case in the bureaucratic arena than in the political arena.[6] Furthermore, bureaucratic decisions normally affect individual firms rather than classes of companies, and this gives business representatives an even greater incentive to press their views in administrative agencies than in Congress.

The common techniques for influencing administrative decisions include the following:

- Participation in the selection of appointees. Industries and interest groups often seek to promote candidates for the administrative posts that affect them and, perhaps more critically, to block the appointment of individuals whom they regard as hostile to their positions.
- Shaping the context of administrative decisions through bureaucratic reorganization. Interest groups seek to have decisions made in an atmosphere that is supportive of their programmatic objectives. Companies involved in international trade would rather have trade policy determined by the Commerce Department, which they regard as supportive of trade, than in the State Department, which they view as unconcerned about trade issues or hostile.
- Service on departmental advisory committees. Most administrative agencies have public advisory committees that allow them to gather the views and expertise of those who are active in their areas of responsibility. Service on these groups allows business people to maintain contacts with administrators and express their policy perspectives.
- Participation in rule making. When agencies draft the formal rules that guide program implementation, they publish these rules in draft form and allow citizens and groups to comment. The steps in the formal rule-making process provide businesses an opportunity to advance their viewpoints on specific issues.
- Maintaining staff contacts. Business representatives work to maintain relations with key individuals at the agency and bureau level in cabinet departments to learn about emerging proposals and changes in agency priorities. Continuing staff relationships help ensure a sympathetic hearing when an emergency arises.
- Influencing administrative decisions through political channels. Administrative agencies are sensitive to the opinions of elected officials. Members of Congress and White House officials can be used to pressure agencies to be more responsive to specific viewpoints than they would otherwise be.

Business representatives are concerned about decisions made in administrative agencies and are energetic in being sure that their opinions prevail. This combination has led many theorists to conclude that business so thoroughly dominates administrative decisions that it can actually be said to have "captured" the agencies.[7]

"Capture" theorists note that business groups are the only organizations that have a continuing financial stake in being informed about an agency's decision making.[8] Other groups appear occasionally to express their views, but, like morning glories, they soon fade from the scene. Since business organizations are the only continuing, nongovernmental factor in an agency's political environment, administrators may come to share business perspectives as they conduct their activities. Furthermore, top administrators usually serve in government for a limited period and then seek to move to private-sector posts. They will probably be searching for employment opportunities in the industry in which they have worked, and this may lead them to avoid anti-industry decisions that could disqualify them from obtaining future employment.

The warning of capture theorists that industry has excessive influence in agency decision making has been quite influential among citizens and scholars for decades. During this time, four bureaucratic principles have emerged to guard against the misuse of administrative discretion: restrictions on decision makers; professionalism; administrative procedure; and congressional oversight.[9]

Various *restrictions on decision makers* in agencies have been enacted to prevent administrators from developing informal contacts with business and being unduly swayed by the arguments of businesspeople. Administrators and business representatives are prohibited from discussing pending cases in informal settings or in off-the-record discussions. Formal logs are kept of telephone calls and written communications with business figures, and most administrators are not allowed to go to work for companies that appeared before them for a year or two after they leave government service.

Another principle for assuring that administrative discretion is not misused to benefit industry is to emphasize the ideal of bureaucratic *professionalism*. Civil servants in departments and agencies are expected to embody the norms of professionalism and objectivity in their decisions. Their expertise is supposed to insulate them from political pressures and allow them to act on the basis of nonpartisan principles. In recent years, statutes have sought to enhance bureaucratic objectivity by requiring agency decisions to be based on cost-benefit and impact analyses.

A third technique for promoting the impartiality of agency decisions is to define the *administrative procedures* that should be used to reach decisions. Agencies are often required to hold formal or informal hearings before they make decisions so that all groups, not just the well-connected, will have an opportunity to express their positions and concerns. Agencies are also instructed to consider certain types of evidence in making decisions and demonstrate "substantial support" for their judgments.

Oversight of agency conduct by Congress is the fourth technique for assuring that administrators do not give in to business pressures. Congress possesses an impressive array of oversight tools.[10] When Congress doubts the appropriateness of administrative actions, it can pass new laws, amend existing statutes, or attach a rider to an appropriations bill reducing the funds of the agency that has offended it. Congress can also pressure agencies into accepting its policy perspective by holding public hearings, conducting investigations, or ordering agencies to submit periodic reports on specific topics. In the past, Congress sought to require agencies to allow Congress to veto specific administrative actions, but the Supreme Court ruled that "legislative vetoes" were an unconstitutional violation of the separation of powers doctrine.[11] Despite the Court, Congress continues to involve itself in the daily administration of public policy to be sure that administrators faithfully carry out the Congress's legislative intent.

The importance of administrative decisions, the principle of the separation of powers, and the absence of a political theory justifying bureaucratic authority mean that administrative agencies often become an arena for conflict over major public policies. Policy disputes that are fought out in Congress when a piece of legislation is being developed are often shifted to the administrative agency once the bill has been enacted. The same opponents who battled in Congress can appear in the corridors of the agency voicing the same arguments they presented earlier. The significance of administrative agencies in the policy process is described by one analysis of environmental legislation in these terms: "When legislation is passed (by Congress) the contestants shift to the administrative agency, and when that goes the wrong way then to the courts."[12] Policy disputes occur in a succession of venues, and business organizations and other groups seek to gain advantage wherever they can. As the AT&T case illustrates, the judiciary can also play an influential hand in this process.

LITIGATION AS A BUSINESS TACTIC

The judicial system is deeply involved in business issues, and the significance of that involvement is growing. Most of this involvement is a product of the general litigiousness of American society, but litigation has also become a nonmarket tactic used by management to secure competitive advantage. As one analyst has commented, "The litigation game is yet another form of nonmarket tactic ever more frequently relied upon by management to assure corporate profitability or simple survival...."[13]

The frequent use of corporate attorneys appears to be a cultural phenomenon rather than a response to specific government actions.[14] The United States has more lawyers per capita than other industrialized countries, but this was the case in the 1920s when government played a minimal role in the economy. The number of lawyers in private industry has grown threefold in recent decades, but the growth was no faster in regulated than in nonregulated industries.[15] There are a variety of possible responses to governmental action. It is often joked that when the Environmental Protection Agency issues new emission standards for automobiles, Japanese firms call their engineers, and American companies assemble their lawyers.

Most corporate legal departments concentrate on ordinary commercial issues such as contracts, leases, patents, trademarks, securities, and tax matters. Other areas of legal attention include antitrust issues, environmental law, product liability, labor-management relations, and international negotiations. Specialized law firms outside the corporation are often retained to deal with these issues. The proportion of corporate legal actions that have strategic or policy relevance is small, but these cases can be hugely significant.[16]

Probably the most frequent corporate litigation situation with public significance involves suits in which one company argues that another has violated a law and seeks damages. The case that resulted in the break-up of AT&T had its origins in litigation brought by MCI, a firm offering long-distance service, alleging that AT&T had violated antitrust laws.[17] The suit was part of a campaign by MCI to attract AT&T's business customers and establish legal precedents that would damage AT&T in other areas of its business. These "private" suits appear frequently in industries that are regulated by government, such as communications and cable television, and they involve the threat that one company will convince administrators to impose additional costs on the other firm through legal action.

The second type of litigation situation with political relevance involves corporate challenges to the legality of governmental action. Such challenges are not new. Southern textile manufacturers mounted a sophisticated and successful challenge to the constitutionality of national child-labor laws in the early decades of this century.[18] Recently, both labor unions and an industry group sued the Labor Department in an effort to invalidate the department's administrative rules covering the exposure of workers to formaldehyde.[19] Other suits challenge the manner in which agencies apply rules in specific situations. Such cases appear frequently in the tax and environmental areas.[20]

Corporate litigation also seeks to shape the rules of marketplace competition. Product-liability standards are now in flux, and countless suits seek to determine if companies are protected from liability by the health warnings on cigarette packages and if companies must pay damages because people who wear lap belts but not shoulder belts in automobile accidents are injured.[21] The objective of some litigation is to impose delays on competitive actions and increase an adversary's costs. Some state laws defending companies from hostile takeovers, for example, were of questionable constitutionality, but their sponsors believed that the laws would result in lengthy litigation. They believed that takeover bids had to be completed quickly or not at all, and the delays imposed by the need to litigate constitutionally suspect antitakeover laws would effectively block the takeover attempts.[22]

The use of litigation as a competitive tactic is a growing phenomenon in business, but it is not without pitfalls.[23] The use of litigation moves the center of managerial decision making toward legal activities and away from product concerns, and it compels managers to learn to make legal judgments as well as economic ones. Litigation is costly, can generate unfavorable publicity, and carries no guarantees of success.

COMPARATIVE ADMINISTRATIVE AND LEGAL TRADITIONS

Legal practices and administrative traditions in the United States differ from those in other countries, and these differences have an important impact on relations between industry and government. A recent study of the international reaction to a specific legal-administrative situation illustrates the nature of the differences.

At the end of the 1970s and the beginning of the 1980s, there was steadily accumulating evidence that vinyl chloride, once widely used in manufacturing plastic-like substances, was a cancer-causing substance.[24] The reaction in the United States to this emerging discovery was a flurry of legal and administrative conflicts. Companies and trade associations challenged the validity of the scientific evidence in lengthy administrative proceedings and objected to the administrative rules that were proposed by the Occupational Safety and Health Administration to control the use of vinyl chloride. Union groups seized on the issue to demonstrate the callousness of management, and both sides used public hearings and the media to "hector each other for the benefit of their constituencies."[25] As technical understanding of the dangers of vinyl chloride grew, limitations on its use were finally accepted and put into effect.

In Germany, Japan, and the United Kingdom, industry and government cooperated to remove the danger posed by vinyl chloride. In each of these countries, business groups worked closely with government agencies to assess the nature of the threat posed by vinyl chloride and develop a plan to check that danger. There was no public acrimony, and there were no appeals to the media. In the end, none of the countries protected its citizens more effectively than the others, but the process of reaching agreement in the United States was more bitter, more costly, and more time-consuming than in the other countries.

Why was this? Why was the administrative process in the United States so much more cumbersome and contentious than in other countries? What features best explain the variations in bureaucratic practice in the four countries? What factors contribute to cooperative relations between industry and administrative agencies in some countries but not others?

This study of the international reaction to the dangers of vinyl chloride identifies three administrative-political factors that shaped the nature of government-industry relations in the United States and the other countries. First is the extent to which the individual countries have an integrated system of governmental decision making in which government has the capacity to make the decisions necessary to solve the problems the society faces. (See Chapter 5.) The second factor is whether the representation of business groups in the country is unified and allows a coherent presentaton of business viewpoints or whether the system of business representation is fragmented. (See Chapter 10.) Finally, the study also concludes that the existence of informal communication networks between government and industry affects the conduct of public policy in the various countries. Table 12–1 ranks the four countries on the basis of each of these factors. The thesis of the study of vinyl chloride is that countries with integrated decison-making systems, unified patterns of business representation, and frequent informal communication will have more cooperative relationships between government and business than those that do not.[26]

TABLE 12–1   Determinants of Industry-Agency Relationships

	INTEGRATED GOVERNMENTAL DECISION MAKING	UNIFIED BUSINESS REPRESENTATION	INFORMAL COMMUNICATION
Germany	Yes, Medium	Yes	Frequent
Japan	Yes, High	Somewhat	Intense
UK	Yes, Medium	Somewhat	Frequent
U.S.	No, Low	No	Limited

Source: Adapted from Joseph L. Badaracco, *Loading the Dice: A Five Country Study of Vinyl Chloride Regulation* (Boston: Harvard Business School Press, 1985).

Integrated Governmental Decision Making

Governmental authority in the United States is more broadly dispersed than in Germany, Japan, or the UK. The doctrine of the separation of powers means that major, long-term policy initiatives in the United States require the support or at least the acquiescence of the president, Congress, administrative agencies, and the judiciary. Disagreement among governmental institutions can produce stalemate or even contradictory policy actions.

American political theory and governmental practice allow administrative agencies a less definitive role than in other countries. The absence of a democratic justification for bureaucratic discretion makes administrative agencies continuously vulnerable to second-guessing by other institutions of government. Business representatives and other political actors know that any agreement reached with administrative agencies can be contested later before judges or politicians.

The U.S. Congress is the world's most assertive national legislature. Like legislatures in other countries, it receives policy recommendations from the chief executive and various executive departments, but, unlike other countries, it then develops its own legislative responses to the problems at hand. In the process of building coalitions to enact legislation, Congress sometimes adopts sweeping policy goals that are impossible to achieve or takes stands that contradict its other positions. A president's opponents are always on the lookout for opportunities to claim credit for well-liked actions and to saddle an administration with responsibility for decisions that are necessary but unpopular.

Congress also devotes more energy to overseeing the administration of legislation than any other major legislature. Germany, Japan, and the UK all have parliamentary systems. Members of parliament select the chief executive on the basis of party, and they then support the actions and proposals of the executive branch. As a rule, executive agencies draft legislation, parliaments adopt what the government submits, and there are no public hearings on how the laws have been implemented.

It should also be noted that congressional involvement in administrative oversight typically occurs at the level of a subcommittee or an individual member rather than through the formal action of the institution. "Congressional" opinions expressed during implementation may be shared by a majority of legislators, or they may simply reflect the atypical sentiments of a handful of members.

Members of Congress are also quick to side with constituents who allege that they have been abused by bureaucrats, as the discussion of the savings and loan industry illustrates. When administrators face a difficult decision, they know that any action they take is likely to result in criticism by a member or a summons from a subcommittee. Under such circumstances, administrators are likely to prefer the most easily defensible course of action rather than taking an option that could be most effective in solving the problem at hand.

The American judiciary is also more deeply involved in administrative issues than are judicial systems in the other countries.[27] Bureaucratic procedures in the United States emphasize the rights of individuals and private parties rather than the requirements of managerial effectiveness. While the basic rule is that courts presume that administrative actions are proper, judges have accepted much of the criticism of the capture theorists that bureaucracies are self-serving, excessively beholden to business interests, unresponsive to citizen concerns, and uninformed about scientific advances. In recent decades, courts have relaxed the rules of standing that limited groups' ability to contest agency actions, entertained cases that challenge administrative procedures, and questioned the substance of agency judgments.[28]

The United States has the most politicized system of judicial selection of any major industrialized country.[29] The common career experience of people appointed to be top judges is their involvement in helping to manage the country's major policy conflicts. As a consequence of their policy orientation, the impact of judicial action on administrative issues is pervasive. By one estimate, 80 percent of all administrative rules issued by the Environmental Protection Agency are challenged in court.[30] Litigation, even if it is unsuccessful, ties up agency resources, delays action, and cautions administrators to proceed carefully. Judicial review has created demands for fuller administrative records, more detailed analyses, and more elaborate justifications for agency decisions, but it has yielded little systematic policy guidance. As a result, parties have little confidence in administrative decisions until they have been sanctioned by the judiciary. Lawyers play a far more prominent hand in administrative relations between corporations and government agencies in the United States than in the other countries because all sides know that every statement made by agency or business figures could later be scrutinized in a courtroom.

Germany, Japan, and England have far narrower and less developed traditions of administrative law.[31] Only in recent decades have judges accepted cases dealing with bureaucratic issues, and, as a rule, they still grant administrators great latitude in their activities.

Departments and agencies in these countries are more influential in drafting legislation than are their counterparts in the United States, and thus fewer grounds for litigation arise from the statutes they administer. Policy styles in Japan and the

United Kingdom stress bureaucratic accommodation and informal decision making. Use of the court system is discouraged. Germany has a somewhat more activist and rule-bound administrative style, but it emphasizes consensus, objectivity, and private negotiations.[32] An expansive judicial role reduces the definitiveness of administrative decisions in the United States, while the narrower range of judicial activity in the other countries strengthens agency judgments.

Germany, Japan, and the United Kingdom also have more respected bureaucratic traditions than does the United States. Top graduates from these countries' most prestigious universities pursue bureaucratic careers, and their nations expect them to preserve the stability and objectivity of the governmental process. In large measure, administrative agencies in these countries are the embodiment of their political communities, and agency officials are expected to defend the state against the schemes and compromises of electoral politics. One authority on Japan has summarized that country's experience in terms that could also be applied, although less strongly, to Germany and the United Kingdom: "For most of the postwar period,...it is accurate to say...that the politicians reigned while the bureaucrats ruled."[33]

In the United States, bureaucrats are more often ridiculed than respected. Lacking a supportive political theory and having their actions constantly reviewed by judges and members of Congress, administrative agencies lack the stature to make the definitive policy judgments.

Business Representation

While American administrative agencies can rarely make definitive decisions in controversial areas, it is also difficult for industry to formulate a cohesive position on divisive issues. As described in Chapter 10, the representation of business interests in the United States is fragmented. Business associations are weak, and individual companies maintain direct relations with the national government.

In Germany, the associations are strong, and they seek to monopolize relations between industry and the national government. Japanese business organizations play an equally prominent role in political and administrative activities, although individual firms also maintain important ties with national agencies. In the UK, both industry associations and major corporations shape policy relationships with administrative agencies.

In the pluralistic, American tradition, individual corporations chart their own course. While some firms might favor legislative actions to deal with a policy problem, others turn toward the bureaucracy, and still others would employ judicial strategies to secure their goals. On most issues, the principal opponents of American companies are other industries or corporations. When business groups are unable to agree among themselves on policy issues, it is difficult to maintain cooperative relations with administrative agencies.

Informal Communications

In the United States, it is difficult for both business and government agencies to develop clear policy positions on controversial subjects. It is also difficult for them to discuss with each other potential areas of agreement. The American public is so distrustful of both government and business that informal communication between bureaucrats and business figures are regarded as a warning sign of conspiracies against the public interest rather than efforts to solve common problems.

The characteristics of American administrative behavior can be seen most vividly in comparison to British practice.[34] The British administrative style stresses informality, flexibility, and accommodation, while American procedures are adversarial and legalistic. The American approach is rigid and rule-bound, and it seeks to restrict agency discretion as much as possible so that administrators will not be swayed by business viewpoints. In contrast, British administrators make extensive use of industry self-regulation and negotiated compliance, and the prosecution of firms for violating rules is extremely rare.

Private consultations with business are built into every stage of the British administrative process. In the United States, agency communication with business are regulated and usually occur under the eyes of the media or at public hearings. In the UK, social and professional communication between industry figures and the senior civil service are a commonplace occurrence. Nonindustry groups have little legal standing in the administrative or legal process. They receive no public funding, and they have limited access to information. These groups have not been as integrated into the bureaucratic process as they have in the United States.

Relationships with administrative agencies are very significant for American corporate and trade association lobbyists, but not as critical as relations with Congress. The opposite is true in the United Kingdom. Administrative agencies are a more meaningful focus of industry communication with government than is Parliament. A handbook for business lobbyists in the UK describes the role of Parliament in these terms:[35]

> Parliament is no longer—except in a few defined circumstances—a decision-maker in the public policy process. Its place in the power structure is that of an institution through which the Executive operates.... Unlike Congress in the United States, it does not lie at the centre of power....real power rests far further down the Civil Service hierarchy than is often believed.

Political figures occupy a smaller number of posts in British departments and agencies than in the United States. Most officials retain their positions when governments change, and these officials are the national government's principal source of expertise on policy questions. Whether communication occurs with representatives of firms or business associations, the bureaucratic tradition emphasizes negotiation and cooperation rather than conflict and enforcement.

Administrative agencies in the United States are weaker and less authoritative than their counterparts in Germany, Japan, and the United Kingdom. Business representation is more fragmented in the United States than in the other countries, and informal communication is more constrained. As a consequence, cooperation between industry and administrative agencies is less instinctive than in the other countries. American executives devote more resources to winning a hearing for their positions in administrative agencies than do their counterparts in other lands, and the conduct of public policy is more adversarial. Are these qualities the inevitable price for the greater openness and diversity of the American corporate system?

SUMMARY

Chapters 9 through 12 have examined relations between government and industry that involve opinion formation, social responsibility, political parties, business associations, lobbying, administrative traditions, and legal practices. Many areas of the discussion have compared behavior in the United States with the patterns of conduct in Germany, Japan, and the United Kingdom.

The argument is not that the arrangements in these countries are necessarily superior to those in the United States. The purpose of the comparisons is to make clear that governing arrangements have specific consequences and that they are the product of national choices. It would not be possible to transplant totally the administrative traditions of Japan, the patterns of business organization in Germany, or political party practices in the UK to the United States, even if that were desirable. It might well be valuable, however, to learn from the accomplishments of other countries and consider whether American practices need reform.

American arrangements for conducting relations between government and industry have emerged in response to the country's unique circumstances, and they embody values that are central to the country's traditions. The comparisons in these chapters are intended to ask whether these arrangements adequately serve the country's needs or whether reforms and adjustments in these arrangements would better help the country achieve its social, political, and economic goals in a rapidly changing international economy.

SELECTED READINGS

Joseph L. Badaracco, *Loading the Dice: A Five Country Study of Vinyl Chloride Regulation* (Boston: Harvard University Press, 1985).

Gary C. Bryner, *Bureaucratic Discretion: Law and Policy in Federal Regulatory Agencies* (New York: Pergamon Press, 1987).

Thomas Petzinger, *Oil & Honor: the Texaco-Pennzoil Wars* (New York: Berkley Books, 1987).

DAVID VOGEL, *National Styles of Regulation: Environmental Policy in Great Britain and the United States* (Ithaca, N. Y.: Cornell University Press, 1986).

JEROLD L. WALTMAN and KENNETH M. HOLLAND (eds.), *The Political Role of Law Courts in Modern Democracies* (New York: St. Martin's Press, 1988).

END NOTES

[1]This description is drawn from Steve Coll, *The Deal of the Century: The Breakup of AT&T* (New York: Atheneum, 1986); and W. Brooke Tunstall, *Disconnecting Parties: Managing the Bell System Breakup*, N.Y.:McGraw-Hill, 1985.

[2]Compare Kenneth Button and Dennis Swann (eds.), *The Age of Regulatory Reform* (Oxford: Clarendon Press, 1989), especially Hudson N. Janisch, "The North American Telecommunications Industry: From Monopoly to Competition," p. 309.

[3]Kay Lehman Schlozman and John T. Tierney, *Organized Interests and American Democracy* (New York: Harper & Row, 1986), p. 272.

[4]David Vogel, *Styles of Regulation: Environment Policy in Great Britain and the United States* (Ithaca: Cornell University Press, 1986), p. 267.

[5]See Gary Bryner, *Bureaucratic Discretion: Law and Policy in Federal Regulatory Agencies* (New York: Pergamon Press, 1987), "The Problem of Bureaucratic Discretion," Chapter 1; and Martin Shapiro, "Administrative Discretion: The Next Stage," *Yale Law Journal*, 92 (1983), 1487–1522.

[6]Edwin M. Epstein, *The Corporation in American Politics* (Englewood Cliffs, N.J.: Prentice Hall, 1969), p. 69.

[7]A fine review of capture theories is found in Barry M. Mitnick, *The Political Economy of Regulation: Creating, Designing, and Removing Regulatory Forms* (New York: Columbia University Press, 1980), Chapters 2–3.

[8]Paul J. Quirk, *Industry Influence in Federal Regulatory Agencies* (Princeton: Princeton University Press, 1981).

[9]Bryner, *Bureaucratic Discretion.*

[10]Bryner, *Bureaucratic Discretion*, pp. 73–78 and 85–87; Lawrence C. Dodd and Richard L. Schott, *Congress and the Administrative State* (New York: Wiley, 1979); and R. Douglas Arnold, *Congress and the Bureaucracy: A Theory of Influence* (New Haven: Yale University Press, 1979).

[11]*Immigration and Naturalization Service* v. *Chadha*, 103 S.C. 2764, 1983; R. Shep Melnick, "The Politics of Partnership," *Public Administration Review*, (November 1985), 653–80.

[12]Samuel P. Hayes, "The Politics of Environmental Administration," in Louis Galambos (ed.), *The New American State: Bureaucracies since World War II* (Baltimore: Johns Hopkins University Press, 1987), pp. 39–40.

[13]David Chadwick-Brown, "Litigation as Private Formulation of Public Policy," *Journal of Contemporary Business*, vol. 10, no. 3 (1981), 121.

[14]B. Peter Pashigian, "Regulation, Preventive Law, and the Duties of Attorneys," in William J. Carney (ed.), *The Changing Role of the Corporate Attorney* (Lexington, Mass.: Lexington Books, 1982), pp. 3–46. See also Antonia Handler Chayes, Bruce C. Greenwald, and Maxine Paisner Winig, "Managing Your Lawyers," *Harvard Business Review*, (January 1983), 84–91.

[15]Pashigian, "Regulation, Preventive Law, and the Duties of Attorneys."

[16]Thomas Petzinger, *Oil and Honor: The Texaco-Pennzoil Wars* (New York: Berkley Books, 1987).

[17]Coll, *The Deal of the Century*, Chapters 2–3.

[18]Stephen B. Wood, *Constitutional Politics in the Progressive Era: Child Labor and the Law* (Chicago: University of Chicago Press, 1968).

[19]Albert R. Karr, "Suits Aim to Alter OSHA's New Rules On Formaldehyde," *Wall Street Journal*, December 3, 1987, p. 12.

[20]See, for example, Vincent R. Zarate, "Four Corporate Tax Challenges Could Cost Jersey More than $150 million," *Star Ledger* (Newark), August 30, 1987, p.27; and R. Shep Melnick, *Regulation and the Courts: The Case of the Clean Air Act* (Washington, D.C.: Brookings Institution, 1983).

[21]"Tobacco group decides against cigarette appeal," *Financial Times* (London), December 28, 1990, p. 3; and "Ford Must Pay Hurt Boy $3.3 Million, Jury Finds," *Wall Street Journal*, December 21, 1987, p. 25.

[22]"Government-Business Relations and the Legal Process," Rutgers University presentation, April 30, 1986.

[23]Samuel A. Bodily, "When Should You Go To Court?", *Harvard Business Review*, May 1981; and Frank Shipper and Marianne M. Jennings, *Business Strategy for the Political Arena* (Westport, Conn.: Quorum Books, 1984), Chapter 7.

[24]Joseph L. Badaracco, *Loading the Dice: A Five Country Study of Vinyl Chloride Regulation* (Boston: Harvard Business School Press, 1985). (The fifth country is France.)

[25]Ibid., p. 131.

[26]Interest representation and administrative integration are also used to examine policy actions in other studies. See Klaus Schubert, "Politics and Economic Regulation," in Francis G. Castles et al. (eds.), *Managing Mixed Economics* (Berlin: Walter de Gruyter, 1988), pp. 169–96.

[27]Jerold L. Waltman and Kenneth M. Holland (eds.), *The Political Role of Law Courts in Modern Democracies* (New York: St. Martin's Press, 1988). See chapters concerning Germany, Japan, England, and the United States. See also Bryner, *Bureaucratic Discretion*, pp. 210–12.

[28]Melnick, *Regulation and the Courts*, "Judicial Capacity and the Regulatory Process," Chapter 10.

[29]Mauro Cappelletti, *The Judicial Process in Comparative Perspective* (Oxford: Clarendon Press, 1989); and Mary L. Volcansek and Jacqueline Lucienne Lafon, *Judicial Selection: The Cross-Evolution of French and American Practices* (New York: Greenwood Press, 1988).

[30]Bryner, *Bureaucratic Discretion*, p. 117; and Badaracco, *Loading the Dice*, pp. 128–31.

[31]Hiroshi Itoh, "The Courts in Japan," and Jerold Waltman, "The Courts in England," in Waltman and Holland (eds.), *The Political Role of Law Courts*; Dieter Lorenz, "The Constitutional Supervision of the Administrative Agencies in the Federal Republic of Germany," *Southern California Law Review* 53 (1980), 543–582, and Hans Linde and Lee Albert, "Commentary," pp. 583–609; and David Vogel, *National Styles of Regulation*, pp. 174 and 287–289.

[32]Kenneth Dyson, "West Germany: The Search for a Rationalist Consensus," and Grant Jordan and Jeremy Richardson, "The British Policy Style or the Logic of Negotiation?", in Jeremy Richardson (ed.), *Policy Styles in Western Europe* (London: George Allen & Unwin, 1982), pp. 17–46 and 80–110.

[33]Clyde V. Prestowitz, *Trading Places: How We Are Giving Our Future to Japan and How to Reclaim It* (New York: Basic Books, 1988), p. 242.

[34]This discussion is based on Vogel, *National Styles of Regulation*, especially pp. 22, 146, 194–95, 267, and 282; Alan Peacock (ed.), *The Regulation Game: How British and West German Companies Bargain with Government* (Oxford: Basil Blackwell, 1984), pp. 101, 108, and 129–30; and Badaracco, *Loading the Dice*, p. 131.

[35]Charles Miller, *Lobbying Government: Understanding and Influencing the Corridors of Power* (Oxford: Basil Blackwell, 1987), pp. 36 and 53. See also Wyn Grant and David Marsh, *The Confederation of British Industry* (London: Hodder and Stoughton, 1977), p. 129.

Chapter 13

International Trade Policies

Government is important to business because public policies affect business operations. Part Four examines three policy areas that have received particular attention in recent years. Chapter 13 reviews the major features of U.S. trade policies and considers whether the existing regime of international trade can survive the fundamental changes now occurring in world politics.

Concerns about the international competitiveness of the U.S. economy have been one of the most influential forces in American politics in the last fifteen years. Chapter 14 examines the history of industrial policy in the United States and industrial policy practices in Germany, Japan, and the United Kingdom in an effort to identify factors that contribute to successful or unsuccessful industrial policy initiatives.

Production decisions, financial judgments, marketing strategies, and human resource choices of business organizations are all embedded in a dense network of social policies. Chapter 15 distinguishes among various social policy objectives in order to clarify the dynamics of social policies and assess their consequences for business.

Nineteen-foot-tall replicas of the seven dwarfs from *Snow White* support the roof of the Walt Disney Company building in southern California.[1] Hollywood has long been the ultimate "dream factory," but behind the carefully crafted facade of fantasy and illusion is an industry whose history is chronicled not only in scripts and screenplays but also in the reports of MBAs and the financial press.[2]

In 1990, Disney Studios ranked number one as measured by domestic box-office attendance, and, that summer, nearly one-third of all theaters were showing Disney films. The year's box-office hit, *Pretty Woman*, was a modern-day Cinderella story, and it became the most successful Disney-Touchstone film ever.

The film industry, however, is changing, and theatrical releases are no longer the industry's principal source of income. Today, the largest earnings come from television productions and home-video sales, and Disney is successful in these areas, too. In addition to providing network shows, Disney's Buena Vista Television airs eighteen hours of first-run programming each week on syndicated television. Disney also accounts for seven of the top-ten home-video best-sellers of all time with *Pretty Woman* selling nearly six million units and *The Little Mermaid* accounting for eight million more.

A second way in which the industry is changing is that it has become a part of the global economy. While it was once dependent on the domestic market, 35 percent of the industry's revenues today come from export sales. *Pretty Woman* was the year's biggest film in such diverse countries as Australia, Singapore, and Venezuela, and it was the most successful American movie ever in Germany, Israel, and Sweden. Tokyo Disneyland has been in operation for seven years, and Euro Disneyland is scheduled to open in Paris in what were once sugar-beet fields outside Paris.

The success of the U.S. film industry in other countries has made it a significant factor in international trade. Film and television businesses now generate an annual trade surplus for the American economy of nearly $5 billion, second only to the aerospace industry. As U.S. firms look to international audiences to provide revenues and cover costs, however, they are encountering more and more trade barriers.

European television was traditionally fragmented into numerous markets, with government-owned networks dominating programming. In recent years, satellites, cable technology, and deregulation have eroded national restraints, and European television has grown rapidly. Changes in Eastern Europe, rising per capita income, and the large number of movie theaters have made the European market particularly attractive to the U.S. film industry, but the European Community has threatened to limit the activities of American firms by imposing new trade restrictions.

In October 1989, the European Commission triggered a trade crisis by proposing to restrict television programs produced outside Europe to 49 percent of transmissions. France, Britain, and other countries then followed with even tighter restrictions on the national origin of films and prime-time programming. What Europeans justified as a measure to preserve their cultural heritage was perceived by the American industry as a salvo in a trade war fired by European producers seeking protection for products they otherwise could not sell. The seriousness of the issue was underlined by Jack Valenti, president of the Motion Picture Association, when he promised to fight the TV quotas "to the death." U.S. firms turned to the government for help.

In the 1980s, the film industry had stepped up its effort to be sure that Hollywood's interests were heard in Washington. The executives of Disney and three other major studios contributed $180,000 to congressional candidates in the 1982 elections. In 1990, they contributed $1.2 million,[3] and the industry also provided stars who drew additional donors to political fundraisers. Disney and other firms have opened Washington offices, and Valenti, Disney officials, and other industry figures have won places on executive branch advisory boards dealing with trade issues. Its celebrity status allows the film industry direct access to public officials, while most corporate representatives must approach officials through their staffs.[4]

U.S. trade representatives complained to the Europeans about the video restrictions, but the issue is complicated by the lack of international rules for dealing with the situation. Traditional trade rules were devised to curtail tariffs—taxes on the import of manufactured goods into a country. The products of the film industry, however, are audiovisual services rather than manufactured items, and the barriers being raised by the Europeans are not tariffs but another form of restriction. How nontariff barriers that limit trade in services are to be handled under the rules of international trade is a problem that has not yet been solved.

This chapter considers the market-access problem of the U.S. film industry by placing it in the broader context of international trade issues. The chapter first examines the rationale for international trade and the basic features of the post–World War II trading system. It then analyzes contemporary pressures on the world trade system and political developments that have made those pressures especially troubling. The chapter concludes by looking to the future. It poses the basic question of whether it is possible to salvage the post–World War II trading system, or whether fundamentally new arrangements are needed to sustain international trade.

FEATURES OF THE INTERNATIONAL TRADING SYSTEM

If the world were a single economic unit, nations would specialize in the economic activities they do best. They would make films, manufacture automobiles, produce wine, or design computers. The nations would trade the surplus in their goods for the products manufactured by other countries. Since each country would concentrate on the goods it produced most efficiently, economic resources would flow to the world's most productive uses, and consumers in every country would gain. *Liberal or free trade policies* are policies that reduce restrictions on the movement of products from country to country so that the world acts more like a single economic unit.

The decades immediately following World War II were a period of unprecedented economic growth in the world. Much of this growth is attributed to the liberal trade policies and stable exchange rates among currencies that then prevailed.

Restrictions on international trade occur because the politics of trade are characterized by an imbalance between those who benefit from liberal trade policies and those who pay the costs.[5] The losers in international trade are manufacturers whose products lose domestic sales to imports. They often enter the political arena to obtain protection for their products, and their very survival can depend on their success in securing governmental help. The beneficiaries of free trade are consumers who can buy products at lower prices and companies that succeed in selling their goods abroad. These groups are less diligent in seeking governmental assistance, even when they encounter trade barriers, because their survival does not depend on governmental action.

History of Trade Policy

Article I of the United States Constitution gives Congress the authority to "regulate commerce with foreign nations" and "lay and collect duties." From the American Revolution through 1820, trade policy was used to support the political objectives of independence and national sovereignty, and imports from European countries were periodically restricted to express political positions and secure American rights.[6] From 1820–1934, trade and tariff policy was governed by domestic political considerations, and Congress reigned supreme. Tariff bills were the major item of congressional business, Congress characteristically responded positively to industry demands for protection, and high duties on imports were the rule of the day.

The culmination of congressional activism in trade matters was the Tariff Act of 1930, better known as the Smoot-Hawley Act. In this bill, Congress ignored the warnings of experts and allowed industry pleas for protection to dominate the legislative process.[7] The bill raised import duties to record levels, set tariffs for twenty thousand different items, and prompted widespread retaliation by the other nations in the form of increased tariffs. As a consequence, U.S. imports between 1929 and 1933 plunged from $4.4 billion to $1.5 billion, and exports collapsed from $5.2 billion to $1.6 billion.[8]

The Smoot-Hawley Act was the last general trade bill ever enacted by Congress. It was followed by a notably different kind of trade law, the Reciprocal Trade Agreement Act of 1934. This legislation lowered U.S. tariffs in exchange for reduced tariffs from other countries and set the pattern for trade policy that would prevail for the next fifty years, from 1934 to 1984.

In this historic law, Congress got out of the business of setting tariffs for specific products. Instead, it authorized the president to negotiate lower tariffs with other nations. Congress also insulated itself from the political pressures brought by the losers in international trade by creating a regulatory agency and directing injured firms to address their complaints there.[9] The delegation of tariff-setting authority to the executive branch did not stop Congress from establishing ground rules for negotiations, and it did not stop members from making speeches to impress constituents back home who faced competition from imports, but the new system relieved Congress of the actual responsibility for setting duties on specific products.

General Agreement on Tariffs and Trade

The new approach to trade policy emerged slowly, and it came to be symbolized by the General Agreement on Tariffs and Trade (GATT). The GATT system remains the basic system of rules governing international trade. GATT had its origins in an Anglo-American dialogue held during World War II on the postwar creation of an international agency to promote trade.[10] When it became clear that there would be no consensus on the authority to be given such an international organization, a less formal agreement was signed in 1947 endorsing a set of broad commercial principles. Individual countries endorsed the GATT principles as they saw fit. Congress has never formally approved the GATT system, but it was put into effect through an executive agreement issued by President Truman.

GATT is composed of guidelines rather than rigid rules. The countries that have signed GATT have not relinquished their sovereignty to a supranational organization.[11] They have not agreed to act in ways that might violate their own laws, damage domestic industries, or hurt their national security. What they have done is to endorse flexible trading principles that can help offset domestic pressures for protectionism.

The central principles on which GATT is based are a commitment to trade liberalization, reciprocity in lowering tariffs, and nondiscrimination in applying tariffs. GATT envisioned a series of trade conferences at which the contracting parties would seek to reduce tariff levels. One member would agree to lower specific tariffs contingent upon the reduction of comparable tariffs by other members. The resulting tariffs were then applied to all imports of those products regardless of the country of origin. GATT has no ability to enforce the negotiated tariffs, but a member can apply to the GATT process for permission to impose an extra duty on goods that come from a country found to have exceeded GATT's tariff levels.

GATT's primary significance over the years has been as a framework for conferences or "rounds" of negotiations on trade issues. The discussions initiated in the late 1980s were the eighth round of negotiations held since GATT was created, and were called the Uruguay Round. The usual practice is for Congress to delegate the president authority to conduct negotiations for a specific period and then agree to accept or reject the outcome of the negotiations as a complete package rather than judging specific tariff items.

When authorizing particular rounds of negotiations, Congress has focused on various trade topics. The Trade Expansion Act of 1962, authorizing participation in the Kennedy Round, considered bureaucratic as well as substantive issues.[12] By 1962, the State Department had been the lead agency on trade issues for three decades, but the Commerce Department charged that the State Department routinely favored foreign over American commercial interests. In response to this criticism, Congress created a Special Representative for Trade Negotiations in the White House to resolve interagency conflicts and coordinate trade policy. The Office of the Special Trade Representative was strengthened in 1974, but executive branch divisions over trade issues persist. The Commerce and Labor Departments typically favor aggressive action to defend American commercial interests, while State and the Treasury usually seek to preserve harmonious relations with trading partners in order to help resolve foreign policy and currency issues.

The 1962 Act also authorized an innovative approach to helping companies and workers hurt by imports. "Trade adjustment assistance" uses tax dollars theoretically generated by international trade to compensate the specific groups that are the losers in the trade process.[13] Firms and employees who have been displaced by international competition can apply for technical and financial aid from government. Firms can request assistance to become more competitive in the marketplace, and workers can use government benefits to learn skills needed to move to new industries. Trade adjustment assistance can diminish political support for protectionism by demonstrating to aggrieved groups that government is responsive to their problems.

As a result of GATT's long-term success at tariff reduction, tariffs have ceased to be the major trade issue. When Congress authorized U.S. participation in the Toyko Round of trade negotiations in 1974, attention focused not on tariff levels but on the administration of the GATT process. Prominent among the issues then under debate were the procedures by which companies obtained relief from international competition.

GATT provisions allow member countries an *escape clause* to limit imports of products that injure their domestic industries. Firms are authorized to apply to their own governments for relief from harmful foreign competition. Article VI of GATT also permits member countries to take account of "unfair" trade advantages given to foreign competitors. If one country subsidizes the manufacture of a product for sale in another country, the receiving country is authorized to impose a *countervailing* duty equal to the amount of the subsidy received in the home country. If the products of one country are sold in another country for less than their actual cost, the receiving country can impose an *antidumping* levy on the product equal to the margin between the production cost and the sale price.

Responsibility for administering GATT provisions and the U.S. trade laws in the United States rests with the International Trade Commission (ITC), an independent regulatory commission. The ITC determines when escape clause, antidumping, and countervailing actions are justified to defend U.S. industry. Before the Trade Act of 1974, American companies had complained that the ITC rarely approved their petitions for relief. In 1974, Congress made it easier for U.S. firms to obtain protection from unfair foreign competition by relaxing the requirements for assistance, but companies still complained that their chances of securing positive ITC judgments were low.

U.S. Trade Policies

GATT supplements rather than replaces a country's own trade policies. Despite GATT, every country has erected barriers to the free flow of trade. While probably more sinned against than sinning,[14] the United States, too, has created policies that restrict imports to the United States and affect exports to other lands.

The United States has established a multitude of specific "Buy American" programs. Many federal statutes require government agencies to purchase American products if they are available at an equal or "reasonable" price. To benefit the merchant marine industry, U.S. flag ships must, by law, be used to transport goods from one U.S. port to another, and American flag vessels must transport half the commodities sent abroad under the foreign aid program. State laws also mandate the use of U.S. materials by state and local government, require the purchase of U.S. automobiles, and restrict the use of foreign steel.

Additional rules limit imports of specific products. U.S. agricultural laws authorize import quotas for products included in price-support programs, and recent years have seen quotas for sugar, peanuts, cotton, and beef. Since the 1950s, imports of textiles have been limited by bilateral accords and the Multifiber Arrangement of 1973. The U.S. government has also persuaded other countries to enter "voluntary" agreements limiting their exports to the United States. Voluntary export restraints (VERs) originated in the textile sector in the 1950s and then spread to steel and automobiles. The most prominent VER appeared in the early 1980s, when Japan agreed to limit auto exports to the United States to head off congressional proposals to legislate comprehensive quotas on Japanese products.

The regulation of the domestic economy is composed of rules that, intentionally or not, also restrict imports. U.S. auto emission standards, testing procedures for pharmaceutical products, and product-liability requirements all constitute barriers to the free flow of goods from other countries. States and localities have building codes drawn up in conjunction with local manufacturers. These codes frequently discriminate in favor of local industry by incorporating specifications for building materials that are only met by products manufactured in the area. International analysts also argue that the general litigiousness of U.S. commercial relationships and the unpredictable administration of U.S. trade laws give U.S. goods an additional measure of protection from foreign competition.[15]

Like other countries, the United States also has policies to promote the export of U.S. goods. The Export-Import Bank (Eximbank) is a federal agency that finances the purchase of U.S. goods by foreign buyers. The Eximbank makes loans to foreign buyers to assist them in purchasing products manufactured in the United States, and it guarantees that foreign companies that borrow money from private sources to purchase U.S. goods will repay their loans. The U.S. also seeks to stimulate exports by linking foreign-aid programs to the purchase of U.S. goods. It encourages the formation of export-trading companies that are exempt from antitrust laws and offers tax preferences for export activities.

Ironically, the United States also disrupts free trade through a well-established program of export controls.[16] In contrast to its efforts to foster a liberal trading order, the United States has frequently restricted exports to promote economic or foreign policy goals. In the wake of the invasion of Afghanistan, President Carter suspended sales of grain to the Soviet Union and imposed controls on all products except medical supplies. The Export Administration Act and the International Emergency

Economic Powers Act provided the legal basis for embargoes against Cuba, Iran, Nicaragua, Libya, and Iraq. Congress has also imposed trade sanctions against South Africa and prohibited the international sale of oil from Alaska's North Slope. While the use of export controls as a tool of international policy is a common phenomenon, the effectiveness of such tactics is a continuing subject of controversy.

The United States was the major world force promoting free trade in the half-century from 1934 to 1984. Since 1984, the international trading system has been subjected to pressures that have eroded the foundations of the postwar arrangements. The next section describes the strains that have appeared in the world trading system, and the section that follows considers whether GATT itself can be salvaged.

THE TRADE SYSTEM UNDER STRESS

Today trade issues stand at the center of the political stage for the first time since the 1930s.[17] More than anything, the new attention is the result of the country's enormous trade deficit. This section first examines the origins of the U.S. trade deficit. It then considers changes in the global trading system and the structure of American politics that have made the deficit an especially difficult problem.

Trade Deficit

The trade deficit reported on the nightly news is the difference between the value of goods or merchandise exported from the United States and value of goods imported from abroad.[18] Every year from 1894 to 1970, the value of U.S. exports exceeded the value of imports. Every year since 1975, in contrast, the United States has had a negative trade balance. The size of that deficit surged in the early 1980s.[19] As reported in Table 13–1, the trade deficit grew from $28 billion in 1981 to $36 billion in 1982, and then it shot up dramatically to $67 billion in 1983 and $113 billion in 1984. The deficit grew at a slower pace in subsequent years and reached a peak of $160 billion in 1987. Since then, the deficit has declined, but in 1990 it still equalled $106 billion.

The extraordinary fourfold increase in the annual trade deficit between 1981 and 1984 was not the result of trade policies but of three broad macroeconomic developments.[20] First was the rise in the value of the dollar. The Reagan administration promised to restore economic growth and reduce inflation when it entered office, which it did, but it achieved these goals at the price of large fiscal deficits and high real interest rates. A consequence of the failure to reduce the budget deficit and lower interest rates when the economy had recovered was an overpriced dollar. The overpriced dollar made it difficult for U.S. firms to sell products abroad and made imports particularly attractive to American consumers.[21] Between 1981 and 1984, the absolute value of U.S. exports fell 7 percent, while the price of goods imported into the United States grew 25 percent.

TABLE 13–1   U.S. Merchandise Exports and Imports, 1981–1990*

	EXPORTS	IMPORTS	BALANCE
1981	$237	$265	$-28
1982	211	248	-36
1983	202	269	-67
1984	220	332	-113
1985	216	338	-122
1986	223	368	-145
1987	250	410	-160
1988	320	447	-127
1989	361	475	-115
1990†	386	491	-106

Source: Economic Report of the President 1991 (Washington, D.C.: Government Printing Office, 1991), p. 405.
* In billions of dollars.
†1990 data based on first three quarters at annualized rate.

The second factor that contributed to the emergence of the trade deficit was the strong stimulus given the U.S. economy in the wake of the 1982 recession. The revival of the U.S. economy in 1983 and 1984 occurred when the rest of the advanced industrial world was still in recession. Economic growth and job creation in the United States stimulated demand for international goods at a time when other countries were urgently seeking to expand markets for their own products. The United States led the industrial world out of the recession of the early 1980s, but it did so through a sharp increase in imports.

Third, the surge in the U.S. trade deficit was also a product of the debt crisis in the developing world. In the 1970s, many developing countries borrowed vast sums in an effort to improve the functioning of their economies. By the early 1980s, however, it was clear that the borrowed funds had not been invested effectively, and the countries were not able to repay their loans as scheduled. The purchase of U.S. goods in Latin America plummeted in these years, as countries such as Brazil, Argentina, and Mexico sought to preserve foreign currency. At the same time, these countries looked to increased sales of their products in the United States to earn money to pay off the international debts.

Trade relations with Japan are now the object of great scrutiny, but there is no reason to believe that Japanese policies played a particular role in the origins of the U.S. deficit. Between 1981 and 1984, the trade deficit with Japan swelled from $16 billion to $37 billion, as Table 13–2 indicates. During these years, however, the deficits with Western Europe and the developing countries of Latin America, Asia, and Africa increased even more rapidly. On the other hand, there is some evidence that Japanese practices have aggravated U.S. trade problems. The US trade deficit with Japan did grow faster between 1984 and 1987 than the deficits with Western Europe and the developing world, and it has fallen more slowly in the years since 1987 than the deficit with Europe.

TABLE 13–2 U.S. Trade Balance by Area, 1981–1990*

	1981	1984	1987	1990†
Total	-$28	-$113	$160	-$106
Canada	-2	-15	-12	-8
Western Europe	+12	-15	-28	+2
Japan	-16	-37	-57	-41
OPEC Countries	-29	-13	-14	-24
Latin America, Asia, Africa (less OPEC)	0	-37	-52	-42
Other	+7	+4	+3	+7

Source: Economic Report of the President 1991 (Washington, D.C.: Government Printing Office, 1991), p. 405.
*In billions of dollars.
†1990 data based on first three quarters are annualized rate.

The growth in the U.S. trade deficit in the early 1980s coincided with basic changes in the world economy. These changes have increased the pressure under which the postwar trade system operates.

Changes in the System of World Trade

In the 1950s and 1960s, major countries defined the value of their currency in terms of the dollar, and the United States supported the value of the dollar by guaranteeing to convert it into gold at a fixed rate.[22] This system of fixed exchange rates pegged to the dollar provided great stability for world trade, but it did not survive changes in the value of the dollar itself.

In the early 1970s, economists concluded that the initial U.S. trade deficits indicated that the dollar was overvalued. To solve the problem, the United States devalued the dollar in relation to other major currencies and ended the convertibility of dollars into gold. These moves forced the world to shift to the current system of floating exchange rates by which the value of the dollar is set every day in the currency markets. Huge pools of international capital have been assembled to speculate in currency fluctuations, and, as a result, manufacturers active in global trade are now less certain of their costs and revenues than they once were.

A second factor that increased instability in world trade was the emergence of new players in the global economy. As noted above, the postwar trading system was the product of agreements between governments in Europe and North America. The rise of Japan as an economic power introduced non-Western cultural assumptions into deliberations over trade issues. Western firms complained in the 1970s and 1980s that Japan pursued unfair trade practices and effectively closed its domestic market to imported goods. Concerns about Japanese practices were multiplied when countries such as Korea, Taiwan, and Singapore and even Brazil and Mexico appeared to be following a similar path. The growing cultural diversity of nations involved in international trade has complicated the process of reaching agreement on contentious issues.

Another change occurring in the 1970s and 1980s was the declining effectiveness of GATT rules and procedures. The GATT had been created as a multilateral device to reduce tariffs, and at this it had been remarkably successful. During these years, however, many governments decided to play a more activist role in improving their nation's economies. This new activism involved preferences and subsidies for domestic industries that often became nontariff restrictions on international trade. The GATT system has never developed effective procedures for dealing with nontariff trade barriers. Furthermore, GATT was conceived to promote trade in manufactured goods. The increasing size of the service sector in the global economy poses problems of definition and analysis that GATT has not solved.

Finally, the GATT principle of nondiscrimination, that each country should grant equal treatment to products regardless of the country of origin, is increasingly subject to challenge. The European Community and other free-trade zones were plainly created to allow their members access to markets under conditions denied to outsiders. Each of these developments has undermined the GATT framework.

The fourth development that has increased pressure on the world trade system is the changed position of the United States. In the decades immediately after World War II, the United States provided leadership to create and maintain the international trade system. As its postwar dominance ended, the United States no longer had the ability to insist on free-trade principles in the world. While the British had defended liberal trade policies in the nineteenth century, and the Americans had promoted free trade in the years after 1934, no single nation now has the power to lead the world to support free trade.

Floating exchange rates, the emergence of new trading nations, the erosion of the GATT, and the decline of U.S. leadership have all complicated the problems of international trade. Political changes inside the United States have also increased the difficulty in managing the world's new trade situation.

Changes in American Politics

Until recently, the politics of trade was rather simple. The Smoot-Hawley lesson from 1930 that restrictions on trade harmed the global economy dominated academic and political thinking. Elite groups endorsed liberal trade policies all but unanimously. The executive branch shaped the nation's trade policies, and protectionism was the central trade issue. Few industries were affected by imports, and Congress established institutions like the International Trade Commission to deflect pressures for legislative action coming from companies hurt by imports.

By the mid-1980s, the situation at home and abroad had changed. The volume of international trade had increased greatly, and the U.S. economy was buffeted by the increases. As the trade deficit exploded, more firms and workers found themselves losers in the trade process. Demands for governmental action multiplied. As governments around the world became more involved in promoting their economies, and the cultural diversity of significant trading nations increased, trade disputes became more complicated to solve.

While trade problems increased, congressional ability to resist protectionist pressures declined. Earlier reforms had weakened the House Ways and Means Committee, which once managed trade legislation, and distributed authority on trade matters to subcommittees responsive to specific interests. Furthermore, trade has also become a more partisan issue. Democrats had once supported international trade. As the Republican administration failed to curb the ballooning trade deficit in the early 1980s, however, trade topics were used by Democrats to criticize a Republican president. As the deficits persisted, some Republicans joined Democrats and made trade a topic of congressional criticism of the executive branch.

The deterioration of the elite consensus in favor of free trade also confused trade issues. The debate has shifted from issues of free trade to questions of fair trade. Multinational enterprises and organized labor had once backed liberal trade policies. The loss of jobs in traditional industries turned unions into champions of protectionist legislation, and the inability of the administration to guarantee access to international markets quieted multinational supporters of free trade doctrines. Contemporary trade disputes are more complex than were earlier issues, and the political ability to respond to these controversies has declined.

CAN THE FREE-TRADE SYSTEM BE SALVAGED?

The Reagan administration strategy for relieving the trade deficit had two elements: reduce the value of the dollar to make U.S. exports more attractive overseas and imports more expensive at home; and press other countries to open their markets to American goods. This strategy has had some success. The trade deficit fell from its height of $160 billion in 1987 to $106 billion in 1990. The deficit equaled 65 percent of the country's exports in 1987, but only 27 percent of exports in 1990.[23] (See Table 13–1.)

Clear progress has been made in reducing the size of the deficit since 1987, but the pace of progress slowed between 1989 and 1990, and the deficit remains at an unsustainably high level. The options for dealing with the continuing trade deficit are two: repair the defects in the existing free-trade system; or move to a system of managed trade.

Free-Trade Option

Proponents of the free-trade option argue that the United States is primarily responsible for creating the trade deficit, and it is its responsibility to eliminate it.[24] In the long term, trade balances are not the product of trade strategies, but of a country's savings and investment policies. The best way—in fact, the only way—

for the United States to lower the trade deficit and prevent the loss of American wages and income is to balance its domestic budget and increase economic productivity.

Champions of free trade acknowledge that protectionism will always be popular among producer groups, but they maintain that the costs of protection to consumers will be greater than the benefits to producers. Import restrictions, they argue, are like a sales tax whose revenues are used to pay a subsidy to the protected industry.[25] The Multifiber Agreement and bilateral accords, for example, limit imports of textiles and clothing. It is estimated that U.S. producers gain slightly more than $4 billion each year from these restrictions, but the costs in higher prices to American consumers exceed $10 billion annually. Protectionism is commonly believed to save jobs. Free-trade advocates argue that the price of preserving jobs in the protected industry is to push up costs throughout the economy and sacrifice more jobs elsewhere. Restrictions on imports of machine tools, for example, are said to cost consumers $120,000 in higher prices for each job "saved" in the industry.[26]

Proponents of the free-trade option agree that the GATT guidelines need to be updated to deal with new conditions. They insist, however, that the trade deficit has been "Made in the USA" and that it can only be remedied through more disciplined fiscal policies.

Managed-Trade Option

Advocates of the managed-trade option for dealing with trade issues contend that free trade is no longer a meaningful policy. While it may be good economic theory, most national governments do not practice free trade. At most, one-half of world trade is currently covered by GATT regulations, and the share appears to be declining.[27] Continuing U.S. efforts to promote free-trade policies in a world that rejects them are simply quixotic, according to managed-trade analysts. They harm U.S. interests and leave essential industries vulnerable to the predatory tactics of international competitors.

The term *managed trade* can be used in three different ways. First, it can simply refer to any system in which government plays an active role in shaping a country's trade flows. Second, more narrowly, managed trade can identify trade strategies that seek to promote specific industries. Trade analysts have recently argued that some sectors, such as high technology, are more important to a country's economy than others.[28] A policy of managed trade might seek to enhance a country's competitiveness in these strategic sectors. Finally, managed trade can refer to a system that establishes quantitative targets for trade flows between nations. A system of managed trade, for example, might insist that the overall trade balance between nation A and nation B be at a certain level. An agreement between the United States and Japan, for example, required the Japanese to purchase a specified share of their semiconductor products from U.S. firms.

Proponents of managed trade maintain that the United States needs an alternative to the laissez-faire attitudes of the past if it is to meet the challenges posed by the trade policies of Japan and the European Community. The significance of the managed-trade and free-trade options for dealing with trade policy can be seen in the context of two current issues: the Uruguay Round of GATT negotiations, and U.S. trade with Japan.

Uruguay Round

The Uruguay Round of negotiations was launched in 1986 and was intended to strengthen, extend, and modernize GATT's rules and procedures.[29] The discussions were to have been completed in 1990, but they broke down at a meeting in Brussels in December 1990 over an impasse in agricultural issues. The talks were suspended, but there are numerous efforts to revive them. The most important topics in the Uruguay Round are the following.

Agriculture: Agriculture makes up 10 percent of world trade, but it has never been subject to GATT rules. The European Community and Japan have a maze of expensive restrictions that create barriers to imports and disrupt the world market in agricultural goods. The United States and agriculture exporting nations have sought to limit internal subsidies to agriculture, eliminate barriers to imports, and reduce the subsidies countries pay to export their products.

Services: Services in such areas as insurance, banking, tourism, and film production account for 20 percent of world trade. The talks have sought to create a broad framework agreement, called the General Agreement on Trade in Services, and a set of annexes laying out rules for governing specific services. The foundation of the agreement holds that countries should not discriminate among service companies of the basis of their national origin.

Intellectual Property Rights: U.S. export earnings from royalties and licensing fees in 1989 reached $12 billion. Most industrial nations allow creators to profit from their products through laws that make it illegal to sell counterfeit goods or pirate patents, computer software, books, records, and tapes. Some other countries have no laws protecting intellectual property rights or do not enforce the laws they have.

Sensitive Industries: Countries in the developing and industrialized world control trade in a few industries that play a sensitive role in their economies, such as textiles, steel, shipbuilding, and automobiles. The Uruguay Round seeks to phase out these special controls.

Dispute Settlement Procedures: GATT's origins as a provisional agreement left it without reliable mechanisms for settling disputes among members. The Uruguay Round seeks agreement on dispute settlement procedures that are swifter and more reliable.

The Uruguay Round of GATT negotiations is perceived in some countries as a means of helping the United States reduce its trade deficit. Thus, a successful outcome is more important to the United States than to Japan and the European Community. Japan is focusing less on GATT than on cutting back exports, moving production abroad, coping with the increased value of the yen, meeting the competition of its recently industrialized neighbors, and managing the process of high-tech innovation.[30] Germany has an export-oriented economy and fears that protectionism in agriculture will lead to retaliation in industrial sectors, but it is currently giving a higher priority to German and European integration than to trade policies. Underdeveloped nations want to expand agricultural exports, but they fear that opening their markets to competition in the service sector will destroy their domestic industries.

The failure of the Uruguay Round is a distinct possibility.[31] It would probably encourage protectionist pressures around the world and result in increased trade barriers. While the collapse of the talks might not be catastrophic, it would indicate that many countries have concluded that their prosperity depends less on a global trading system than on regional and bilateral arrangements. Among the most important of these relationships is trade between the United States and Japan.

U.S.–Japanese Trade

The emergence of the trade imbalance between the United States and Japan in the mid-1980s has hurt political relations between the two countries. The bond with Japan has been the foundation of U.S. security arrangements in the Pacific since World War II, and the economic interdependence of the two countries makes harmonious relations important for the future.[32]

Japan maintains that U.S. trade problems are the result of the failure of U.S. macroeconomic policies. The United States, according to Japan, should balance its domestic budget, increase savings and investment, and improve the education and training of workers to cure the trade deficit, not blame the Japanese. Japan did not create the U.S. trade deficit, and it should not be expected to adopt policies to eliminate it.

United States trade negotiators have argued that the trade deficit is compounded by Japanese policies and practices. Japan, they maintain, has adopted a series of unfair commercial tactics that exploits its access to international markets and effectively closes Japanese markets to foreign firms. Certain structural features of the Japanese economy are also identified by U.S. representatives as barriers to U.S. firms including the structure of the Japanese distribution system, which restricts the operations of large retail stores; the behavior of the conglomerates, called keiretsu; the lax enforcement of Japanese antitrust laws; restrictive land use laws; and the cumbersome patent system.[33]

Regardless of the conflicting perceptions of specific topics, it is clear that Japan does indeed exhibit a trade pattern that differs from those of other major nations.[34] Japan's exports to the United States are quite normal, but it displays a clear aversion to importing manufactured products, especially in sectors in which the United States has technical superiority. Despite journalist rhetoric about the "flood" of imports from Japan, the United States received more goods in 1990 from both Canada and Western Europe than from Japan. The striking difference in U.S.

trade with Japan is that Japan imports from the United States only half as much as Canada and Western Europe. The United States trade deficit with Japan has fallen from $57 billion in 1987 to $41 billion in 1991, but it remains at an unacceptably high level

What role can free-trade and managed-trade approaches play in dealing with this problem? Is the trade deficit with Japan the result of U.S. macroeconomic policies, as the Japanese claim; or of Japanese trade barriers, as U.S. representatives contend? Is the emergence of a small U.S. trade surplus with Europe in 1990 evidence that the persistent deficit with Japan is a structural, rather than a macroeconomic, problem? The U.S. film industry's ability to maintain access to international markets will be a telling indicator of the future viability of the current system of international trade.

SUMMARY

Liberal or free-trade policies are policies that facilitate the movement of products from country to country and allow the world to act more like a single economic unit.

The Smoot-Hawley Act of 1930 sharply increased tariffs on goods coming into the United States. This led to an overall reduction in the volume of international trade and aggravated economic conditions that were then moving toward depression.

The Reciprocal Trade Agreement Act of 1934 established the pattern of lower tariffs that was to prevail for a half-century. This new approach was symbolized by the General Agreement on Tariffs and Trade. GATT was based on a commitment to trade liberalization, reciprocity in lowering tariffs, and nondiscrimination in applying tariffs among member countries. Since its creation, GATT has sponsored eight conferences or "rounds" of negotiations on trade issues. GATT is based on a series of voluntary guidelines rather than on a set of obligatory rules.

The United States deficit in merchandise trade grew enormously during the 1980s and placed trade issues back at the center of the political stage. While the U.S. trade deficit was not caused by Japanese policies, Japan's practices have aggravated U.S. trade problems.

Changes in the world trading system including floating exchange rates, the emergence of new trading nations, the erosion of GATT coverage, and the decline of U.S. leadership have all complicated the process of dealing with trade problems at the global level. Developments in U.S. politics have also complicated trade issues and reduced the capacity of the political system to respond to these problems effectively.

Whether the free-trade system of the last half-century can be salvaged through reforms and improvements in GATT, or whether the GATT system will be slowly replaced by a system of "managed trade" remains an open question.

SELECTED READINGS

I.M. DESTLER, *American Trade Politics: System Under Stress* (Washington, D.C.: Institute for International Economics, 1986).

ROBERT Z. LAWRENCE and CHARLES L. SCHULTZE (eds.), *An American Trade Strategy: Options for the 1990s* (Washington, D.C.: Brookings Institution, 1990).

EDWARD J. LINCOLN, *Japan's Unequal Trade* (Washington, D.C.: Brookings Institution, 1990).

HENRY R. NAU (ed.), *Domestic Trade Politics and the Uruguay Round* (New York: Columbia University Press, 1989).

ROBERT M. STERN (ed.), *U.S. Trade Policies in a Changing World Economy* (Cambridge, Mass.: MIT Press, 1987).

END NOTES

[1]Statements about The Walt Disney Company come from the firm's *1990 Annual Report* (Burbank, Calif.: Disney, 1990).

[2]Statements about the industry are drawn from Bruce Stokes, "Tinseltown Trade War," *National Journal*, February 23, 1991, pp. 432–38.

[3]Ibid., p. 435.

[4]Ronald Brownstein, *The Power and the Glitter: The Hollywood-Washington Connection* (New York: Pantheon, 1990).

[5]This chapter relies on the basic text on trade issues: I.M. Destler, *American Trade Politics: System Under Stress* (Washington, D.C.: Institute for International Economics, 1986); here, pp. 3–5.

[6]See Richard N. Cooper, "Trade Policy as Foreign Policy," *U.S. Trade Policies in a Changing World Economy*, Robert M. Stern (ed.), (Cambridge, Mass.: MIT Press, 1987), pp. 291–322.

[7]The classic account is E.E. Schattschneider, *Politics, Pressures and the Tariff: A Study of Free Private Enterprise in Pressure Politics, as Shown in the 1929–1930 Revision of the Tariff* (New York: Prentice-Hall, 1935).

[8]Destler, *American Trade Politics*, p. 9.

[9]I.M. Destler, "United States Trade Policymaking in the Uruguay Round," in Henry R. Nau (ed.), *Domestic Trade Politics and the Uruguay Round* (New York: Columbia University Press, 1989), pp. 191–207.

[10]Kenneth W. Dam, *The GATT: Law and International Economic Organization* (Chicago: University of Chicago Press, 1970), Chapters 2–3.

[11]Stefanie Ann Lenway, *The Politics of U.S. International Trade: Protection, Expansion and Escape* (Boston: Pitman, 1985), pp. 4–7.

[12]Claude E. Barfield and John H. Makin (eds.), *Trade Policy and U.S. Competitiveness* (Washington, D.C.: American Enterprise Institute, 1987), Chapters 2–5.

[13]Barfield and Makin (eds.), *Trade Policy and U.S. Competitiveness*, Chapters 22–24; and Robert Z. Lawrence and Robert E. Litan, *Saving Free Trade: A Pragmatic Approach* (Washington, D.C.: Brookings Institution, 1986).

[14]For an alternative view, see Sima Lieberman, *The Economic and Political Roots of the New Protectionism* (Totowa, N.J.: Rowman & Littlefield, 1988).

[15]Alan M. Gurman and Andrew D.M. Anderson, *Administered Protection in America* (London: Croom Helm, 1987).

[16]William J. Long, *U.S. Export Control Policy: Executive Autonomy vs. Congressional Reform* (New York: Columbia University Press, 1989).

[17]Destler, "United States Trade Policymaking in the Uruguay Round," in Nau (ed.), *Domestic Trade Politics and the Uruguay Round*, p. 192.

[18]The current accounts balance includes trade in both goods and services such as tourism, transportation, financial services, and film industry services. A surplus or deficit in the current accounts balance is offset by a shift in the capital account that represents a movement of investment funds.

[19]Specific data in this section is drawn from *Economic Report of the President 1991* (Washington, D.C.: Government Printing Office, 1991), pp. 404–406.

[20]Destler, *American Trade Politics*, pp. 181–82; and William R. Cline, *United States External Adjustment and the World Economy* (Washington, D.C.: Institute for International Economics, 1989), pp. 51–75.

[21]Benjamin Friedman, *Day of Reckoning: The Consequences of American Economic Policy* (New York: Random House, 1988).

[22]This section draws from Destler, *American Trade Politics*, pp. 37–55.

[23]*Economic Report of the President 1991* (Washington, D.C.: Government Printing Office, 1991), p. 405.

[24]Robert Z. Lawrence and Charles L. Schultze, "Evaluating the Options," in Lawrence and Schultze (eds.), *An American Trade Strategy: Options for the 1990s* (Washington, D.C.: Brookings Institution, 1990), pp. 1–41.

[25]This and the following statements come from the *Economic Report of the President 1991*, pp. 240–41.

[26]Ibid., p. 241.

[27]Laura D. Andrea Tyson, "Managed Trade: Making the Best of the Second Best," in Lawrence and Schultze (eds.), *An American Trade Strategy*, pp. 142–85; here, p. 144.

[28]See Paul Krugman, "Strategic Sectors and International Competitiveness," in Stern (ed.), *Trade Policies in a Changing World Economy*, pp. 207–32; and Martin Wolf, "Academics now advocate trading blocs," *Financial Times* (London), October 30, 1989, p. 19.

[29]This section is based on the *Economic Report of the President 1991*, pp. 243–52.

[30]Bunroku Yoshino, "Japan and the Uruguay Round," pp. 111–34, and Frank D. Weiss, "Domestic Dimensions of the Uruguay Round: The Case of West Germany in the European Communities," pp. 69–89, in Nau (ed.), *Domestic Trade Politics and the Uruguay Round*.

[31]Bruce Stokes, "Après GATT, le Deluge?" *National Journal*, January 12, 1991, pp. 75–78.

[32]This discussion is based on Edward J. Lincoln, *Japan's Unequal Trade* (Washington, D.C.: Brookings Institution, 1990).

[33]*Economic Report of the President 1991*, p. 255

[34]Lincoln, *Japan's Unequal Trade*, pp. 3, 16, 68–69, and 137.

Chapter 14

Competitiveness and Industrial Policy

Worries about the international competitiveness of the American economy have prompted much of the attention now focused on relations between government and industry. The deterioration of traditional industries, diminished market share in conspicuous product areas, and perceptions that other nations have pulled ahead in critical technologies have aroused fears about America's future. The competitive achievements of other countries have led commentators to ask whether their governments' policies have contributed to their economic success.

Political economists classically assumed that the factors that determined the success of a nation's economy were fixed and immutable.[1] A country would produce the goods for which it had the greatest natural advantages, and then buy the goods from other countries for which it had the least advantages. Countries that were endowed with the advantages needed to produce the most highly prized goods would be most prosperous.

The success of Germany and especially Japan in reshaping their economies convinced analysts that a nation's competitive advantages were not all predetermined. Through the appropriate mix of public policies, some countries have been able to create the comparative advantages needed to produce high-value goods. The recognition that comparative advantage was an acquired rather than a foreordained quality draws attention to the policies those countries adopted to upgrade their economies and enhance their industrial performance.

This chapter examines *industrial policies* to promote economic well-being. Industrial policy is both an analytic concept and a political symbol. It represents the view that government should play an expanded role in shaping the economy.

Authors often choose sides and announce whether they support or oppose industrial policy.[2] The effort here is not to stand for or against industrial policy but to distinguish successful industrial policies from policies that have fallen short. By identifying the common features of successful industrial policies, it is possible to consider whether such policies could boost the American economy in the years ahead.

This chapter first examines the idea of industrial policy and then turns to a closer analysis of industrial policies in the United States. It reviews the history of policies affecting specific industries, the administrative tools used to carry out industrial policies, and current arguments about industrial policy proposals. An analysis of industrial policies in Germany, Japan, and the United Kingdom provides helpful contrasts to American practice, and it helps explain why industrial policies have succeeded in some circumstances but not others. The final section of the chapter concentrates on one area of industrial policy that usually receives special consideration, high-technology policies.

WHAT IS INDUSTRIAL POLICY?

Industrial policy is policy designed to improve economic growth. There are two basic definitions of *industrial policy*. One is broad, and the other narrow. From the first perspective, the term includes all government activities that have an impact on the competitiveness of a nation's economy.[3] Here industrial policy is broadly defined as governmental "programs that affect the pattern of economic development."[4]

Followers of this definition of industrial policy identify various features of the American economy that they believe limit its competitiveness. They then advocate governmental programs to remedy these failings. Encompassed within the broad definition of industrial policy are the following topics:

- Macroeconomic policies. Bruce Scott and George Lodge maintain that the competitive problems of the American economy are the result of unsound macroeconomic policies.[5] U.S. policies emphasize leisure, consumption, and the redistribution of the economic pie. Improved competitiveness, according to Scott and Lodge, requires the United States to stop responding to the short-term consumption desires of the marketplace and adopt economic strategies based on increased saving, investment, growth, and productivity.

- Labor-management relations. Lester Thurow traces the competitive problems of American industry to adversarial relations between labor and management.[6] Poor employee motivation, high labor-turnover rates, and unstable organizational arrangements are the result of the absence of a sense of equity in major corporations. From Thurow's perspective, the acceptance by both labor and management of their interdependence is crucial both for the prosperity of individual firms and the long-term success of the nation's economy.

- Education and infrastructure. Among the factors that Michael Porter believes determine the competitive advantage of nations are advanced educational skills and specialized infrastructure investments.[7] Highly educated personnel and facilities such as university research institutes are essential to design and develop a steady flow of sophisticated products. Without such resources, Porter maintains, a country's prosperity will pass as its natural advantages lose their significance in an increasingly complex world economy.

- Production technology. Stephen Cohen and John Zysman argue that competitiveness is determined by the manner in which a nation produces goods and services.[8] They believe that the main cause for the deteriorating U.S. competitive position is the failure to modernize production technologies in critical industries. The failure to promote new production technologies limits the attractiveness of current products and closes off avenues for future economic progress.
- Cultural patterns. Robert Reich contends that the United States suffers from a conflict between its business and civic cultures.[9] The cultures embody conflicting notions of freedom, responsibility, citizenship, and community, and tensions between them surface in continuing struggles over the competing claims of economic prosperity and social justice. According to Reich, the failure of the United States to develop a mode of accommodation between these two cultures has hindered the country's economic progress.

The broad definition of industrial policy includes macroeconomic policies, labor-management relations, education and infrastructure, production technologies, cultural patterns, and more. Unfortunately, this definition is so encompassing as to be unwieldy. When almost everything is seen to be an aspect of industrial policy, the concept loses much of its utility.

The second meaning of industrial policy is narrower.[10] According to the narrower definition, industrial policy is governmental action intended to improve a country's economic well-being through its impact on *specific industries*. Industrial policies may launch new, high-technology industries, enhance the competitiveness of existing industries, or sustain jobs and firms in declining industries. The phrase *industrial policy* is used in this chapter in this narrow, sector-specific sense.

INDUSTRIAL POLICY: AMERICAN POLICIES AND PROPOSALS

The United States is often thought to have shunned special assistance to individual firms and industries.[11] In fact, the country has a long history of stunningly successful efforts to enhance the nation's economic well-being through policies based on particular industries. As noted in Chapter 1, earlier generations accomplished such impressive economic feats as building transcontinental railroads and modernizing the nation's agricultural production and distribution systems. In the last half-century, no nation has had a record of more innovative and successful industrial policies than the United States. The chronicle of sector-specific industrial policies reveals impressive triumphs, costly flops, and some cases that are still too close to call.

Industrial Policy Examples

In the two decades after World War II, government policy improved dramatically the quality of private American housing stock. U.S. housing was transformed from marginally adequate to probably the best housing in the world. With political support based on efforts to reward veterans for wartime service, government devised a series of financial arrangements and tax concessions that reduced the risks at each step in the housing construction and sales process. As a result, the housing industry thrived, and a large fraction of the American public obtained quality housing that had previously been unaffordable.

In 1961, the United States pledged to land a person on the moon before the end of the decade and return that person safely to earth. This objective required the rapid development of the nation's space industry and a considerable expenditure of public funds. The first lunar landing occurred in 1969 and was followed by a series of televised landings that symbolized the era's enthusiasm for space exploration. The attainment of the nation's goal was made possible by NASA's flexible administrative structure, new patterns of government-business collaboration, the imaginative cultivation of political support for the space program, and the unusual perseverance of public officials.

Government policies to enhance the nation's telecommunications system have changed from generation to generation, but the result is a telephone system that is unmatched in quality and accessibility anywhere in the world.[12] The original patents awarded Alexander Graham Bell expired at the end of the nineteenth century, and this ushered in an era of competition in the telephone industry. After World War I, state and national regulators allowed AT&T to create a fully integrated telephone system and achieve monopoly status in virtually every aspect of telephone service and equipment. In the 1950s, competition began to reappear in the industry, and this development led in 1984 to the break-up of AT&T and the divestiture of the local telephone operating companies. The disruption of the nation's phone service that occurred then was followed by the introduction of revolutionary new telecommunications technologies.

Not every instance of government assistance to specific industries has been successful. Some policy initiatives, in fact, have been expensive failures. These failures were sometimes the result of economic factors and on other occasions the product of political calculations.

The steel industry turned to government for assistance when it encountered severe competitive pressures.[13] Working with steel unions, the companies succeeded in obtaining costly tax concessions, procurement preferences, trade protection, and adjustment assistance. The effort expended in gaining these preferences distracted the industry from the need to develop a strategy to meet international competition. The principal result of government aid was to reduce the industry's urgency in improving its products and procedures. As a result, the industry's eventual adjustment was probably more painful and traumatic than would otherwise have been the case.

In 1980, Congress created the U.S. Synthetic Fuels Corporation to make the country less dependent on imported oil by developing technologies to obtain oil from domestic shale and coal.[14] The Synfuels Corporation was authorized to seek $68 billion to meet the goal of producing two million barrels of oil per day by 1992.

President Carter declared that the Synfuels project would dwarf NASA's lunar-landing program. In 1985, Congress eliminated funding for the Synfuels Corporation, and the next year the agency went out of business. It then had just one project in commercial production that yielded only 4,300 barrels of oil per day. Congress approved the Synfuels project when the price of oil was $30 a barrel, but it lost interest when the price of crude fell below $15 a barrel. However valuable experts say synthetic fuels may be in the future, officeholders turned their attention to more popular problems.

Some industrial policies can be labeled successes or failures rather easily, but the country's most celebrated industrial policy initiative, assistance to the Chrysler corporation during the period 1979 to 1980, still resists easy characterization.[15] As the smallest of the three major American automobile manufacturers, Chrysler had long faced a difficult competitive situation. It had many of the overhead costs of larger companies, but it enjoyed fewer economies of scale and sold fewer cars with which to pay its costs. For a half-decade, the firm had sought government aid in the form of development grants, tax credits for car buyers, reductions in its own tax obligations, and administrative relief from regulatory requirements. As its situation became more acute, Chrysler worked with its unions, local auto dealers, and professional lobbyists to step up its campaign to secure government aid. During the presidential primary season, the Carter administration agreed to a package of $1.5 billion in loan guarantees and mandatory concessions to the firm from Chrysler unions, suppliers, and lenders.

Chrysler survived its crisis and was able to repay its loans before the required dates. The company improved its product line, but it also reduced its number of workers from 122,000 to 84,000.[16] The recovery in the firm's situation resulted from plant closings, increases in sales, tax concessions, and import quotas on Japanese cars approved during the Reagan presidency. The costs of public assistance to Chrysler and the automobile industry during these years were enormous, but the industry continues to face enormous challenges.

The review of policies involving housing, the NASA lunar landing, telecommunications, the steel industry, synthetic fuels, and Chrysler confirms that the United States has, indeed, pursued a series of sector-specific industrial policies. Furthermore, these policies are remarkably diverse. They have employed a lengthy catalogue of policy tools: direct subsidies, credit assistance, government procurement, tax concessions, trade protection, the use of unappropriated funds, and regulatory preferences. In contrast to the ideological animosities often provoked by discussions of industrial policy, these policies display a pragmatic willingness to rely on government agencies, corporations, nonprofit institutions, or some innovative public-private mechanism whenever it promises to help achieve a program's objectives. Finally, these policies, especially the successful ones, are unusual in their creativity. They are not standard government responses to routine problems, but imaginative solutions to unique situations. They are part of the long history of public action to boost economic well-being through policies directed toward specific industries.

Contemporary Issues

One prominent American scholar has reviewed the history of industrial policies in the United States and the success of other governments in enhancing their business environments and concluded, "The confidence that we can be competitive without a national strategy...no longer accords with present reality."[17] The United States, it is said, must follow the lead of other governments and devise a coherent strategy to improve its industrial performance if it is to remain competitive in the world marketplace.[18]

Industrial policies provide start-up aid for new industries, offer adjustment assistance to traditional industries, or restructure the marketplace for specific goods. Contemporary proposals for an American industrial policy concentrate on providing an administrative framework for the policies.[19] Most proposals call for a *federal investment bank* to target financial aid to companies facing structural problems. The creation of a federal investment bank implies that the traditional financial markets do not provide adequate capital to distressed industries or new firms.

A second feature of many industrial policy programs is the establishment of a *new technologies foundation* modeled after the National Science Foundation. This foundation would select and subsidize new technologies that promise broad economic benefits. This proposal assumes that existing financial markets undervalue the societal benefits of new technologies.

Finally, industrial policy packages ordinarily include a proposal to create an *economic coordination council*. The council would be responsible for dampening labor-management animosities, coordinating federal programs affecting industry, and conducting industry-by-industry analyses of domestic trends and international developments.

Other industrial policy proposals endorse a range of sector-specific initiatives. Companies would receive public aid, according to these proposals, when they promise extraordinary public benefits or face unusual domestic or international competition. Individual authors also invoke the term "industrial policy" to characterize initiatives to aid distressed regions, expand federal support for infrastructure expenditures, improve the nation's education system, and subsidize child-care costs.

Industrial policy proposals are supported by policy analysts, liberal office-holders, labor union officials, and representatives of companies and regions that expect to receive aid.[20] Such figures argue that markets and macroeconomic policies do not adequately address the problems of specific groups and do not acknowledge the reality of government involvement in international economic competition. They point to the hardships faced by unemployed workers and abandoned communities through no fault of their own.

Champions of industrial policy applaud successful initiatives from past decades and argue that the country has nothing to fear from an expanded role for government in economic decision making. It is far cheaper, they maintain, for government to rescue troubled companies today than to pay the costs of unemployment assistance, job retraining, and pension bailouts in the future. Moreover, if prominent corporations are allowed to fail, it might panic financial markets and lead to significant disruptions of the economy. If the government stands by and does nothing to halt the collapse of basic industries, the nation's prosperity and its place in the world will inevitably deteriorate. Unless government helps American companies today obtain start-up capital and enter foreign markets, they will not be able to lead the world economy in the twenty-first century.

Opposition to industrial policy proposals is spearheaded by economists who maintain that the proposals are unfair and simply will not work.[21] They stress that corporations and industries facing hardship do so for fundamental reasons that will not be cured by short-term support. Programs of temporary assistance distract business, government, and the public from the need to address fundamental problems.

Opponents of industrial policy maintain that government does not have the fortitude to manage industrial policy programs properly. According to this view, the adoption of industrial policy measures is likely to produce a series of expensive payoffs to declining but politically influential industries. The result will be increased costs for healthy firms, consumers, and the general economy as government channels scarce resources into inefficient activities. Charles Schultze forecasts, "...the surest way to multiply unwarranted subsidies and protectionist measures is to legitimize their existence under the rubric of industry policy."[22]

The review of the industrial policy debate and past examples of industrial policy suggest that the success of industrial policies depends less on technical judgments than on the context in which industrial policies are conducted. It appears that American industrial policies have been successful when used to accomplish a broadly accepted public goal.[23] They have also been effective when programmatic decisions were shielded from particularistic political pressures and when corporations were constrained to behave in economically efficient ways. If these three conditions were not met, the adverse results predicted by the critics of industrial policy have often appeared. Further evidence on the factors that contribute to the effectiveness of industrial policies is gained by examining experiences in other countries.

INDUSTRIAL POLICY: INTERNATIONAL EXPERIENCE

Germany

German industrial policies are intended to accomplish three goals: maintain production and employment in existing industries; promote the growth of new industries and technologies; and subsidize specific consumer goods.[24] The Ministry of Economic Affairs provides large subsidies to traditional "sunset" industries such as coal, steel, and shipbuilding. While these subsidies have occasionally helped firms and regions adjust to new economic realities, they have usually just delayed the day of reckoning.

The Ministry of Research and Technology assists "sunrise" industries, including computers, aerospace, and nuclear energy, through a system of subsidies, project grants, and tax concessions. German involvement in the European Airbus program to manufacture airliners has been successful, but the record in other areas has been mixed, with some public research and development funding simply replacing previously available private support.

The postal, communications, and rail systems in Germany receive massive subsidies. These subsidies have lowered immediate costs to consumers, but the subsidies have also reduced the incentives for these systems to improve the efficiency of their operations. As a result, the total costs of these services remain high, and the quality of service is uneven.

The German economic system achieved an impressive record in the quarter-century after World War II and in the entire postwar era. The country's sector-specific industrial policies, however, have made a smaller contribution to this success than the country's sound macroeconomic policies, consensual policy style, and constructive system of labor-management relations.[25] Policies to sustain older industries, promote new technologies, and reduce the costs of consumer items have had only mixed results. When we turn from Germany to Japan, we encounter a country in which targeted industrial policies have played a more prominent role in economic success.

Japan

The significance of industrial policy in Japan is a subject of considerable controversy. Some scholars attribute Japan's economic success to the country's institutional arrangements that facilitate effective government decision making and allow close cooperation between firms and government.[26] Other authors trace Japan's economic success to its macroeconomic policies that stress personal saving, holding down interest rates, and limiting consumption.[27] Still other analysts maintain that Japan's economic achievements result from sector-specific industrial policies that explicitly target individual industries for governmental assistance.[28]

In Japan's high-growth decades, the Ministry of International Trade and Industry (MITI) identified a series of industries whose well-being it thought was important to the country's economy. MITI sought to reorganize traditional industries such as sugar refining, textiles, cement, and chemicals that had lost their competitiveness. The agency sponsored corporate agreements to restrict output and offered firms subsidies to adopt new practices. MITI also identified sunrise industries such as computers, biotechnology, and new building materials. These industries were thought to be critical because they were likely to grow in the future as national income increased, offered potential economies of scale, would benefit other sectors of the economy, and could become a significant source of future exports.

Having targeted key industries, MITI offered the industries government assistance in exploiting the long-term potential of their markets. They received tax incentives, special depreciation rules, government-funded research assistance, and direct financial subsidies. Favored industries also benefited from submarket interest rates, preferences in public procurement, a domestic market protected from international competition, and incentives to export unneeded production.

Another critical feature of Japanese policy was that official action supplemented marketplace competition rather than displacing it.[29] Public decisions were intended to establish conditions of investment and risk that promoted corporate productivity and enhanced competition. The Japanese state pervades the economy, but markets remain fluid, competition among firms and enterprise groups is fierce, and corporate bankruptcies are frequent.

Japan has won first place in global competition in numerous industries, and industrial targeting has contributed to this achievement.[30] Economic success in Japan, however, has also depended upon a well-educated workforce, effective coordination between industrial and macroeconomic policies, successful industry practices in the areas of personnel, product engineering, and quality control, and corporate discipline that results from domestic and international competition.

While Japan's record in targeting governmental assistance to individual industries can count many successes, the UK's record has been failure-strewn. When attention shifts from Japan to the United Kingdom, our effort is to determine why industrial policies have contributed to decline rather than growth.

United Kingdom

British industrial policies before the 1980s involved frequent actions to cure the problems of specific industries.[31] Government agencies tried to remedy lagging productivity and check the declining British share of world trade by establishing public-private planning procedures. Governments also sought to promote international competitiveness through mergers and reorganizations of existing industries, procurement preferences, and large subsidies for both declining and emerging industries. Assistance was given to such diverse industries as textiles, computers, cement, semiconductors, steel, supersonic aircraft, and even John deLorean's ill-fated automobile venture in North Ireland. Unfortunately, the aid programs responded more fully to the claims of politically influential groups than to the requirements of economic growth. A typical assessment of these programs concluded that "the industrial policies of the 1970s involved much waste of public money, and also often had the effect of slowing down the process of industrial adjustment."[32]

During the Thatcher years of the 1980s, the United Kingdom abandoned its most ambitious efforts to aid specific industries. Prime Minister Thatcher sought to improve British competitiveness through macroeconomic policies, the privatization of nationalized industries, deregulation, and governmental assistance to small firms and new technologies.

Factors Associated with Success

Sector-specific industrial policies can make only a limited contribution to a country's prosperity. Enough American, German, and Japanese industrial policies have had positive results, however, to warrant an examination of the factors associated with economic success. We concluded above that successful industrial policies in the United States were associated with broad public support, protection from political pressure, and constraints on corporate decision making. Does the international experience confirm these factors? If so, why are these factors important?

Policy success in both Germany and Japan rested on broad political agreement about the importance of economic growth. In contrast, economic stagnation in the United Kingdom was associated with intense conflict over the priority to be given to economic issues. Why is public support for economic goals important? Modern governments are composed of semiautonomous agencies with diverse objectives, and industrial societies are based on complicated arrangements among increasingly rigid organizations. Successful industrial policies require coordination among these institutions and agencies. Public enthusiasm for industrial policy goals is a critical mechanism for winning bureaucratic support and achieving administrative coordination.

Industrial societies are also characterized by aggressive groups and political leaders who seek to exploit public policies for their own benefit. Industrial policies require some groups to make short-term sacrifices to achieve long-term economic gains for the broader society. Such policies are vulnerable to efforts of groups seeking to use policy resources to enhance their own position. The authoritative role of administrative agencies in Japan and of banks, state ministries, and rational policy making in Germany shielded industrial policy judgments from short-term political pressures. Industrial policy judgments in the UK were highly politicized, and the resulting policies usually failed to achieve positive results.

Corporations are profit-maximizing institutions. They are also bureaucratic entities that respond to managers, product organizations, nonmanagement employees, shareholders, and lenders. Each constituency makes claims on the corporation, and corporations sometimes placate their constituencies by sacrificing the resources they need for long-term growth. Firms need to resist the excessive demands of their constituents to maintain the efficiency of their operations. The export-orientation of the German and Japanese economies and competitive pressures in both countries forced companies to make the economically responsible decisions needed for industrial policy success. When governments subsidize firms indiscriminately, the firms are prone to use the resources to appease their constituencies. In such situations, industrial policies may slow or even halt economic modernization.

The review of German, Japanese, and British experience confirms the view that successful industrial policies are associated with broad support for program goals, protection of program judgments from political pressures, and mechanisms to ensure economically disciplined corporate behavior. To conclude this discussion, it is necessary to consider how industrial policies relate to government support of high technology.

HIGH-TECHNOLOGY POLICIES

High-technology industries are a critical element in the current discussion about industrial policy.[33] High-technology industries are those that have high research and development expenditures and experience rapid technology change. Even though high-tech industries account for only a small share of employment, exports, or value-added in manufacturing, they receive special governmental attention.

Modern economies depend less on raw materials than on technique and know-how. New technologies can generate efficiencies that spread throughout an economy and produce strategic advantages for a country over its competitors. Since the benefits to a society from new technologies are greater than the returns received by individual investors, governments often help finance a country's research-and-development program. The ability of the United States to maintain wage levels and living standards depends on its success in developing a stream of new technologies that yield products that can be sold to other countries.

Government support for technology in the United States is grounded in traditional backing for technical and scientific education, assistance for industrial modernization, and public purchases of new products.[34] Traditional activities became more focused during World War II. At that time, the Department of Defense launched a series of successful R&D projects designed to help the military perform its responsibilities.[35] Military resources helped launch the country's electronics, computer, communications, and aircraft industries, and military spending sustained these industries until their products developed commercial markets.[36] The Defense Department funded corporate and academic research, arranged preferential loans and tax concessions, and offered large procurement contracts.

Military agencies developed close working relationships with corporations and then used the knowledge they gained to invite the most successful research labs to work on their projects. Military procurement shaped production strategies and moved new technologies from the laboratory to the production line. The Defense Department persuaded other government agencies to relax enforcement of antitrust laws for critical industries and to protect domestic markets from international competition, and the Department itself acted to sell the products of favored firms to other countries.

Analysts disagree about the impact of military spending on the economy, but the defense record does show that government has the capacity to manage successful industrial policies. Pentagon procedures resembled the practices now used in Japan to promote new technologies: the selection of a narrow segment of an expanding industry; systematic exploitation of new techniques; reliance on rapid economies of scale in production; and public subsidies and trade protection for emerging industries.[37]

Contemporary accounts from individual industries demonstrate that American domination of new product technologies has ended. These examples, however, do not warrant sweeping conclusions about American scientific decline.[38] A larger share of Nobel Prize laureates in the sciences came from the United States between 1976 and 1988 than in any earlier period, and more Nobel recipients came from the United States than from all other nations combined.[39] The United States continues to have a vibrant and well-funded scientific community.

In 1988, expenditures for research and development totaled $126 billion.[40] Following the pattern of the decade, 48 percent of these funds came from the federal government, 47 percent from industry, and the balance from other private and governmental sources, including universities.

Growth in R&D expenditures in recent decades has been substantial. Before World War II, federal R&D spending equalled less than one-tenth of 1 percent of gross national product, and funding for agricultural R&D exceeded the funds available for military research. Since World War II, the large increases in research and development outlays have been focused on defense technologies. The military and space share of all R&D expenditures reached a high of 56 percent in the early 1960s, declined to 28 percent in 1980, and rebounded to 37 percent in 1987, as a result of the Reagan defense build-up. While military and space projects still receive the greatest share of federal R&D spending, the largest percentage increases in the 1980s occurred in health care and energy research.

Total public and private outlays for R&D are substantially higher in the United States than in other nations because of larger size of the American economy. Today, R&D expenditures equal 2.6 percent of GNP. This is an increase from the 2.2 percent which characterized the mid-1970s and represents clear growth over 1955, when only 1.5 percent of GNP was devoted to R&D. How does U.S. R&D spending compare to other nations as a share of GNP?

Total U.S. R&D expenditures as a percent of GNP are very similar to those of Germany and Japan, as is displayed in Table 14–1. In 1987, the United States expended 2.6 percent of GNP for R&D, Germany spent 2.8 percent, and Japan spent 2.9 percent. In 1986, the United Kingdom had lagged somewhat behind, with R&D spending at 2.4 percent of GNP.

A major difference in R&D spending is the share that goes to military purposes. One-third of U.S. R&D funds was used for space and defense projects in 1987. In contrast, only a negligible portion of R&D expenditures in both Germany and Japan go to defense purposes. Civilian, nondefense R&D spending in Germany and Japan equals 2.6 percent and 2.8 percent of GNP respectively, as indicated in Table 14–1. Outlays for civilian R&D in the U.S. and the UK were a full percent lower.

TABLE 14–1   National R&D Expenditures as a Percent of GNP, 1975–1987

	TOTAL R&D				NONDEFENSE R&D			
	U.S.	*Germany*	*Japan*	*UK*	*U.S.*	*Germany*	*Japan*	*UK*
1975	2.2%	2.2%	2.0%	2.1%	1.6%	2.1%	2.0%	1.5%
1981	2.4	2.5	2.3	2.4	1.8	2.4	2.3	1.7
1986	2.7	2.7	2.8	2.4	1.8	2.6	2.8	1.8
1987	2.6	2.8	2.9	N/A	1.7	2.6	2.8	N/A

Source: U.S. Department of Commerce, *Statistical Abstract of the United States 1990* (Washington, D.C.: Government Printing Office, 1990), page 585.

Most economists argue that the benefits to a nation's economy from civilian R&D expenditures are greater than those realized from military R&D. As the national security situation changes, the United States may reconsider its investment in military R&D expenditures and refocus governmental resources on civilian activities.

The commercial spinoffs from defense expenditures do not justify past outlays, but the procedures used by the Department of Defense to promote new technologies are applicable to civilian areas. Defense Department statements have begun to emphasize the civilian benefits of its R&D program, and some officials have proposed that the Pentagon's high-technology center, the Defense Advanced Research Projects Agency (DARPA), should play a direct hand in the development of civilian technologies. One area in which this has already occurred is in the development of high definition television (HDTV).

Advanced, high-resolution display screens figure prominently in military crisis centers, but they may also be a foundation for industrial success in the twenty-first century.[41] HDTV technology may be an critical component of the next generation of computer, television, telecommunications, and electronics products. Large Japanese companies have invested hundreds of millions of dollars in efforts to develop large, thin, extra-sharp screens that will be light enough and affordable enough to be hung on the wall of an average home. If the United States loses out in this new technology, it may lose, by one estimate, more than two million jobs.[42]

Some U.S. companies are developing existing HDTV technologies beyond the point reached by Japanese firms, and others are devising newer, even more exotic technologies. The Pentagon's DARPA has contributed $15 million to these development efforts, but it is not clear if the technical hurdles in perfecting the various strategies can be overcome. Once the technical problems have been solved, the shift from development to large-scale production will then require additional resources. While American scientists have often produced stunning breakthroughs, Japan and other countries have moved more quickly to put science to work in their economies.[43]

The Bush Administration has opposed proposals to subsidize the competitiveness of the American electronics industry, and it sought to kill governmental efforts to assist HDTV.[44] The administration seeks instead to increase private research funds by reducing the capital gains tax. It maintains that the resources to propel an industry to international leadership through the brute force of money are not available and responding to political pressures by distributing small amounts of money to various industries would be futile.

Some leaders in Congress and industry agree that DARPA should not be used to help domestic industries, but they favor the creation of a civilian version of the agency to promote commercial development of new technologies.[45] A National Technology Office could monitor international competition in key industries, facilitate joint research ventures, designate projects worthy of public support, and safeguard the public interest in publicly supported research areas. The President's Commission on Industrial Competitiveness has proposed the creation of a super-agency to preside over all nonmilitary research receiving public assistance.[46]

SUMMARY

Industrial policies have been successful in promoting economic development. Examples of such success appear in sector-specific industrial policies in the United States, in the experience of other nations, and in the record of government support for new technologies.

Our conclusion is that industrial policies are most successful when they have broad public support, are protected from special-interest political pressures, and include restraints to ensure responsible corporate conduct. The challenge facing the United States is to create the conditions in which industrial policies are likely to succeed. Failure to do so merely allows such policies to become payoffs to politically influential industries.

Declining defense expenditures present both challenges and opportunities. Military spending has had a record of success in promoting new industries. Reduced defense outlays could destroy an agency that has had a noteworthy track record in advancing new technologies, or these cuts could simply release resources into the civilian economy. How the United States manages the decline in defense expenditures could be an important indicator of its ability to utilize industrial policies to enhance its international economic competitiveness in the years ahead.

SELECTED READINGS

CLAUDE E. BARFIELD and WILLIAM A. SCHAMBRA, (eds.), *The Politics of Industrial Policy* (Washington, D.C.: American Enterprise Institute, 1986).

KENNETH FLAMM, *Targeting the Computer: Government Support and International Competition* (Washington, D.C.: Brookings Institution, 1987).

RICHARD R. NELSON, *High-Technology Policies: A Five-Nation Comparison* (Washington, D.C.: American Enterprise Institute, 1984).

BRUCE L. R. SMITH, *American Science Policy Since World War II* (Washington, D.C.: Brookings Institution, 1990).

SHERIDAN M. TATSUNO, *Created in Japan: From Imitators to World-Class Innovators* (New York: Harper & Row, 1990).

END NOTES

[1]James A. Brander, "Shaping Comparative Advantage: Trade Policy, Industrial Policy, and Economic Performance," in Richard G. Lipsey and Wendy Dobson (eds.), *Shaping Comparative Advantage* (Scarborough, Ont.,Canada: Prentice Hall Canada, 1987), pp. 1–55.

[2]For a review of the arguments and positions, see R. D. Norton, "Industrial Policy and American Renewal," *Journal of Economic Literature* (March 1986), pp. 1–40.

[3]Aaron Wildavsky, "Squaring the Political Circle: Industrial Policies and the American Dream," p. 28, in Chalmers Johnson (ed.), *The Industrial Policy Debate* (San Francisco: ICS Press, 1984).

[4]Ira C. Magaziner and Robert B. Reich, *Minding America's Business: The Decline and Rise of the American Economy* (New York: Harcourt Brace Jovanovich, 1982), p. 255.

[5]Bruce R. Scott and George C. Lodge, "Introduction", in Scott and Lodge (eds.), *U.S. Competitiveness in the World Economy* (Boston: Harvard Business School Press, 1985), pp. 1–11.

[6]Lester Thurow, *The Zero-Sum Solution: Building a World-Class American Economy* (New York: Simon and Schuster, 1985), pp. 119–25. See also D. Quinn Mills and Malcolm R. Lovell, "Enhancing Competitiveness: The Contribution of Employee Relations," in Scott and Lodge (eds.), *U.S. Competitiveness in the World Economy*, pp. 455–78.

[7]Michael E. Porter, *The Competitive Advantage of Nations*, (New York: Free Press, 1990), pp. 73–85.

[8]Stephen S. Cohen and John Zysman, *Manufacturing Matters: The Myth of the Post-Industrial Economy* (New York: Basic Books, 1987), pp. 3–11 and 59–65.

[9]Robert B. Reich, *The Next American Frontier* (New York: Times Books, 1983), pp. 4–21.

[10]See Chalmers Johnson, "Introduction: The Idea of Industrial Policy," pp. 3–26, in Johnson (ed.), *Industrial Policy Debate* (San Francisco: ICS Press, 1984); and Jeffrey B. Freyman, "Industrial Policy: Patterns of Convergence and Divergence," pp. 44–68, in Jerold L. Waltman and Donley T. Studlar (eds.), *Political Economy: Public Policies in the United States and Britain* (Jackson, Miss.: University of Mississippi Press, 1987).

[11]See Ezra F. Vogel, *Comeback: Case by Case: Building the Resurgence of American Business* (New York: Simon and Schuster, 1985).

[12]See Gerald W. Brock, *The Telecommunications Industry: The Dynamics of Market Structure* (Cambridge, Mass.: Harvard University Press, 1981); and Steve Coll, *The Deal of the Century: The Breakup of AT&T* (New York: Atheneum, 1986).

[13]See, for example, John Strohmeyer, *Crisis in Bethlehem: Big Steel's Struggle to Survive* (New York: Penguin Books, 1986).

[14]Eric M. Uslaner, *Shale Barrel Politics: Energy and Legislative Leadership* (Stanford, Calif.: Stanford University Press, 1989).

[15]Robert B. Reich and John D. Donahue, *New Deals: The Chrysler Revival and the American System* (New York: Penguin Books, 1985).

[16]Ibid. p. 265 and pp. 243–47.

[17]Vogel, *Comeback: Case by Case*, pp. 269–70.

[18]Bruce R. Scott, "National Strategies: Key to International Competition," in Scott and Lodge (eds.), *U.S. Competitiveness in the World Economy*, p. 71.

[19]See, for example, James K. Galbraith, "Congress and the Industrial Policy Debate," in Sharon Zukin (ed.), *Industrial Policy: Business and Politics in the United States and France* (New York: Prager, 1985), pp. 99–106; and Congressional Budget Office, *The Industrial Policy Debate* (Washington, D.C.: Government Printing Office, 1983).

[20]Richard E. Foglesong, "The Politics of Industrial Policy in the United States," in Foglesong and Wolfe (eds.), *The Politics of Economic Adjustment*, pp. 27–64.

[21]The most prominent statement of opposition came from Charles L. Schultze, "Industrial Policy: A Dissent," *The Brookings Review*, Fall 1983, pp. 3–12.

[22]Ibid., p. 11.

[23]See Robert B. Reich, "Why the U.S. Needs An Industrial Policy," *Harvard Business Review*, January 1982, pp. 74–81.

[24]This section is drawn from Andrew P. Black, "Industrial Policy in W. Germany. Policy in Search of a Goal?," in Graham Hall (ed.), *European Industrial Policy* (London: Croom Helm, 1986), pp. 84–127.

[25]See Francois Duchene, "Policies for a Wider World," pp. 213 and 228, in Duchene and Shepherd (eds.), *Managing Industrial Change in Western Europe*.

[26]Chalmers Johnson, "The Institutional Foundation of Japanese Industrial Policy," in Claude E. Barfield and William A. Schambra (eds.), *The Politics of Industrial Policy* (Washington, D.C.: American Enterprise Institute, 1986), pp. 187–205.

[27]Philip H. Trezise, "Industrial Policy Is Not the Major Reason for Japan's Success," *Brookings Review* (Spring 1983), 13–18.

[28]Clyde V. Prestowitz, *Trading Places: How We Are Giving Our Future to Japan and How to Reclaim It* (New York: Basic Books, 1988), Chapter 5, "Mandarin Strategies: Japan's Industrial Policy."

[29]Robert S. Ozaki, "How Japanese Industrial Policy Works," pp. 47–70, in Johnson (ed.), *The Industrial Policy Debate*; and Zysman, *Governments, Markets, and Growth*, p. 237.

[30]Clyde V. Prestowitz, *Trading Places* (New York: Basic Books, 1988).

[31]Michael Utton, "Developments in British Industrial and Competition Policies," in Hall (ed.), *European Industrial Policy*, pp. 59–83; Jeffrey B. Freyman, "Industrial Policy: Patterns of Convergence and Divergence," in Waltman and Stydlar (eds.), *Political Economy: Public Policies in the United States and Britain* (Jackson, Miss.: University of Mississippi Press, 1987), pp. 44–68; and Francois Duchene, "Policies for a Wider World," in Shepherd and Duchene (eds.), *Managing Industrial Change in Western Europe*, pp. 220–24.

[32]Wyn Grant, *Government and Industry: A Comparative Analysis of the US, Canada and the UK* (Hants, England: Edward Elgar, 1989), p. 112.

[33]This section is drawn from Richard R. Nelson, *High-Technology Policies: A Five-Nation Comparison* (Washington, D.C.: American Enterprise Institute, 1984).

[34]Bruce L. R. Smith, *American Science Policy Since World War II* (Washington, D.C.: Brookings Institution, 1990).

[35]Harvey Brooks, "Technology as a Factor in U.S. Competitiveness," in Scott and Lodge (eds.), *U.S. Competitiveness in the World Economy*, p. 333.

[36]Ann R. Markusen, "Defense Spending as Industrial Policy," in Zukin (ed.), *Industrial Policy*, pp. 70–84.

[37]See Harvey Brooks, "Technology as a Factor in U.S. Competitiveness," pp. 330–33, in Scott and Lodge (eds.), *U.S. Competitiveness in the World Economy*.

[38]Nelson, *High Technology Policies*, Chapter 3, "Policies Supporting High-Technology Industries: Quantitative Aspects".

[39]U.S. Department of Commerce, *Statistical Abstract of the United States 1990*, p. 591.

[40]This section is drawn from U.S. Department of Commerce, *Statistical Abstract of the United States 1990*, pp. 583.

[41]This example is drawn from Sheridan M. Tatsuno, *Created in Japan: From Imitators to World-Class Innovators* (New York: Harper & Row, 1990), pp. 129–48; "Bigger, Wider, Flatter, Brighter: The Key to Making it in HDTV," *Business Week*, February 26, 1990, pp. 82–85; and from David S. Cloud, "Washington Policy on R&D Proving Divisive Issue," *Congressional Weekly Quarterly Report*, May 13, 1989, pp. 1107–11.

[42]"Congressmen unite to fight cuts in research funding," *Financial Times*, November 21, 1989, p. 26.

[43]Richard Florida and Martin Kenney, *The Breakthrough Illusion: Corporate America's Failure to Move from Innovation to Mass Production* (New York: Basic Books, 1990).

[44]See "U.S. semiconductor industry fears confirmed," *Financial Times*, December 1, 1989, p. 6; and "High-Tech Business Loses A Friend at the Pentagon," *New York Times*, April 29, 1990, p. E5.

[45]See Kenneth Flamm, *Targeting the Computer: Government Support and International Competition* (Washington: Brookings Institution, 1987), Chapter 6, "National Technology Policy."

[46]President's Commission on Industrial Competitiveness, *Global Competition: The New Reality*, vol. 1, (Washington, D.C.: Government Printing Office, 1985), pp. 22–24, 50–51.

Chapter 15

Social Policies Affecting Business

Social policies impact business operations at every turn. Production decisions, financial judgments, marketing strategies, and human resource choices are all embedded in a dense network of government policies.

Government programs affecting industry do not emerge from a single set of concerns. They are the result of numerous efforts to accomplish a multitude of objectives. Only by identifying the *objectives* of social policies is it possible to appraise the issues raised by such policies. Table 15–1 identifies three basic objectives of business-related social policies: accomplish broad societal goals; protect society from business; and safeguard workers.

Some social policies use industry to achieve societal objectives that have no necessary relationship to business. Governments need revenues, and businesses can be used to collect the needed funds. Modern governments provide retirement and health-care programs, and businesses are often required to assist these efforts. The United States has been slow to adopt family policies, but current proposals to provide maternity, parenting, and child-care assistance often rely on industry. The first section of this chapter explores health-care issues and the role of business in achieving broad societal goals.

Other social policies are designed to protect society from injury caused by the activities of business. Governments maintain service quality by requiring occupational groups such as doctors, lawyers, plumbers, and schoolteachers to secure licenses. Numerous consumer products may not be sold unless certified by government to be safe or, at least, not dangerous. Government also protects citizens by regulating product labeling and advertising, and it attempts to preserve the environment by controlling business operations. To illustrate this type of social policy and appraise different policy approaches, the second section of this chapter examines policies that protect the environment from damage caused by business.

TABLE 15–1   Objectives of Social Policies Affecting Business

---

Policies to achieve societal goals

Revenue systems
Retirement programs
Health care
Family policies

Policies to protect society from business

Occupational licensing
Product safety
Deceptive advertising and labeling
Environmental protection

Policies to protect workers

Minimum wage and hours
Labor-management relations
Equal employment opportunity
Safe working conditions

Still other social policies define the relationship between workers and employers. Individual workers are at such a disadvantage dealing with large employers that government has established procedures to assure some measure of equity. Laws prevent the employment of children, establish minimum-wage levels, and specify the hours that can be worked. Equal opportunity laws forbid employers from treating workers according to gender, race, or ethnicity, and occupational safety measures require firms to protect the health of employees in the workplace. Government also guarantees employees the right to form labor unions and bargain collectively. The final section of this chapter considers different means of protecting employees in the workplace. The theme of this chapter is that the manner in which business organizations are used to promote the country's social goals has often come to complicate or even frustrate the realization of those goals.

POLICIES TO ACHIEVE SOCIETAL GOALS

Commentators usually describe U.S. social policies as less developed than policies in comparable nations.[1] Most U.S. social policies, they point out, were not inaugurated until late in the game, had only limited significance until the 1930s, and involved relatively low levels of public spending. In comparison to other countries, the United States is said to have an incomplete system of social-security policies that provides neither comprehensive health care nor support for the costs of raising families.[2] The United States is also depicted as a country that is willing to tolerate high levels of unemployment in order to hold down inflation.

Like many stereotypes, this description contains elements of truth, but it also ignores key features of American historical experience. A distinctive factor in fashioning relations between government and business in a country is the sequence of development.[3] The United States witnessed a broad measure of male suffrage and the emergence of popularly based political parties early in the nineteenth century. Industrialization, the advent of corporate hierarchies, and the growth of labor unions occurred in the second half of the 1800s. Large government bureaucracies did not appear until the first half of the twentieth century.

The sequence of historical development saw democracy appear first in the United States, then industrialization, and finally public bureaucratization. In other countries, governmental bureaucracies appeared earlier in the process of development, and industrialization and democracy came later. The differences in the sequence of development had important implications for social policies and relations between government and business.

In the United States, established companies viewed the growth of government bureaucracies as a threat to their autonomy and a danger to their ability to achieve their economic goals. German corporations, in contrast, regarded previously existing government agencies as a natural part of their environment and a source of commercial assistance. The pattern of historical development helps explain the tensions between government and industry in the United States and the pattern of collaboration observed in European countries.

The democracy-industrialization-bureaucracy sequence of development can also help correct the impression of the United States as a country with delayed social policies. The early appearance of popularly based political parties resulted in the establishment in the nineteenth century of significant social policies that are usually overlooked.[4] The most expensive program was a Civil War pension system that consumed more than 40 percent of federal revenues and 1 percent of GNP by the mid-1890s. The system was intended to benefit war widows and disabled veterans, but eligibility requirements were relaxed, and the actual number of recipients multiplied well beyond those originally eligible.

A second kind of nineteenth-century social policy created jobs in the public sector and then exchanged those jobs for political support. Blatant use was made of the Post Office, then accounting for more than 60 percent of federal civilian employment, to reward party workers for their political efforts. Political standards were also used to award jobs in urban governments and in businesses that provided public services. A final feature of nineteenth-century social policy that reflects the impact of democracy was the growth of public primary education. American education stood out from other countries at this time for its high enrollment levels and substantial expenditures.

The early appearance of democracy provided an impetus to launch expansive social policies, but other characteristics of American government hindered the growth of these policies. The underdeveloped federal bureaucracies denied these policies national administrative support until the 1930s. The early emergence of private institutions also meant the public social bureaucracies, when created, usually had to accommodate well-established private-sector programs. The combination of public and private programs has often complicated the development of social service policies. A review of health-care policies illustrates the pitfalls of blending public programs and private institutions to secure social goals.

Health Care

The original model for providing public health care was established in Germany in 1883.[5] This program was employment-based. Workers and employers in particular industries were required by law to contribute to an insurance fund for their industry that would cover the full costs of medical care and pay half of the salary of incapacitated workers. Newer health-care systems in countries such as Canada have created national insurance programs that cover all residents and pay for medical services on a national or state basis. A third type of scheme is a national health service plan patterned after the program in the United Kingdom. Here a national health service covers all residents and directly provides medical and hospital care free of charge.

The United States is the only major industrial country that does not have a national health care system. American procedures for providing health care do not fit under any of the major classifications outlined above.[6] Health-care costs in the United States were originally assumed to be the responsibility of the individual and the individual's family.

Private health insurance funds appeared in the United States in the 1930s. They grew rapidly during World War II, when offered as a fringe benefit by employers who were prohibited by wartime controls from raising employee salaries. Although most Americans are now covered by employment-related health programs, these plans are not mandated by law.

In 1965, two national programs were enacted to provide health care to groups that had difficulty participating in the private insurance market, the aged and the poor. The aged have very high health-care costs and face exceptionally high insurance premiums, and the poor, who also have high health-care costs, simply lack the resources to purchase private insurance. Medicare provides insurance benefits for the aged, and Medicaid offers grants to states to cover part of the cost of medical assistance to the poor.

The United States spent $483 billion for health care in 1987, as is reported in Table 15–2. This expenditure reflects a sevenfold increase from the amount spent in 1970. In 1970, health-care costs consumed 7.4 percent of the country's gross national product. Since then, health-care costs have taken an ever-increasing share of national income and national budgets, and in 1987, 11.1 percent of GNP was devoted to health-care expenditures.

TABLE 15–2   United States Health-Care Expenditures, 1970–1987

YEAR	TOTAL ($ IN BILLIONS)	PERCENT OF GNP	SOURCE OF PAYMENTS, BY PERCENT		
			Patient	*Insurance*	*Government*
1970	$70	7.4%	38%	26%	36%
1975	124	8.3	31	28	41
1980	236	9.1	27	32	41
1985	403	10.4	26	33	41
1987	483	11.1	25	34	41

Source: Statistical Abstract of the United States 1990 (Washington, D.C.: Government Printing Office, 1990), pp. 92–93.

In 1970, as is reported in Table 15–1, patients paid directly 38 percent of the nation's health-care costs. In that year, 26 percent of costs were covered by insurance premiums, and 36 percent came from government expenditures. By 1987, the share of health-care costs paid directly by patients had fallen to 25 percent, the proportion covered by insurance premiums had risen to 34 percent, and the portion coming from government coffers had grown to 41 percent. In large part, the insurance premiums for health care in the United States are paid by employers.

In 1987, more than three out of every five Americans were covered by employment-related health insurance.[7] Medicare provided assistance to the 15 percent of the population who were senior citizens, and about 8 percent were covered by Medicaid. Approximately thirty-three million citizens were not covered by any form of health plan.

These data highlight two fundamental problems with the U.S. health-care system: the lack of a health plan for thirty-three million Americans, and the continually rising costs that endanger other necessary expenditures by citizens, business, and government.

In comparative perspective, the extraordinarily high price of medical care in the United States is one of the distinctive features of the system.[8] For fifteen years, government and industry have been talking about "cost-containment" programs for health-care expenditures, but the results have been uneven.[9]

Business has pursued two strategies to contain health-care costs: one to encourage patients to seek less expensive care, and the other to persuade providers to become more efficient. Businesses originally offered health care to employees as a fringe benefit without requiring employees to pay any share of the costs. As a technique to restrain the unnecessary use of medical care, businesses have recently sought to compel employees to contribute to the payment of medical costs by requiring employees to pay themselves the first few hundred dollars of medical costs per year and also to pay 10 or 20 percent of subsequent bills.

Businesses have also supported the creation of prepaid group health pro-grams, sometimes called health maintenance organizations (HMOs). HMOs bring together groups of physicians who provide medical care in a single location. Proponents argue that HMOs can take a long-term view of the health of a patient, realize economies of scale in providing care, and benefit from more systematic supervision of the provision of care.

Each time business groups think that they have made progress in restraining health-care costs, however, they see government changing the policy rules and pushing their costs back up.[10] Workers covered by employer-sponsored health plans do not pay income tax on the premiums paid by employers for health coverage, even though these premiums are a form of employee compensation. This exemption has given the federal government legal grounds to regulate employer-sponsored health plans. Government has required business to extend coverage to include psychiatric services, alcohol- and drug-abuse treatment, home health care, and the insurance costs of high-risk groups. In addition, federal programs to reduce the government's medical expenditures have limited the rates government pays to doctors and hospitals under Medicare and Medicaid. The subsequent government rates are less than the costs charged to private health plans and often, critics say, less than the actual costs of providing the services. Doctors and hospitals make up the shortfall by increasing the prices charged to private-sector patients, and an increasing share of these costs are ultimately paid by employers. When Congress decided in 1991 to cut $42 billion out of the Medicare budget as part of its five-year plan to reduce the federal deficit, the group that grumbled most was the business community, which feared that the reductions would simply be tacked onto the health-care bills they would eventually have to pay.

Some large companies and insurance carriers have the market power to negotiate their own discounts with health-care providers. One consequence of these discounts, however, is that more health-care costs are being pushed onto small business and individuals. Faced with skyrocketing costs, an increasing number of small businesses, whose workers are usually young and healthy, are choosing not to buy any health insurance at all.[11] This trend is adding to the number of workers not covered by any health care plans and compounding the problems of the existing system.

Mistrust of government has made most companies wary of proposals to expand the role of government in the health-care system.[12] The spiraling costs of health insurance, however, have recently led firms to consider proposals they once would have rejected outright. One idea gaining attention acknowledges that businesses cannot control health-care costs without government help. This pro-posal envisions the creation of an "all-payers" coalition, in which government and employers would create a formal alliance to negotiate lower prices with doctors and hospitals. Another plan calls for legislative restrictions on the volume of health-care services now funded for each individual. These "managed-care" pro-posals would require more emphasis on preventing unnecessary and inefficient patient care than is present in current public and private programs.

Political figures are reluctant to address the problems of the thirty-three million citizens with no health-care coverage without the support of business, but business groups do not want to expand medical expenditures without a credible system for controlling costs. At the same time, various groups are seeking to persuade Congress to require businesses to provide employees new coverage involving maternity, parenting, and child-care assistance.

There is no magic formula for determining which social programs should be funded by employers. At the beginning of this century, employers began to contribute to retirement programs. In the 1940s and 1950s, businesses began to pay employee health-care bills. Now businesses are starting to adopt programs to ease the burdens of an employee's family life. Politicians find federal mandates expanding the health coverage business must provide appealing because they can vote for benefits whose costs must be borne by the private sector. Excessive mandates, however, can build inefficiencies into the economy, damage specific businesses, and hinder the international competitiveness of key industries. Deciding the proper role for business in achieving the nation's social goals has been an ongoing task for policymakers for more than a century. Surging expenditures require that the role of business in providing health care be reexamined.

POLICIES TO PROTECT SOCIETY FROM BUSINESS

American consumers have begun to demonstrate their clout as environmentalists. Almost 90 percent of consumers tell opinion researchers that they prefer to buy environmentally safe products.[13] In 1991, they convinced corporate managers that they would back their words with actions. In that year, tuna companies started to declare their products "dolphin safe," a telephone firm promised to contribute a fraction of its revenues to environmental groups, McDonald's announced forty initiatives to cut the volume of waste generated in its restaurants, and laundry detergents claimed to be phosphate-free, made of biodegradable cleaning agents, and produced through energy-efficient processes.

Consumers have recently demonstrated a new appreciation of environmentally safe products, but environmental pollution is not new. Pollution comes from many sources. One is the high concentration of population. Living generates wastes, and densely settled areas overwhelm nature's ability to process such wastes. Pollution is also a by-product of an industrial society.

Air pollutants are discharged by automobiles, industrial plants, and electric power facilities, and such pollutants increase rates of respiratory disease, damage the atmosphere, and produce "acid rain". Water pollutants consist mainly of organic wastes and chemical discharges. Organic wastes are naturally degradable, but when degradation occurs in water it consumes the dissolved oxygen that is necessary to support aquatic life. The presence of excessive organic wastes can destroy a body of water as a habitat for fish and other life forms. Chemical discharges often persist for lengthy periods. They can enter the food chain, harm the reproductive system of animals, and cause disease. The land can also be contaminated by toxic wastes, and it has been ravaged by solid-waste disposal, strip mining, urban development, negligent agricultural practices, and careless recreation uses.

Environmental pollution is a problem that requires government intervention in the marketplace. The failure of markets to prevent pollution results from the fact that polluters do not pay all the costs of fouling the environment. Both the drivers and the manufacturers of automobiles, for example, are responsible for air pollution that aggravates the misery of people who have asthma, emphysema, and pulmonary diseases, but they are not required to pay for the suffering they cause.

The problems of preventing pollution are further complicated by a mismatch in the incidence of the costs and benefits of controlling pollution. The costs of preventing pollution must be paid now by an identifiable group of voters, while the benefits accrue to future citizens who are often unappreciative of what they receive. Since the benefits of a clean environment are usually available to everyone regardless of their contributions, people have an incentive to evade the burdens of environmentally responsible action.

Governmental interest in the environment goes back to the nineteenth century, but contemporary concerns crystallized in 1970 with the creation of the Environmental Protection Agency (EPA). The pattern for modern environmental legislation was set in that year with the enactment of the Clean Air Act of 1970.[14] This law required the EPA to perform three tasks. First, it was to establish national air quality standards to protect public health and safeguard the general welfare. Second, the EPA was to set limits for the emission of air pollutants from stationary sources such as factories and incinerators and from nonstationary sources, including automobiles. The agency's third task was to approve state plans to achieve the national standards within four to six years. In carrying out these tasks, the EPA was instructed to act on the basis of public health and not on the basis of economic or technical feasibility.

A similar approach to environmental protection was seen in the Water Pollution Control Act of 1972. This act established two national goals: to improve water quality so that all waters would be "fishable and swimmable" by 1983; and to eliminate the discharge of all pollutants into navigable waters by 1985. The legislation instructed the EPA to create an interim permit system that would specify the amount of pollution individual factories and municipal waste-treatment plants would be allowed to discharge into waterways until the total ban came into effect. The statute authorized grants to assist state agencies in developing waste-treatment programs, but it also directed the EPA itself to order companies to comply with its permit restrictions if state governments did not act to enforce the standards. A novel feature of the legislation was that firms and municipalities were required to use the best practicable technology and then the best available technology to control pollution, but these terms proved difficult to define.

Two laws from 1976 established federal responsibility for controlling toxic substances. The Toxic Substances Control Act instructed the EPA to protect people and the environment from "unreasonable" chemical risks. The agency made an inventory of 50,000 commercial chemicals, and it then restricted or even banned the use of substances that violated its safety standards. The Resource Conservation and Recovery Act required the safe disposal of hazardous wastes. The EPA created a regulatory system that included standards and record-keeping requirements for generating hazardous wastes, for transporting wastes, and for facilities that stored, treated, or disposed of hazardous wastes. To clean up disposal sites that were created before 1976, Congress also passed the Comprehensive Environmental Response, Compensation, and Liability Act of 1980. Often called the "Superfund Bill", this legislation made all "responsible parties" who contributed to a dump site liable to pay the costs of cleaning it up. If no one was proven to be liable for causing the hazard, the EPA itself would clean up the site with financing provided by a special tax on petroleum and chemical companies. (See Chapter 11).

Business and the Environment

Business is often regarded in the United States as the enemy of the environment.[15] Threats to the environment are not seen, as they are in the UK, as the inevitable consequence of consumption in an affluent society or production in an industrialized economy.[16] In the United States, threats to the environment are usually attributed to the profit motive of large corporations. "We will kill ourselves and all those around us," one environmental commentator despairs, "for a profit."[17] The only way to protect the environment, it is said, is with rigid laws and steep fines. This perspective is associated with an image of corporations as cost-minimizing entities that willfully ignore the social consequences of pollution.

Recently, an alternative view of corporations has emerged among some sectors of the environmental community. The National Wildlife Federation has created a Corporate Conservation Council made up of senior corporate figures. A Wildlife Federation aide commented: "We discovered that there is a lot we have in common and very little about which we were at odds.... Alliances between corporations and organizations like ours...are not difficult to make because the differences between the corporate world and the environmental world are not as broad as some may believe."[18]

A senior economist from the Environmental Defense Fund has also pointed out that companies are more than just cost-minimizing institutions.[19] They are also a source of creative energy, sensitive to a variety of constituencies, that can be harnessed to solve environmental problems. Recognizing that the environmental movement's traditional reliance on government has reached the point of diminishing returns, the chairman of the Sierra Club has recently proposed that the environmental movement bypass stalled government programs and focus instead on corporate behavior.[20] An acknowledgment of the diversity of corporate concerns suggests new approaches to environmental policy.

Environmental policies have traditionally relied on "command-and-control" regulation. This type of regulation takes two forms. The responsible regulatory agency may require the use of specific technologies to limit pollution, or it may establish emission levels for individual pollutants and/or general environmental quality standards. The "command-and-control" approach to checking environmental pollution is quite popular, but it has inevitable shortcomings. The designation of a specific technology to solve pollution problems may not be *the* most effective or even *an* effective way of achieving the desired goals. In addition, setting emission standards or general environmental quality standards leads to endless technical and procedural disputes that often frustrate the accomplishment of statutory goals.

The features of "command-and-control" regulations are illustrated by EPA efforts to deal with chlorofluorocarbons (CFCs). In 1974, a research report from the University of California argued that CFCs, a chemical widely used in aerosol sprays, was the main cause of the depletion of the ozone layer in the stratosphere.[21] After some controversy, the EPA banned the use of CFCs in nonessential aerosols in 1978, and the European Community established a overall production limit for certain CFCs in 1980. The most striking feature of these policies was that they actually resulted in an increase in the production of CFCs. By 1985, the reduced use of CFCs in aerosols was matched by increased use of CFCs for nonaerosol purposes. Governments on both sides of the Atlantic were slow to act against new CFC uses because of their desire not to disrupt their firms and industries. Furthermore, some of the compounds developed to replace CFCs also resulted in environmental problems that rivalled those of the original CFCs. "Command-and-control" regulations are often necessary elements of solutions to environmental problems, but their use in specific situations usually requires a detailed understanding of the technologies and the industries affected by the proposed rules.

A second approach to achieving environmental policy goals relies on the doctrine of legal liability. Liability standards determine who is responsible for the harm caused in a particular situation. As noted above, the Superfund bill passed in 1980 employs a liability approach to determining who is responsible for paying the costs of cleaning up toxic dump sites. Any company that contributed in any way to a dump site is responsible for paying all the costs of the cleaning up that site. This strict liability standard makes companies that have acted in good faith and have had only minimal involvement in a site decades ago responsible for all of the costs of cleaning up that site. It may also allow other firms whose behavior may have been more negligent to escape responsibility when the necessary legal standards cannot be satisfied. Liability approaches to environmental protection generate litigation, but the slow pace of cleaning up Superfund sites illustrates their weakness is achieving environmental goals.

The third approach to improving environmental quality relies on the use of marketplace incentives. Many economists argue that "command-and-control" regulations are inherently inefficient because they substitute the judgment of bureaucrats for the operations of the market. Greater reliance on economic incentives and private-sector decisions, they maintain, can improve environmental quality more effectively at less cost. The dynamics of this approach are illustrated by plans to reduce hydrocarbon emissions by 85 percent at fifty-two DuPont plants.[22] Traditionally, the EPA would have ordered the company to reduce emissions by 85 percent at each of 548 sources of hydrocarbon emissions within the plants. The cost would have been $106 million. Requiring the same 85 percent reduction on a plant-by-plant, instead of a source-by-source, basis allowed plant managers to decide how best to cut back emissions and would have cost less than half as much, $43 million.

The most ambitious market-based program for improving environmental quality is contained in the Clean Air Act of 1990.[23] The bill promises to check the damage done by acid rain to forests and lakes in the Northeast by requiring emission sources, mostly midwestern power plants, to cut their discharges of sulfur dioxide by ten million tons per year. After capping the nation's total sulfur-dioxide discharge, the legislation then sets up an emission-credit trading system. Under the system, utilities that cut emissions below the required ceiling could sell the extra credits to other firms. These provisions broke the decade-long deadlock over the bill, helped the utilities finance the $5 billion annual costs of reducing emissions, and provided industries flexibility in deciding which technologies to use to achieve the required improvements.

One weakness of market-oriented approaches to environmental protection is that they may be inequitable. "Command-and-control" regulations demand an equal proportionate sacrifice from all manufacturers, but market-oriented approaches provide an advantage to low-cost producers who are usually the best financed. While the society may receive more pollution abatement for less cost through market-oriented approaches, representatives of small business sometimes regard such proposals as inequitable to smaller, poorly financed firms.

A journalist wrote that the battle over the acid-rain provisions of the 1990 Clean Air bill was a battle between Democrats and Republicans "over who can best protect the environment at least cost to their constituents."[24] Government has usually relied on direct regulation to improve environmental quality. The acid-rain provisions of the 1990 Clean Air Act is the first extensive test of the effectiveness of economic, market-based incentives in accomplishing environmental goals. It symbolizes an obligation to acknowledge the characteristics of business organizations when designing social policies

POLICIES TO PROTECT WORKERS

Each morning one hundred million Americans rise and travel to their place of work. Their relationships with employers reflect interests that are both antagonistic and interdependent. Their relationships with other employees are also partly cooperative and partly competitive. One objective of social policy is to guarantee satisfactory workplace relationships. Procedures for assuring equity and safety in the workplace focus on both labor unions and government standards.

Labor Unions

Labor unions are intended to protect the interests of their members in the workplace. Unions gained effective immunity from prosecution under antitrust laws with the passage of the Norris–La Guardia Act in 1932. The modern system of labor relations is based on the National Labor Relations Act (Wagner–Connery Act) of 1935. This law guaranteed employees the legal right to organize labor unions and bargain collectively with employers. It also required employers to deal with legally constituted labor organizations and prohibited them from engaging in a series of "unfair labor practices," such as seeking to dominate a union or firing a worker for being a union member. The Wagner–Connery Act established a permanent National Labor Relations Board (NLRB) to administer the law, investigate complaints, and issue orders to halt actions that violated the law.

The Labor Management Relations Act (Taft–Hartley Act) of 1947 made unions liable for damages resulting from breach of contract, banned a variety of restrictive union practices, and authorized an eighty-day cooling-off period for strikes that might affect the national health or safety. Unions were required to submit annual financial reports, hold fair elections, and conduct their business in accordance with basic democratic rules. The act also created a Federal Mediation and Conciliation Service to reduce the number of strikes by providing a federal mediator when labor and management sides could not agree on the terms of a contract.

Collective bargaining, rather than submitting to compulsory arbitration or governmental decisions, has been the preferred choice of American unions in resolving labor-management disputes. Labor contracts usually govern the terms and conditions of employment, including such items as wages, hours, fringe benefits, vacations, and grievance procedures. Contracts can also include specific work rules defining the tasks performed by workers, specifying the number of available employees, restricting the work load to be performed in a given time period, and stipulating the amount of work space required to perform various tasks.

The interpretations of the National Labor Relations Act by the NLRB over the years have determined the precise meaning of provisions defining the coverage and requirements of the law. Even though the NLRB's rulings often reflect the policies of the incumbent administration, the nation's collective bargaining system has remained essentially unchanged since the 1930s.

While unions usually rely on collective bargaining to advance the interests of their members, they occasionally pursue legislative strategies to secure specific goals. The Davis-Bacon Act, for example, requires contractors to pay high union wage rates on federal construction projects, even though equally skilled workers may be available at lower wage rates. Government regulation of labor-management relations spurred the growth of labor unions in the 1930s and 1940s, and it also resulted in the expansion of corporate personnel departments and the hiring of specialists in various aspects of the personnel process.

Government Standards

Safety and equity in the workplace is achieved through government standards as well as through the operations of labor unions. An early example of legislative action to protect workers was the Fair Labor Standards Act of 1938, which forbade child labor, guaranteed a minimum wage, and instituted a maximum forty-hour work week for businesses operating in interstate commerce. Other examples of government standards to protect workers appear in the areas of equal employment opportunity and occupational safety.

Equal Employment Opportunity. According to theory, rewards in American society are supposed to be based on merit, and everyone is to have a fair opportunity to demonstrate his or her worth in the marketplace. The 1960s and 1970s witnessed a growing public awareness that the ideal of equal opportunity was more preached than practiced.

The Civil Rights Act of 1964 is the cornerstone of federal policy to prevent discrimination in the workplace. Title VII forbids employers, labor unions, and government agencies from discriminating among employees on the basis of race, color, sex, religion, or national origin in regard to hiring, firing, wages, promotions, fringe benefits, and the like. At the same time, Section 703 of the statute also states that the title does not require "preferential treatment" to be given to any group or individual because of an "imbalance" in employment patterns. The Civil Rights Act created the Equal Employment Opportunity Commission (EEOC) and charged it with the responsibility to implement the law. The EEOC is a five-person board whose members are appointed for five-year terms by the president, but the powers of the Commission were originally limited to investigating complaints and promoting conciliation.

The enforcement powers of the EEOC were greatly increased by the Equal Employment Opportunity Act of 1972. The new law gave the Commission power to initiate court actions and to investigate company records to uncover patterns of discrimination. The EEOC's jurisdiction was also expanded in 1972, and it was given authority over all private employers with more than fifteen workers, educational institutions, employment agencies, labor unions, and apprenticeship programs.

A series of other laws extended nondiscrimination principles to other situations. The 1963 Equal Pay Act prohibited wage discrimination among workers because of gender, and the Pregnancy Discrimination Act of 1978 required employers to treat pregnancy and childbirth as a disability under fringe-benefit plans and to guarantee reinstatement to women on leave for pregnancy-related reasons. The Age Discrimination in Employment Act of 1967 outlaws job discrimination on the basis of age, and the Vocational Rehabilitation Act of 1973 seeks to ensure equal opportunity for handicapped persons. The Veterans Readjustment Assistance Act of 1974 requires government contractors to take affirmative action to employ and advance veterans of the Vietnam era.

More difficult employment problems come when the issue shifts from non-discrimination to more positive forms of affirmative action. The 1964 Civil Rights Act prohibits "preferential treatment" to correct imbalance in employment patterns, but affirmative actions are frequently authorized to compensate for past discrimination. Defining the nature of past discrimination and shaping appropriate remedial programs remain controversial. The U.S. Supreme Court, for example, endorsed by a five-to-four margin a court order requiring a local sheetmetal union to meet a minority-hiring target of 29 percent.[25] The majority justified the order by writing that the union had practiced "pervasive and egregious" discrimination, but the minority maintained that remedies short of quotas should be used when warranted and that such remedies were only permissible when they did not harm innocent nonminority workers.

Occupational Safety and Health. The Occupational Safety and Health Act of 1970 was passed by lopsided votes in both the Senate (83 to 3) and the House of Representatives (383 to 5). Its purpose was "to assure so far as possible every working man and woman in the nation safe and healthful working conditions."[26] The Occupational Safety and Health Administration (OSHA) was instructed to reduce hazards in the workplace, improve existing health and safety programs, and establish mandatory health and safety standards.

OSHA combines both executive and judicial functions. It establishes standards for particular substances such as benzene or cotton dust that might harm workers' health and bars workplace practices it regards as unsafe. The enforcement of OSHA standards occurs through inspections of company facilities by OSHA compliance officers who determine if the appropriate standards have been met or whether citations should be issued for probable violations. If an employer contests a citation, the case is sent to the Occupational Safety and Health Review Commission, OSHA's judicial arm, where an administrative law judge hears the case. The law judge's decision may then be appealed to the full Commission, the U.S. Court of Appeals, and the U.S. Supreme Court.

Workplace health and safety are serious issues, and OSHA's good intentions win wide praise, but OSHA has become one of the most controversial agencies in the federal government. Business groups charge that OSHA has established trivial standards that are unrelated to health and safety, that enforcement is so inconsistent as to constitute harassment, and that the agency has not produced results that are commensurate with the costs it has imposed. Union representatives insist that the OSHA statute is sound and that the agency has helped defend the health and safety of American workers. They maintain that OSHA would have even greater impact if its standards were tightened up and its enforcement procedures strengthened.

Controversy centers on two issues. The first is whether or not OSHA's standards should emerge from a process that includes an evaluation of the costs and benefits of specific rules. The original legislation does not explicitly recognize the possibility of a trade off between costs and benefits. OSHA has interpreted the language of the statute to mean that costs should not be considered in establishing most health and safety standards. When business organizations protested that it was unreasonable to ignore costs, the Supreme Court ruled that Congress could have included a cost-benefit test for OSHA standards if it had intended such a standard to be invoked.[27] Cost-benefit tests, the justices wrote, would inevitably lead to less rigorous standards, and Congress had sought more protection for workers, essentially regardless of cost.

The second area of controversy involves OSHA's record. Academic researchers do not agree on whether OSHA's activities have actually reduced the incidence of workplace injuries. Researchers who rely on aggregate data use statistical analyses that have been unable to link improvements in injury and illness rates with OSHA's efforts. Other studies have examined specific plants or pieces of machinery before and after the inauguration of OSHA standards. These studies have discovered improvements in health and safety, but they do not consider whether these improvements would have occurred without OSHA action.

Labor unions were originally created to protect the interests of workers. In recent decades, the catalogue of government programs designed to enhance the status of employees in the workplace has grown substantially. Recently, employers have also been more conscious of the need to enhance job satisfaction and improve the quality of the work experience if their companies are to succeed in the increasingly competitive international environment.

SUMMARY

Much public debate about the relationship between business and social policy emerges from partisan disputes over political symbols. This chapter argues instead that it is necessary to distinguish the objectives of social policies in order to evaluate the role of business in those policies.

In the health-care field, corporations are used as a means of funding a social program that has no necessary relation to business. How great a burden should business bear in such policy areas? What are the political and economic consequences of requiring businesses to shoulder these costs?

Some social policies are designed to protect society from business. Numerous restrictions have been placed on business operations to prevent businesses from damaging the environment. Are specific restrictions the most effective way of limiting industrial pollution? Does the emphasis on preventing industrial pollution lead the public to ignore other sources of pollution more important than industrial pollution?

Still other social policies try to correct the imbalance between corporations and workers that is inherent in the employment relationship. The conflicts between unions, corporations, and government agencies over protecting the interests of employees often distract from the more basic issues of what sorts of safeguards are desirable and how these safeguards can best be provided. A clearer analysis of the role business plays in various social policy areas is a prerequisite to more effective social policies.

SELECTED READINGS

FRANCIS G. CASTLES (ed.), *The Comparative History of Public Policy* (New York: Oxford University Press, 1989)

MARGARET S. GORDON, *Social Security Policies in Industrial Countries: A Comparative Analysis* (New York: Cambridge University Press, 1988).

SAMUEL P. HAYS, *Beauty, Health, and Permanence: Environmental Politics in the United States* (New York: Cambridge University Press, 1987).

ELLEN FRANKEL PAUL, *Equity and Gender: The Comparable Worth Debate* (New Brunswick, N.J.: Transaction, 1989).

MARK SAGOFF, *The Economy of Earth* (New York: Cambridge University Press, 1988).

END NOTES

[1]This section relies on Edwin Amenta and Theda Skocpol, "Taking Exception: Explaining the Distinctiveness of American Public Policies in the Last Century," in Francis G. Castles (ed.), *The Comparative History of Public Policy* (New York: Oxford University Press, 1989), pp. 292–333.

[2]Margaret S. Gordon, *Social Security Policies in Industrial Countries: A Comparative Analysis* (New York: Cambridge University Press, 1988).

[3]Mansel G. Blackford, *The Rise of Modern Business in Great Britain, the United States and Japan* (Chapel Hill, N.C.: University of North Carolina Press, 1988); and Alfred D. Chandler, Jr., "Government Versus Business: An American Phenomenon," in John T. Dunlop (ed.), *Business and Public Policy* (Cambridge, Mass.: Harvard Graduate School of Business Administration, 1980).

[4]Amenta and Skocpol, "Taking Exception…," in Castle (ed.), *Comparative History of Public Policy*, pp. 296–99.

[5]Gordon, *Social Security Policies*, pp. 198–204.

[6]Gordon, *Social Security Policies*, pp. 216–22.

[7]*Statistical Abstract of the United States 1990* (Washington, D.C.: Government Printing Office, 1990), p. 100.

[8]Gordon, *Social Security Policies*, pp. 223–24.

[9]Patricia Munch Danzon, "Health Policy in 1984: The Crisis in Costs," in John H. Moore (ed.), *To Promote Prosperity: U.S. Domestic Policy in the Mid-1980s* (Stanford, Calif.: Hoover Institution Press, 1984), pp. 125–36.

[10]Julie Kosterlitz, "Softening Resistance," *National Journal*, January 12, 1991, pp. 64–68.

[11]Julie Kosterlitz, "Unrisky Business," *National Journal*, April 6, 1991, pp. 794–97.

[12]Kosterlitz, "Softening Resistance," *National Journal*, January 12, 1991, pp. 64–65.

[13]Michael McCloskey, "Consumers as Environmentalists," in W. Michael Hoffman, Robert Frederick, and Edwards S. Petry (eds.), *Business, Ethics, and the Environment: The Public Policy Debate* (New York: Quorum Books, 1990), pp. 139–44.

[14]Charles O. Jones, *Clean Air: The Policies and Politics of Pollution Control* (Pittsburgh: University of Pittsburgh Press, 1975).

[15]Samuel P. Hays, *Beauty, Health, and Permanence: Environmental Politics in the United States* (New York: Cambridge University Press, 1987); and Charles S. Pearson (ed.), *Multinational Corporations, Environment, and the Third World: Business Matters* (Durham, N.C.: Duke University Press, 1987).

[16]David Vogel, *National Styles of Regulation: Environmental Policy in Great Britain and the United States* (Ithaca, N.Y.: Cornell University Press, 1986), pp. 254–55.

[17]Nancy W. Anderson, "Worldwide Responses to the Environmental Crisis," in Hoffman, Frederick, and Petry (eds.), *Business, Ethics, and the Environment*, p. 151.

[18]Lynn A. Greenwalt, "An Environmental Agenda for the 1990s," in Hoffman, Frederick, and Petry (eds.), *Business, Ethics, and the Environment*, pp. 146–47.

[19]Daniel J. Dudek, Alice M. LeBlanc, and Kenneth Sewall, "Business Responses to Environmental Policy: Lessons from CFC Regulation," in Hoffman, Frederick, and Petry (eds.), *Business, Ethics, and the Environment*, p. 36.

[20]Michael McCloskey, "Customers as Environmentalists," in Hoffman, Frederick, and Petry (eds.), *Business, Ethics, and the Environment*, pp. 139–44.

[21]Dudek, et al., "Business Responses to Environmental Policy," in Hoffman, Frederick, and Petry (eds.), *Business, Ethics, and the Environment*, pp. 34–60, especially p. 45.

[22]M.T.Maloney and Bruce Yandle, "Cleaner Air at Lower Cost: Bubbles and Efficiency," *Regulation* (May/June 1980), pp. 49–52.

[23]Margaret E. Kriz, "Dunning the Midwest," *National Journal*, April 14, 1990, pp. 893–97; and George Hager, "Wheels Begin Rolling Again on House Clean Air Bill," *Congressional Quarterly Weekly Report*, March 17, 1990, pp. 828–29.

[24]Kriz, "Dunning the Midwest," *National Journal*, April 14, 1990, p. 897.

[25]*Sheetmetal Workers of N.Y. Local 28* v. *EEOC*, 54 U.S. 3596 (1986).

[26]Occupational Safety and Health Act, Public Law 91–596.

[27]*American Textile Manufacturers Institute, Inc.* v. *Donovan*, 69 U.S. 185 (1981).

Conclusion

THE CONTEST FOR FUTURE SOLUTIONS

Academic books usually emphasize the failures that occur in the governmental and corporate arenas. This tendency should not distract us from the fact that the American political and economic system has produced a lifestyle that is widely envied and imitated. The U.S. system has shaped world events for decades and remains a model for peoples struggling to chart their own destinies. The past achievements of the U.S. system, however, are no guarantee of future success.

Spectacular changes have occurred in the international environment in which the United States operates. Germany has come together, and the Soviet Union has come apart. Europe is continuing its process of regional integration, while Japan is testing its stature as a regional leader. The globalization of economic activity and the emergence of new technologies have altered the international division of labor and redistributed the global economic pie. Within the United States, economic organizations, governmental institutions, and traditional public policies have taken on new characteristics and reflected new dynamics. As a result of these changes, there is much work to be done.

The changes occurring at home and abroad require new thinking about the operations of the U.S. political-economic system. For example, the preceding chapter argued that the role of business in social policy areas needs to be reevaluated. Earlier chapters examined the pressures that are leading to the restructuring of the international trading system and to the reconsideration of industrial policy proposals. In these policy domains and in a long list of other economic and political areas, old ways of doing business do not provide an adequate response to new realities. The United States does indeed face a daunting series of challenges, but there is no reason to believe that today's challenges are more stubborn than those that were met in earlier eras.

It has been the theme of this book that the solutions devised for problems in past eras were not the product of a single doctrine or ideology. Solutions to nineteenth- and twentieth-century political and economic problems were not dictated by the governmental arrangements constructed at the end of the eighteenth century. Popular sovereignty and a competitive marketplace have been key elements in the U.S. political and economic framework, but American responses to societal problems have often contradicted the principles associated with these symbols.

This book has argued that the achievements of the American political and economic system have not been based on an ideology but a process. The American tradition recognizes that both government and business are imperfect institutions. To compensate for these defects, Americans have created a surprisingly subtle pair of procedural rules: government has been authorized to make the country's ultimate economic decisions, and economic groups have been allowed to influence the most basic political judgments.

These procedural rules have led to an unending struggle about how to solve best the country's most pressing problems. Government, business interests, and nonbusiness groups have competed in each era to champion alternative solutions to the issues facing the country. The ultimate outcome of the skirmishes in this process of *contested solutions* has depended upon the ability of the various actors to demonstrate that their proposals satisfy in some manner the long run interests of a majority of the American people.

The conflicts that make up this process of *contested solutions* have provided the foundation for the successes of the American system. The continued existence of diverse, partially autonomous sectors of the society has guaranteed alternative perspectives on public issues and assured competing proposals for guiding governmental policy. The recognition that societal decisions must produce results that satisfy, at some level, the standards of public opinion has introduced a measure of accountability into the system. The political and economic conflicts among government, business, and nonbusiness groups have helped sustain the dynamism of the American economy and helped ensure responsiveness to public opinion.

The *process of contested solutions* safeguarded in the past the nation's political choices and promoted its economic well-being, but whether it can solve the problems of the 1990s remains to be seen. Since the bonds between government and business are always changing, the future shape of those relations necessarily remains uncertain. While it is always dangerous to predict future events, four possible scenarios for relations between government and business appear likely.

The Victory Scenario

The contest among government, business, and nonbusiness groups to promote policy solutions to public problems might produce a decisive victory for one group or another. Business organizations may come to dominate public affairs by convincing the rest of society that the country's international economic position is so precarious that economic problems must take precedent over other concerns. Business representatives could also persuade the public that business should become the basic source of expertise and judgment about what needs to be done to sustain a prosperous economy.

Alternatively, the role of business groups in public affairs might be severely restricted. Popular acceptance of the political role of business rests on its ability to provide the material benefits of a consumer society. If American corporations, in general, visibly lose out in international economic competition, the position of business in the domestic political arena will be severely eroded.

Corporations are expected to provide citizens reasonable value for the goods and services they deliver. If firms are too greedy and retain too large a share of the benefits of economic activity, their political position will also decline. The Wall Street scandals of the 1980s and the conspicuous salary increases for chief executives of declining firms are evidence that some business people have already lost touch with popular values and expectations.

The erosion of the role of business in public affairs could be accompanied by the increased influence of nonbusiness groups. Noneconomic groups might contend that a successful economy rests on an effectively functioning society and that expansive social policies are needed to maintain such a society. Or they might insist that government has paid too much attention to materialistic values in recent decades. The country would be healthier, they could argue, if less concern were given to consumption patterns and more attention paid to the nation's cultural and spiritual values. Either way, representatives of nonbusiness groups might convince people that business can contribute little to the country's future and that the nation's public policies should be placed in other hands.

Finally, the growth in the role of government in society that has characterized the twentieth-century could continue or even accelerate in the decade ahead. The growing complexity of the domestic and international environment will probably prod government to assume a more activist role, and domestic political interests could succeed in forming coalitions that would propel government into more and more areas of society. The continued expansion of government could restrict the activities of private groups and institutions to such an extent that they are no longer able to be autonomous actors in public affairs.

The ultimate victory of either government, business, or nonbusiness groups in capturing control of the nation's public policy process would represent a substantial departure from the nation's basic values. Such an imbalance could lead to a set of public policies that would aggravate the very problems it was intended to solve.

Cooperation/Collaboration Scenario

Analyses of the economic achievements of Germany and Japan stress the close cooperation between government and business and the extensive collaboration among business organizations that occurs in those countries. Business interest associations in Germany and government agencies in Japan facilitate the exchange of information, the development of common organizational perspectives, and the coordination or even the joint sponsorship of projects intended to advance the countries' economies.

In contrast, the image of relations between government and business in the United States is one of conflict and antagonism. The distrust and the litigiousness among government, business, and nonbusiness groups hinder the development of solutions to public problems and impose unnecessary costs on the conduct of public policy. American corporations increasingly find themselves competing in the international marketplace not against corporations but against government-assisted consortia. The increasingly close alignment between international companies and their governments is said by some to place U.S. firms at a considerable competitive disadvantage.

For these reasons, some American commentators advocate programs to promote cooperation between business and government and encourage formal ties among American corporations. Such proposals often involve public funding of projects beneficial to corporate development, government assistance in international marketing activities, exemptions from antitrust laws, and public policies to coordinate corporate operations.

Proposals that the United States should become more like Germany or Japan are superficially appealing, and some practices from other countries can certainly be used to reform the conduct of American corporations and government institutions. But as the United States adopts some international practices, it should recall that its past successes have rested on its differences with German and Japanese practices as much as on its similarities. The United States has much to learn from its international competitors, but the individualism of American entrepreneurs and the adaptiveness of U.S. firms have made critical contributions to the country's past achievements. It might be unwise or even futile to abandon American practices in an ill-considered effort to transplant corporate and governmental practices that are inconsistent with American cultural traditions.

Particularism Scenario

The view that the United States government has lost the capacity to manage the country's policy process is supported by its inability to deal with such basic problems as the budget deficit, energy supply, the trade deficit, and the savings and loan crisis. The development that threatens the traditional success of the American economy most severely is the deterioration in the social environment from which the U.S. economic system draws its strength. Measures of social disorganization, educational failure, and institutionalized waste provide accumulating evidence that the public decision-making process is not providing adequate solutions to the country's most pressing problems.

Numerous groups and organizations have gained the ability to block policy initiatives that do not satisfy their interests. Other elements of the society have been able to use the election process, the legal system, and other strategically placed social institutions to impose costs on the public that enrich them without providing commensurate public benefits.

Relations between government and business in the future will probably display the competitive tensions that have characterized past decades. The internationalization of business activity will probably increase the significance of government as a factor in society. The fragmentation of governmental authority, government's piecemeal approach to public policy, and the instability of government policy judgments could all become increasingly disruptive factors.

It is possible that the practice of specific groups and institutions to insist on receiving their particular policy benefits without regard for the impact of their positions on the broader community could become even more frequent. So many groups could assert their individual right to receive a generous share of the rewards of a prosperous society that the conditions necessary to sustain a successful community will be undermined. The U.S. political process is a mirror that reflects how Americans see themselves. They have the ability to change the reflection they see, but whether they have the will to reform the political process is not clear.

Refurbished Contested Solutions Scenario

Successful societies devise some formula to align the rewards that flow to individuals with the actions that best promote the interests of the society. Some nations have relied on cultural homogeneity to link individual self-interest and collective good. Other countries are characterized by a deference to established authority that leads to the widespread acceptance of judgments that reflect the interests of limited segments of the society. These options are not open to a society that celebrates diversity and teaches citizens to challenge authority.

The basic glue that has held the United States together has been a sense of opportunity. The United States has always been a land of possibilities, a land of aspiration and entrepreneurship. The sense that individuals could improve their position by making some type of contribution has been the essence of that notion of opportunity.

In recent years the sense of opportunity has become disengaged from the belief that individuals should make some contribution to justify the benefits they receive. The most provocative symbols in contemporary politics involve people who are seen to exploit the society for personal advantage without providing an honest return for their benefits. The public sense that some groups are exploiting public and private institutions leads citizens to withdraw their support for critical social processes and encourages them to seek out ways in which they too can exploit their communities.

One way to refurbish the process of contested solutions is to restore the notion that opportunities and benefits in a society must be, in some way, commensurate with the contribution that has been made. Corporations, the media, the entertainment industry, the legal system, interest group advocates, and the political world need to be reminded that it is inherently destructive to grant benefits that have not been in some way earned.

The process of contested solutions could be further refurbished by the explicit recognition that the policy process should provide significant value for resources expended. Squandering money on the Defense Department or the savings and loan industry is a social offense. We should acknowledge, as well, that government can waste money in the health care industry, in education institutions, and on infrastructure projects. There needs to be a new emphasis by both government and business on value as a basis for conducting social activities. Ignoring the contributions needed to sustain society encourages groups to engage in socially destructive actions and impose costs on the general society which it will eventually be unable to bear.

As we reach the end of this book, it is clear that the relationship between business and government has been a linchpin of American society. To date this relationship has reflected the basic judgment that the relative independence of industry provides citizens greater benefits than would be achieved through tighter government controls. Each era reconsiders this judgment as it addresses the era's problems. Through a process of contested solutions, citizens evaluate the claims of government, business, and nonbusiness groups to guide the country into the future. More than in most eras, the next decades judgments about the proper role of government and business will be based on how individual citizens interpret the events now occurring in the global ecomony, the domestic political arena, government bureaucracies, and corporate boardrooms. This book has sought to help readers play their role in the tasks ahead. Their success will be important for them and for the future well-being of our national community.

Index